SCHOLARS AT WAR

AUSTRALASIAN SOCIAL SCIENTISTS, 1939-1945

SCHOLARS AT WAR

AUSTRALASIAN SOCIAL SCIENTISTS, 1939-1945

**Edited by Geoffrey Gray,
Doug Munro and Christine Winter**

E PRESS

Published by ANU E Press
The Australian National University
Canberra ACT 0200, Australia
Email: anuepress@anu.edu.au
This title is also available online at: http://epress.anu.edu.au

National Library of Australia Cataloguing-in-Publication entry

Title: Scholars at war : Australasian social scientists, 1939-1945 /
            edited by Geoffrey Gray, Doug Munro and Christine Winter.

ISBN: 9781921862496 (pbk.) 9781921862502 (ebook)

Subjects: Anthropologists--Australia--Biography.
            Anthropologists--New Zealand--Biography.
            Historians--Australia--Biography.
            Historians--New Zealand--Biography.
            World War, 1939-1945--Science.
            Social sciences--Australia.
            Social sciences--New Zealand.

Other Authors/Contributors:
            Gray, Geoffrey G.
            Munro, Doug.
            Winter, Christine.

Dewey Number: 301.0922

All rights reserved. No part of this publication may be reproduced, stored in a retrieval system or transmitted in any form or by any means, electronic, mechanical, photocopying or otherwise, without the prior permission of the publisher.

Cover design and layout by ANU E Press

Cover image: Canberra, ACT, 1945-05-29, Members of the Instructional Staff of the Land HQ School of Civil Affairs at Duntroon Military College. Australian War Memorial ID 108449.

This edition © 2012 ANU E Press

Contents

Preface vii

Contributors ix

Acknowledgments xi

Abbreviations and Acronyms xiii

Introduction 1
    Geoffrey Gray, Doug Munro and Christine Winter

Part I: The Australians   29
    Geoffrey Gray and Christine Winter

1. A. P. Elkin: Public morale and propaganda 35
    John Pomeroy

2. Conlon's Remarkable Circus 55
    Cassandra Pybus

3. H. Ian Hogbin: 'Official adviser on native affairs' 73
    Geoffrey Gray

4. W. E. H. Stanner: Wasted war years 95
    Geoffrey Gray

5. Camilla Wedgwood: 'what are you educating natives for' . . . 117
    David Wetherell

6. Ronald Murray Berndt: 'Work of national importance' 133
    Geoffrey Gray

7. The Road to Conlon's Circus—and Beyond:
   A personal retrospective 149
    J. D. Legge

Part II: The New Zealanders   163
    Doug Munro

8. Derek Freeman at War 169
    Peter Hempenstall

9. J. W. Davidson on the Home Front 187
   Doug Munro

10. Neville Phillips and the Mother Country 207
    Jock Phillips

11. Dan Davin: The literary legacy of war. 225
    Janet Wilson

Consolidated Bibliography. 243

Index. 279

Preface

The idea for this book was initiated when Geoff Gray and Doug Munro first met, at a workshop on Pacific biography, 'Telling Pacific Lives', held at The Australian National University in December 2005. There was an apparent synchronicity, and certainly a meeting of minds. One of us was writing biographies of Pacific historians and, in passing, their wartime experiences; the other had written on Australian anthropologists and how the war impacted on the discipline and its development in Australia. Christine Winter, who joined in the project later, was writing about National Socialism in New Guinea and Oceania. By the time we next met, 12 months later in Dunedin at the Pacific History Association Conference, the idea for the present volume had congealed. We agreed that an examination of the war work done by Australian and New Zealand social scientists—especially anthropologists and historians during World War II—would enable a discussion of the way in which war affected the lives and careers of a selected group of scholars from the two countries.

We were aware that, in Australia, the readjustments of war provided opportunities for intellectual talent to play a role in government policy and in the plans for postwar reconstruction that would not otherwise have been available. This group of mostly men was confident of their ability to influence the course of events—if not during the war then certainly in the postwar period; they saw themselves as liberal, reform-minded progressives, with a nationalist agenda and a bias for state intervention. They were representative of the new academic and professional elite that emerged during the war and which was to play an influential part in public life during the decades following the war. The different circumstances of New Zealand limited the mobilisation of scholarship for the war effort. The majority of university graduates served in the armed forces in combat roles. Only occasionally were their talents channelled into war work more in keeping with their scholarly callings, be it scientific research or security intelligence.

The fact that we live in different countries has encouraged a trans-Tasman approach that allows comparisons that might not otherwise have been evident. That said, there is an element of pragmatism—unavoidably—in the selection of the individual scholars represented in this collection. Others could conceivably have been included but the final line-up was, in the last resort, a function of the availability of contributors. We hope that this volume will inspire further work on the broad subject of scholars at war and, in particular, attention to those individuals (such as the Australian museum anthropologist Norman Tindale and the New Zealand historian Angus Ross) not included in the pages that follow.

Geoffrey Gray, Canberra
Doug Munro, Wellington
Christine Winter, Canberra

Contributors

Geoffrey Gray

Geoffrey Gray is Research Fellow at the Australian Institute of Aboriginal and Torres Strait Islander Studies, and Adjunct Professor of History, University of Queensland. His publications include *A Cautious Silence: The politics of Australian anthropology* (Canberra, 2007).

Peter Hempenstall

Peter Hempenstall is Conjoint Professor of History, University of Newcastle, NSW. His publications include *The Lost Man: Wilhelm Solf in German history* (Wiesbaden, 2005), co-authored with Paula Tanaka Mochida.

John Legge

John Legge is Emeritus Professor of History at Monash University. Publications include *Australian Outlook: A history of the Australian Institute of International Affairs* (Canberra, 1999).

Doug Munro

Doug Munro is a Wellington-based biographer and historian, and an Honorary Associate Professor, University of Queensland. Publications include *The Ivory Tower and Beyond: Participant historians of the Pacific* (Newcastle upon Tyne, 2009).

Jock Phillips

Jock Phillips is the General Editor of *Te Ara* (the *Encyclopedia of New Zealand* project), Ministry of Culture and Heritage, New Zealand. Publications include *Settlers: New Zealand immigrants from England, Ireland and Scotland, 1800–1945* (Auckland, 2008), co-authored with Terry Hearn.

John Pomeroy

John Pomeroy is an independent scholar and author of 'Morale on the Home Front in Australia During the Second World War', PhD thesis, University of Sydney, 1995.

Cassandra Pybus

Cassandra Pybus is Australian Research Council Professorial Fellow in the Department of History, University of Sydney. Publications include *The Devil and James McAuley* (Brisbane, 1999).

David Wetherell

David Wetherell is Senior Lecturer in History at Deakin University. Publications include *Charles Abel and the Kwato Mission of Papua New Guinea, 1891–1975* (Melbourne, 1996).

Janet Wilson

Janet Wilson is Professor of English and Postcolonial Studies at the University of Northampton, UK. Publications include (as editor) *The Gorse Blooms Pale: Dan Davin's Southland stories* (Dunedin, 2007).

Christine Winter

Christine Winter is a Postdoctoral Research Fellow in the School of History, Philosophy, Religion and Classics at the University of Queensland, and a Visiting Fellow in the School of Culture, History and Language, College of Asia and the Pacific, at The Australian National University.

Acknowledgments

First and foremost we thank Tim Causer, then at the Menzies Research Centre, for his outstanding research assistance among archival repositories in London. We have also incurred debts of gratitude to numerous archivists, especially to Sarah Walpole (Royal Anthropological Institute, London), Julia Mant and Tim Robinson (University of Sydney Archives), Maggie Shapley and Karina Taylor (Australian National University Archives), and Malcolm Underwood (St John's College, Cambridge). More generally, we acknowledge the assistance of the staff of the Manuscripts Section, National Library of Australia; the Alexander Turnbull Library, Wellington; Archives New Zealand, Wellington; the Department of Defence Library, Wellington; the National Library of New Zealand; and Special Collections, Barr Smith Library, University of Adelaide. We are also grateful to Justin Cargill of the Victoria University Library for bibliographic assistance.

An especial word of thanks goes to the contributors, many of whom put aside current engagements in order to write their chapters. Without exception they were cordial and cooperative. We are further indebted to Peter Hempenstall and Janet Wilson, Melanie Nolan and unnamed referees for comments on earlier drafts.

Abbreviations and Acronyms

2NZEF	2nd New Zealand Expeditionary Force
AIATSIS	Australian Institute of Aboriginal and Torres Strait Islander Studies
AIF	Australian Infantry Force
ANGAU	Australian New Guinea Administrative Unit
ANRC	Australian National Research Council
ANU	Australian National University
ANUA	Australian National University Archives
APB	Aborigines Protection Board (South Australia)
APTRC	Australian Pacific Territories Research Committee
ArchivesNZ	Archives New Zealand (Wellington)
ASAO	Association for Social Anthropology in Oceania
ASIO	Australian Security Intelligence Organisation
ASOPA	Australian School of Pacific Administration
ATL	Alexander Turnbull Library (Wellington)
AWB	Aborigines' Welfare Board of New South Wales
AWM	Australian War Memorial (Canberra)
BBCAU	British Borneo Civil Affairs Unit
BSIP	British Solomon Islands Protectorate
CCC	Commonwealth Coal Commission
CIB	Commonwealth Investigation Branch
CNM	Committee on National Morale
CSIRO	Commonwealth Scientific and Industrial Research Organisation
CSSRC	Colonial Social Sciences Research Council
DOI	Department of Information

DORCA	Directorate of Research and Civil Affairs
FELO	Far Eastern Liaison Office
LSE	London School of Economics and Political Science
NAOU	North Australia Observer Unit
NMC	National Morale Committee
NAA	National Archives of Australia
NLA	National Library of Australia (Canberra)
NSW	New South Wales
NTSRU	Northern Territory Special Reconnaissance Unit
RAF	Royal Air Force
RAAF	Royal Australian Air Force
RAI	Royal Anthropological Institute (London)
SAMA	South Australian Museum Archives
SPC	South Pacific Commission
TNG	Territory of New Guinea
UAP	United Australia Party
UCSD	University of California, San Diego
WAAAF	Women's Auxiliary Australian Air Force
WAVES	Women Accepted for Volunteer Emergency Service

Introduction

Geoffrey Gray, Doug Munro and Christine Winter

> So much Australian history is written by intellectuals, so little is written about them.[1]

During the twentieth century, intellectuals were mobilised during times of war. They had a number of choices: conscription in the armed forces that compromised their status as intellectuals; contribution to the war effort by adapting their role as intellectuals to a new set of circumstances and needs of the nation;[2] or opposition to the war. While there 'is copious evidence of intellectuals' desire to contribute to the war effort qua intellectuals, there is not always agreement about the precise role of the intellectual in the wartime order of things'.[3] Australian and New Zealand social scientists—our primary focus— were conscripted or volunteered for armed duty, or contributed by adapting their expertise to the war effort. *Scholars at War* explores the use of Australian and New Zealand social scientists, and contextualises their experiences and contributions within wider examinations of the role of intellectuals in war.

Scholars at War links a group of social scientists through geography, transnational, national and personal scholarly networks, and shared intellectual traditions. A collective or group biography involves 'a comparison of several lives or analysis of a number of lives together, linked through a central theme'.[4] This grouping enables comparisons to be made, similarities and differences to emerge, and connections to be revealed. These connections in the main are disciplinary based, emphasise transnational (in our case, empire) links that predate the war, and are based on shared war service, and shared outlook and desires. *Scholars at War* is structured around historical portraits of individual Australasian social scientists. They are not a tight group; rather a cohort of scholars serendipitously involved in and affected by war who share a point of origin.

---

1 G. C. Bolton, 'Foreword', in John A. Moses, *Prussian-German Militarism, 1914–18, in Australian Perspective: The thought of George Arnold Wood* (Peter Lang/Bern, New York, 1991), p. 5.
2 For example, Robin W. Winks, *Cloak & Gown: Scholars in the secret war, 1939–1961*, 2nd edn (New Haven, Conn., 1996).
3 David Drake and Debra Kelly, 'Editorial: Intellectuals and war', *Journal of War and Culture Studies*, 2:1 (2009), pp. 5, 6–8.
4 Lois W. Banner, 'History as Biography', *American Historical Review*, 114:3 (2009), p. 583. For historical analysis using collective biography, see Richard Hofstadter, *The American Political Tradition and the Men Who Made It* (New York, 1948); and Lois W. Banner, *Intertwined Lives: Margaret Mead, Ruth Benedict, and their circle* (New York, 2003). For transnational history and the importance of biography, see David Lambert and Alan Lester (eds), *Colonial Lives Across the Empire: Imperial careering in the long nineteenth century* (Cambridge, 2006); also William Palmer, *Engagement with the Past: The lives and works of the World War II generation of historians* (Lexington, Ky, 2001).

Analysing practitioners of the social sciences during war brings to the fore specific networks, beliefs and institutions that transcend politically defined spaces. Individual lives, we argue, can help us to make sense of a piece of the historical process. It helps us illuminate particular events and the larger cultural, social and even political processes of a moment in time.[5] Deacon, Russell and Woollacott remind us that biographies can illustrate that the Antipodes 'has never existed in isolation from conflicts and crises elsewhere around the globe. Australian [and New Zealand] lives are intricately enmeshed with the world, bound by ties of allegiance and affinity, intellect and imagination.'[6]

When we first conceived of *Scholars at War*—the first scholarly publication to examine the effect World War II had on the careers of social scientists—we did not start with a firm hypothesis; rather we wanted to examine their contribution to World War II, the impact war had on them personally and professionally, and the effect war had on the development of social sciences in Australasia.[7] In order to explore these themes, the main biographical focus is on early to mid-career academics, though scholars more advanced in their careers and social scientists who came into academia in the postwar period are also discussed. We therefore invited authors working on biographies or with interest in the war work of social scientists to focus on this particular period and these specific issues. With the exception of Aldophus Peter Elkin and Camilla Wedgwood, none of the social scientists portrayed in *Scholars at War* has had a biography written about them that details their war involvement and war experiences, and none has written an autobiography.

World War II was a major turning point of national outlook, patriotism and belonging. Many of the scholars discussed in this volume, however, particularly those from New Zealand, served abroad during the war, and some continued their professional lives outside the nations they had grown up in. *Scholars at War* investigates how World War II impinged on a group of Australian and New Zealand intellectuals—namely, social anthropologists and historians, most of whom were at the beginning of their careers: Derek Freeman, J. W. Davidson, Neville Phillips, Dan Davin, Ronald Berndt, and J. D. Legge (the youngest of our group), and, in the case of W. E. H. Stanner, H. Ian Hogbin and Camilla Wedgwood, midway. There are two exceptions: one was Elkin, who had an

---

5   Alice Kessler-Harris, 'Why Biography?', *American Historical Review*, 114:3 (2009), p. 626.
6   Desley Deacon, Penny Russell and Angela Woollacott (eds), *Transnational Ties: Australian lives in the world* (Canberra, 2008), pp. xiii–xiv.
7   In the literature on war and society, there is no book that we know of that deals with the use of social scientists in the Pacific War, apart from Roy MacLeod (ed.), *Science and the Pacific War: Science and survival in the Pacific, 1939–1945* (Dordrecht, 2000), which is largely a study of the natural sciences. There are nonetheless a large number of articles that touch on aspects of this but focusing on the United States and Britain, on the Atlantic rather than the Pacific. Few scholars have tracked postwar national and social-scientific developments in the Asia-Pacific region.

established career, the other Alfred Austin Joseph Conlon, a mature-age student (often described as a perennial student) who was enrolled in a medical degree and was a student representative on the University of Sydney Senate.

I

Historical geographer Matthew Farish avers that the Pacific War showed that, of all the social sciences,

> anthropology's relevance…was singled [out] by the discipline's unusual, lingering treatment of the 'whole man', and the ease with which it could shift to accommodate the rudimentary 'universal cultural patterns' favored by…planners. Even more crucial, however, was the experience anthropologists possessed in contact situations and field methods… [anthropologists] held 'an informant's view of culture', a particularly relevant approach for those soldiers who would be engaging in 'social control at the local level'.[8]

The use of anthropological knowledge in war, as pointed out by Farish, was an extension as well as a continuation of the use of anthropologists by colonial governments in the Pacific in the interwar years.[9] Colonial governments readily accepted—although did not necessarily embrace fully—the usefulness of anthropology or advice from anthropologists in the control, management and advancement (uplift) of colonised peoples.[10] This is illustrated by the appointment of government anthropologists—initially to the Australian Territory of Papua (F. E. Williams, 1922), and soon after in the League of Nations Mandated Territory of New Guinea (E. W. P. Chinnery, 1924).[11] On the Australian mainland, it was a period of incremental growth and steady professionalisation of the discipline, and a move away from museum anthropology that was largely confined to physical anthropology and the collection of material artefacts. The new, modern discipline of social anthropology was established at the University of Sydney. A.

---

8   Matthew Farish, 'Archiving Areas: The Ethnogeographic Board and the Second World War', *Annals of the Association of American Geographers*, 95:3 (2005), p. 673.
9   Matthew Farish, *The Contours of America's Cold War* (Minneapolis, Minn., 2010), especially pp. 101–46.
10 See various chapters in Naomi McPherson (ed.), *In Colonial New Guinea: Anthropological perspectives* (Pittsburgh, Pa, 2001).
11 See, for example, Geoffrey Gray, 'There Are Many Difficult Problems: Ernest William Pearson Chinnery—government anthropologist', *Journal of Pacific History*, 38:3 (2003), pp. 313–30; I. C. Campbell, 'Anthropology and the Professionalisation of Colonial Administration in Papua and New Guinea', *Journal of Pacific History*, 33:1 (1998), pp. 69–90.

R. Radcliffe-Brown was Foundation Professor (1926–31), followed by Raymond Firth as Acting Professor (1931–32), its third professor, A. P. Elkin (1934–56), and lecturer in Melanesian ethnography, H. Ian Hogbin.[12]

War, nevertheless, brought forth a different set of requirements and specialisations needed by the armed forces.[13] The Australian Army's use of social scientists (particularly anthropologists) covered a diverse range of tasks from how to best use Australian colonised peoples in support of the war effort to their suitability as soldiers in the service of the defence of Australia—defined at that time to include the territories of Papua and New Guinea.[14] F. E. Williams, E. W. P. Chinnery and the educationalist and anthropologist W. C. Groves were recruited, at varying times, to assist in the production of propaganda for the Far Eastern Liaison Unit (FELO) or to the Allied Geographical Unit or the Education Unit.[15] The closest to frontline fighting was the establishment of the North Australia Observation Unit (NAOU) commanded by the anthropologist Major W. E. H. Stanner and the NT Special Reconnaissance Unit (NTSRU) commanded by the Melbourne University-based anthropologist Squadron Leader Donald F. Thomson. The NAOU was to assist in the protection of Australia's north from

---

12 The situation in the United States and Britain was different, especially Americanist traditions that were heavily influenced by Boas with their emphasis on culture and personality (behaviour) and concentration on salvage anthropology among dispossesed Native Americans in the south-west of North America. Moreover, the number of practising anthropologists was greater than in Australia and New Zealand, where museum anthropology was taught only at the University of Otago, Dunedin. Regna Darnell, *Invisible Genealogies: A history of Americanist anthropology* (Lincoln, Nebr., 2001); George W. Stocking jr, *After Tylor: British social anthropology 1888–1951* (Madison, Wis., 1995); Geoffrey Gray, *A Cautious Silence: The politics of Australian anthropology* (Canberra, 2007); Caroline Thomas, 'Professional Amateurs and Colonial Academics: Steps towards academic anthropology in New Zealand, 1860–1920', MA thesis, University of Auckland, 1995.

13 Jan van Bremen, 'Wartime Anthropology: A global perspective', in Akitoshi Shimizu and Jan van Bremen (eds), *Wartime Japanese Anthropology in Asia and the Pacific* (Osaka, 2003), pp. 13–48; David Price, 'Lessons from Second World War Anthropology: Peripheral, persuasive and ignored contributions', *Anthropology Today*, 18:3 (2002), pp. 14–20; Glenn Petersen, 'Politics in Postwar Micronesia', in Robert C. Kiste and Mac Marshall (eds), *American Anthropology in Micronesia: An assessment* (Honolulu, 1999), pp. 145–96. American anthropologists were sent into Japanese internment camps during World War II. See Peter Suzuki, 'Lessons from WWII', [Letter], *Anthropology Today*, 18:6 (2002), p. 26; Murray Wax, 'Rosalie H. Wax (nee Rosalie Amelia Hankey), 1911–1998', *Anthropology Today*, 19:1 (2003), p. 25. Further sources on the wartime mobilisation of anthropologists include: Margaret Mead, 'Anthropological Contributions to National Policies During and Immediately After World War II', in Walter Goldschmidt (ed.), *The Uses of Anthropology. A special publication of the American Anthropological Association*, no. 11 (1979), pp. 145–57; also Geoffrey Gray, 'Managing the Impact of War: Australian anthropology and the South West Pacific', in Roy MacLeod (ed.), *Science and the Pacific War: Science and survival in the Pacific, 1939–1945* (Dordrecht, 2000), pp. 187–210; Geoffrey Gray, '"The next focus of power to fall under the spell of this little gang": Anthropology and Australia's post war policy in Papua New Guinea', *War & Society*, 14:2 (1996), pp. 101–17; Geoffrey Gray, 'Australian Anthropologists and WWII', *Anthropology Today*, 21:3 (2005), pp. 18–21; Geoffrey Gray, '"The army requires anthropologists": Australian anthropologists at war, 1939–1946', *Australian Historical Studies*, 37:127 (2006), pp. 156–80; Noah J. Riseman, 'Colonising Yolngu Defence: Arnhem Land in the Second World War and transnational uses of indigenous people in the Second World War', PhD thesis, University of Melbourne, 2008; Brian Jinks, 'A. A. Conlon, the Directorate of Research and New Guinea', *Journal of Australian Studies*, 12 (1983), pp. 21–33.

14 Robert Hall, *The Black Diggers: Aboriginal and Torres Strait Islanders in the Second World War* (Sydney, 1989).

15 Alan Powell, *War By Stealth: Australians and the Allied Intelligence Bureau 1942–1945* (Melbourne, 1996), pp. 343–44 (re FELO), 315–64.

invasion by the Japanese. Stanner was chosen to command the unit in part because of his anthropological expertise and a belief by the military commanders that he had the ability to lead Aboriginal people and command their loyalty. Thomson established a guerilla force (NTSRU) of some 50 Yolgnu (Arnhem Land) warriors who were armed with spears (he did not provide them with guns) to work behind the lines should the Japanese invade. Thomson also advised, early in the war, the British Solomon Islands Protectorate (BSIP) Defence Force but had returned to Australia by the time Japan attacked Pearl Harbor. The biggest think tank of social scientists advising the Army and planning for the postwar period—particularly in Australia's colonies and the wider South-West Pacific region—was, however, the Directorate of Research and, from October 1944, the Directorate of Research and Civil Affairs (DORCA). The directorate advised the Commander-in-Chief, Thomas Blamey, on matters to do with, for example, future policy and constitutional problems associated with a postwar military and civilian government in Papua and New Guinea.[16]

In New Zealand the situation for social scientists was somewhat different to that in Australia. In 1944, mapping out the central role of social scientists for a postwar Pacific—particularly applied anthropology—the New Zealand scholar Ernest Beaglehole contrasted British and Australian prewar and war developments with those of New Zealand:

> The British Colonial service has in the past been able to make use of anthropologists in the service of colonial administration, notably in Africa. Administrators have also often profited by training in anthropology at one of the English universities. Australia again, has had its government anthropologist in Papua and in New Guinea. It has been able to make use of additional skilled anthropological surveys in various sections of both mandate and territory. The New Zealand government and its island administrations have remained consistently and continuously unaware of the benefits that would accrue to Pacific administration by the use of a government anthropological service.

Beaglehole sarcastically suggested that the reason for this lack of interest in New Zealand to utilise social scientists was either 'an already incredibly efficient island administration, or, a certain myopic insensitiveness to the skills of the modern anthropological and socio-psychological field worker'.[17] In New Zealand there were, for example, no war-born institutions similar to the Australian Army's Directorate of Research to provide a haven for intellectuals.

---

16 Brian Jinks, 'Policy, Planning and Administration in Papua New Guinea 1942–52, with Special Reference to the Role of Colonel J. K. Murray', PhD thesis, University of Sydney, 1976; Gray, 'Managing the Impact of War', pp. 187–210. See chapter by Pybus in this volume.
17 Ernest Beaglehole, 'The South Seas Regional Commission', *Journal of the Polynesian Society*, 53:2 (1944), pp. 69–70.

Nonetheless, the experiences of New Zealand social scientists during World War II were profound, and even though they had less opportunities than their Australian colleagues to work in specialised units together with other intellectuals, clusters and group formation also eventuated. They served at home, in Britain, and to some degree in the region, especially in the Solomon Islands and Fiji. In particular, there was a young cohort (born in the early 1920s), which enlisted in the New Zealand Territorial Army and went on to distinguished academic careers. The New Zealand historian Keith Sinclair wrote that 'few of us doubted the importance of winning the war or that we would soon need to serve'.[18] He also points out that New Zealand did not send young men aged under twenty-one overseas. This meant that some of the cohort remained in New Zealand until quite late in the war. Sinclair and Bruce Biggs, an old friend from school and inaugural lecturer in Maori language at Auckland University College, organised an informal reading group while they were at Army School. When Sinclair turned twenty-one, he volunteered to go abroad with the Navy's Scheme B—an officers' training course in the United Kingdom. In this, he was joined by the anthropologist J. Derek Freeman.[19] Biggs was sent to Fiji. New Zealand looked to Fiji as its first line of defence against invasion and attack. Other members of this cohort include Cyril Belshaw and William Geddes. Cyril Belshaw (b. 1921) commented recently that 'volunteering to join the British Solomon Islands Defence Force…was probably the best career decision I have ever made'. It enabled him to accept an offer from the Institute of Pacific Relations to take a survey of colonial government and reconstruction in New Caledonia, New Hebrides and the British Solomon Islands, which resulted in *Island Administration in the South West Pacific* (1950). His father, an economics professor in New Zealand, was a friend of W. L. Holland, Director of the Institute of Pacific Relations in New York, and this association was to Cyril's benefit. When Belshaw arrived at the London School of Economics (LSE) to undertake doctoral studies, Raymond Firth 'was of the opinion that my life in the Solomons gave me a sense of the reality in the field'. His wartime work acted as a substitute of sorts for fieldwork, and Belshaw completed a library thesis.[20]

Similarly, deployment turned into fieldwork opportunity for W. R. Geddes (1916–89) who put H. D. Skinner's one-year anthropology course at Otago University to good use during his service (1941–45) in the 2nd New Zealand Expeditionary Force. Rising to staff sergeant, he spent most of his time in Fiji. This experience was the basis for his Polynesian Society memoir, *Deuba: A study of a Fijian village* (1945), written during the Bougainville campaign,

---

18 Keith Sinclair, *Halfway Round the Harbour: An autobiography* (Auckland, 1993), p. 54.
19 Ibid., pp. 84–5; see also Hempenstall this volume.
20 Cyril Belshaw, *Bumps on a Long Road* (Self-published: <www.lulu.com>, 2009), pp. 31, 54–8. The thesis was published as 'The Great Village: The economic and social welfare of Hanubada, an urban community in Papua' (London, 1957).

and his University of London (PhD, 1948) thesis, 'An Analysis of Cultural Change in Fiji', written at the LSE. In 1947–48, he lectured in psychology at Birkbeck College, University of London, and returned to Auckland in 1951 as a lecturer in anthropology at Auckland University College, rising to Professor of Anthropology at the University of Sydney in 1958. The work of women scientists and social scientists, as in Australia, was marginalised and elided, and it is to this we now turn.

II

While war opened up new home-front opportunities and work environments for women of all ages and classes, in the world of the sciences and social sciences war exacerbated a pre-existing gendered divide. A scarcity of trained and experienced female social scientists in Australia and New Zealand and a lack of units and deployments open to women had the consequence that the number of female scholars at war this volume portrays is small indeed. The opportunities for education during the war, which were enhanced through an absence of men, and the academic postwar environment of unusual students—namely, returned soldiers enrolling as mature-age students—opened new avenues for female social scientists, particularly in the new discipline of sociology. The main cohort of female social scientists came into professional careers in the postwar period, and is therefore not part of the biographical chapters. In order to understand the impact of war on a gendered development of social sciences, the main directions and research agendas undertaken by these postwar women scholars are set out and contextualised here.

The war work of women scientists and social scientists, despite the war work of eminent American anthropologists such as Margaret Mead and Ruth Benedict, is frequently overlooked, undervalued and under-researched. It reflects a perceived maleness of war and a desire to domesticate women; men went overseas, and women, with few exceptions, stayed at the home front.[21] It also mirrors the lack of suitably qualified university-educated women. The naval historian Kathleen Broome Williams has written on women scientists who worked for the US Navy during the war. In her group biography, she singles out four women who went on to distinguished careers. Nonetheless, there were few women with scientific qualifications, and those who were qualified found

---

21   Libby Connors, Lynette Finch, Kay Saunders and Helen Taylor, *Australia's Frontline: Remembering the 1939–45 war* (St Lucia, Qld, 1992); Marilyn Lake, 'Female Desires: The meaning of World War Two', in Joy Damousi and Marilyn Lake (eds), *Gender and War: Australians at war in the twentieth century* (Cambridge, 1995), pp. 60–80.

work in laboratories—a space largely denied women before the war.[22] A further restriction was the refusal of the Navy to enable women to enlist like the men; rather they were attached to auxiliary units, such as Women Accepted for Volunteer Emergency Service (WAVES).

The situation in Australia was no better—if anything, worse. For example, in Australia, women—educated or not—were encouraged to join the Australian Women's Land Army to provide labour to rural areas. Nevertheless, historian Marilyn Lake has judged World War II to be one of the high points of feminist mobilisation—that is, women entered public life as men conventionally conceived it.[23] Despite such a judgment, there were few opportunities for women scientists during the war,[24] and the rules against the employment of married women created great difficulty in obtaining tenured positions in universities, which lasted into the 1960s, at least.[25] Cambridge-educated physicist Rachel Makinson, for example, who later had a distinguished career in wool research at the Commonwealth Scientific and Industrial Research Organisation (CSIRO) Division of Textile Physics, came to the University of Sydney in 1939. She commented in an interview with Anne Sarzin:

> The prejudice in Australia against married women working was colossal…But apart from that, I wasn't allowed to have a decent position in the University because my husband was already there. They had fathers and sons in the same department but not husbands and wives. It was an unwritten but definite policy.[26]

Women social scientists were few in number in Australia and New Zealand. Camilla Wedgwood is the most well known of the small number of women social scientists in Australia and New Zealand at the outset of the war.[27] The Australian anthropologist Phyllis Kaberry, the most senior and best qualified of all the Australian women social scientists, carried out fieldwork (1939–40) in

---

22 Williams notes that, in contrast, the Manhatten Project actively recruited and employed a number of women scientists. Kathleen Broome Williams, *Improbable Warriors: Women scientists and the U.S. Navy in World War II* (Annapolis, Md, 2001). See, for example, Jane S. Wilson and Charlotte Serber (eds), *Standing By and Making Do: Women of wartime Los Alamos* (Los Alamos, NM, 2008 [1988]).
23 Lake, 'Female Desires', p. 75.
24 See, however, Nessy Allen, 'Test Tubes and White Jackets: The careers of two Australian women scientists', *Journal of Australian Studies*, 52 (1997), pp. 126–34. See also interviews with Australian scientists: viewed 22 April 2011, <http://www.science.org.au/scientists/interviews/w/gw.html> There are seven women interviewed who were active during the war; only two—Dorothy Hill and Jean Laby—were employed for their scientific expertise.
25 Patricia Crawford and Myrna Tonkinson, *The Missing Chapters: Women staff at the University of Western Australia, 1963–1987* (Perth, 1988).
26 Anne Sarzin, 'Review [of *Profiles: Australian women scientists*, by Ragbir Bhathal]', viewed 22 April 2011, <http://www.wisenet-australia.org/issue52/bookrev.htm> A similar situation confronted Catherine Berndt when her husband, Ronald, obtained a position at the University of Western Australia in 1956. In a more general sense, Roy MacLeod's volume *Science and the Pacific War* is silent on the work of individual women scientists, with the exception of passing references in individual chapters.
27 See Wetherell this volume.

the Sepik district of the League of Nations Mandated Territory of New Guinea. The need for an eye operation forced her to return to Sydney, where she spent 1940–41 writing up field reports and working for the university's Department of Anthropology as an honorary assistant lecturer. War precluded her return to the Sepik. While successively holding Sterling and Carnegie Fellowships (1941–43) at Yale University, USA, she gave lectures and edited *The Dynamics of Culture Change* (New Haven, Conn., 1945)—a posthumous collection of Malinowski's unpublished papers. Despite attempts by Elkin to lure her back to Sydney (in late 1947, he offered her a senior research fellowship to establish 'a sociological department'),[28] she travelled to London where she became a research associate (1943–44) at the Royal Institute of International Affairs. She then worked in the Office for Colonial Affairs and conducted fieldwork in the Cameroons. After a short period as a lecturer, she was appointed, in 1951, Reader in Anthropology at University College, London—a position she retained until her retirement in 1976. And despite a solid record of achievement, the English anthropologist Audrey Richards' claims to consideration for the vacant Chair of Anthropology at The Australian National University (ANU) were summarily dismissed by the Vice-Chancellor, L. G. Melville: 'Do you not think that Audrey Richards, especially in view of her sex, might be a little old to take over a young department in an area where she is unfamiliar?'[29] She was, however, under consideration for the ANU Foundation Chair of Anthropology, supported by Raymond Firth and Keith Hancock, advisors to the Interim Council, who saw no problems in appointing Richards.[30]

Or else, women academics took a subservient role. A young New Zealander, Catherine Helen Webb, was enrolled in the Diploma in Anthropology at the University of Sydney. She had completed a Certificate of Proficiency in Anthropology at the University of Otago, Dunedin, under H. D. Skinner and had a BA from Victoria University College, Wellington.[31] She married fellow anthropology student Ronald Murray Berndt in April 1941; he was twenty-four, Catherine twenty-two. They became Elkin's long-desired husband-and-wife combination: 'I realized that this field-work combination of man and wife was an ideal one, for their particular gifts were complementary, just as their opportunities for working respectively with native men and women were also complementary.'[32] Catherine, like Ronald, completed her Diploma in

---

28 Kaberry to Elkin, 11 January 1948, Papers of A. P. Elkin, University of Sydney Archives [hereinafter EP], 197/4/2/373.
29 L. G. Melville to W. K. Hancock, 19 March 1956, Hancock Papers, Australian National University Archives [hereinafter ANUA], 19/18.
30 School of Pacific Studies, Notes on discussion between the Vice-Chancellor [Douglas Copland] and Professor Firth, Monday, 23 May 1949, FIRTH7/5/8.
31 Victoria University Calendar, 1936, pp. 121, 123, 125; 1937, pp. 129, 134; 1938, pp. 134, 136, 141; University of Otago Registry and Administration Records, MS-1632/024.
32 A. P. Elkin, 'Foreword', in Ronald M. Berndt and Catherine H. Berndt, *Sexual Behaviour in Western Arnhem Land* (New York, 1958 [1951]), pp. 9–10.

Anthropology in April 1942; her anthropological research was only marginally linked to the war effort, and is one of the few cases of a female—or male—social scientist being able to conduct non-war-related research unhindered by the war.[33] As their careers took shape, Catherine, perhaps putting aside her ambitions, increasingly devoted herself to actively developing and making Ronald's career. Ronald acknowledged his debt often—for example, by dedicating *Love Songs of Arnhem Land* to her: she 'has been and continues to be my constant companion on all our fieldwork'.[34] In 1956, Ronald accepted a position as senior lecturer at the University of Western Australia; Catherine and he remained there for the rest of their lives. Their nearly 50-year partnership was one of the most industrious ever encountered in anthropology.[35]

Elkin gathered together the largest group of women social scientists. During the war, he developed an interest in the assimilation of recent European immigrants to Australia. It reflected Elkin's long-held desire to include sociology as integral to the department's functions.[36] Elkin's sociological research program during the war examined 'problems connected with the assimilation of alien groups'; it was supported, and in part funded, by the Commonwealth Department of Post-War Reconstruction. In spite of his long-held interest in sociological problems, it was also a force of circumstance brought about by wartime exigencies and a shortage of research funds; most of the Rockefeller Foundation and Carnegie funds had dried up. The Department of Post-War Reconstruction headed by H. C. Coombs identified three commissions of inquiry: into housing, rural reconstruction and secondary industry.[37] Elkin's students were able to provide information on the first two. This sociological research was conducted by recent—mostly women—graduates in the department: Jean Craig (later Martin), Caroline Tennant Kelly, Mona Ravenscroft, Florence Harding, Vere Hole, John McDonald

---

33 Geoffrey Gray, '"You are...my anthropological children": A. P. Elkin, Ronald Berndt and Catherine Berndt, 1940–1956', *Aboriginal History*, 29 (2005), pp. 77–106; also Gray on Berndt, this volume.
34 Ronald M. Berndt, *Love Songs of Arnhem Land* (Chicago, 1978), p. xx.
35 For a list of their publications, see Robert Tonkinson and Michael Howard (eds), *Going It Alone? Prospects for Aboriginal autonomy* (Canberra, 1990), pp. 45–63.
36 *Our Opinions and the National Effort* (Sydney, 1941) was Elkin's first attempt at non-Aboriginal sociology. It was 'based on a survey and analysis of opinions of individuals of the typical and various sections and ages of the community in which the author was assisted by twenty observers mostly graduates in anthropology. The results of the survey were sent in the first instance to the Commonwealth authorities. Amongst other things the book shows the necessity for basing all appeals and calls to the nation on a knowledge of the various divisions of opinion and the types of reaction which exist.' 'Notes and News', *Oceania*, 12:2 (1941), p. 187. See also A. P. Elkin, 'The Need for Sociological Research in Australia', *Social Horizons*, (July 1943), pp. 5–15. *Social Horizons* was the journal of the Australian Institute of Sociology, of which Elkin was President.
37 H. C. Coombs, *Trial Balance: Issues of my working life* (Melbourne, 1983 [1981]), pp. 26–32.

and Jim Bell.³⁸ Craig also researched problems associated with rural housing,³⁹ as did Ravenscroft.⁴⁰ In early 1945, Craig was appointed Teaching Fellow at the University of Sydney so she could continue aspects of her rural research.⁴¹ Since 1942, Kelly had researched 'into problems connected with the assimilation of alien groups, which has been of high standard and national importance'.⁴² This research was under the auspices of the Department of Post-War Reconstruction with the assistance of the Department of the Interior. After the war Kelly did field research on migrants in Victoria and Queensland.⁴³ Elkin's support of research into 'alien groups' did not cease with the abandonment of the Department of Post-War Reconstruction. Hole and Harding, both MA graduates, spent the academic year 1947–48 in the Department of Sociology and Anthropology, University of Chicago, as did Jean Craig: 'in particular they are studying the method of social science research which have [sic] developed in these schools.'⁴⁴

Craig was lured into identity and migration studies. Other sociological investigations supported by the Sydney Anthropology Department included John McDonald's 'research in Italy in districts from which immigrants come to Australia', and that of Jim Bell, who was 'engaged in a sociological study of an old township near Sydney'.⁴⁵ The sociology of recent immigrant groups faded from Elkin's view but not from that of the Foundation Professor of Anthropology at the ANU: the Vienna and Berlin trained ethnomusicologist and London trained anthropologist S. F. Nadel. He had developed a detailed research program that included investigating the process of assimilation of recent migrant groups. Soon after his arrival, the department in Canberra was renamed to embrace both anthropology and sociology so such research as assimilation of migrant groups could be studied. Soon after, Craig enrolled to do her doctoral research on 'role assumption and fulfillment among European migrants in Australia'.⁴⁶ She was awarded her PhD in 1954.

---

38 'Notes and News', *Oceania*, 14:2 (1943), p. 182; 15:3 (1945), p. 276; 16:4 (1946), p. 353. Kelly was awarded the Diploma in Anthropology in 1945—her first and only formal qualification in anthropology. 'Notes and News', *Oceania*, 15:3 (1945), p. 276. Kelly was a friend of Margaret Mead, who stayed with her when she came to Australia; she had also worked for Elkin, as a research assistant, since the early 1930s.
39 Elkin noted that she 'has specialised in the social-anthropological (sociological) study of rural communities'. 'Notes and News', *Oceania*, 15:3 (1945), p. 276.
40 Mona Ravenscroft, 'The Housing Problem', *Social Horizons* (July 1943), pp. 48–53. She was for several years a tutor and research assistant in the Department of Anthropology.
41 'Notes and News', *Oceania*, 15:3 (1945), p. 276. See Jean Craig, 'Some Aspects of Life in Selected Areas of Rural New South Wales', MA thesis, University of Sydney, 1945.
42 'Notes and News', *Oceania*, 15:3 (1945), p. 276.
43 'Notes and News', *Oceania*, 16:4 (1946), p. 353.
44 'Notes and News', *Oceania*, 18:2 (1947), p. 176; 18:4 (1948), p. 358.
45 'Notes and News', *Oceania*, 24:1 (1953), p. 78.
46 S. F. Nadel, *Report on Activities in 1952, Department of Anthropology and Sociology, ANU*, Copy in authors' possession; Jean Craig, 'Assimilation of European Immigrants: A study in role assumption and fulfilment', PhD thesis, Australian National University, 1954.

Others worked in Indigenous studies during the war. Elkin pursued an interest in Aboriginal people of mixed descent, which he regarded as sociological rather than anthropological. Ronald and Catherine Berndt and Marie Reay, a recently graduated student, mainly undertook this research. Certainly, it was not considered orthodox social anthropology and those who conducted this type of research were not thought of as 'real' anthropologists.[47] Post war, there were only meagre funds available for anthropological research and Elkin believed that the best use of these funds was pursuing research on Aboriginal people of mixed descent living in rural and urban New South Wales, especially north-western New South Wales. Most of this work was associated with the NSW Aborigines' Welfare Board (AWB), of which Elkin was Vice-Chairman, and focused on problems specific to the implementation of the assimilation policy of the NSW Government. Funding for research therefore came mainly from the University of Sydney, the AWB and what limited funds were available from the Australian National Research Council (ANRC). A case in point is Pamela Nixon's 1947 MA thesis, which dealt with the history of the community, family and kinship, economics, religion, authority and leadership, and recreational activities at La Perouse.[48] The impact of war opened up opportunities for female scholars in the postwar period, particularly in the new and growing discipline of sociology and related fields in social anthropology. This development, however, is not at the core of *Scholars at War*, which examines social-science professionals during World War II.

III

The New Zealanders discussed in *Scholars at War* were in Britain before the war, or, in Freeman's case, arrived during the war, and remained there (as did some Australians, such as Keith Hancock). The Australians who found themselves in Britain at the beginning of the war, by and large, endeavoured to return to Australia, which reflects, in part, a desire to help defend Australia and a new nationalism that developed during the war; this nationalism was reflected by an optimism that as the war ended Australia and the world generally would provide new opportunities. A number of organisations were established during the war that recruited social scientists, besides DORCA; the Department of Post-War Reconstruction mapped out new structures and directions for peacetime Australia. As H. C. Coombs noted: the task of the Department of Post-War

---

47   Geoffrey Gray, '"[The Sydney school] seem[s] to view the Aborigines as forever unchanging": Southeastern Australia and Australian Anthropology', *Aboriginal History*, 24 (2000), pp. 176–200.
48   Pamela Nixon, 'The Integration of a Half-caste Community at La Perouse, NSW', MA thesis, University of Sydney, 1947.

Reconstruction, established soon after John Curtin was elected Prime Minister, 'was to ensure an economic and social context in which positive opportunities were present rather than merely an absence of constraints'.[49]

The Pacific War therefore provided an opportunity for intellectual talent to play a role in running and shaping Australia. 'The growth of services, the expansion of government…gave the younger generation chances which it would never have had in the stagnant society between the wars.' In the Public Service, the Department of External Affairs, for example, 'was picking up bright young men… there was a spirit of optimism about Australia's future. The new generation was confident that past mistakes would be avoided.'[50] This new generation perceived themselves as progressive and able to direct a postwar agenda in the development of the nation.[51] Notwithstanding, the intellectual, cultural, social and political networks linking Australia to Britain and the Empire were not loosened. The Empire remained—as it had before the war—a large conglomerate of nations interlocked through intellectual, social and cultural networks that bound the British world together, beyond the 'mother country'.[52] Consideration, for instance, of empire (transnational) networks of scholarly patronage indicates less difference between New Zealand and Australia than Belich suggests and perhaps more than Mein Smith's work would allow, especially when early to mid-twentieth-century academic appointments in Australia and New Zealand are considered.[53] *Scholars at War* shows the intellectual and scholarly links not just across the Tasman but also the transnational networks in which all our subjects were in some way intertwined and interweaved. It links two neigbouring countries through a network of scholars based in Britain, Australia, New Zealand and the United States, whose histories are seldom reflected in the

---

49 Coombs, *Trial Balance*, p. 26 ff. See also papers from the conference on 'The Seven Dwarfs and the Age of the Mandarins, 1940s–1960s', 4–5 November 2010, Old Parliament House, Canberra.
50 Richard Hall, *The Real John Kerr: His brilliant career* (Sydney, 1978), pp. 43–5, 53.
51 John Pomeroy, 'Morale on the Homefront in Australia During the Second World War', PhD thesis, University of Sydney, 1995, p. 231; see also Paul Hasluck, *Diplomatic Witness: Australian foreign affairs, 1941–1947* (Melbourne, 1980).
52 Carl Bridge and Kent Fedorowich, 'Mapping the British World', *Journal of Imperial and Commonwealth History*, 31:2 (2003), pp. 1–15; Keith Jeffrey, 'The Second World War', in Judith M. Brown and Wm. Roger Louis (eds), *The Oxford History of the British Empire. Volume 4: The twentieth century* (Oxford, 2001), pp. 306–28; Simon Potter, 'What Did You Do in the War, Professor? Imperial history and propaganda, 1939–45', in Robert Blyth and Keith Jeffery (eds), *The British Empire and its Contested Pasts* (Dublin/Portland, 2009), pp. 24–42; cf. Jim Davidson, *A Three-Cornered Life: The historian WK Hancock* (Sydney, 2010), pp. 186–227.
53 James Belich, *Paradise Reforged: A history of the New Zealanders from the 1880s to the Year 2000* (Auckland, 2001); Philippa Mein Smith, Peter Hempenstall and Shaun Goldfinch, with Stuart McMillan and Rosemary Baird, *Remaking the Tasman World* (Christchurch, 2008); Peter Hempenstall, 'Overcoming Separate Histories: Historians as "ideas traders" in a trans-Tasman world', *History Australia*, 4:1 (2007), pp. 4.1–4.16; Geoffrey Gray and Doug Munro, 'Australian Aboriginal Anthropology at the Crossroads: Finding a successor to A. P. Elkin, 1955', *Australian Journal of Anthropology*, 22:3 (2011, forthcoming); see also Belshaw to Gray, Emails, 2010, re University of British Columbia anthropological appointments.

historiographies.⁵⁴ Even at a personal level, young scholars such as Sinclair and Freeman, in their brief stopover in Melbourne, established intellectual and social links with the Melbourne academy, which were carried into postwar relations.

These networks stretched far and wide, within a small circle of anthropologists and historians in Australia and New Zealand, to the 'mother' country. They were often inclusive but were equally often fractious due in part to personal, intellectual and political tensions.⁵⁵ London committees routinely did the work of selecting suitable candidates for senior postings in Australian and New Zealand universities. The appointment in 1925 of A. R. Radcliffe-Brown to the Foundation Chair of Anthropology at the University of Sydney was decided by a London-based committee that included an Australian, Elliot Grafton Smith (the other members were the Cambridge anthropologist A. C. Haddon and J. T. Wilson, Professor of Anatomy, Cambridge). Haddon was consulted over most empire appointments, including the Chair in South Africa, and the government anthropologist positions in Papua and New Guinea. Elkin's appointment to the Sydney Anthropology Chair in 1933 was an exception, with a local selection committee making the appointment, although his referees were British (including Radcliffe-Brown) as were those of the other applicants, who were part of the international cohort of anthropologists. The then Vice-Chancellor, Sir Mungo MacCallum, was determined to have Australians appointed when possible. These empire networks were not diminished by war but rather were strengthened and invigorated by war. The ANU Interim Council sought advice over academic appointments from London-based advisers, namely the New Zealander Raymond Firth and the Australians Howard Florey, Mark Oliphant and Keith Hancock. The appointment, in 1949, of Ralph Piddington as Foundation Chair at Auckland University College is a case in point. The governing council sought advice from the Association of the Universities of the Commonwealth, which was asked to convene a committee to advise on the appointment of the professor. The committee was London based and consisted of Raymond Firth as Chairman, E. Evans-Pritchard and Darryll Forde.

The key figures in these empire (transnational) networks of scholarly patronage and appointment were Haddon, Bronislaw Malinowski and A. R. Radcliffe-Brown before the war, and, after the war, Raymond Firth and to a lesser degree Keith Hancock.⁵⁶ Elkin was a central figure, too, as all the anthropologists in *Scholars at War* other than Freeman either were taught by Elkin or worked in the Sydney department under Elkin. He was the dominant figure in prewar

---

54 Hempenstall, 'Overcoming Separate Histories'.
55 Gray, *A Cautious Silence*, pp. 13–76.
56 See Geoffrey Gray and Doug Munro, 'Your own position is not being overlooked': The politics of choosing a successor to S. F. Nadel, 1957, Unpublished manuscript; and generally Davidson, *A Three-Cornered Life*; S. G. Foster and Margaret M. Varghese, *The Making of The Australian National University, 1946–1996* (Sydney, 1996).

and postwar Australian anthropology, exercising his authority over funding, choice of field site, patronage, academic positions, even controlling the material published in the journal *Oceania*, which he edited from 1933 to his death in 1979. He was consulted over the establishment of the Chair in Auckland, and the University of Western Australia developing anthropology there.[57] Elkin is the oldest of the social scientists discussed in *Scholars at War*—born a decade before the end of the nineteenth century—while there is a generation gap between Elkin and the other Australian and New Zealand social scientists who were by and large of the same cohort. The youngest was born in 1926. In the terminology of the academy in the early 2000s, they were early to mid-career scholars. With the exception of Elkin, the anthropologists are second generation. The Australian anthropologists were trained under Radcliffe-Brown, Firth and/or Elkin at Sydney, furthering their studies under Malinowski and Firth at the LSE. With the exception of Hogbin, who returned to a position in Australia, the Australian anthropologists found African-oriented work through the British Colonial Office, which supported anthropological research through the universities, or, in the case of Piddington, appointed to the University of Aberdeen. Hogbin, when he was an undergraduate at Sydney, was taught by, and later became a colleague of, Wedgwood. Hogbin was the first Australian scholar to attend the LSE under Malinowski. The Australian anthropologists were Durkheimian in theoretical outlook when they left for London. When they returned, they had taken a Malinowskian functionalist turn. Piddington remained a devout Malinowskian functionalist all his life.

Attendance at the LSE created other networks by bringing the Australians and New Zealanders into contact with anthropologists such as Lucy Mair, Audrey Richards and S. F. Nadel—scholars of considerable eminence before the war; or establishing connections with Hancock, who was to play a key role in the appointment of J. W. Davidson to the ANU. Towards the end of the war, Mair, an expert on colonial administration, was brought out to Australia to conduct a survey of Papua and New Guinea as well as to advise on the courses at the Army's School of Civil Affairs.[58] It is most likely that Hogbin suggested her; Hogbin and Mair's friendship dated to their time at the LSE in the early 1930s. Certainly, it was Hogbin who enabled Piddington to be appointed Deputy Principal of the Army's School of Civil Affairs; he arrived in 1944 after spending the war working for the British Army. Ronald and Catherine Berndt—the youngest of the anthropologists—were heavily influenced by Elkin, were

---

57   Geoffrey Gray and Doug Munro, 'Establishing Anthropology and Maori Language (Studies), Auckland University College: The appointment of Ralph Piddington, 1949', in Regna Darnell and Frederic W. Gleach (eds), *Histories of Anthropology Annual*, volume 7 (Lincoln, Nebr., forthcoming); Geoffrey Gray, '"You are… my anthropological children"', pp. 77–106.
58   Lucy Mair, *Australia in New Guinea* (London/Melbourne, 1948).

awarded doctorates from the LSE and were supervised by Firth and Kaberry. (Elkin encouraged them to make as many contacts as possible, as this was in his opinion more important than a doctorate from the LSE.)[59]

New Zealand, in contrast with Australia, was characterised by dispersal and expatriation. Similarly to the Australians, New Zealand social scientists went to London to pursue their education—most notably, to obtain postgraduate qualifications; other factors were the cultural cringe and a yearning to see a wider world, particularly to visit the 'mother country'. Davin, Davidson and Phillips were all in London at the outbreak of war and were caught up in the war mobilisation. Freeman, as alluded to earlier, was in Samoa at the outbreak of war. He shared Davidson's distaste for war. Nonetheless, he enlisted in the Navy and arrived in England for an officers' training course. It enabled him, in retrospect, to pursue a career in anthropology at the LSE.

These intellectual and academic networks were further enhanced post war. Stanner, Davidson and Freeman were all appointed to the newly established ANU; Stanner and Freeman were appointed largely on the recommendation of their old teacher and mentor Firth with some input from Hancock. Hogbin turned down a readership at the ANU to remain at Sydney—a strange decision considering he had such an appalling relationship with Elkin, which was a matter he frequently commented on in his personal correspondence.[60] The Berndts expanded their empire network, spending six months on a Carnegie Travelling Grant investigating anthropology teaching in the United States. While opportunities for social scientists in Australia were limited, they were even more so in New Zealand. Davin lived in England. Davidson and Freeman moved to the ANU where they remained all their academic lives. Only Neville Phillips returned to New Zealand.

IV

The experience of individual anthropologists during the Pacific War accelerated and consolidated the emergence of anthropology as an applied discipline. Australia had long had an interest in Papua (an Australian territory from 1906; until then it had been administered by Britain) and New Guinea (a German territory until 1914 when Australia occupied it on the declaration of war, and then, from 1921, a League of Nations 'C' Mandate under Australian administration). The appointments of government anthropologists in Papua

---

59 Elkin to R. M. Berndt and C. H. Berndt, 3 August 1954; also R. M. Berndt to Elkin, 2 May 1954, EP, 41/4/2/375.
60 There is a belief he turned the position down because he would not have been able to hide his homosexuality in such a small city as Canberra.

and New Guinea reflect a growing acceptance by colonial governments of anthropology as a helpful discipline useful in governing colonised peoples. Anthropology, as a way of justifying its scholarly and practical credentials, presented itself to colonial administrations and metropolitan governments—Britain, the United States and Australia—as a discipline that was able to help in the control, management and advancement of colonised peoples in the African colonies and indigenous people in settler nations such as Australia, Canada and the United States.

It is during the interwar period that Australian anthropology, slowly but surely, became a recognised academic discipline with the accoutrements of professionalisation: specialised and specific qualifications and training, specific funding for research problems, a growing body of specialists, a journal devoted to publishing the results of research, and various attempts to 'control a market for their expertise'.[61] The interwar years saw also the demise of the amateur ethnographer, usually associated with museum anthropology.

War therefore opened up spaces in which a new academic and professional elite was established. It gave a younger generation chances it would never have had in the stagnant societies of New Zealand and Australia between the wars.[62] War enhanced the developing professionalisation of anthropology and an increasing interest in regional and national histories. Post war saw anthropology expanding its academic and disciplinary authority, knowledge and power. The Pacific War thus created an unprecedented opportunity for Australia's anthropologists. David Price has noted that World War II provided American anthropology with an impetus for its expansion not only in the academy but also within the military and government. Before the war American universities and museums were few in number and funds for research were scarce, especially for overseas research. It was localised, inward rather than outward looking, with most socio-cultural research as salvage ethnography on American Indians. War also placed an emphasis on the practical applications of anthropology and ethnographic knowledge, which saw an increase in applied anthropology after the war—a shift that by the end of the 1950s had given way to sociological ethnographic research on culture and what were perceived as people with minimal European contact.[63] This is so for Australia, which combined both an applied interest in

---

61 Magali Sarfatti Larson, *The Rise of Professionalism: A sociological analysis* (Berkeley, Calif., 1977), p. xvi; Donald Wright, *The Professionalization of History in English Canada* (Toronto, 2005), pp. 4–5. Also Legge in this volume.
62 Hall, *The Real John Kerr*, pp. 43–5. Such stagnation included Australian universities—described as 'small and extremely parochial institutions where men of strong personality could build up excessive power bases for the implementation of their views'. Leonie Star, *Julius Stone: An intellectual life* (Sydney/Melbourne, 1992), p. 67.
63 Robert C. Kiste and Mac Marshall, 'Introduction', in Kiste and Marshall, *American Anthropology in Micronesia*, p. 2.

governing colonised peoples in mainland and external territories and pursuing what might be thought of as major questions concerning people with minimal European contact—found in the Highlands of New Guinea.[64]

Some observers expected that in the wake of the war the hour of social sciences had come. Ernest Beaglehole in 1944 saw a trend developing in Europe and South-East Asia that he hoped would extend to the Pacific region:

> It is already clear that the reconstruction of the post-war world is likely to demand the solution of an enormous number of extremely complex problems. These problems are of all kinds: some of them economic, some political, some educational, some health problems—but all of them, in their fundamentals, human problems…Statesmen will hopefully use the advice, the knowledge and the skilled techniques of the scientist in solving this world-wide human problem. The social sciences, in particular psychology, anthropology, economics and medicine, will thus have to meet large scale responsibilities in this post-war world.[65]

The extended use of the social sciences, and anthropology in particular, as occurred in America, in the service of government and the military, however, did not occur in Australia and New Zealand. Certainly, post war, there was an expansion in the social sciences and increased student numbers.

> Australian universities experienced a remarkable renaissance in 1946, 1947 and 1948, resuming the flowering of academic and student life interrupted in early 1942 by national mobilisation…The Universities were bulging. At Sydney a record 3,600 first year students enrolled in 1946, 1200 of them ex-servicemen and women. The largest group was in the Arts, with 790 first year enrolments.

By 1948, enrolments were 10 450.[66] Anthropology was a popular subject; the Anthropology Department was overflowing with students and its small staff was overloaded. To be sure, some of the younger scholars, such as Ronald and Catherine Berndt, Mona Ravenscroft and Jean Craig, were given teaching opportunities as a consequence. During these years, Hogbin dithered over his future, teaching part-time at the Australian School of Pacific Administration (ASOPA) to the detriment of his teaching duties at the university. Elkin was furious with him for not pulling his weight.

Opportunities for social scientists—economists, historians, sociologists, psychologists and anthropologists—were limited. Nevertheless, in the first

---

64 See Terence Hays (ed.), *Ethnographic Presents: Pioneering anthropologists in the Papua New Guinea Highlands* (Berkeley, Calif., 1992).
65 Beaglehole, 'The South Pacific Commission', p. 59.
66 Alan Barcan, *Radical Students: The Old Left at Sydney University* (Melbourne, 2002), p. 174.

decade after the end of the war, anthropology in particular was courted by the PNG Administration even to the extent of contemplating (and arranging for) a husband-and-wife team as government anthropologists. There appeared to be a defined role and future for anthropology and its usefulness and practical application in the governance of colonised peoples. Elkin, who, in 1949–50, had undertaken a survey of anthropological research in Melanesia, recommended not only that colonial administrations appoint permanent anthropologists to research positions but also that mission societies appoint 'mission anthropologists' to help in their 'approach, in their difficulties, and to evaluate functionally the effects of their activities'.[67] He advocated—as he had before the war—that colonial officials and mission staff be trained in anthropology and associated subjects before embarking on their work. This represented some continuity with prewar colonial governments and the place of anthropology but there was an added dimension: an interest in social change.

The establishment of an Army School of Civil Affairs at Duntroon in December 1944 illustrated the success of the DORCA in convincing military authorities of the wisdom of such a training school; it provided further opportunities for social scientists and was part of the expansion of the social sciences in Australia. The School of Civil Affairs was, however, short lived and, after a rather prolonged negotiation over the future of the school post war, it was placed under the control of the Department of External Territories, renamed the Australian School of Pacific Administration (ASOPA) and located at Mosman on Sydney Harbour. The school trained officers, especially cadets and patrol officers for service in Papua and New Guinea.[68] Various members of the ASOPA hoped the school would be incorporated into the ANU as a centre for colonial studies and training along the lines of that offered at Oxford. This did not occur.

The new Administrator of Papua New Guinea, J. K. (Jack) Murray, who had been a member of DORCA, was keen to get a set-up that would allow 'routine anthropological work being done in the territory, research work directed to the answers to specific questions such as those related to depopulation, health and the status of women'; there was, he opined, 'practically [an] open field being presented to any research workers in anthropology who wish to undertake work here'.[69] In these circumstances, Elkin recommended a husband-and-wife team, Ronald and Catherine Berndt, who were eminently suitable to undertake such research. A formal appointment for the Berndts was in the air. The upshot was that the Berndts were not considered. Rather, Charles Julius, who had done his MA under Elkin before the war, was appointed in 1950 to a position often described as government anthropologist. Rather than making it an administration-wide

---

67 A. P. Elkin, *Social Anthropology in Melanesia: A review of research* (Melbourne, 1953), p. x.
68 A history of ASOPA awaits its historian.
69 J. K. Murray to Elkin, 10 July 1951, EP, 183/4/2/338.

one, the position was confined to the Department of District Services and Native Affairs and 'limited to District Services' requirements, which emphasises the point that no GA [Government Anthropologist] being available for the purposes of other departments such as Health and Education'. The terms of Julius's appointment cut across the plans of the Director of Education, W. C. Groves, who envisaged a research section in the Education Department in which Julius would have represented anthropology, the Viennese-educated Stephen Wurm linguistics, and a 'third person specialised in Applied or Educational Psychology'.[70] Julius retained his position as anthropologist in the Department of District Services until his death in 1965. Unlike his predecessors, Chinnery and Williams, he acted as neither gatekeeper nor active researcher; he appears not to have engaged in any serious long-term anthropological research.[71] Groves pointed out to Elkin that as far as he could determine the newly appointed Minister for Territories, Paul Hasluck, squashed the proposal: 'anthropology has no place in his administration.'[72]

There had been calls in New Zealand before the war to provide training for colonial officials but until the establishment of the Department of Anthropology at Auckland University College, in 1949, there was no facility available. Even then, despite lip-service, the department did not provide such specialised training. Certainly, the usefulness of anthropology in the administration of New Zealand's colonial territories was prominent in the thinking of Auckland's University College Council when they discussed the creation of the Chair of Anthropology and its functions. Before the war various scholars such as Ernest Beaglehole, psychologist and anthropologist at Wellington, had argued that training in anthropology was important for all officials dealing with indigenous peoples; added to this was a discussion on the role of anthropology in preserving Maori culture[73] and more generally as part of the armoury of colonial administration.[74] That is, anthropology could enable a sympathetic and wise governance of colonised peoples under New Zealand rule. These ideas were taken up by Auckland, which also added the need for teaching Maori language.[75] The 1950s and 1960s saw growth in social anthropology and national histories in both Australia and New Zealand.

---

70   W. C. Groves to Elkin, 28 August 1951, EP, 182/4/2/325.
71   See the file from PNG National Archives that contains most of his lectures to the School of Civil Affairs, ASOPA and local induction courses for patrol officers, plus notes from research he conducted in Busama in 1947. Government Officers, Mr Charles Julius (Government Anthropologist), Papua New Guinea National Archives, Port Moresby.
72   Groves to Elkin, 28 August 1951, EP, 182/4/2/325.
73   Steven Webster, *Patrons of Maori Culture: Power, theory and ideology in the Maori renaissance* (Dunedin, 1998), pp. 73–102; A. T. Ngata, 'Anthropology and the Government of the Native Races in the Pacific', *Australasian Journal of Psychology and Philosophy*, 6:1 (1928), pp. 1–14.
74   M. P. K. Sorrenson, 'Polynesian Corpuscles and Pacific Anthropology: The home-made anthropology of Sir Apirana Ngata and Sir Peter Buck', *Journal of the Polynesian Society*, 91:1 (1992), pp. 17–23.
75   See Gray and Munro, 'Establishing Anthropology and Maori Language (Studies), Auckland University College'.

V

The Pacific was the last part of the world to be colonised and the last to be decolonised.[76] At the start of the war in the Pacific there were six colonial nations occupying the islands in the Pacific: those under the British flag (including Australia and New Zealand); France; Japan; the United States; the Netherlands and Portugal.[77] Yet, at the time, decolonisation was seen as a predominantly British problem, focused primarily on its African colonies, India and parts of South-East Asia such as Burma. Australia and New Zealand, however, had gained additional territories—New Guinea and Samoa—to administer only two decades earlier after World War I, and did not see the same urgency to deal with issues of decolonisation or even consider self-government for their colonies, despite mounting discontent, particularly in the mandated territory of Samoa.[78] Nevertheless, they were drawn into a wider debate on political change and future policy for the various South-West Pacific colonies under their administration, which was fuelled by a crisis of legitimacy of the League of Nations during the 1930s and gained further momentum once war was declared in 1941.[79] At the end of the war, Japan lost her Micronesian colonies, the French remained entrenched in their territories that were portrayed as being part of metropolitan France, the United States had extended the size of its empire with the acquisition of Micronesia, and Portugal remained in Timor (now Timor Leste). The Netherlands, while granting independence to Indonesia in 1948, held onto the western half of New Guinea (West Papua).

A crisis of colonialism was a consequence of World War II. War had destabilised the prewar order as well as enabling colonised peoples to see the weakness and frailties of colonial governance and its rulers in the South-West Pacific.[80] Assisting the return of the colonial governments, anthropology had a critical role to play. Anthropologists believed (a belief accepted by military and civilian authorities) they were best situated to provide advice on controlling and managing colonised populations disrupted and dislocated by the impact of war. War—cataclysmic event—offered an opportunity for regeneration, renewal

---

76   Roger C. Thomson, *Australia and the Pacific Islands in the 20th Century* (Melbourne, 1998), p. 189 ff.; Donald Denoon (ed.), *Emerging from Empire? Decolonisation in the Pacific* (Canberra, 1997); Stewart Firth, 'The War in the Pacific', in Donald Denoon et al. (ed.), *The Cambridge History of the Pacific Islanders* (Cambridge, 1997), pp. 291–323; Hugh Laracy, 'World War Two', in K. R. Howe, Robert C. Kiste and Brij V. Lal (eds), *Tides of History: The Pacific Islands in the twentieth century* (Honolulu, 1994), pp. 149–69.
77   See Dorothy Woodman, *An A. B. C. of the Pacific* (Harmondsworth, UK, 1942), pp. 79–107.
78   I. C. Campbell, 'Resistance and Colonial Government: A comparative study of Samoa', *Journal of Pacific History*, 40:1 (2005), pp. 45–69.
79   Michael D. Callahan, *A Sacred Trust: The League of Nations and Africa, 1929–1946* (Sussex, UK, 2004), especially pp. 63–96.
80   Geoffrey M. White and Lamont Lindstrom (eds), *The Pacific Theatre: Island representations of World War II* (Melbourne, 1990).

and reform.[81] It is not surprising therefore that there developed a tension between re-establishing colonial rule and an international push for the reform of colonialism with the eventual aim of decolonisation. Anthropology, of all the social sciences, was able to bridge both by mapping out reforms and supporting the strength (the good bits) of the old order. This brought about a further expansion and professionalisation of social anthropology—the dominant social science on colonised peoples and colonial rule. At war's end, most Australian social scientists—especially those connected with DORCA and ASOPA—were confident that their voice had acceptance and authority over matters to do with Papua and New Guinea (albeit over Aboriginal Australia Elkin retained his authority). Australian anthropology, however, rarely examined colonial legitimacy and its own place in colonialism; rather there was an acceptance that enlightened colonial rule was beneficial for indigenous peoples.[82]

Notwithstanding, there is no historical consensus on the position of DORCA regarding independence for Melanesian colonies, particularly Papua and New Guinea. Certainly, members of the directorate such as Hogbin and Wedgwood in particular, and Julius Stone to a lesser degree, argued for increasing indigenous control, and possibly some form of self-government. We do not think they envisaged that these colonies could be independent nations, rather some form of self-government and association with the colonial nation. Throughout the war discussion and debate, muted as they might have been, continued on the future of colonies and this debate occurred particularly within the Directorate of Research.[83] Certainly, the members of DORCA argued for an enlightened postwar colonial policy and practice.

Anthropologists had a particular interest in examining what was variously described as a clash of cultures, culture contact and the consequence of these events: cultural or social change—that is, the modification of cultural practices to make them compatible with modernity. Understanding these events and the processes associated with them assisted colonial administrators to advance the

---

81   Michael Barnett, *Empire of Humanity: A history of humanitarianism* (Ithaca, NY, and London, 2011), p. 28.
82   Gray, *A Cautious Silence*, passim. See also Max Pinkowski, 'American Colonialism at the Dawn of the Cold War' (pp. 62–88), and Frank A. Salamone, 'In the Name of Science: The Cold War and the direction of scientific pursuits' (pp. 89–107), both in Dustin M. Wax (ed.), *Anthropology at the Dawn of the Cold War* (London/Ann Arbor, Mich., 2008).
83   See especially Gray on Hogbin and Stanner, and Pybus on Conlon, in this volume. Also Gray, '"The next focus of power to fall under the spell of this little gang"', pp. 101–17. Geoffrey Bolton, Dr Evatt and Mr Hasluck at the United Nations, Unpublished paper. Bolton comments: 'I think it possible that Coombs because of his subsequent eminence has been a little over-rated and Hogbin a little under-rated as influences on the early shaping of post war policy for PNG.' Email, 15 November 2010. Cf. Tim Rowse, *Nugget Coombs: A reforming life* (Melbourne, 2003), pp. 178–81, who ascribes some unwarranted importance to the role of Coombs vis-a-vis the directorate and its work.

'native' down the road of civilisation. It was not merely a matter of pacification. The Australian-born political scientist Linden Mander believed that past colonial policy had

> been…administered without a realisation that…the impact of Western life upon native life has unleashed forces which cut far deeper than can be effectively dealt with through the traditional methods of Western law and order. Today the Western powers are paying the penalty for this lack of imagination and insight. Those who studied colonial policy years ago within the dimension of the political and legal are now confronted with situations which these methods are relatively powerless to control.[84]

This was a plea for social science and its practitioners to help identify the problems of colonial administration and the advancement and welfare of the colonised peoples.

A number of monographs, booklets and pamphlets were published during the war and in the period immediately after the war extending until the mid-1950s. Imbued with optimism and idealism, Australian and New Zealand social scientists, writers, intellectuals and church leaders with interest in the Pacific set out arguments and put out moral calls for a new future and a 'new deal' for Pacific Islanders. Among some writers was a belief that the colonial powers were indebted to the indigenous populations who had assisted and sacrificed for the Allied war effort.

The New Zealand-born and American-based anthropologist Felix M. Keesing, for some years on the staff of the Institute of Pacific Relations,[85] was one of the first into this field with his *The South Seas in the Modern World* in 1941. Keesing attempted to 'define comprehensively the political, strategic, and economic role these Oceanic islands play in the world today, and especially the modern experience and problems of the peoples native to them'.[86] During the war,

---

84   Linder [sic] A. Mander, 'Review [of *Island Administration in the South West Pacific*, by Cyril S. Belshaw]', *Pacific Historical Review*, 19:3 (1950), pp. 315–16. Linden A. Mander, a South Australian, was Professor of Political Science at the University of Washington (Seattle) and authored *Some Dependent Peoples of the South Pacific* (Leiden/New York, 1954). At a Pacific History Workshop—'1945 to 1965: The Defining Years'—held at the ANU in December 2003, three views were expressed about Eddie Ward, the Minister for External Territories in the Labor Government (1941–49), and implicitly postwar policy in Papua and New Guinea. Donald Denoon made reference largely by omission in arguing that Paul Hasluck, Minister for External Territories in the second Menzies Government (1951–66), was the best of all postwar Ministers for Territories. He did not think Ward was up to Hasluck. The New Guinean historian August Kituai started and finished his paper with Ward's 1945 policy statement and its inherent promise to Papua New Guineans that things would change for the better. It was a moral statement about the failure of the Australian Government rather than a statement about Ward. This was implicit also in the story about Tom Kabu—promises made during the war and the failure to implement these promises on the ground. Outside these views, the period 1945–49 was not discussed, and no paper addressed the immediate postwar policy in Papua New Guinea.
85   Woodman, *An A. B. C. of the Pacific*, p. 86.
86   Felix M. Keesing, *The South Seas in the Modern World* (New York, 1941), p. xiii.

he worked as an analyst in the Research and Analysis Branch's Pacific Island section, where he 'directed the compilation of information...on "all phases of psychological warfare, morale, politics, diplomacy, public administration, law personnel and social affairs in the area"', which was designated the South-West Pacific during the war.[87]

The Institute of Pacific Relations sponsored research into identifying problems of colonial administration and had a number of publications that focused on the impact of the Pacific War on colonial administration, which were part of a wider push for long-term change. Social anthropologists such as Stanner, Elkin, Hogbin and Wedgwood, the New Zealand-born Cyril Belshaw and the British expert on colonial administration Lucy Mair, and a number of missionaries including J. W. Burton and the Anglican Bishop of Sydney George Cranswick all addressed political and social change in the South-West Pacific in some detail, with differing motives and outcomes.[88]

An analysis of the similarities and differences between the models developed by individual scholars, missionaries and public intellectuals would give us a more nuanced understanding of the contribution of social scientists to this short but intense debate surrounding a 'new deal', which was soon overshadowed by different concerns and political necessities.

A direct result of the war was the shift of power in the Pacific: an increasing dependency on America coinciding with the demise of British military power, and, as the 1940s ended, the onset of the Cold War. The difficulty for Australia and New Zealand during and after the war was balancing American power and influence in the Pacific with an attachment to Britain. That is, the US Navy and American troops in the streets of Australia and New Zealand were 'a constant reminder that New Zealanders lived in a Pacific country'. Australia and New Zealand faced a common dilemma:

> [H]ow to pay their dues in this new, dangerous American sphere of dominance while remaining members of the British Commonwealth.

---

87 David H. Price, *Anthropological Intelligence: The deployment and neglect of American anthropology in the Second World War* (Durham, NC, 2008), pp. 222–3.

88 A. P. Elkin, *Wanted—A charter for the native peoples of the South-West Pacific* (Sydney, 1943); H. Ian Hogbin and C. V. Wedgwood, *Development and Welfare in the Western Pacific* (Sydney, 1943); J. W. Burton, *The Atlantic Charter and the Pacific Races* (Sydney, 1943); [H. E. Hurst], *The Pacific Islander: After the war what?* (Geelong, Vic., 1944); Julius Stone, *Colonial Trusteeship in Transition* (Sydney, 1944); Lucy Mair, *Australia in New Guinea* (London, 1948); G. H. Cranswick and I. W. A. Shevill, *A New Deal for Papua* (Melbourne, [1949]); H. Ian Hogbin, *Transformation Scene: The changing culture of a New Guinea village* (London, 1951); Cyril Belshaw, *Island Administration in the South West Pacific: Government and reconstruction in New Caledonia, the New Hebrides, and the British Solomon Islands* (London, 1950); W. E. H. Stanner, *The South Seas in Transition: A study of post-war rehabilitation and reconstruction in the Pacific territories* (Sydney, 1953). Of course, various articles appeared in the journal *Pacific Affairs*. This is by no means a comprehensive listing of works dealing with postwar colonial policy and practice in the South-West Pacific or Oceania generally. There were also a number of pamphlets on the postwar future of Aboriginal people in Australia.

> Added was the sense of Britishness inhabiting New Zealanders, their direct economic interests, and the need to cling in self-defence to the power of the Royal Navy [that all] kept New Zealand comfortably under direct British control longer than other settler Dominions.[89]

How the Cold War impacted on Australian and New Zealand anthropologists and social scientists generally is under-researched, although some individual cases have been addressed in the scholarly literature.[90] As one writer so succinctly put it: 'Western countries underwent a period of anti-communist hysteria.'[91] Nevertheless, intellectual suppression during the Cold War in Australia and New Zealand was relatively benign compared with the often public humiliation American social scientists were frequently subjected to in the 1950s.[92] To be sure, some scientists and social scientists were publicly accused of being communists and their careers were curtailed and hindered.[93] It is well known that the Australian Security Intelligence Organisation (ASIO) engaged in covert investigation of social scientists and scientists. Some of the social scientists in *Scholars at War* were subjected to such investigations but the impact these investigations had on the careers we have so far been unable to ascertain.[94]

VI

American social scientists, particularly anthropologists, have been reluctant to discuss and analyse their involvement in war. David Price finds this attitude confusing: 'The silence surrounding American anthropology in the Second World War is especially curious, given widely held feelings of honor and support for those American men and women who contributed to the fight against tyranny.'[95] Despite a large body of anthropological literature analysing conflict and war, there is a 'surprising lack of scholarly documentation and analysis of anthropology's contribution to the wars of the twentieth century'.[96] Australian and New Zealand anthropologists are similarly reticent. We are reminded of

---

89 See Hempenstall, 'Overcoming Separate Histories'.
90 See, for example, Jean Buckley-Moran, 'Australian Scientists and the Cold War', in Brain Martin, C. M. Ann Baker, Clyde Manwell and Cedric Pugh (eds), *Intellectual Suppression: Australian case histories—analysis and responses* (Sydney, 1986), p. 11; Phillip Deery, 'Scientific Freedom and Postwar Politics: Australia, 1945–55', *Historical Records of Australian Science*, 13:1 (1986), pp. 1–18; Geoffrey Gray, '(This Often) Sympathetic Collaboration: Anthropologists, academic freedom and government', *Humanities Research*, 2 (1998), pp. 37–61.
91 Buckley-Moran, 'Australian Scientists and the Cold War', p. 11.
92 See David H. Price, *Threatening Anthropology: McCarthyism and the FBI's surveillance of activist anthropologists* (Durham, NC, 2004); Wax, *Anthropology at the Dawn of the Cold War*.
93 Intellectual/academic suppression might involve the blocking of funds, the denial of promotion or publication, outright harassment, the subtle undermining of reputation or, in extreme cases, dismissal.
94 Lachlan Clohesy, 'Australian Cold Warrior: The anti-communism of W. C. Wentworth', PhD thesis, Victoria University (Melbourne), 2010.
95 Price, *Anthropological Intelligence*, p. xii.
96 Ibid., p. xii.

Roy MacLeod's observation that 'for many of the men and women caught up in war work it was an aberration, a regrettable interruption to the normal flow of scientific and academic work'.[97] Australian and New Zealand social scientists have downplayed any role they had during World War II. When Jeremy Beckett, a younger colleague, asked Hogbin about his war work, he quickly passed over it.[98] Some of the experiences examined in this volume might also lead to the answer that a practical use of expertise by the armed forces—and in war propaganda, despite the high esteem applied social science developed—was seen as undermining scholarly standing. Hogbin's reluctance to answer might be found there, and his association with DORCA and its political ideals seen by conservative elites during the Cold War period as radical and left-wing.

Besides the central question of how war affected the careers of a selected group of social scientists, there are five thematic matters that are addressed in the contributions to *Scholars at War*: the way in which some Australian and New Zealand social scientists sought to involve themselves in war and the war effort both at home and abroad; the role of Australian and New Zealand social scientists in World War II and the way in which they were used by the military authorities; the way anthropologists in particular assisted Australian (and Allied) military forces in the effective use of indigenous peoples during war; the way in which war enlarged anthropology's role as an informing and advising discipline and some of the consequences war had on the institutional structures of the discipline, including transnational ties and networks; and the influence war had on the individual scholar, their scholarship and the wider discipline.

We take a biographical approach to allow a nuanced appraisal of individual experiences and wider trends. No-one was left unaffected. No given person's war experience was the same as another's. Certain generalisations, however, emerge. Those caught up in frontline duties usually have far more negative memories of their wartime experience than those who served in non-combat roles.[99] Apart from Phillips and Davin, none of the scholars in this book had to confront the physicality of war and they tended to look back more benignly on their wartime years.

The war often enhanced careers, providing opportunities and preferment that would not otherwise have arisen. The social scientists in this book were able to continue as anthropologists or historians because the state needed their expertise and scholarship. Accordingly, they were drafted into duties that were closely related to their callings, creating continuity rather than disruption or disjunction. The youthful J. D. Legge used his experiences in DORCA as the

---

97 MacLeod, *Science and the Pacific War*, pp. 1–3.
98 Personal communication, Jeremy Beckett, 3 February 1993.
99 This point emerges unmistakably in Jeremy D. Popkin, *History, Historians, & Autobiography* (Chicago/London, 2005), pp. 187–204.

springboard to a successful academic career first in Pacific history before moving onto South-East Asian history. Ian Hogbin, Camilla Wedgwood and Bill Stanner did not have to make up on lost time after the war, because they were able to continue their callings—if in a different guise and under different circumstances. Indeed, they achieved a great deal during the war. Stanner, it is true, bemoaned his wasted war years but he was prone to blaming others for his setbacks and for allowing circumstances to get the better of him. Elkin—at the peak of his power both within the academy and with government before the outbreak of war—saw his importance and influence diminish. He was disappointed at being unable to influence events to any extent, although his patronage did help Ronald Berndt—who was lucky enough not be called up—to engage in fieldwork during and after the war. The one whose career unravelled in the postwar period was also the one whose star was most on the ascendancy in wartime Australia. Conlon preferred working outside established hierarchies and structures; as Peter Ryan states, Conlon 'drew perverse enjoyment from the deliberate pursuit of the winding ways instead of the straight path. He would use the back stairs even when the grand front door had been opened for him.'[100] Conlon cultivated personal support and loyalties both with his superiors and with members of the directorate; he failed, however, to establish a broader support base from which he could launch an organisational structure that would survive in postwar Australia. He had limited success, nonetheless, with the creation of the Pacific Territories Research Council and the School of Civil Affairs, both of which excluded him when taken over by the Department of External Territories.

Finally, we hope that *Scholars at War* stimulates further debate and research into the development of the social sciences in Australasia and the Pacific and the work of Australasian social scientists.

---

100   Peter Ryan, *Brief Lives* (Sydney, 2004), p. 61.

Part I: The Australians

Geoffrey Gray and Christine Winter

The Pacific War created an unprecedented opportunity for Australia's anthropologists. Before 1939, anthropology in Australia was dominated by Adolphus Peter Elkin, the country's only professor in the subject, at the University of Sydney, and Chairman of the Australian National Research Council (ANRC)[1] committee for anthropology, which oversaw anthropological research in Australia and Melanesia. Elkin's department exercised a key role in training administrators and missionaries for Australia's overseas territories, which reflected the cardinal justification of anthropology in assisting colonial administrations in their control and development of indigenous peoples. The war wrought key changes in his position and in the discipline over which he ruled. From 1942 onwards, war-born organisations such as the Australian Army's Directorate of Research and, from October 1944, the Directorate of Research and Civil Affairs (DORCA; including the School of Civil Affairs established in December 1944) began to recruit anthropologists, which challenged Elkin's university monopoly on research and training, and placed them in a challenging cross-disciplinary environment that also included economists, geographers and legal experts.

The day after Australia declared war against Germany, in a reply to a request from the Manpower Committee of the Department of Defence, Elkin compiled on behalf of the ANRC a list of anthropologists in Australia.[2] It is unclear why this information was sought other than seeking to assemble a list of scientists and their fields of expertise for use in the war effort.[3] It was an extensive list; included were anatomists, physical anthropologists, physiologists and psychologists, archaeologists and social anthropologists. The list illustrates not only the paucity of positions, but also the elasticity of professional definitions. Notwithstanding only a few on the list were used in war work.

Of the anthropologists listed, only Elkin and H. I. Hogbin—both at the University of Sydney—had permanent positions in the discipline. Included

---

1 The ANRC was formed in 1919 as a representative body of the most eminent scientists in Australia. Among its many functions was to provide advice to government on scientific matters. It was disbanded in 1955 and replaced with the Australian Academy of Science. See A. P. Elkin, 'The Australian National Research Council', *Australian Journal of Science*, 16:6 (1954), pp. 203–11.
2 Elkin to A. B. Walkom, Hon. Sec., ANRC, 4 September 1939, EP, 156/4/1/14. See also Geoffrey Gray, 'Managing the Impact of War: Australian anthropology and the South West Pacific', in Roy M. MacLeod (ed.), *Science and the Pacific War: Science and survival in the Pacific, 1939–1945* (Dordrecht, 2000), pp. 187–210.
3 Michelle Freeman, 'Australian Universities at War: The mobilization of universities in the battle for the Pacific', in MacLeod, *Science and the Pacific War*, pp. 119–38.

also were those who were anthropologically trained such as the NT Director of the Native Affairs Branch and Advisor to the Commonwealth Government on Native Affairs, E. W. P. Chinnery, who assisted the Far Eastern Liaison Office (FELO). The educationalist and anthropologist W. C. Groves and Australia Museum curator Fred McCarthy were coopted into the Australian Army Education Service where they produced booklets and pamphlets for the use of soldiers fighting at the frontline. The Papuan Government Anthropologist, F. E. Williams, who was with the Allied Geographic Unit, was killed in an air crash in March 1943.[4] Camilla Wedgwood, who had not worked as an anthropologist since 1936, was Principal of Women's College at the University of Sydney. Elkin excluded anthropologists such W. E. H. Stanner, Ralph Piddington and Donald Thomson who were overseas.[5] Although not on Elkin's list, these three men went on to make significant contributions to Australia's war effort.[6]

At the outbreak of war, Stanner was in East Africa undertaking research for Oxford University, Thomson was completing a PhD at Cambridge (and returned to Australia via America) and Ralph Piddington was lecturing at the University of Aberdeen; each made his way back to Australia to play a part in the war effort. With the exception of Thomson, who was attached to the Merauke (West Papua) Force of the Australian Army, no anthropologists were engaged in overseas combat duty. Stanner was commander of a mobile coastal-watching force in northern Australia—the North Australia Observer Unit—and acted as an advisor on colonial policy and civil affairs. He was appointed to the Australian Army's Directorate of Research in October 1944, where he joined the anthropologists Hogbin and Wedgwood. Piddington, who had enlisted in the British Army's psychology unit, was brought out at the end of 1944 to be Deputy Principal of the School of Civil Affairs.[7] Members of the directorate took short trips to Papua New Guinea, although both Hogbin and Wedgwood undertook extensive research as the war drew to a close. Most members of the directorate, however, remained in Australia at Land Army Headquarters (LHQ), Victoria Barracks, Melbourne.

In New Zealand the situation for anthropologists was somewhat different. Individual examples demonstrate. The New Zealand (and now Canadian) anthropologist Cyril Belshaw (b. 1921) commented that 'volunteering to join the

---

4 A. P. Elkin, 'A. R. Radcliffe-Brown, 1880–1955', *Oceania*, 26:1 (1956), pp. 239–51.
5 See Gray, 'Managing the Impact of War', pp. 187–9.
6 D. J. Mulvaney (ed.), 'Donald Thomson's Report on the Northern Territory Coastal Patrol and the Special Reconnaissance Unit 1941–3', *Aboriginal History*, 16:1 (1992), pp. 1–57.
7 The linguist and self-made anthropologist T. G. H. Strehlow lectured at the School of Civil Affairs: 'I was in charge of army cadets destined for service in New Guinea, and my knowledge of Aborigines was supposed to serve as a platform between the cadets and their relationship with the New Guinea natives…When I pointed out that there was really no similarity between the two peoples, I was told to teach the cadets the best I could to get along with the natives. There was some very woolly-headed thinking among army top-brass, I soon learnt.' Quoted in Ward McNally, *Aborigines, Artefacts and Anguish* (Adelaide, 1981), p. 73.

British Solomon Islands Defence Force…was probably the best career decision I have ever made'. It enabled him to accept an offer from the Institute of Pacific Relations to take a survey of colonial government and reconstruction in New Caledonia, New Hebrides and the British Solomon Islands, which resulted in *Island Administration in the South West Pacific* (1950). His father, an economics professor in New Zealand, was a friend of W. L. Holland, Director of the Institute of Pacific Relations in New York, and this association was to Cyril's benefit. When Belshaw arrived at the London School of Economics (LSE) to undertake doctoral studies, Raymond Firth 'was of the opinion that my life in the Solomons gave me a sense of the reality in the field'. His wartime work acted as a substitute of sorts for fieldwork; Belshaw completed a library thesis.[8] It was a similar case for W. R. Geddes (1916–89), who put H. D. Skinner's one-year anthropology course at Otago University to good use during his service (1941–45) in the 2nd New Zealand Expeditionary Force. Rising to staff sergeant, he spent most of his time in Fiji. This experience was the basis for his Polynesian Society memoir, *Deuba: A study of a Fijian village* (1945), written during the Bougainville campaign, and his University of London (PhD, 1948) thesis, 'An Analysis of Cultural Change in Fiji', written at the LSE. In 1947–48, he lectured in psychology at Birkbeck College, University of London, and returned to Auckland in 1951 as a lecturer in anthropology at Auckland University College, rising to Professor of Anthropology at the University of Sydney in 1958.

Such a direct impact on a career is not so obvious for Australian social scientists discussed in this volume other than Ronald M. Berndt (b. 1916) who was not called up for military service. He was fortunate as it gave him time to develop as an anthropologist; he focused on field research, most of which had little to do with the Australian war effort although it was presented as such to government authorities. The careers of Hogbin and Wedgwood were unimpeded by the war although in Wedgwood's case she shifted from being Principal of Women's College at the University of Sydney to taking a more active teaching role at the Australian School of Pacific Administration (ASOPA). Hogbin briefly toyed with the idea of an appointment to ASOPA but decided to remain at the University of Sydney. The periods during the war and post war were highpoints in Hogbin's career as an applied anthropologist: he advised both the Minister for (Eddie Ward) and the Administrator of Papua and New Guinea (J. K. Murray) on policy and its implementation (not forgetting his work for the British Solomon Islands Protectorate in 1943). By 1950, however, he withdrew from policy work and advice and no longer undertook field research, concentrating on teaching, writing and university politics. Stanner looked upon his war years as 'wasted years', and struggled after the war to find himself a permanent position in

---

8   Cyril Belshaw, *Bumps on a Long Road* (Self-published: <www.lulu.com>, 2009), pp. 31, 54–8. The thesis was published as *The Great Village: The economic and social welfare of Hanubada, an urban community in Papua* (London, 1957).

colonial administration or the academy. He obtained a position as director at Makerere University College but resigned a year into his appointment. He was offered the Chair of Anthropology at Auckland University College, which he rejected in favour of a readership at the recently established Australian National University (ANU) in Canberra.[9] John Legge, the most junior member of this group, provides a personal account of his war work, especially with the Directorate of Research and Civil Affairs, and how that influenced his interest in Pacific history. He went on to a distinguished career, having made a switch to South-East Asian history.

Elkin responded to the necessities of war work with patriotic duty and fervour.[10] His biographer, Tigger Wise, writes that he 'threw himself into an almost jingoistic campaign to whip up the Australian war effort'. He made a statement in his 1940 presidential address to the Royal Society of New South Wales that highlighted the role of scientists 'as citizens to do their utmost to press their knowledge on both government and people…we should not sit aloof adopting the attitude that if the country does not want our knowledge or help it can leave it'. Elkin subsequently devoted himself to 'a four year campaign of patriotic speeches, surveys, questionnaires and the pressing of unsolicited advice on the government and the public'.[11]

Australian social scientists were utilised, by and large, during the war as experts in their field but for an agenda outside their choosing and control. John R. Kerr, second-in-command to Conlon, lamented that '[t]he war of course interrupted most people in their chosen course, and Conlon had interfered with my plans to return to the Bar'.[12]

Many of the individual experiences of Australian scholars were linked through the energy and vision (and charisma) of Alfred Austin Conlon (1908–61) who recruited most of them initially to a research section in the Australian Army, expanding later into the Directorate of Research and Civil Affairs, which was located at Victoria Barracks, Melbourne.[13] It never had a war establishment or a war diary. H. G. Conde, Chairman of the Army's Establishment Investigating Committee in November 1945, observed that 'appointments had been made individually. In this respect it is…quite the exception to any other Army organisation.'[14] Conlon, an extraordinary and singular individual described by Kerr as 'a psychological magician', oversaw much of the work undertaken

---

9   See chapters on Hogbin and Stanner in this volume.
10 See Pomeroy, in this volume; Gray, 'Managing the Impact of War', pp. 187–210.
11 Wise, *The Self-Made Anthropologist*, p. 147; see also Geoffrey Gray, '"The army requires anthropologists": Australian anthropologists at war, 1939–1946', *Australian Historical Studies*, 37:127 (2006), pp. 156–80.
12 John Kerr, *Matters for Judgment: An autobiography* (Melbourne, 1978), p. 110.
13 Geoffrey Gray, 'Australian Anthropologists and WWII', *Anthropology Today*, 21:3 (2005), pp. 18–21; Gray, '"The army requires anthropologists"', pp. 156–80.
14 Conde to Minister for the Army, 14 November 1945, National Archives of Australia, MP 742/1, 240/1/2267.

by members of the directorate.[15] Dorothy Shineberg, who joined ASOPA as a twenty-year-old lecturer in 1947, comments that 'Alf's greatest gift was that of making one feel important'.[16] Conlon assembled around him an exceptional group of talented people, among them the future judge and Governor-General (Sir) John Kerr, the diplomat (Sir) James Plimsoll, the poets James McAuley and Harold Stewart, and the famed Mitchell librarian Ida Leeson.[17] And some lifelong friendships—such as the Professor of Jurisprudence and International Law at the University of Sydney, Julius Stone, and R. D. ('Panz') Wright, Professor of Physiology at the University of Melbourne—developed during these years.[18] In late 1944, Conlon arranged for the British colonial administration specialist Lucy Mair to lecture on colonial administration at the School of Civil Affairs and prepare a report. She wrote that her lectures were to 'show the problems of New Guinea are those which every colonial administration has to face, and to indicate what experience elsewhere could contribute to their solution'. The research she conducted for these lectures formed the groundwork for her report, published as *Australia in New Guinea* (1948).[19] The School of Civil Affairs (later ASOPA) was the outcome of the directorate's war-born interest in reforming colonial policy in the South-West Pacific, especially in Papua and New Guinea, which reached into postwar policy and practice. The school ostensibly was to train colonial officials and civil affairs officers to assist in the government of occupied territories. It was anticipated that the Pacific Territories Research Council would supply much-needed research into problems of policy and practice.

Kerr points out that a key role of the directorate was to provide policy advice on the postwar military government of Papua and New Guinea and other occupied nations of the South-West Pacific including British Borneo.[20] DORCA prepared studies that Blamey had ordered and provided reports on a broad range of topics that Conlon judged to be of national importance. His staff dealt with such subjects as army health and nutrition, the study of terrain, dietary standards for Papuans and New Guineans employed by the Army, trends in Allied, imperial and international relations, and a host of other matters great and small.

> Work of enduring value was performed: the Territories were placed under one administration; their laws were consolidated and codified; and the

---

15 Kerr, *Matters for Judgment*, p. 100. It does not surprise that the longest chapters by far in two biographical collections are those on Conlon. John Thompson (ed.), *Five to Remember* (Melbourne, 1964), pp. 91–162; Peter Ryan, *Brief Lives* (Sydney, 2004), pp. 28–61.
16 Dorothy Shineberg, 'The Early Years of Pacific History', *Journal of Pacific Studies*, 20 (1996), p. 2.
17 For a more comprehensive list, see Gray, 'Managing the Impact of War', p. 205 n. 34.
18 Leonie Star, *Julius Stone: An intellectual life* (Sydney and Melbourne, 1992), pp. 56–80; Peter McPhee, *'Pansy': A life of Roy Douglas Wright* (Melbourne, 1999), pp. 59–66, 223–4.
19 L. P. Mair, *Australia in New Guinea* (London, 1948).
20 Kerr, *Matters for Judgment*, pp. 97–8.

L.H.Q. School of Civil Affairs, established in Canberra in 1945 to train service personnel to be colonial administrators, became in peacetime the Sydney-based Australian School of Pacific Administration.[21]

Cassandra Pybus's chapter reveals Conlon's quite astonishing personality, which mesmerised many but deeply alienated others, and the networks he cultivated to achieve his ambitions and visions, all of which explain why he was a man for the moment rather than the hour. The wartime edifice that he constructed through personal influence and backstairs intrigue came tumbling down when the circumstances that permitted its existence no longer obtained. He attempted to revive his wartime influence when, in 1948–49, he took over from John Kerr as principal of the ASOPA. This proved disastrous.[22]

In Australia the themes of power, influence and their loss accompany the use of social scientists during the war. The experiences outlined in this section underline—beyond personal power struggles—the importance of research as the foundation of colonial policy advice and formulation, dominated nonetheless by Australia's role in the administration of colonial Papua and New Guinea.

---

21   Peter Ryan, 'Conlon, Alfred Austin Joseph (Alf) (1908–1961)', *Australian Dictionary of Biography. Volume 13* (Melbourne, 1993), pp. 479–80.
22   Cassandra Pybus, *The Devil and James McAuley* (St Lucia, Qld, 1999), pp. 87–96.

1. A. P. Elkin: Public morale and propaganda

John Pomeroy

Late in 1941, Sir Thomas Blamey, Commander of the 2nd Australian Infantry Force (AIF) in the Middle East, was back in Australia for consultations when he publicly condemned complacency about the war, accusing his fellow Australians of leading a 'carnival life', comparing them with 'a lot of gazelles grazing in a dell, near the edge of a jungle'.[1] Blamey's indignation might have been partly coloured by the fact that Melbourne Cup week was in full swing and because proposals to curtail race meetings for the duration of the war met strong opposition in both Sydney and Melbourne. At the same time, while the new Curtin Government was cognisant of the need to strengthen civilian morale, its propaganda arm, the Department of Information (DOI), was in disarray, without a clear remit and widely viewed as ineffectual. The new Minister for Information (and Postmaster-General), Senator W. P. Ashley, known in Australian Labor Party (ALP) circles as 'Bill the Fixer', promised a reorganised DOI would provide 'a virile service both through the press and broadcasting stations'.[2] But the department's ability to function effectively was so circumscribed by events as to make it both a scapegoat and the target of competing elites—both individuals and agencies—aiming to take over or abolish its functions.

One of those anxious to take over, or at least direct, the DOI's propaganda role was A. P. Elkin, Professor of Anthropology at the University of Sydney. In 1941, Elkin conducted a survey of public attitudes to the war called *Our Opinions and the National Effort*[3] and its findings vindicated Blamey's bleak assessment of civilian morale. It was not the first time that Elkin, then aged fifty-one, had analysed contemporary patterns of thought; his Honours thesis was titled 'Australia's National Consciousness' (1915).[4]

In 1940 Elkin described Australians as 'astonished and bewildered by the apparent lack of industrial unity…even after a year of war'[5]—a situation he believed was caused by the lack of a broad consensus as to the significance of what he regarded as activities and events of great moment. Searching for

---

1 *The Argus*, 17 November 1941.
2 *Sydney Morning Herald*, 10 January 1942.
3 A. P. Elkin, *Our Opinions and the National Effort* (Sydney, 1941). The booklet, 80 pages in length, was printed by the Australasian Medical Publishing Company, which undertook most university printing.
4 Tigger Wise, *The Self-Made Anthropologist: A life of A. P. Elkin* (Sydney, 1985), p. 20.
5 A. P. Elkin, *Society, the Individual and Change with Special Reference to War and other Present-Day Problems. The Livingstone Lectures* (Sydney, 1941), p. 5.

a means of understanding community attitudes and the processes of change in society, Elkin looked to the experience of cultural change in 'primitive' settings. He concluded that the same groupings in industrialised societies—political, economic and religious—also existed in pre-industrial communities. He noted that in general, individuals followed cultural patterns developed by a long historical process but that individual differences of temperament, intellect and energy affected the way individuals experienced and reflected that culture. For Elkin, motives for warfare stemmed from 'culturally produced' factors and not from 'biological or psychological excuses'. And, he was alert to the dangers inherent in the organisation of a democracy at war—the risk that those fighting totalitarianism could be 'driven to adopt much of its method of organisation'—a point that would be made more publicly and forcefully by John Anderson, Challis Professor of Philosophy (1927–58), two years later.[6]

From his research on factors influencing cultural change in society, Elkin drew firm conclusions about the role of intellectuals in wartime. In his 1941 presidential address to the Royal Society of New South Wales, he outlined the responsibilities of scientists, declaring that 'we should not sit aloof adopting the attitude that if the country does not want our knowledge or help it can leave it'.[7] He lamented the lack of any government response to his call, but added that scientists who could speak with authority would eventually be heard. Elkin saw the ineffectuality of the DOI as a call to arms for the intelligentsia; its failure to rise to the occasion had created a vacuum—both ideological and organisational—one that Elkin believed himself well qualified to fill.

Elkin was a workaholic with a strong sense of public duty and moral rectitude. In addition to being Professor of Anthropology at the University of Sydney, he was President of Australian Mass Opinion, Foundation President of the Australian Institute of Sociology, editor of the journal *Oceania*, an active member of the Anglican Diocese of Newcastle (where he had been ordained a priest 20 years before) as well as representing the Newcastle Bishop on the Sydney Diocese, advisor on Native Affairs to both the Anglican Board of Missions and the Protestant National Missionary Council, President of the Association for the Protection of Native Races, Vice-Chairman of the Aborigines Protection Board (APB) of New South Wales, a member of various academic boards and committees, and a prolific writer of articles and letters to journals and newspapers.[8] He was at

---

6   Ibid. Anderson's polemic *The Servile State* was published in 1943. See also Brian Kennedy, *A Passion to Oppose: John Anderson, philosopher* (Melbourne, 1995).
7   A. P. Elkin, Presidential Address to the Royal Society of New South Wales, quoted in Wise, *The Self-Made Anthropologist*, p. 147.
8   For background on the Department of Anthropology's activities during this period, see A. P. Elkin, 'The Emergence of Psychology, Anthropology and Education', in *One Hundred Years of the Faculty of Arts* (Sydney, 1952), pp. 21–41; also Elkin, 'The Journal Oceania: 1930–1970', *Oceania*, 40:4 (1970), pp. 245–79; Geoffrey Gray, *A Cautious Silence: The politics of Australian anthropology* (Canberra, 2007). Although Elkin was Foundation President, the Australian Institute of Sociology was established by Miss Aileen Fitzpatrick,

the top of his game. But these worthy activities did not redeem him in the eyes of critics, such as his biographer, Tigger Wise, who has described his contribution to the war effort as 'a four year campaign of patriotic speeches, surveys, questionnaires and the pressing of unsolicited advice on the government and public'.[9] An examination of his collected papers confirms this assessment but does not explain his need to play a leadership role in the development of public policy and opinion. Wise does suggest, however, by way of explanation, that Elkin 'had come to believe that his country possessed in him one of its finest minds' and he believed that 'scientists as citizens are bound to do their utmost to press their knowledge on both government and people'.[10] It could be said that his independent, strongly motivated approach was a product of his upbringing and of his admiration for the work of the Anglican theologian and social reformer F. D. Maurice and the works of Charles Darwin and Charles Kingsley. Gregory Melleuish wrote that Elkin 'believed that the role of religion was to counter the disunity of modern society' and that his ultimate goal was 'social integration'. Melleuish argues that 'the history of political liberalism in Australia is tied to the history of liberal Protestantism' and that this connection can be seen in the writings and influence of Francis Anderson, who was Professor of Philosophy at Sydney when Elkin was a student. Quoting from Elkin, Melleuish notes that the latter saw religious consciousness as the means 'to transform all social groups and relationships so that they will express the highest ideals that the saints and seers of society have seen'.[11] In common with radical clergymen Bishop E. H. Burgmann[12] and R. S. Lee, and with Francis Anderson, Elkin shared 'the quest for a humanistic rather than a theistic rationale for religious belief'. He also shared their strategy—that of the liberals prominent in the Australian Institute of Political Science—one of 'seeking a rapport with the rest of society in order to educate public opinion along civic lines and so lead society into the Promised Land of consensus'.[13]

Elkin was bent upon shaping public policy on a range of subjects, but most particularly, propaganda. The genesis of Elkin's survey can be traced to his concern about the poor performance of the Government's 1941 war-loan appeal

---

Foundation Director of the NSW Board of Social Study and Training. See K. S. Cunningham, *The Social Science Research Council of Australia 1942–1952*, ([Canberra], 1967), p. 10. Elkin was also a member of the Panel for Psychological Propaganda. National Archives of Australia [hereinafter NAA], SP 112/1/1, item 429/1/1.
9   Wise, *The Self-Made Anthropologist*, p. 147. Wise has described Elkin's personal philosophy as 'adaptation to the system'. See, however, Jonathan Lane, 'Anchorage in Aboriginal Affairs: A. P. Elkin on religious continuity and civic obligation', PhD thesis, University of Sydney, 2008, pp. 44–70.
10   Wise, *The Self-Made Anthropologist*, p. 147.
11   Gregory Melleuish, 'Conceptions of the Sacred in Australian Political Thought', *Political Theory Newsletter*, 5:1 (1993), pp. 39–51. See also Lane, 'Anchorage in Aboriginal Affairs'. Francis Anderson was inaugural Professor of Philosophy at the University of Sydney. He was appointed in 1890 to a position he held for the next 30 years. <http://www.library.usyd.edu.au/libraries/rare/philosophy/sectionsydney.html> (viewed 20 October 2010).
12   See Peter Hempenstall, *The Meddlesome Priest: A life of Ernest Burgman* (Sydney, 1993).
13   Tim Rowse, *Australian Liberalism and National Character* (Melbourne, 1978), p. 159.

and a recruitment campaign for the Australian Infantry Force (AIF), which, in both cases, senior officials had attributed to 'apathy'. But Elkin felt this was more 'an effect rather than a cause' and could be masking other attitudes that should be assessed if the lack of commitment to the war effort was to be understood and remedied.

He undertook his survey without government financial support to test public opinion on matters that he regarded as essential to the war effort. Elkin was well informed about the use of public opinion surveys and techniques, particularly the work of Mass-Observation, an outfit set up in Britain in 1937 by Tom Harrisson and Charles Madge and later commissioned to provide information on public opinion to the British authorities in the early stages of the war.[14] Elkin saw himself as fulfilling a similar role and, borrowing Mass-Observation's methodology (without acknowledgment), Elkin conducted his survey using teams of 20 observers recruited from people known to him either as graduates of the Department of Anthropology or from his many other professional and business contacts; they were volunteers who gave up evenings or weekends to carry out the surveys. Elkin told them their work could influence government policies, that the survey would be 'important for the maintenance of morale and the attainment of a greater degree of unity of national effort' and urged them to 'do what you can, as quickly as you can'. The individuals and groups surveyed were located in Sydney, Newcastle, eight country towns and a 'few country districts'. The interviews were based on a long questionnaire with responses obtained 'not by direct questioning, but as a result of guided conversations' with those surveyed; all up, the attitudes and opinions of 400 individuals of various ages and groups were recorded.[15] His biographer has noted that 'the whole thing smacked strongly of being a questionnaire interpreted by the preconceptions of the surveyor' and that the survey's reception from the press and professional journals was minimal[16]—a conclusion not borne out by the press clippings and reviews in the Elkin Papers.[17]

The survey results convinced Elkin that the poor response to the war effort constituted nothing less than 'a grave national problem' that required close analysis, preferably by sociologists and other social scientists. He recommended

---

14 See Angus Calder and Dorothy Sheridan (eds), *Speak for Yourself: A mass-observation anthology, 1937–1949* (London, 1984). Elkin's publication *Our Opinions and the National Effort* contains no acknowledgment of, or reference to, the pioneering work of Mass-Observation, whose first major survey of public opinion in Britain was: Charles Madge and Tom Harrisson, *Britain by Mass-Observation* (Harmonsdworth, UK, 1939). For a critical assessment of the methodology and application of this form of public opinion sampling, see Raymond Firth, 'An Anthropologist's View of Mass-Observation', *Sociological Review*, 31:1 (1939), pp. 166–93; Penny Summerfield, 'Mass-Observation: Social research or social movement?', *Journal of Contemporary History*, 20:3 (1985), pp. 439–52.
15 Elkin, 'Guidance Notes for Mass Observation "Observers"', [c.1941], Papers of A. P. Elkin, University of Sydney Archives [hereinafter EP], 104/1/15/1.
16 Wise, *The Self-Made Anthropologist*, p. 149.
17 EP, 104/1/15/1.

that all government appeals to the community be followed up with social surveys to evaluate public opinion and that the effectiveness of campaigns in the media and other outlets (churches, cinemas and public meetings) should be measured. For him, apathy was not confined to any one class or group, although occasionally there were examples of a town or settlement—usually isolated—where negative attitudes could be accounted for in both class and family terms. Such people might be 'cynical and even antagonistic' or 'disillusioned and helpless', arising out of their experience in the Depression, and any campaign to win their support for a national war effort would need to take account of these factors.[18]

The survey had revealed considerable distrust and lack of confidence in politicians and political leaders. Speculating as to the origins of this negativity, Elkin suggested envy, rumour or scandal, parliamentary behaviour and 'intrigues between parties' as possible causes; and, he said, the remedy lay in politicians performing their duties 'with resoluteness and single hearted devotion' while the public was enjoined to 'give all respect to those whom we elect'. Elkin's solutions were often expressed in this pious and unrealistic fashion. In one of his many articles and letters to newspapers, he called on the Australian people to 'identify their political and social ideals with the country as a whole' and blamed the 'over-segmentation of society' for obstructing the war effort.[19]

Elkin's polling had also shown that cynicism and antagonism were all too prevalent: a working-class, female aged pensioner saw the war as 'unnecessary' and caused by business leaders being greedy and selfish; a twenty-eight-year-old woman said 'there is not much in life, we were on the dole for three years and couldn't get enough to eat; my husband joined up so that the family would have enough money to live on; the "country" doesn't want you, except for "their" own ends'. Some young mothers were highly critical of the war, making it clear they were too busy raising children with meagre resources and having to cope with rising prices. Working-class women saw the war as yet another burden and were generally contemptuous of politicians; the less privileged saw 'apathy' as the main problem and the well-off as complacent and hedonistic. Conversely, an affluent woman complained about working-class men 'down in the village' who, since they would not work, 'should be made to go to the war', and, she said, '[f]ascism seems a lot better than communism, it's more stable anyway and the lower classes don't get such a hold on things'. And, there were prosperous males who wanted to discipline lazy workers who, although they earned good wages, dissipated them at 'the dogs'.

---

18 Quotes from Elkin in this and following paragraphs are from *Our Opinions and the National Effort*, unless otherwise referenced.
19 *Sydney Morning Herald*, 12 September 1941.

Elkin had exposed the absence of any general sense of peril or challenge. But, even allowing for the unsatisfactory political situation, he thought it unfair to lay the blame for all such problems on the Government; 'in a democracy, political instability is an effect, more than it is a cause, of social instability and individual uncertainty'. His results had shown there was some doubt as to the efficacy of democracy and Elkin thought the most serious and immediate problem was to achieve unity by giving democracy a 'spiritual content' and making it a 'social ideal'. That way, he argued, 'indecision will be swallowed up with enthusiasm', producing a national unity where vested interests and privileges were sacrificed for the greater good.

Elkin was an innovator and he was also an opinionated man who expected his advice to be taken seriously by politicians and the public, and he set about bringing the results of his survey to the notice of senior members of the Government. He argued that 'the national effort must be directed not only at destroying Nazis, but also at building a better social and economic structure'—a perspective drawn from observation and experience during the Depression; it was a perspective he shared with many of his contemporaries who were to exert influence on government policies at this time. But he was adamant that if the people of Australia wanted democracy there had to be greater conviction and commitment, which in turn required people to 'express it, work for it, fight for it and trust it'. A full understanding of the moral and political objectives in the war depended on a more informed attitude promoted through propaganda—propaganda that he conceived as 'designed to unify and prepare a people intellectually, emotionally and physically to recognise, resist and defeat actual aggressors'.

Others might have thought this a tall order, but Elkin was supremely confident of his ability to deliver the goods. But first, political leaders had to face the fact of widespread 'disillusionment, disappointment, futility, distrust, diffidence and indifference' in the minds of the community (or at least the small survey sample) concerning 'politics in general and the war in particular'. Further confirmation of these attitudes came from other sources. The first Gallup Poll, conducted in October 1941, revealed that 68 per cent of those interviewed were dissatisfied with the performance of the United Australia Party (UAP)–Country Party coalition and that 77 per cent favoured a national all-party wartime government, while another survey, conducted by the Sydney *Daily Telegraph*, concluded that 'the greatest problem to be solved in Australia is a psychological one—and that this problem is very great'.[20]

The political context had indeed created such a climate, one in which, according to Paul Hasluck, 'the Australian Government did not possess and was unlikely

---

20 'You, Me and this War', *Daily Telegraph*, October 1941, p. 212.

to gain the full confidence and united efforts of Australians'.[21] At the time of Elkin's survey, the short-lived Fadden administration was on its last legs before being defeated on the floor of the House of Representatives. Its demise brought to an end almost two years of internecine party bickering on the part of the Coalition and frustrated attempts (ironically by Robert Menzies and H. V. Evatt) to form a national government. This is why Elkin was convinced his task was one of 'national significance' although he seems to have prejudged, or at least assumed, the positive connection between 'opinions and attitudes' on the one hand and 'national effort and national unity' on the other. Surveys of public opinion were still in their infancy but the fact that a survey was conducted at all (and published) represents an innovative and determined effort to focus on a subject that was giving cause for concern at a critical stage of the war.

Elkin believed that manifestations of 'apathy' (identified in about 7 per cent of the total opinion analysed) could be traced back to the Depression years. While there was a segment of the population whose existence was 'vegetative', there were many young men, unable to find work, who did not feel themselves 'part of the nation'. And it was also possible, he argued, that the dole had made young and old dependent on the state, with the consequence that they did not understand or accept the reciprocal contract 'that the State is dependent on them'. Elkin was at odds with the conclusion of the Joint Committee on Social Security that there was 'abundant evidence that economic security is fundamental to the survival of Democracy' and that the chief cause of 'apathy' was to be found in social economic deprivation.[22]

Elkin argued that 'the seed of a better attitude' had to be sown among people who needed to appreciate the present danger and the ideological conflicts 'being fought out in blood and iron'. Such an approach constituted 'propaganda', but 'the association of this term with lying must not blind us to the fact that it is used on us in advertising and in religion, and is employed by the British as well as the enemy'. Most important, he wrote, was a campaign that would 'bring forth the fruits of service, sacrifice and complete self-devotion'.

For Elkin, the lack of national unity demonstrated the need for propaganda. Disunity was evidenced by profiteering, industrial disputes, political bickering and lack of cooperation in forming a national government, over-segregation of society and a general selfishness; people would not commit themselves totally to the war effort and this attitude was exemplified by the poor response to recruiting and war-loan appeals. For example, the average number of subscribers

---

21 Paul Hasluck, *The Government and the People, 1939–1941* (Canberra, 1952), vol. 1, p. 381.
22 The first (interim) report of the Joint Parliamentary Committee on Social Security was published in September 1941. The quotation is at page 5 of the report and at page 759 of *Parliamentary Papers—General*, vol. 2, 1940–43.

to war loans was less than half that of the Great War—a deficit Elkin attributed to the 'many thousands of citizens whose minds and hearts, as well as pockets, are not in the war'.[23]

In an article published in the *Sydney Morning Herald* on 12 September 1941, Elkin summarised the survey and his conclusions with the caption 'A Real War Effort—Call For National Awakening'. On 11 October, Elkin wrote to the Melbourne *Herald* suggesting the establishment of a Commonwealth Government Department of Propaganda. A few days later, he wrote to Prime Minister, John Curtin, forwarding a copy of *Our Opinions and the National Effort* and asking him to consider the formation of a department responsible for propaganda. Curtin replied on 16 October, advising Elkin that he had referred his suggestion to the Minister for Information, Senator W. P. Ashley.[24] Concerned that senior bureaucrats might shelve his proposal, Elkin wrote a four-page letter to Ashley offering advice as to how the minister and his department might proceed:

> I think you have two tasks: one is propaganda, and that is absolutely essential; the second is to get information regularly regarding the reaction and attitudes of people of all types to all your propaganda efforts whether these deal with recruiting, war loans, ARP, maintenance of morale and the unifying of thought regarding the urgency of the situation and the call which it makes upon us. As I said before, I should be willing to help in this matter and I know a number of trained and well balanced people who would do likewise.[25]

Elkin argued that a Department of Propaganda should adopt an activist stance, using newspapers, radio, cinema and public meetings to inspire the community. He thought this could be achieved at the cinema by placement of appeals immediately after the playing of the National Anthem and by screening photographs of the King and the Queen—with the proviso that the promotion or propaganda was 'not spoilt by a speaker's face or voice which causes laughter or irritation'. Similarly, speakers at public meetings 'must be gifted with the power to hold and inspire audiences' in addition to possessing a good knowledge of events and must be of sufficient status. Elkin saw himself as head of the new Department of Propaganda, as someone who, though not a Member of Parliament, 'should be given Cabinet rank'.[26] He saw the new department as 'concerned not only with sieving and releasing news for consumption at home and abroad, but with stirring us into thought and action with regard to every aspect of the conflict in which we are engaged'.

---

23 Elkin, Lack of Unity: The need for propaganda, (typescript, c. 1941, 8 pages), EP, 104/1/15/5.
24 Elkin to Curtin, 13 October 1941; and Curtin to Elkin, 16 October 1941, EP, 104/1/15/2.
25 Elkin to Ashley, 11 November 1941, NAA, A1608/1, item AK 29/1/2.
26 Elkin, Lack of Unity.

To press his claims for government appointment, Elkin cited numerous examples from his folders of press clippings and notebooks of counterproductive advertising and propaganda on the radio, in the press and at the cinema; of mistakes made by the DOI and of radio announcers whose 'manner of utterance' resembled that of 'driving a nail into people's heads with the result that they pull their heads away'. Similarly, there were 'forced' or 'melodramatic' appeals by radio announcers or officials of the DOI and others were 'too comforting'; such appeals oversimplified the situation and the impression conveyed was that if people worked harder the war was an episode that could be concluded 'quickly or slowly as we were inclined'.[27] Some broadcasts met his approval; he was so impressed with Chester Wilmot's introduction in the first part of the dedication of the cemetery at Tobruk that he recommended its use throughout the following weeks on different stations—but not the second part of the ceremony because 'the voices of the speakers were not as good as they might be'.[28] Elkin concluded his lengthy epistle with a further reminder about his availability to assist.

Nothing came of his approach but he was undeterred and wrote to both Curtin and Ashley again on 17 December.[29] He pointed out that recent events (the attack on Pearl Harbor and the sinking of *HMS Repulse* and *HMS Prince of Wales*) had subjected morale to 'much strain' and there were signs that it would not 'stand up to the strain sufficiently well'. The Elkin analysis was that there was widespread concern over the fate of Malaya and Singapore, worry that America was not prepared, anti-British sentiment was widespread, air-raid shelters were inadequate and equipment for fire fighting was not being made. As if this was not enough for the wilting recipients, he threw in a few more problems: 'There is a feeling that a fifth column is acting…the opinion is even expressed that some leaders, apparently business leaders, would be willing to seek peace in the interests of trade with Japan.' All the more reason, argued the indefatigable Elkin, for tackling the problem by strengthening public morale so as 'to ensure a sound basis for our efforts and sacrifices'. Why not establish a section in the DOI dealing specifically with morale, he asked, stressing again the urgency of the matter and reiterating his offer of assistance.

Again, he received only a formal acknowledgment. In January 1942, he took up the cudgels once more, sending more proposals and a four-page outline for a 'Department of Morale', having apparently had second thoughts about its standing. He reiterated his view that there was no united war effort and that there was 'widespread concern that this war is not the concern of the working

---

27   Elkin to Ashley, 11 November 1941, NAA, A1608/1, item AK 29/1/2.
28   Elkin to Ashley, 11 November 1941, NAA, A1608/1, item AK 29/1/2. The 'well worded introduction' by Chester Wilmot is quoted in full in Wilmot's *Tobruk, 1941: Capture, siege, relief* (Sydney, 1945), pp. 315–17.
29   Elkin to Curtin and Ashley, 17 December 1941, NAA, A1608/1, item AK 29/1/2.

man'.³⁰ An even longer silence followed. On 5 March, he decided to pursue the Prime Minister again, this time with a five-page letter containing more observations on current concerns affecting public morale. He complained that the DOI had not faced up to the problem of morale on the home front; the Government should be concerned because 'unless positive measures are taken to rally people's morale against the enemy, a feeling of frustration is going to be so widespread that we shall not be able to make the resistance that is essential'. He also mentioned that in addition to the lack of effective propaganda and publicity there was a growing morale problem among Australian-based troops, some of whom he claimed had 'no positive idea of why they are in camp' or were 'worrying about leave' and there was 'the unbridling of the passion for drink and women'.³¹

Elkin asked Curtin's pardon for the length of the letter but claimed to represent 'very many citizens' who supported the proposal for a Department of Morale, which, if staffed by qualified people who 'understood Australian people and facts of psychology and sociology', could ensure that publicity and propaganda avoided the blunders made by the DOI. Since the publication of his pamphlet, Elkin had undertaken further opinion sampling, which revealed that government radio appeals were regarded as unconvincing and too much of a 'hard sell' to be effective; moreover, people criticised their artificial tone and content. They were 'written by people with upper class outlooks' who should 'get into uniform instead of talking so much'.³²

Concurrently, Elkin was analysing the causes of absenteeism in the coal industry and corresponding with the Commonwealth Coal Commission (CCC) on working conditions in that industry.³³ His investigation identified five principal contributory factors: the 'irresponsibility' of coalminers, especially the younger men; overstrain ('some medical men say "miners are done at 45"'); personal maladjustment, causing irritability and a disinclination to commence work; the after effects of drink or 'the lure of the races and such like for those who devote themselves to these forms of excitement'; and, finally, the distrust and hostility of miners towards mine owners, which he saw as an expression of the class attitude to war.³⁴

Elkin examined the historical background including the use of strikes as a weapon to achieve better conditions. In a climate of industrial disputation, he argued, there was 'good ground for the seed of the class war and Marxian

---

30   Elkin to Curtin, 14 January 1942, EP, 104/1/15/6.
31   Elkin to Curtin, 5 March 1942, NAA, A1608/1, item AK 29/1/2.
32   Elkin, Radio Scatters, 30-page typescript, EP, 104/1/15/1.
33   See correspondence, Elkin to Chief Executive Officer, Commonwealth Coal Commission (CCC), 14 and 15 January 1942, and R. P. Jack (CCC) to A. P. Elkin, 14 and 17 January 1942, EP, 104/1/15/5.
34   Elkin, Coal, (typescript, c. January 1942), EP, 104/1/15/5.

doctrines'; and he thought the arbitration system exacerbated the problems by institutionalising class confrontation. He recommended that the Government assure miners that they are 'producing for themselves and not just to fill the coffers of owners and big capitalists' and that they were making a significant contribution to the defence of Australia. He recommended implementing a policy of security and continuity of employment and suggested it might be necessary to 'promise sincerely that profits will be controlled in peace time as in war time'; he also recommended decentralisation of industry so that factories did not crowd around coalfields and advised that any appeals to the miners should be made 'at their level and from their point of view'.

To meet the need for increased production, Elkin proposed nationalisation as the way to bridge the gulf between workers and employers.[35] But this would require a 'moral revolution' because miners needed inculcation with the ideal of service. Such an approach would have been in line with Elkin's religious-ethical views and, as his biographer has recalled, would also have arisen 'out of his pragmatic approach, a wish to cooperate and compromise with government'.[36]

The CCC was not entirely convinced by Elkin's identification of socioeconomic factors as the chief cause of the problems facing the industry; they saw it as not so much a problem of morale but more a residual antagonism from the Depression heightened by the perception that 'the owners are the hammer and the miners are the anvil'. The coal industry identified strikes as a relatively small factor in production problems, pointing out that absenteeism had accounted for 19 per cent of lost production in one area.[37] The application of sociological method to the production front attracted Elkin. He was familiar with developments in the United States, especially the work of Taylor, Gantt, Emerson, Bath and others who had adopted a scientific approach to industrial management problems. He saw 'departmentalism and lack of central coordination' as having a serious effect on the war effort, and recommended an industrial policy based on a realistic assessment of wartime needs.[38]

Elkin continued his research, or coordinated that of others, into the problems of the coal industry as well as those of the steel and munitions industries. On the basis of his growing interest and knowledge about the sociology of the workplace, Elkin also wrote to Wallace Wurth, Director-General of Man Power, about production problems in Sydney, Newcastle and Lithgow where 'lack of morale' had been identified as 'the greatest single contributing factor in restricting production'. To solve this problem, he had formulated a five-point

---

35 See Alan Walker, *Coaltown: A social survey of Cessnock* (Melbourne, 1945); Robin Gollan, *The Coalminers of New South Wales: A history of the union, 1860–1960* (Melbourne, 1963).
36 Telephone conversation, John Pomeroy/Tigger Wise, 30 March 1994.
37 Jack to Elkin, 17 January 1942, EP, 104/1/15/1.
38 The Sociological Approach to the Production Problem, (typescript, c. 1942), EP 104/1/15/5.

plan involving the coordination of all human and material resources to achieve maximum output for the war effort (a theme that dominated his speeches and writing throughout the period 1941–43).[39]

He identified stress as a growing problem for production-line workers whose morale was being undermined by increasingly long shifts (some were 12 hours); he argued that the only available solution was to train women for the workforce, and, together with his letter to Wurth, he provided a draft scheme for training women in munitions production. Thanking Elkin for his proposals, Wurth said that women's employment was under review but the process was 'complicated by the difficulties associated with a determination of their conditions of employment'.[40]

In yet another research project, Elkin summarised the opinions of 126 people who were asked a series of questions around the theme 'What are we fighting for?' Twenty-eight people expressed the view that Australia was fighting for its survival, its existence as a nation, to keep the Japanese out, to defeat aggression or just simply 'to save our skins'. Elkin viewed these responses as defeatist; instead, people should have indicated they were 'mentally and physically defiant'.[41] Five respondents said 'we are fighting for Britain…because we are part of the British Empire', while a majority asserted that 'we are fighting for democracy and freedom' and the 'Australian way of life'. Twelve respondents put the view that the war was being fought for capitalists and financiers and another 10 were dubious about the real aims of 'freedom and democracy'. Elkin seemed disturbed by these findings despite the fact that they indicated a keen appreciation of why Australia was at war. Again, he expatiated on the meaning of democracy:

> We must restore mutual trust and confidence, for justice and liberty depend on the manifestation of these qualities between those who are chosen to govern and those who consent to be governed…unless we can replace the present widespread lack of confidence by a freely-given and sincere deserved trust, democracy must be a sham.

Citizens should be more politically aware, since democracy required as many 'democrats' as possible. 'No one', he argued, 'can be a democrat by proxy', and apathy would result in fascism. Elkin's brand of social responsibility emerges most clearly in his elaboration of the purpose of democracy. He argued that it had to 'signify some definite social content and purpose—and not merely a condition of life'. Democracy, he believed,

---

39 Elkin to Wurth, 16 February 1942, EP, 104/1/15/5.
40 Wurth to Elkin, 25 February 1942, EP, 176/4/2/203.
41 A. P. Elkin, What Are We Fighting For?, (typescript, c. 1942), EP, 104/1/15/3. The following two quotations come from this source.

combined on the one hand with economic security for a large minority, the socially disinherited, and on the other hand with effective power held in the hands of a very small minority, is no longer thought to be an undisguised blessing, or a desirable goal. Nor are the majority of us satisfied with the advertising view that democracy is mainly a matter of freedom in trading, of unrestricted commercialism. Greater and greater numbers are maintaining that if democracy is to be worthwhile it must ensure social and economic security to all individuals, and put the welfare of human personality above all the dogmas of economic and political theories.

Elkin also analysed—a modest 24 pages this time—the DOI promotional series *On the Production Front*, posing the question: 'Are we on the production front, fighting the nation's enemies, or just doing our job in the old peacetime way?' He posed a series of rhetorical questions:

> Is our attitude that of the soldiers, sailors and airmen, whether they be defending with their backs to the wall or furiously attacking the enemies' position, using all their energy, thought, initiative and strength? Or are we merely concerned with receiving our pay and fulfilling our working hours' contract, but without zest? Are we still interested mainly in our sectional quarrels between groups within our industry, and in fighting the 'bosses', or are we toiling to win victory over the external enemy ignoring all the petty irritations of our employers, fellow workers and union delegates and even the shortage of beer?[42]

To ascertain what was being done, Elkin organised a study of the opinions of a selected panel on the question 'Are we making an all-in war effort?' Ninety-five per cent thought not, citing inefficiency in administration and production, too much politics and squabbling, too much 'business as usual', too much emphasis on luxury and non-essential production and too many strikes and stoppages. 'In other words', Elkin concluded, '[g]overnment administrative authorities, employers, workers and most of us were failing to make that "all-in effort" on which our national existence depended'.

Elkin reviewed what had happened since the survey was carried out in the 'gloomy days' of February–March 1942 and observed that conditions had changed considerably 'in the past few months', including the creation or conversion of factories to munitions or war-related production. More than half the workforce was so engaged and management and labour were cooperating, longer hours and shifts were being worked and the impact of rationing was taking effect. While these developments were heartening, Elkin pointed to

---

42 A. P. Elkin, On the Production Front, (typescript, n.d.), EP, 104/1/15/5.

some emerging problems—for example, working conditions were damaging the health of workers, and so, 'duodenal trouble...is widespread amongst munitions workers'. He also worried about 'the Class Division', which reflected 'an underlying antagonism' in which 'two sides are poised, suspicious of one another, and even in the face of a threat to national existence, still find it impossible to work out and adopt a satisfactory means of cooperation, freed from mutual suspicions and recriminations'.[43] As an expert, if not Australia's leading authority, on Aboriginal society, he reflected on the contrast in social cohesion between the European and Aboriginal cultures—something that has been elsewhere described as 'nostalgia for a lost wholeness'.[44]

Elkin had also been studying the effect on morale of Japanese radio propaganda. In some cases, 'Radio Tokio' pre-empted local media with news of events, such as the sinking of *HMAS Perth* and *HMAS Hobart*, which, at the time he was writing, remained rumour only, since news of their loss had not been admitted or released by the Australian authorities. Not that Elkin had any practical solution since it was a 'difficult problem of whether to ignore or deal with Japanese propaganda', but in his opinion 'no fixed rule can be established but great care should be taken with any answers'.[45] By now, having read Elkin's letter, Curtin was probably apprehensive that all the criticism might be undermining national morale.

In the absence of a positive response to his lengthy letter of 5 March, Elkin led a deputation to lobby the Minister for Information on the need to do something urgently about morale and the DOI. The deputation was well publicised in the Sydney press and included Bishop C. Venn Pilcher (Anglican Diocese of Sydney), Professor Ian Clunies Ross (Dean of the Faculty of Veterinary Science at the University of Sydney), Reverend D. MacDonald (MLA for Mosman) and Dr C. R. McRae (Principal of the Sydney Teachers' College). This meeting, held on 7 April 1942, might have been the proverbial last straw that prompted action since, soon after, Curtin decided to appoint a subcommittee of Cabinet to report on the work and the cost of the DOI.

Elkin's correspondence and complaints had in the meantime been passed by Curtin to J. H. Scullin, who, although without portfolio, was a close confidant of Curtin and was used to undertake several tasks and inquiries (including into uniform taxation) to which the Prime Minister was unable to devote full time or attention.[46] On behalf of the Prime Minister, Scullin asked Alfred Conlon to

---

43   Ibid. Elkin's biographer noted 'a lifelong aversion for divisiveness' in her subject, which she believes might be explained by Elkin's unhappy childhood. Wise, *The Self-Made Anthropologist*, p. 8.
44   Melleuish, 'Conceptions of the Sacred in Australian Political Thought', pp. 40–1.
45   Elkin to Curtin, 5 March 1942, NAA, A1608/1, item AK 29/1/2.
46   Rt Hon. J. H. Scullin (Member of Parliament, 1910–13, 1922–49; Prime Minister, 1929–32). See John Robertson, *J. H. Scullin: A political biography* (Perth, 1974).

undertake preparation of an interim report on the problem of civilian morale for submission to the Prime Minister.[47] There is no record presently available that suggests that Elkin was aware of this development. Had he known of it, there is every reason to suppose that his reaction would have been neither calm nor congratulatory. Apart from the fact that Elkin believed that he was the pre-eminent authority on morale, he disliked Conlon and the feeling was reciprocated. Three weeks later, on 22 May 1942, the Cabinet subcommittee, chaired by Scullin, had completed its report and recommended the abolition of the DOI, with its functions to be dispersed to appropriate departments.

By the time news of the appointment of the Conlon Committee reached him, Elkin had seen the writing on the wall and moved his energies and attentions elsewhere. According to Wise, 'in a bid for power outside his strict field, he had lost ground' and, as he had done at several other critical points in his life, he returned to his own domain to lick his wounds and reflect on his personal scrupulosity.[48] His high moral stance would not have commended him as a suitable candidate for a task requiring pragmatism and an ability to deal with the public and politicians alike. Except for a few small tasks and surveys for government authorities, Elkin now confined himself to public speaking, letter writing, teaching, editing *Oceania* and welfare work. In late May 1942, it was reported that he had recommended to the Diocese of Newcastle that it should establish an advisory committee to discuss the Church's contribution to morale.[49]

In April, Elkin had written to the Prime Minister about another matter more directly related to his field of study. As a member of the Aborigines' Welfare Board of New South Wales, he was aware of proposals that an Aboriginal mixed-blood battalion might be formed. The idea attracted his support and he suggested that every opportunity should be taken to provide Aborigines 'with a chance of helping their country either in the fighting services or in auxiliaries to these services or in factories'. In support of his argument, Elkin pointed to the fact that there was growing support for full citizenship rights for Aborigines and that these included responsibilities that meant allowing them 'to fight and work with us'; such inclusion, he argued, would demonstrate that 'the citizenship we talk about is the real thing and not a species of segregation'.[50] Noting media

---

47   The evidence for this chronology comes from Conlon to Curtin, 4 April 1942, NAA, A1608/1, item AK 29/1/2.
48   Wise, *The Self-Made Anthropologist*, p. 154, and telephone conversation, Pomeroy/Wise, 30 March 1994. For adverse comments on Elkin's scrupulosity, see Geoffrey Gray, '"Piddington's Indiscretion": Ralph Piddington, the Australian National Research Council and academic freedom', *Oceania*, 64:3 (1994), pp. 217–45.
49   *Newcastle Morning Herald*, 27 May 1942. Although Drew Cottle has claimed that Elkin was 'an influential member of the Morale Committee', there is no evidence presently available to substantiate such a claim. See Drew Cottle, 'A New Order for the Old Disorder: The state, class struggle and social order, 1941–1945', in Richard Kennedy (ed.), *Australian Welfare History: Critical essays* (Melbourne, 1982), p. 276.
50   Elkin to Curtin, 2 April 1942, NAA, MP 508/1, item 240/701/217. For an estimate of Elkin's policy of social assimilation for the Aborigines of Australia, see Russell McGregor, 'The Concept of Primitivity in the

speculation that the Aboriginal population might help the Japanese in the event of a land invasion, Elkin—while not discounting the possibility—said it could be avoided if the military authorities were prepared to utilise the services of trained anthropologists who could act as liaison officers and who might train Aborigines as coast watchers.[51]

Elkin's proposals were forwarded to the relevant government departments (Army, Interior and Labour and National Service) for advice. They received support from Wallace Wurth, Director-General of Man Power, and also from Military Intelligence advisers who observed that 'the fact that there are only a few scattered thousand of abos does not make the thing unimportant...if we do not get hold of them there is little doubt that the enemy, if he gets a chance, will'.[52] This insight was informed by recent experience in Malaya and Burma and would also be critical in New Guinea where the campaign depended on the support and sympathy of the indigenous population. From the Army's point of view, it was accepted that mixed bloods could form a fighting unit with good morale and that, moreover, the training and possible employment of full-blooded Aborigines as a unit 'might serve to heighten morale in general'.[53]

Although Elkin's proposal received support from these quarters, E. W. P. Chinnery, the Commonwealth Advisor on Native Matters, was more cautious, pointing out that while the Army could expect a good response if it decided to enlist Aborigines for special armed units in the north, there was some doubt as to whether they 'could be relied upon to serve consistently for any length of time'. He saw a real danger in friendly contacts between Japanese and Aborigines, especially those who were not under the supervision of reliable Europeans, such as missionaries. Despite these reservations, Chinnery argued for the establishment of 'watching posts with wireless sets under trained Europeans at strategic points along the coastline known to be frequented by wandering Aboriginals'.[54]

Early Anthropological Writings of A. P. Elkin', *Aboriginal History*, 17:2 (1993), pp. 95–104.
51   D. J. Mulvaney has described Elkin's professional approach as 'narrowly defined' and 'willing to be guided by expediency'. He regards Elkin as 'someone who frequently hindered research by any but those in, or from his own department'. D. J. Mulvaney, 'Australian Anthropology: Foundations and funding', *Aboriginal History*, 17:2 (1993), p. 125.
52   Summary file note, 13 May 1941, NAA, MP 508/1, item 240/701/217.
53   Robert A. Hall, *The Black Diggers: Aborigines and Torres Strait Islanders in the Second World War* (Sydney, 1989), pp. 26–8.
54   Chinnery to Barrenger, 29 April 1942, NAA, MP 508/1, item 240/701/217. See also discussion on allegations of disloyalty in Robert A. Hall, *Fighters from the Fringe: Aborigines and Torres Strait Islanders recall the Second World War* (Canberra, 1995), pp. 45–51, 131–2. For anthropologists and the war effort, see Geoffrey Gray, 'Australian Anthropologists and WWII', *Anthropology Today*, 21:3 (2005), pp. 18–21; Gray, '"The army requires anthropologists": Australian anthropologists at war, 1939–1946', *Australian Historical Studies*, 37:127 (2006), pp. 156–80.

1. A. P. Elkin: Public morale and propaganda

Chinnery was also supportive of the enlistment of both full-blooded and mixed-blood Aborigines in heavily populated European districts, and was confident that 'many of them would make excellent soldiers'.[55] He referred to the good work they had done in the last war and, more recently, in the Middle East. This argument, however, did not impress C. L. A. Abbott, the Administrator of the Northern Territory. Citing the recent bombing of Darwin and, while failing to mention that the behaviour of the white population, including members of the Administration and military forces, was deserving of even closer scrutiny and censure, Abbott declared, 'Aboriginals would not hold their ground against bombing and machine gunning'; but he did say he supported 'closer contact between natives and Army personnel under certain circumstances'.[56]

On 2 July 1942, Elkin wrote to the Treasurer, J. B. Chifley, about his opinion surveys and the Second Liberty Loan, which he and his team of observers had begun to analyse as soon as it was obvious the public response had not fulfilled expectations. He enclosed a brief report on the 'lag' and identified some of the issues that had emerged from the survey. First, it was clear that the idea of a war loan had to be sown in people's minds well before it was launched and then, when launched, it should be accompanied by as much fanfare and as many public rallies as possible. Advertising for the loan should focus not only on the need to pay for weapons but also on the challenge, and dangers, to be faced as well as the ultimate goal; and appeals should be tailored according to the financial abilities of people to contribute.[57]

Elkin argued that while public appeals by government leaders influenced the success of war loans, their success was very much 'tied up with the whole problem of morale', with the idea of winning the war, not only to defeat the Axis powers, 'but also to bring into being a better social and economic system of our own people in which the supremacy of the human personality over all economic laws should be established'. He added that the majority of people would not work and fight merely to defeat somebody; 'moreover, many people say that this is a capitalists' war and to say the least, are not enthusiastic about it'. Concluding his letter to Chifley, Elkin stressed that the key to framing successful appeals lay in having a solid grasp of public opinion. Writing on the subject in the *Australian Journal of Science* in August 1942, Elkin reiterated the

---

55 Hall, *The Black Diggers*, pp. 113–33. See also Noah J. Riseman, 'Colonising Yolngu Defence: Arnhem Land in the Second World War and transnational uses of indigenous people in the Second World War', PhD thesis, University of Melbourne, 2008. Others were attached to the North Australia Observation Unit raised in May 1942 under the command of Major W. E. H. Stanner. Richard Walker and Helen Walker, *Curtin's Cowboys: Australia's secret bush commandos* (Sydney, 1986), pp. 138–50.
56 Abbott to Secretary, Department of Interior, 17 April 1942, NAA, MP508/1, item 240/701/217. See Douglas Lockwood, *Australia's Pearl Harbour: Darwin 1942* (Melbourne, 1966); and Timothy Hall, *Darwin 1942: Australia's darkest hour* (Sydney, 1980). For a contrary view to Hall's, see Alan Powell, 'The Darwin "Panic", 1942', *Journal of the Australian War Memorial*, 3 (1983), pp. 3–9.
57 Elkin to Chifley, 2 July 1942, EP, 104/1/15/6.

view that such surveys were particularly useful in wartime since 'a knowledge of people's opinions and reactions is essential if their wholehearted cooperation is to be maintained.'[58]

Elkin did meet with success with his work for the Recruiting Drive Committee of the RAAF (NSW) on factors affecting recruiting for the Women's Auxiliary Australian Air Force (WAAAF). His report drew letters of appreciation from the Minister for Air, Hon. A. S. Drakeford, and the Chairman of the Recruiting Committee, Sir Donald Cameron. His research and opinion polling were carried out under subject headings, which included 'moral stigma', 'sex hostility', 'selfishness', 'snobbishness', 'fear of unemployment after the war', 'glamour', 'marriage' and 'discipline'. The report revealed perceptions about the WAAAF indicative of contemporary prejudices about women's place and the nature of service life. Grouped into moral, financial, social and organisational factors, they were judged, by Elkin, to be 'equally potent in deterring girls from enrolling'.[59] High on the list of negatives was the reputation of the WAAAF, which, according to one respondent, was that 'its members have an extremely smutty reputation due to tales spread by members of the RAAF'.

Noting the WAAAF's public image problem, Elkin summarised some of the more lurid stories about pregnancies, several about the propensity of WAAAF women to overindulge in liquor and the rumour that a maternity wing was being built at Richmond Air Base. Elkin concluded that a standard of conduct when off duty is 'accepted as the standard for and by many men of the fighting services, and apparently some women in uniform have adopted the same standard for themselves'. Hence 'men will be men' and possibly 'women will be women', or is it possibly the fear that 'women will be men?' he asked. Male resentment was also identified as a factor undermining the morale and image of the WAAAF; while some men simply 'disliked their women folk joining the service', there was a certain amount of 'sex hostility' from RAAF men who believed that women were encroaching too far into their traditional domain. Elkin recommended remedial action be taken to dispel fears and prejudices and to improve the image of the WAAAF.[60]

The Recruiting Committee established a subcommittee to consider Elkin's findings and, on the subject of the 'moral aspersions', Sir Donald Cameron said that 'every possible action should be taken to squash and wipe out' such

---

58 Elkin, 'Study of Public Opinion', *Australian Journal of Science*, 5:1 (1942), pp. 16–18.
59 Elkin, Enrolment in the WAAAF: Objections and difficulties, (typescript, 12 August 1942), EP, 104/1/15/4. Again, Elkin used a team of 'observers' to obtain the raw data on which he based his report.
60 Summary of views as recorded by Elkin's team of observers, (n.d.), EP 104. See also Joyce A. Thompson, *The WAAAF in Wartime Australia* (Melbourne, 1991), pp. 182–4. Thompson notes that despite Elkin's efforts, 'recruiting still lagged behind the RAAF's expanding requirement, malicious rumours of misconduct continued to circulate and the report itself had little or no effect on the drafting of constitutional legislation and conditions of service for the women's auxiliaries' (p. 185).

1. A. P. Elkin: Public morale and propaganda

criticism; this sort of adverse comment often emerged in wartime and was 'an influence to damage any movement, particularly one which is unusual and new, as is certainly the case with the amazing job the women are doing to help us come out victorious in this conflict'.[61] Recommendations were sent on to the Recruiting Committee and, with a few amendments, were adopted unanimously, and the Director of Recruiting of the Air Board commended Elkin's role.[62]

At the start of the 1943 academic year, Elkin was fully occupied. Although he had lost Hogbin to war service, there were 30 students enrolled in the Department of Anthropology, several of whom were engaged in war-related research work. Areas of research included the assimilation of immigrants, especially wartime refugees, production and morale in factories, studies of attitudes towards Aborigines in country towns and a survey of all sources of food and water and the prevalence of poison plants in combat areas. Inspired by the principles of the Atlantic Charter, Elkin was also preparing a booklet on the need for a similar charter for the peoples of the South-West Pacific, and was examining the training needs of administrators for the Australian New Guinea Administration Unit (ANGAU)—a project sponsored jointly by the Department of External Territories and the Australian National Research Council.[63] At the same time, he was corresponding with F. M. Forde (Minister for the Army), E. J. Ward (Minister for External Territories) and H. V. Evatt (Minister for External Affairs), outlining his views on the future of Papua, New Guinea and the islands of the South-West Pacific.[64]

In his analysis of the role of 'middle class moderates' involved in public affairs in the period leading up to the war, Stephen Alomes has noted that their stance included 'a strong element of moral correction in the desire to uplift the masses, improve their speech and educate their minds'.[65] As a member and founder of organisations that provided a focus for debate on public issues and as a prominent participant in that debate, Elkin held similar views and fits this description. Although most of his attempts to influence government at the highest levels, especially in relation to propaganda, were fruitless, his campaign to convince his fellow Australians of the dangers of apathy continued unabated. He spoke from a wide variety of platforms and wrote numerous articles and letters on what he saw as the priorities to build morale and win the war. He promoted the concept of morale, linking it to duty, sacrifice and patriotism at every opportunity. He called for greater sacrifice, moral restraint and control.

---

61 Cameron to Elkin, 28 August 1942, EP, 104.
62 Cameron to Elkin, 17 September 1942, and Chadwick to Cameron, both in EP, 404.
63 A. P. Elkin, *Wanted—A charter for the native peoples of the South-West Pacific* (Sydney, 1943).
64 Elkin to Halligan, Department of External Territories, 21 May 1943, and correspondence with Forde, Ward, Evatt, 1943–44, EP, 176/4/2/210. This correspondence is focused on Elkin's views of what Australia should do in Papua New Guinea after the war. See Gray, '"The army requires anthropologists"', pp. 166–8.
65 See Stephen Alomes, '"Reasonable Men": Middle class reformism in Australia 1928–1939', PhD thesis, Australian National University, 1980. See also Rowse, *Australian Liberalism and National Character*, pp. 158–9.

He believed in the responsibility of the state to influence public opinion, as evidenced in his proposals to establish a Department of Propaganda (or Morale), and he was concerned about what the mass of people might do if not instructed or at least warned about their responsibilities in a time of crisis.

As a member of this group of 'middle class moderates', Elkin wanted to be taken seriously, play a prominent role in public affairs and influence public culture and mores. He was highly critical of complacency, apathy, greed and moral decay, and believed that people of his qualifications and standing were obliged to assume positions of power and responsibility and to provide moral leadership. In this sense, he was exercising, or attempting to exercise, moral and ideological leadership—an approach that, through his opinion sampling and surveys, incorporated the views and interests of those groups over which he, and other contemporary elites, intended to exercise guidance and control. In his personal quest for influence and recognition during wartime, however, Elkin had been spectacularly unsuccessful.

Elkin's view of the masses as politically apathetic and inclined to habitual or 'vegetative' behaviour was not exceptional among elites but at least he recognised that economic conditions—notably those created by the Depression—were a potent causal factor. He would have agreed with J. S. Mill—an early influence on his thinking—who wrote:

> [T]he most important point of excellence which any form of government can possess is to promote the virtue and intelligence of the people themselves. The first question in respect to any political institutions is how they tend to foster in the members of the community the various desirable qualities…moral, intellectual and active.[66]

Elkin's dealings with the political and bureaucratic elite of wartime Australia demonstrate a limited grasp of the dynamics of political power and influence. He was socially and politically inept, was neither a 'fox' nor a 'lion' in terms of Pareto's taxonomy and certainly not a political adventurer or entrepreneur. He was the quintessential Victorian public moralist.[67] A new elite, akin to the New Deal intelligentsia in America, was emerging to play an important role in the higher direction of the war and policies for postwar reconstruction. Elkin's inability or unwillingness to play practical politics and secure an effective power base meant that, while his academic career continued to provide him with a platform from which to speak out on issues of concern to him, he was increasingly isolated from the development and implementation of public policy.

---

66 Quoted in Peter Bacrach (ed.), *Political Elites in a Democracy* (New York, 1971), pp. 74–5.
67 Collini has described the characteristic preoccupations and assumptions of Victorian public moralists as 'an obsessive antipathy to selfishness, and consequently their reflections were structured by a sharp and sometimes exhaustive polarity between egoism and altruism'. Stefan Collini, *Public Moralists: Political thought and intellectual life in Britain, 1850–1930* (Oxford, 1991), p. 5.

2. Conlon's Remarkable Circus

Cassandra Pybus

Alf Conlon (1908–61) was a visionary. He would not have known it, but his ideology had similarities with the Italian Marxist Antonio Gramsci. Conlon had a belief that the ideas that shape society come from a fairly small elite united by shared intellectual premises, and he sought to use the chaos of the war to establish a new kind of elite in Australia. What Gramsci termed 'organic intellectuals' Conlon thought of as his intellectual underground. When the war had begun to pose a direct threat to Australia, he could see that the fallout was going to destroy the credibility of the existing elites and undermine the derived power of the conventional establishment. He recognised the possibility of using the chaos to build a new power group with progressive ideas, organic to Australian society and based on intellect. No Marxist, Conlon insisted his 'New Men' would be a classless elite, yet those he had in mind were lower-middle-class boys like himself who had come to university through the selective State school system. The poet James McAuley was typical of Conlon's incipient elite: brainy, ambitious, contemptuous and, most importantly, a product of Conlon's alma mater, Fort Street Boys High, Sydney, as were Hal Stewart, Ian Hogbin, Jim Plimsoll and a brilliant law graduate named John Kerr.

Born and bred in Sydney, Conlon probably thought himself *sui generis*. That was certainly how he was seen by his admiring friends at Sydney University. The most obvious accoutrement of the Conlon persona was his pipe: occasionally sucking on it between words, more usually, using it to point, to rub the back of his neck, scratch his balls, or stick it, stem first, into his ear or nostril. Once in verbal flight, Conlon could be mesmerising, especially for impressionable minds, as Donald Horne recounts:

> He seemed an ordinary man, yet when he talked he could conjure up great visions, as if the smoke from his pipe was being shaped into the mirages of wisdom…'what this country needs is a good sociology'. He would linger over 'sociology', with a long stress on each syllable, chew his pipe for a while, then point it. 'And it's people like you who will provide it'. I had scarcely heard of the word 'sociology' but I would wave my glass of beer in general agreement and wait silently for Alf's next statement. He was talking some of the language of planning—words like 'scientific manpower control' that did not seem to have meaning—enlivened the imagination with the romance of manipulation and the

language of change, peering into the future of the war for exciting possibilities. New ideas were coming up. New things would happen. And we would be among them.[1]

With this kind of technique, Conlon managed to entrance minds more worldly than wide-eyed, young Donald. He had a real gift for talking on any subject with apparent insight and intellect, drawing on an astonishing range of superficial knowledge and convincing his audience, one to one, of their own special importance in the scheme he had envisaged. A physically nondescript man with a crew cut and horn-rimmed glasses, he was married with a child and was rather old to be an undergraduate. This curious spellbinder probably would have remained nothing more than a great talker and engaging eccentric were it not for the war. In the anxieties of that special time, Conlon found his metier.

It was his position as student representative on the University of Sydney Senate that provided his springboard to power. From the time of his election in 1939, he showed no interest in student concerns; he went straight for the main game: negotiating influence, especially when the university became embroiled in controversy over the appointment of Julius Stone to a chair in jurisprudence in 1940–41. Stone had been the unanimous choice of the appointment committee, but the implacable opposition of the NSW Bar to this Jew saw his appointment blocked by the Chancellor and three senior legal members of the Senate. Conlon lobbied tirelessly on Stone's behalf, leaking Senate information to Stone in Auckland and his student friends in Sydney; the latter undertook a robust campaign in support of Stone, devoting an entire special issue of the student newspaper, *Honi Soit*, to the scandal. Professors Richard Mills and Alan Stout led the academic response. Stone's appointment was upheld and the various conservatives on the Senate were forced by circumstance to resign, which did wonders for Alf Conlon's position on the Senate. From that time, Mills and Stout were among Conlon's most staunch supporters. No-one was more staunch in his support than Julius Stone. Once installed in the Chair, he gave Conlon the job of hand picking the students to be reserved from call-up to go into law.[2]

Together with Mills from Economics and Stout from Philosophy, he formed the military subcommittee in 1940—established to consider the utilisation of personnel in the university. Conlon was able to convince his professorial colleagues of the need for a proper manpower policy within the university to best direct the talent pool. He had himself appointed Manpower Officer—to the astonishment and envy of his student friends—with a suite of rooms in the quad, staff and filing cabinets. And access to the top military brass. His maxim was that every door was open. Early in 1940, he walked through the door of

---

1 Donald Horne, *The Education of Young Donald* (Sydney, 1967), p. 243.
2 Leonie Star, *Julius Stone: An intellectual life* (Sydney and Melbourne, 1992), p. 57.

2. Conlon's Remarkable Circus

Brigadier Victor Stantke, who was in charge of the administration of Eastern Command, to put to him the idea that the Army should establish a research section to utilise the intelligent young men at university, rather than wasting them as artillery fodder. Stantke was impressed, although the best he could do, at that time, was put Conlon on a committee investigating an army education scheme that might keep up the morale of the troops.[3]

Conlon was also a key figure in the establishment of a National Union of Australian University Students, and used his contacts in this sphere to develop his visionary plans. In Melbourne for meetings at various times during 1941, he held heavy drinking soirees with Melbourne intellectuals. Some thought him a blowhard; others were instant converts. 'Panzee' Wright, Professor of Medicine at Melbourne University, found a kindred soul when a student took him to meet Conlon at a house in Toorak. He and Conlon fell into an excited discussion about how to handle the military situation:

> It traversed the whole field from reactions of various types of individuals to the sort of effect the war would have on the economy of the country to problems of the psychology of Australian soldiers fighting from Australia instead of the back streets of Paris, and all the rest of it. What would be the difference between the Digger legend of this war and the previous war? All sorts of stuff about herd psychology, problems of tropical medicine. The lot.[4]

They finished talking about 4 am and Wright finally got home to find that his anxious wife had rung the police.

When General Stantke became Adjutant-General in 1941, Conlon's prospects began to look up. Stantke set up the Army Education Service in the Land Army Headquarters (LHQ) in Melbourne and Conlon happily took the credit.[5] At Ushers, the downtown bar where Conlon's circle drank, he would sound forth about the important work that could be done from within the military. His talk was peppered with the phrase 'Army Education', by which he meant something altogether different from imparting a few skills to the diggers. Whatever the task he had in mind, Conlon could always make it sound thrilling when talking to the boys in Ushers bar, as Donald Horne remembered:

> It might be necessary for intellectual integrity to put on its uniform, he explained, and hide itself in the Army for the duration of the coming Barbarians, against which we saw Alf as the main bulwark. 'Have you

---

[3] General Stantke, in John Thompson (ed.), *Alfred Conlon: A memorial by some of his friends* (Sydney, 1963), pp. 102–3.
[4] Roy Douglas Wright, in Thompson, *Alfred Conlon*, p. 27. Wright was universally known by his nickname, variously spelt 'Pansy' or 'Panzee'. Conlon addressed him as 'Panz'.
[5] Conlon's CV, September 1943, National Archives of Australia [hereinafter NAA], A1608/1, item AK29/1/2.

ever thought'…he pulled his ear thoughtfully as he spoke to us in the pub. 'Have you ever thought of chaos? That's a word we should get used to boys. Chaos.'[6]

The war had become a grim reality for Australia by February 1942. The Labor Government of John Curtin faced the appalling prospect of a Japanese invasion following the fall of Singapore and the bombing of Darwin. Australia's Eighth Army Division had been destroyed and 22 000 Australian troops had been taken prisoner. The country was in a state of alarm verging on panic. Ironically it fell to Curtin, who had never completely shed his pacifist, anti-conscription convictions, to intensify his nation's identification with the Allied war effort and boost morale on the home front. Professor A. P. Elkin of the Anthropology Department at Sydney University bombarded Curtin with proposals for the establishment of a Department of Morale under Elkin's direction. Conlon also had an interest in massaging the community morale, although in his scheme of things there was no place for Elkin; he was yesterday's man. Curiously, Conlon won the day and it was to Sydney University's Manpower Officer and not to its Professor of Anthropology that the Prime Minister turned, in March 1942, for a report on the problem of morale, giving Conlon the opportunity to secure a key role for himself in wartime policy.

Throughout March and April, Conlon was engaged in feverish activity in Canberra, Sydney and Melbourne, 'carrying on a single-handed struggle to establish myself in the hierarchy', as he told his friends at Ushers.[7] When Conlon was duly appointed to chair the Prime Minister's Morale Committee, he hand picked its members from among his personal allies: Alan Stout, 'Panzee' Wright and Ian Hogbin, with Julius Stone as deputy chair. Elkin was pointedly ignored. Under Conlon's verbose guidance, the Morale Committee held a two-day meeting in June to discuss such weighty matters as a campaign to turn suburban gardens into vegetable plots to offset the loss of workers, and the negative attitude of housewives. Towards the end of the second day, Conlon mused: 'If we could think of another name for information we could get a new department.' Money for staff and resources would not be a problem, he said.[8] Northern Australia was seen to be vulnerable to the twin evils of Japanese spies and American soldiers, so Ian Hogbin and Panzee Wright were dispatched to report on the particular problems of morale in north Queensland. Another two-day meeting in July got down to more substantial issues, especially Conlon's notion that there should be a strong national body to influence the Federal Government on education policy. A subcommittee was established to make recommendations. A research committee was also established. A paid consultant

---

6 Horne, *The Education of Young Donald*, p. 283.
7 Conlon to Stone, 11 April 1942, Stone Papers, National Library of Australia [hereinafter NLA], MS 5516.
8 NAA, 1608/1, item AK 29/1/2.

was necessary for this committee, Conlon insisted, and he arranged for his brilliant friend Jim McAuley to get the job. In December the committee coopted several more of Conlon's allies: John Kerr as well as 'Nugget' Coombs and Brian Fitzpatrick from the new Department of Post-War Reconstruction.

Having a special project from the Prime Minister did wonders for Conlon's aura. Brian Fitzpatrick enjoyed drinking with Alf, yet he always had an uneasy feeling that the Prime Minister's Press Secretary was probably desperately paging somewhere for Conlon: '"*Are you there? Won't you come? Jack wants to see you. When can you come?*" One had this feeling because Alf didn't pretend to be the great panjandrum and the backroom boy, that he was.'[9] His friends at Sydney University thought so, too. The rumour mill had it that his next move was to a top job in the Army.

It is doubtful that Conlon did have a great deal of influence with Curtin. There is not a jot of real evidence for it, even though numerous historians have looked. It probably required just a few minutes of Curtin's time to agree to Conlon's idea about a committee to consider morale, if only to get rid of him. The official war historian, Paul Hasluck—who loathed Conlon—examined all the documents he could locate and could find no evidence that the Morale Committee had any influence on the Prime Minister or that its members were effectively in touch with him.[10] Conlon did call on the Prime Minister in December 1942 to discuss his proposals. Curtin seems to have been bemused and alarmed by Alf's grandiose ideas for creating a Department of Public Relations, responsible to the Prime Minister and costing £2 million, and referred the idea to Arthur Caldwell who proved the death knell for the idea.[11] Conlon's one claim to success was the establishment of the Commonwealth Department of Education, with his staunch ally Richard Mills as its first director, although the direct impetus for this move came from Nugget Coombs in his capacity as Director-General of Post-War Reconstruction. Otherwise the Morale Committee's recommendations proved to be something of a dead end for Conlon's ambitions. No matter. Alf always had other fish to fry, having managed to persuade General Stantke to establish a research section at Victoria Barracks LHQ, Melbourne, with himself appointed as a major on the special list. Whatever it was Conlon was doing in Melbourne, he wanted it kept hush-hush, giving his friends to understand it was TOP SECRET. He had been able to second a number of ex-academics and lawyers from other army units and had set them the task of working out a plan for the northern regions of Australia in the event of invasion. His team included

---

9   Brian Fitzpatrick, in Thompson, *Alfred Conlon*, p. 7.
10 Paul Hasluck to J. W. Burton, 16 August 1967, from the private papers of Nicholas Hasluck.
11 Curtin to Conlon, 11 March 1943, NAA, A1607/1, item AK 29/1/2.

John Andrews, a geographer, cartographer Edgar Ford and lawyer Frank Hutley. In addition, he had contrived the transfer of two Fort Street old boys, John Kerr and John Ryan. These two were to become his right-hand men.

Even so, early in 1943, when General Lloyd succeeded Stantke as Adjutant-General, Conlon's outfit looked very shaky. Lloyd could not abide Conlon and thought his research unit a lot of nonsense; he was determined to be rid of it. Staff were whittled away. Conlon made a characteristic countermove and got a friend to introduce him to Brigadier Eugene Gorman, a close friend of the Commander-in-Chief, General Thomas Blamey. Over a few drinks, Conlon put it to Gorman that what Blamey needed was a special intelligence unit to help him deal with the non-orthodox problems of the Army, such as the administration of occupied areas. In February 1943, Conlon's group was transferred to the Directorate of Military Intelligence, LHQ, where they occupied an old weatherboard building known as L Block, beside the Victoria Barracks in St Kilda Road.

By the time the year was out, everyone in Conlon's outfit had been given a considerable leg-up by General Blamey. The story of how this happened has become the centrepiece of the Conlon legend—more parts myth than fact. It is said that the battle-hardened, no-nonsense Commander-in-Chief, just back from the war zone, paid a visit to the research unit and gruffly demanded an explanation of what it was they actually did. Alf replied—so some versions of the story go—'We just bugger about.' In other versions, Conlon, feet on desk, scratching his bum with his pipe, gives a rather more blunt response: 'Fuck all.' Again, the Conlon magnetism worked. On 6 October 1943, the unit was transformed into the Directorate of Research and made responsible directly to Blamey himself. The directorate had no actual establishment; staff were appointed on the Commander-in-Chief's special list, at Conlon's discretion. Whatever it was that Conlon did say—and it seems Alf went to see the General rather than the other way about—it reinforced Blamey's own view that as the Australian head of the armed forces, not just as an appendage of the British, he had a historic and politically sensitive role. Moreover, Conlon's ideas spoke directly to Blamey's belief that Australia must have a key role in the Pacific once the Japanese had been driven out. Where the other army brass regarded Conlon as a nuisance and a fraud, Blamey could see his usefulness. Always vulnerable to criticism and intrigue, Blamey saw the benefit of having a sort of intelligence unit on the margins of the military to assist him to deal with civil and political issues.[12] The directorate was to be his eyes and ears and its charter was vague and broad. Major Conlon could do pretty well what he liked, as long as General Blarney could reap a benefit.

---

12 See John Hetherington, *Blamey, Controversial Soldier: A biography of Field Marshal Sir Thomas Blamey…* (Canberra, 1954); Gavan Long, *The Final Campaigns* (Canberra, 1963).

In January 1944, Lieutenant Colonel Julius Stone was brought into the directorate full-time for what he explained to a Harvard colleague were '[s]pecial duties of an expert and secret nature'.[13] Professor Keith Murray, an agriculturalist recruited from Queensland University, already held the rank of a full colonel. Other lieutenant colonels appointed were Professor Keith Isles, an economist from Adelaide University, and the anthropologists Ian Hogbin and Camilla Wedgwood from Sydney University. Not to be outranked by his subordinates, Conlon was promoted to lieutenant colonel. Bill Stanner was unwillingly drafted into the position of assistant director of research. It says much for Conlon's pulling power that he could compel the transfer of Stanner, who had been the advisor to the Minister for the Army and had developed the remarkable North Australia Observer Unit as a bush commando unit on the front line of defence in the Northern Territory. It was a move Conlon might well have come to regret. Stanner was a man of considerable experience, a few years older than Alf, and he already held the rank of lieutenant colonel. He never was beguiled by the Conlon charisma.

This rash of highly placed appointments was a direct result of Conlon's trips to New Guinea with Blamey towards the end of 1943. Blamey had encountered serious trouble in his command in New Guinea just as the campaign against the Japanese was at a precarious point, with desperate fighting on the Kokoda trail across the Owen Stanley Range. General Douglas MacArthur, as the Supreme Allied Commander in the Pacific, had pressured Curtin to send Blamey to New Guinea to take control—a move that had resulted in a confrontation with Major General Rowell, the commander of the New Guinea force. Rowell had a longstanding antipathy to Blamey, whom he saw as debauched and unstable; Blamey had him removed. With no shortage of politicians and military officers looking for Blamey's head, he needed Conlon's help to ensure his command would be judged a success.

As the Japanese retreated in the final months of 1943, the whole of New Guinea had come under the control of the Australian New Guinea Administrative Unit (ANGAU). Conlon saw his opportunity to be the architect of a 'New Deal' for Australia's colonial territories and moved swiftly to establish his unit as the policy arm of ANGAU. In February 1944, Blamey presented a verbose paper, written by Conlon, to alert the Government to the 'tremendous political vistas' presented in the Pacific and the need for imagination, insight and ingenuity. The paper argued that with the Japanese all but defeated in the South-West Pacific, the Australian Government was strategically placed to seize the initiative to influence the future activities of the United States and other imperial powers in the Pacific basin, as well as commercial development in the region. The war had

---

13   Star, *Julius Stone*, p. 75.

given Australia a unique opportunity to exercise a moral policy as a justified weapon of power politics to protect not only the future of native people in the Pacific but also the strategic security of Australia:

> It may be we are confronted with one of those rare moments in history where morality coincided with expediency. The strategic importance of New Guinea could not be overstated in the chain of islands from Timor to the Solomon's [sic] and New Caledonia which were the forward line of defence for Australia. The reoccupation and military administration of New Guinea must be approached as a critical phase in Australia's colonial policy.[14]

The paper hinted at a colonial policy that included more than the territories of Papua and New Guinea at a time when colonial expansion for Australia was in the air. H. V. (Bert) Evatt, the Minister for External Affairs, had made no secret of his ambition to secure a security zone in the South-West Pacific and had consistently identified Dutch New Guinea, Timor, the Solomons and New Caledonia as areas that Australia should be given to administer following liberation from the Japanese. US President Franklin Roosevelt had indicated to the Pacific War Council in February 1943 that there should be a redistribution of sovereignty in the Pacific and he had raised the possibility of Australia taking over responsibility for Portuguese Timor. The idea of Australia and New Zealand being given postwar control of both French and British Pacific possessions was mooted again at the Pacific War Council in January 1944.[15]

Conlon was convinced that preparing the ground for a radical and expanded postwar colonial policy was the job of his Directorate of Research. Everyone was set to reading some aspect of colonisation and the Pacific. Ida Leeson, recruited from the Mitchell Library through the good offices of Julius Stone, was given the rank of major and the task of rapidly building a research library. Orders were placed for close to 200 books on criminology, sociology, colonial policy, anthropology, philosophy, international law, administration and labour, as well as copies of all journals on Africa, Oceania, Asia and the Pacific. Any book the staff wanted, Leeson would try to get. Jim McAuley, for whom reading was a consuming passion, could not have been more delighted, since Alf's research brief dovetailed nicely with his burgeoning interest in aesthetics and the philosophy of Asia. Hal Stewart was as happy as a sand-boy in his job as the librarian's assistant.

On one idle afternoon in October 1943 when Corporal Stewart and Lieutenant McAuley found they had L Block to themselves, they hit upon the idea of constructing some hoax surrealist poems that they would pass off on their

---

14   The Situation of Australian Colonies as at January 1944, NAA, CP637, item 45.
15   See Richard Hall, *The Real John Kerr: His brilliant career* (Sydney, 1978), p. 57.

literary *bête noire*, Max Harris, as the work of an unknown, deceased poet, Ern Malley.[16] The whole collection was called *The Darkening Ecliptic* and carried an epigraph of 'an old proverb' that they concocted: 'Do not speak of secret matters in fields full of little hills.'

Directorate colleagues were given a reading. Conlon was absolutely delighted. Ian Hogbin and Camilla Wedgwood expressed surprise that the Malley oeuvre had taken only an afternoon to write and set themselves the task of duplicating the experiment. As Stewart recalled, they had no difficulty whatsoever in producing as many poems 'of a very much higher quality than ours in rather less time'.[17] Kerr gave sage legal advice not to accept any money for publication of this fake drivel and suggested that they could invite an important public figure to write a preface to the book.[18] Conlon, with his 'no hands approach to life', had the idea to involve Bert Evatt, the Minister for External Affairs and Attorney-General.

The atmosphere of heady tomfoolery generated by the Malley hoax seems to have infected most of the directorate with fanciful ideas. Not content merely to subvert colonial policy, Conlon had notions that postwar policy for Australia was also grist for his mill. A draft paper from Julius Stone proposed a series of huge research projects that touched on every conceivable aspect of domestic and foreign policy. In just some of Stone's proposals, Isles was to investigate industrial and agricultural capacity, the role of economic collaboration with the United States and the implications of US involvement in the Pacific; Conlon was to elaborate questions of stability and instability of postwar government policy, strategic and imperial policy towards the United States and ties with Britain; Kerr was directed to the constitutional issues of defence and other strategic aspects, as well as the relationship between the bureaucracy and government and manpower allocation; Stanner was to overview the colonial issue in terms of its obligations and commitments, economic capacity, manpower requirements and policy imperatives. And this was only the tip of the policy iceberg; there was plenty more.

Stanner, the outsider within Conlon's empire, responded as if it were another hoax, calling it 'a gargantuan essay in quantitative colossalism which out-Conlons Conlon'. With contemptuous ridicule, he dismissed Stone's project as fantasy, which illustrated 'the increasing erectility of the Directorate's libido…likely to afford equal assistance to the bounding megalomanias or the melancholias between which we now alternate'. Stanner felt that the sooner Stone was returned to the officer reserve the better. 'I am now strongly anti-

---

16 For a full account of the Ern Malley hoax, see Michael Heyward, *The Ern Malley Affair* (St Lucia, Qld, 1993).
17 Harold Stewart, quoted in ibid., p. 100.
18 John Kerr, *Matters for Judgement: An autobiography* (Melbourne, 1978), p. 11.

Semitic', he concluded.[19] There was no love lost between Conlon and his acerbic assistant director. To Stanner's relief, Stone returned to his university duties in February 1944 and his grand plan languished for want of Alf's attention.

Conlon was determinedly pursuing his own radical plans for Australia's territories, which he was not about to let fall back into the hands of the old planters and colonial administrators. He wanted new policies in place that emphasised native welfare, as well as Australia's strategic interests, and he saw it as his job to create a new generation of enlightened administrators. Reg Halligan, the unimaginative head of the Department of Territories, found himself out-manoeuvred, with his minister, Eddie Ward, completely seduced by Conlon's vision of a 'New Deal' for New Guinea.[20] Now Conlon had two powerful patrons in Blamey and Ward. As these men did not see eye to eye, it was one of Conlon's roles to act as a conduit of information between them, further enhancing his power and greatly increasing the enmity directed towards him from within the Army and from the bureaucrats in Canberra.

Eddie Ward was a pugnacious, old-style labour man with a foul tongue and a reputation as a radical firebrand, for whom colonialism was an anathema. Curtin disliked Ward, who had been foisted on his Cabinet by the Caucus, and the territories portfolio was his way of repaying Ward for his disloyalty. As expected, Ward found this portfolio an embarrassment. He was disinclined to take the advice of Reg Halligan, nor was he inclined to take the readily proffered advice of Professor Elkin, whose policy of compromise and restraint had no appeal. Instead, he turned to Conlon to deliver a policy that would redeem the portfolio from the stigma of colonial exploitation. Halligan and Conlon were meant to work closely together; they did not. As far as Alf was concerned, Reg Halligan would not have recognised a good idea if it were held out to him on a fork.

In mid-April 1944, Conlon and two senior officers in the directorate had accompanied Ward on a tour of Papua and New Guinea where the ANGAU top brass was openly annoyed at what they saw as the directorate's radical meddling in the Army's business. The diary entries of ANGAU officer Eddie Stanton give a flavour of the general opinion on this subject. Like the settler community, he was outraged at the idea that indigenous workers were going to be paid compensation, 'as if we, the white man, owe the natives anything'. And again, specifically concerning Hogbin: 'He advocates that natives are our equals and that we should regard them as our brothers, and do everything in our power to elevate them.' Hogbin was seen as the driving force behind the push for compensation and concern for indigenous welfare. His homosexuality did not

---

19 Notes and Correspondence, March 1944, Stone Papers, NLA, MS 5516.
20 NAA, CP 637/1.

escape comment. 'He likes native boys', Stanton pointedly observed.[21] As far as most in ANGAU and the settler community were concerned there was too much bleeding-heart anthropology in the directorate and altogether too much Conlon everywhere.

Conlon's other powerful patron, General Blamey, needed help to advance his ambitious plan for regional security, which sought a much more potent role for Australia in the Asia-Pacific region. How much Blamey's vision of Australia as the dominant power in the postwar Pacific was a product of the fevered enthusiasm of the directorate, and how much was his own idea, it is hard to tell, but the Commander-in-Chief received determined support in the directorate. The whole thrust of their activity was to provide a radically new approach that would sweep away the exploitative colonial system of the past and establish structures and policies to facilitate the process of self-government, as sketched in Hogbin and Wedgwood's book *Development and Welfare in the Western Pacific*, published in 1943, which argued that Australia's obligations to the people of its Pacific territories could be honoured 'only if we abandon all thought of developing the region ourselves and train the islanders to do so'.[22]

Conlon had suspicions that the bureaucrats in Ward's department were sympathetic to the return of civil government in the territories, since this would hand control of administration back to them. Here Conlon was able to use his close relationship with the Commander-in-Chief, getting Blamey to persuade the Prime Minister that General MacArthur wanted ANGAU to remain in control of New Guinea. He knew that Curtin would defer to MacArthur's wishes, even when it was against his own judgment and advice.[23] Conlon also fought a determined campaign against the Department of External Territories to make sure that all applications for re-entry to areas under Australian Army control be referred to the directorate for action, so that he controlled the movements of civilians to the South-West Pacific, as well as to Malaya, Borneo and the Dutch possessions. Even the Rajah of Sarawak had to get Conlon's permission to visit his own country.[24] Throughout 1944 Conlon was running lines of interference on many different fronts. In April 1944 he had dispatched Bill Stanner to London, to precede Blamey in talks associated with the Commonwealth Prime Ministers' Conference. Since Conlon did not trust Stanner to see things his way, he also sent John Kerr to keep watch and to use his own initiative, if need be.

---

21   Hank Nelson (ed.), *The War Diaries of Eddie Stanton: Papua New, 1942–45, New Guinea, 1945–1946* (Sydney, 1996), pp. 269, 275–6.
22   Ian Hogbin and Camilla Wedgwood, *Development and Welfare in the Western Pacific* (Sydney, 1943), pp. 2–3.
23   Curtin to Ward, 31 October 1944, NAA, A518/1, item A800/1/7.
24   NAA, MP742, items 274/1/249 and 274/1/247.

Among the top-secret reports that Conlon received from his emissaries in London was Stanner's report on the high-powered Social Sciences Research Committee in the Colonial Office.[25] This was just the kind of thing Conlon was looking for: a process to mastermind progressive policy in Papua and New Guinea after the war. By September 1944, he had got Eddie Ward to secure the agreement of the War Cabinet to the establishment of an External Territories Research Council, chaired by Conlon. The members made a familiar roll call of his friends: Richard Mills, Panzee Wright, Keith Isles, Keith Murray and Camilla Wedgwood, as well as Nugget Coombs representing the Department of Post-War Reconstruction; it had functions so broad and ill-defined they would make any bureaucrat blanch.[26]

The External Territories Research Council was only one element in Conlon's grand plan to redesign the intellectual landscape of postwar Australia. Back in 1943 Conlon had floated with Richard Mills of the Universities Commission the prospect of setting up a special research council. Conlon had been keen to impress upon his old friend that tertiary education failed to give weight to 'what might be called Australia's strategic position' and that the emerging intelligentsia lacked the knowledge base for an appreciation of Australia's position in the Pacific; he proposed a research committee to attempt to redress those limitations.[27] The compliant Mills agreed to be a nominal chair, as long as he did not have to do anything.[28] In a characteristic move, Conlon then got Julius Stone to propose that the Australian National Research Council set up the Social Sciences Research Committee to be chaired by Richard Mills. By the time the first meeting convened, this group had expanded to include Alf Conlon, Panzee Wright, Nugget Coombs and Keith Isles.[29]

As with every project of Conlon's devising, here much of the work was done informally in late-night drinking sessions in Melbourne. Panzee Wright remembers one such session in the middle of 1944 when he and Alf were speculating about what might happen after the war if the northern hemisphere was really wrecked. 'Why shouldn't Australia be ready to be the new Constantinople?' they asked themselves. They devised a plan to 'put up a new university and put it in the front garden of the Commonwealth government and try and staff it with people of such eminence that when they asked for six million the government would have to take it seriously'. Then and there they

---

25   NAA, MO729/8, item 49/439/73; see also Geoffrey Gray, 'Managing the Impact of War: Australian anthropology and the South West Pacific', in Roy M. McLeod (ed.), *Science and the Pacific War: Science and survival in the Pacific, 1939–1945* (Dordrecht, 2000), pp. 187–210.
26   NAA, A518, item R815/1/1.
27   Conlon to R. C. Mills, 25 October 1943, NAA, A1608/1.
28   Stout Papers, University of Sydney Archives, p. 180, item 210; also the correspondence in relation to the Social Sciences Research Committee in the Wright Papers, University of Melbourne Archives, A.1968.0003.
29   Australian National Research Council Papers, NLA, MS 482, box 24; Stuart Macintyre, *The Poor Relation: A history of social sciences in Australia* (Melbourne, 2010), pp. 48–9.

drafted a proposal for such an institution, which would attract back to Australia its outstanding intellectual expatriates. Next morning the proposal was with General Blamey, who enthusiastically undertook to persuade the Prime Minister to the idea. Central to the concept was a world-class medical research institute. And who better to head it up than Howard Florey, whom Blamey was able to persuade to make a special visit to Australia in September 1944, ostensibly to discuss the latest developments in penicillin. It was Conlon who met Florey when he arrived in Adelaide and briefed him while they travelled to Melbourne for further discussions with Blamey. The following year, when negotiations with Florey began in earnest, Conlon was the go-between.[30]

The School of Civil Affairs was prompted by another top-secret report leaked from London, about a similar set-up in Whitehall. Conlon's plan in the short term was to put together a training course in civil affairs for personnel in areas liberated from the Japanese. When the war was over, the grand plan was to make this an Institute of Colonial Studies like the one at Oxford, which would become one of the institutes at the new national university. He was determined to cut out Professor Elkin, whose department at Sydney University had traditionally trained men for colonial administration. With his own anthropologists on staff, Conlon was able to tap excellent networks for training materials and personnel. Camilla Wedgwood obtained a prospectus detailing courses for training in colonial administration from Margaret Mead, and Ian Hogbin arranged for Ralph Piddington—yet another anthropologist antipathetic to Elkin—to be brought out from the University of Aberdeen to the directorate.[31] In early January 1945, Lucy Mair, who was an expert in colonial administration in Africa, was brought out from the London School of Economics (LSE).

The next move was to persuade the War Cabinet subcommittee to provide funding for a School of Civil Affairs in Canberra. At the War Cabinet meetings, Blamey did the talking, but Conlon was invariably present at his elbow. By September 1944, the skeleton of the School of Civil Affairs was in place: Keith Murray was the principal, with Ralph Piddington as his deputy and Ian Hogbin, Camilla Wedgwood, John Andrews, John Legge and Jim McAuley as the lecturing staff. The absence of the directorate's other anthropologist, Bill Stanner, was notable. Conlon was unconcerned about Stanner, for whom he had other plans, and he continued to make high-ranking appointments of academics, lawyers and other persons whose skills he needed. Since there was nothing in the military to compare even remotely with the Directorate of Research, it attracted rancour from within the military and from without. It was not just that the directorate did not hold parades, or that its staff would not salute and wore their uniforms askew; what really infuriated was the high elevation of their ranks. There was

---

30 The correspondence is in the Florey Papers, Parcel 10/11, Australian National University Library.
31 Margaret Mead to Camilla Wedgwood, 15 August 1944, Wedgwood Papers, NLA, MS 483.

no war establishment for the directorate and appointments were made on the Commander-in-Chief's special list. According to Wing-Commander White, who raised the matter in Parliament in September 1944, among the 24 officers in the directorate, nine of whom were colonels, there was not an overseas service stripe or a wound to be seen. White's fulminations against this 'excrescence' greatly annoyed the Minister for the Army, Frank Forde, who did not appreciate having to defend this bunch of oddballs in the Parliament. The attack also made Conlon alert to the advantages of recruiting men with overseas service or wound stripes. When Peter Ryan, a sergeant who had distinguished himself in combat in New Guinea, presented himself at the directorate, Alf took him on immediately. Ryan recalls that he was one of four new recruits to the directorate at that time, each of whom had distinguished overseas service. For a few weeks, he had 'no duties whatsoever' and then Conlon directed him to a pile of books to read on history and colonial policy. He read diligently and in no time was promoted to the rank of lieutenant as an instructor at the School of Civil Affairs. His job was to teach Pidgin.[32]

Jim McAuley was promoted to captain and his job was as instructor in colonial administration—not that he really knew anything about colonial administration. None of them did. Hogbin, Wedgwood and Piddington gave instruction in aspects of anthropology and Andrews taught geography. The teaching ratio was one staff for every two students. Professor Elkin was quick to see the negative implications for his anthropology department. 'If this kind of set up remains after the war', he bitterly complained to a colleague, 'then the age of miracles has arrived'.[33]

Blamey had approved £10 000 from the Army budget for permanent premises for the school on a site chosen by Conlon within the grounds of the proposed national university, but in the short term they used facilities at Duntroon. The behaviour of both staff and students was, however, decidedly unmilitary. Ralph Piddington had a serious drinking problem, and sometimes on parade he was too drunk to stand. Almost immediately there was conflict over the refusal of the directorate officers to recognise the authority of the commanding officer at Duntroon. Soon they were banned from that site with nowhere to go.[34] In June 1945, Conlon was desperately trying to negotiate a new home for the next training intake, at the same time as he was establishing a radical new policy for the administration of Australia's Pacific territories, including an ambitious

---

32   Peter Ryan, in Thompson, *Alfred Conlon*, p. 19.
33   Quoted in Tigger Wise, *A. P. Elkin: The self-made anthropologist* (Sydney, 1985), p. 160.
34   NAA, MP742, item 323/21/27.

legal project to consolidate the legal systems of Papua and New Guinea. Simultaneously, he was getting into terrible hot water over a lunatic project to control the civil administration of British colonies in Borneo.[35]

As the commander of the armed forces in Borneo, Blamey was in a strong position and he was not a man to show deference to the British. He insisted that Conlon was to control civil affairs in Borneo or the Australians would withdraw all support.[36] In April 1945, Blamey bluntly informed the British Colonial Office that the civil affairs unit they had detached to Australia, including a former chief justice and deputy governor of North Borneo, was unsuitable and an ANGAU senior officer was ordered to the directorate to raise a detachment for Borneo. When the forward party of British officers arrived in Australia, they found that an Australian unit, the British Borneo Civil Affairs Unit (BBCAU)—known colloquially as the Bastards, Bludgers, Cunts and Arseholes Unit—had been created to do the job in Borneo in their stead. To their fury, the British officers found themselves confined to Ingleburn Barracks while a rookie Australian unit was dispatched to Borneo. They were incensed at being placed under the command of an Australian officer and even more outraged to be told the authority of the Colonial Office would not be recognised. They sent complaints back to London that Conlon was unpredictable, power-hungry and unreasonable. There was talk of mounting a formal complaint to the Australian Government about the way Conlon was running the show.[37]

By the middle of 1945 Conlon's chaotic administration had caught up with him. The size of the directorate had blown out fourfold, with 60 staff in the School of Civil Affairs and a further 70 in the directorate. His operation was exposed on several fronts with no clear lines of responsibility. John Curtin was seriously ill and Conlon's political patronage looked increasingly fragile. Ida Leeson observed his great distress when she told him that Curtin had an occlusion: 'He looked most pained and said "Don't say that Ida, don't say it. Don't say the word", because he thought it might mean the end of their planning if Curtin died.'[38] On the ground in Borneo, the civil affairs situation was disastrous. The forward BBCAU party had arrived on 30 April, hopelessly understaffed, without unit stores, equipment or transport, and with no knowledge of the nature and area of the impending operation except that it was to be in British Borneo.[39] The despairing commanding officer begged to have the British personnel released to join the unit, but at the end of June there were still 40 British officers penned up at Ingleburn.

---

35 NAA, MP742, item 274/1/246.
36 NAA, MP742, item 274/1/246.
37 Kerr, *Matters in Judgement*, p. 103.
38 Ida Leeson, in Thompson, *Alfred Conlon*, p. 14.
39 Long, *The Final Campaigns*, p. 403.

The notion of Australia holding on to British Borneo was lunatic, for any number of reasons, but Conlon's plan had a certain logic. If Australia was able to secure control of North Borneo then it would be in a position to trade territory with the Dutch: North Borneo for Dutch New Guinea. Evatt had already tried to negotiate Australian postwar control over the Dutch colonies in New Guinea and Timor, which were central to his and Blamey's concept of Australia's postwar regional security. Conlon confidently expected another 18 months of war, with MacArthur's forces driving the Japanese back, island by island. This would give him the necessary time to put in place new administrative and legal structures in New Guinea and, perhaps, to negotiate with the Dutch. As the expert on Dutch New Guinea, John Legge was very aware of Conlon's desire to see New Guinea united under one administration. He felt that by the middle of 1945 Alf was 'alive to the issue of a possible trade with Dutch Borneo'.[40] That said, it was highly unlikely that Prime Minister Curtin would ever have entertained the idea of holding on to Borneo, for all his loyalty to Blamey. As it was, Curtin was out of action. In his place, Frank Forde was acting as Prime Minister. Forde could not stand Blamey and despised Conlon. When Curtin died on 5 July 1945, Conlon's schemes stood absolutely no chance.

Following Curtin's death, Forde immediately ordered an investigation into the directorate. On 25 July, Conlon was requested to supply the Chief of the General Staff with a list of his staff and an outline of their duties and responsibilities. He did not comply with this request. The War Establishment Committee continued to press the directorate for information, reporting with some exasperation that 'the Director is absent and there appears to be no deputy'; various officers were signing memos for Conlon but he was not in evidence.[41] At the School of Civil Affairs they were disturbed by Conlon's state of mind. McAuley had been concerned for some time that Alf had 'lost control of himself and was courting disaster…the magic touch had gone, the spellbinding powers and the operational judgment'.[42] He had been aware of some clandestine activity over Borneo, but he was not aware how serious it was until he began to hear rumours from England that Conlon 'had fallen foul of the Colonial Office'.[43] It was now too late to do anything to help. Alf was no longer functioning in any coherent way. On 15 August, the War Establishment Committee reported that Lieutenant Colonel Conlon had been admitted to hospital. It seems he had suffered some kind of nervous breakdown. Knives were being sharpened all over town.

Conlon never returned to his position at the directorate. The atomic bombs that were dropped on Japan early in August put the finishing touch to his

---

40   John Legge, correspondence with the author.
41   NAA, MP742, item 1/1/1808.
42   James McAuley, 'John Kerr's Judgement', *Quadrant*, 20:1 (1976), p. 26.
43   James McAuley, Interview with Catherine Santamaria, 5–7 May 1976, Oral History Collection, NLA, TRC 576.

plans. General Blamey travelled to Tokyo Bay to sign the surrender document on behalf of Australia—a token gesture, since the Australian Government had been basically ignored when the surrender terms had been formulated. Blamey made it clear he would step down immediately when he returned. Conlon, discharged from hospital, drafted the letter of resignation. The Commander-in-Chief considered that his job was done and did not wish to continue under a prime minister who did not have complete confidence in him. The new Prime Minister, Ben Chifley, did not, however, accept the resignation, indicating that he wished to retain Blamey to deal with the complexity of the immediate postwar period. The Commander-in-Chief was thus able to repay his debt of gratitude by promoting Alf Conlon to the rank of full colonel. He was placed on the regimental supernumerary list on 14 September.

On 19 September, the Minister for the Army fielded a barrage of questions in Parliament about Conlon and his organisation. The honourable members demanded to know the exact situation with the Directorate of Research—described as an organisation that had 'inquired into everything in Heaven and on earth', under the command of someone who was 'in civil life a third year medical student', who had recently been seen in Canberra 'wearing the full uniform of a staff Colonel'. Surely, they demanded of the minister, this unit of 'highly paid professors disguised as temporary Lieut-Colonels and Majors' was a luxury the taxpayers should be rid of.[44]

Forde was furious. He had anticipated questions about the directorate and was ready to report that it was being rapidly dismantled. He was unaware that Conlon had become a colonel. No-one seemed able to account for it. Forde determined to have the promotion rescinded and wrote Blamey a strong letter to that effect. The Commander-in-Chief replied on 14 November with three closely typed pages of wounded invective in typical Conlon-esque prose, claiming that the minister's demand to rescind the promotion was

> a gratuitous insult to an officer who has served with selfless devotion… No officer had a better record of understanding and pioneering effort in the development of a sound administrative approach to difficult problems derived from some of the novel circumstances of modern warfare…he possesses imagination, tenacity and administrative skill considerably beyond the ordinary. This was manifest in advice and assistance in problems of mobilization and in introducing scientific services into the Australian Army.[45]

Conlon kept his rank as a colonel. His services were never again sought by the Army or anybody else with any real power in the postwar world. He was

---

44 Abbott, in *Hansard*, 19 September 1945.
45 Blamey to Forde, 14 November 1945, NAA, MP742, item 1/1/1808.

cut out of the planning for The Australian National University. Donald Horne recalled an afternoon and evening he spent drinking with Conlon at the Hotel Canberra in 1945. Into the early hours of morning the drinking continued, creating a scene rich in ironic symbolism with Horne, incapable of coherent speech, grunting the odd sceptical aside and Alf still holding forth about the need for Australian foreign policy even as he was 'staggering in the shadows'.[46]

Kerr remained principal of the Australian School of Pacific Administration (ASOPA) but resented Alf's trickery in holding back his career at the Bar; finally, in 1948, he resigned, leaving the position open for Alf. It was not welcomed by all and many predicted it would be disastrous. It was, with his old friend Jim McAuley leading the charge to oust him. Alf turned his attention to completing his medical degree, finally graduating in 1951. He was not suited to general practice and set himself up as a psychiatrist, but his ramshackle lifestyle and lack of concern for his own general health caught up with him and he died prematurely in his own home, aged fifty-three.

---

46   Donald Horne, *Confessions of a New Boy* (Ringwood, 1985), pp. 155–7.

3. H. Ian Hogbin: 'Official adviser on native affairs'[1]

Geoffrey Gray

Herbert Ian Priestley Hogbin[2] was born in England in 1904 and emigrated with his family to Australia in February 1914. He attended school in Leeton, in country New South Wales, and then Fort Street High School in Sydney. He attended the University of Sydney, on an education bursary, where he completed, in 1926, a Bachelor of Arts and a Diploma in Education.[3] Hogbin attended Radcliffe-Brown's lectures on social anthropology—Anthropology I and Anthropology II—in the newly formed Department of Anthropology.[4] Faced with a shortage of fieldworkers, Radcliffe-Brown persuaded—as Hogbin remarked later—a scarcely prepared twenty-two-year-old to join an expedition to Rennell Island and Ontong Java in 1927. Hogbin's fieldwork was the first research conducted under the auspices of the Australian National Research Council (ANRC). Those scholars considered for fellowships 'should be men of unusual promise [who] should be assured of either a definite University post or of a connection with teaching, research or scientific work having a direct bearing on some biological aspect of human welfare'.[5] He was awarded his MA in Anthropology (for his work on Ontong Java) on 12 August 1929, the same year he left for the London School of Economics (LSE) to write his doctoral dissertation under Bronislaw Malinowski—later published as *Law and Order in Polynesia* (1934).

Hogbin considered himself a Malinowskian functionalist, although he owed his interest and development in social anthropology to Radcliffe-Brown. In

---

1 H. Ian Hogbin to Camilla Wedgwood, 20 April 1944, Wedgwood Papers, National Library of Australia [hereinafter NLA], MS 483, box 1.
2 Hogbin changed his name by deed poll. He informed the Registrar: 'I recently discovered that my name is not what I had thought it was. Would you therefore have it altered in future editions of the [University] Calender. I am entered as "Herbert William Hogbin": my name is really "Herbert Ian Hogbin".' H. Hogbin to Registrar, University of Sydney, 18 March 1929, University Administration, File G3/187, University of Sydney Archives. He inexplicably added 'Priestley'. His birth certificate names him Herbert William Hogbin, b. 17 December 1904. Against how the rest of the family pronounced their name Hogbin, he pronounced it 'Hobben'. Personal communication, Rosemary Stanley (Hogbin), 1 April 1994.
3 He thanked Dorothy Griffith Taylor: 'You know quite well that if it had not been for you I could not have been an anthropologist, don't you? If you had not come to my rescue with a loan when Radcliffe Brown first made me the offer I might now be teaching! (awful thought).' Hogbin to Taylor, 10 September 1934, Hogbin Papers [hereinafter HP], University of Sydney Archives.
4 Hogbin took his lecture notes with him to Rennell and Ontong Java, where they fell overboard, but he successfully retrieved them. They are deposited in the Hogbin Papers, University of Sydney Archives.
5 Edwin E. Embree to Orme Masson, 27 May 1926, Elkin Papers [hereinafter EP], University of Sydney Archives, 155/4/1/1.

September 1934, soon after *Law and Order* was published, he wrote to Dorothy Griffith Taylor, younger sister of Thomas Griffith Taylor, associate professor and foundation head of geography in the University of Sydney:

> I do not know if I have told you before…I have completely lost respect for Radcliffe Brown's scientific theories and with that tumbled all regard for his person. He is a vain silly man—also I fear a very unhappy one. At the same time…I have a regard for him in that he made me an anthropologist. The book [*Law and Order*] of course *ought* to have been dedicated to Malinowski, only that would not have been right—I owe too much to Radcliffe Brown. Also naturally it was impossible when he wrote the Introduction, I wrote and told [Malinowski] how sorry I was that I could not at least group his name with Radcliffe Brown, and he very kindly wrote back to say that he would like to have me dedicate my next book to him, and he was sure that it would be a better one anyway.[6]

Hogbin returned to Sydney in 1931. He spent most of 1932 and 1934 first in Guadalcanal and Malaita in the British Solomon Islands Protectorate (BSIP) and then in Wogeo (Schoutten Islands) in the Australian-administered Territory of New Guinea (TNG), a League of Nations mandate. On his return, he was appointed temporary lecturer in the Department of Anthropology at the University of Sydney to teach Melanesian ethnography—a position made permanent in 1936. Hogbin made the University of Sydney his academic base for the rest of his career, while regularly visiting London on sabbatical leave. He used these visits to develop his love for Italian Renaissance painting in the galleries of Europe, Baroque architecture, the theatre and opera.[7]

Notwithstanding Sydney being close to his geographical areas of interest, he was on the lookout for other academic positions. In 1937 he applied unsuccessfully for the Chair at Johannesburg, and was undecided about an opening at Aberdeen; he asked Raymond Firth to keep him in mind should there be 'any [other] suitable openings'.[8] He also applied for a position at Cambridge in early 1938.[9] It indicates that not all was well with Sydney, particularly Hogbin's professional and personal relationship with his Professor, A. P. Elkin.

Like anthropologists of the time, he spent long periods in the field, rarely returning, however, to conduct follow-up research, which is a feature of

---

6   Hogbin to Taylor, 10 September 1934, HP.
7   Jeremy Beckett and Geoffrey Gray, 'Hogbin, Herbert Ian Priestley (1904–1989)', *Australian Dictionary of Biography. Volume 17* (Melbourne, 2007), p. 539.
8   Hogbin to Firth, 16 July 1937, Archive of Sir Raymond Firth, British Library of Political and Economic Science, London School of Economics, London School of Economics and Political Science [hereinafter FIRTH], 8/1/52.
9   Hogbin to Firth, 3 May 1938, Reference for H. I. Hogbin (application to University of Johannesburg), 18 March 1937, FIRTH8/2/2.

present-day anthropology. His primary anthropological interests were social and cultural change, depopulation and colonial administration, which shifted after the war into a more orthodox ethnography, illustrated by his publications in the 1960s and 1970s.[10] He published widely on many of these topics and his Malaita study was published as *Experiments in Civilisation: The effects of European culture on a native community of the Solomon Islands*, published in the same year as World War II was declared.[11] *Experiments in Civilisation* was a 'pioneer study of a society in the process of change'.[12] It was, in his own estimation, of

> theoretical importance, in that the process of culture change is a phenomenon of great sociological significance; but it has in addition practical relevance, since the analysis of the actual results of attempts by European agents to transform native societies along lines they consider desirable shows whether they are in fact achieving what they seek and whether there are any unsuspecting developments of their activities.

He drew on African colonial policy and practice, which 'for the most part [were] more progressive than in the South Seas, with the object not only of indicating possible lines of development, but also furnishing…practical assistance to administrators and missionaries'.[13] We see this suite of interests appear in his war research in the BSIP and in his advice to the Australian New Guinea Administrative Unit (ANGAU), which carried out all the functions of the prewar government as well as providing assistance and advice to the civilian postwar PNG Government.

At the outbreak of war with Germany, Hogbin was teaching, his career seemingly secure and promising. Hogbin enlisted on 17 April 1942 several months after war with Japan was declared. Before the war, Hogbin had developed a loose association with a literary coterie at the university that included A. A. 'Alf' Conlon, Ian Maxwell from the English Department, the poets Alec Hope, Harold Stewart and James McAuley and a young Donald Horne; it seemed to Horne that 'everyone in this circle adopted a pose of contempt for everything that was happening in the intellectual wasteland it was their misfortune to find themselves in'.[14] Hogbin fell into the category of people Elkin 'disapproved of strongly: the "anti-personality"—people who questioned the system'. The relationship between Elkin and Hogbin was, not surprisingly, fraught. Elkin was

---

10   See list of publications in Fisher Library card catalogue, University of Sydney.
11   He had not returned to the Solomon Islands after 1943 and was 'therefore in no position to prepare a major revision…and bring it up to date'. H. Ian Hogbin, *Experiments in Civilization: The effects of European culture on a native community of the Solomon Islands* (London, 1939), p. xiv.
12   Ibid., p. xiv.
13   Ibid., p. 3.
14   Cassandra Pybus, *The Devil and James McAuley* (St Lucia, Qld, 1999), pp. 9–10; also Alan Barcan, *Radical Students: The old left at Sydney University* (Melbourne, 2002).

the antithesis of the more refined and elegant Hogbin, and Elkins' biographer concedes that Hogbin had advantages of style and substance over his more senior colleague: 'striding up and down in front of the students with a cigarette between his fingers, [Hogbin] was widely read, cultured, liberal, brilliant, a witty lecturer.'[15] Theirs was a mutual dislike that predated the war,[16] and was exacerbated by it.

War

Soon after he enlisted, Hogbin was appointed to the National Morale Committee (NMC), headed by Conlon.[17] Conlon hand-picked its members from among his personal allies: Alan Stout (Sydney University philosopher), Roy ('Pansy') Wright (Professor of Physiology at the University of Melbourne),[18] Hogbin and Julius Stone (Professor of Jurisprudence at the University of Sydney). Hogbin and Stone had written the interim report on the need for such a committee. In January 1943, Hogbin and Wright were sent to northern Queensland to investigate morale. They spent three weeks in Cairns, Townsville and Rockhampton, and 'although in that short period a full and complete investigation of the problem was not possible, we feel that we can, with confidence, put forward a number of recommendations'. They delivered their report to Conlon on 1 February.[19] Perhaps the lack of action is explained by the Morale Committee and its members, especially Conlon, being seen as intruders by the traditionalists in the bureaucracy.[20] As a first foray into influencing the formulation of policy by Conlon, it was hardly successful. Notwithstanding, it created the beginnings of a network of intellectuals, academics and professional men who would influence government policy during and after the war.[21]

Early in 1943, as Hogbin remembered it, he 'offered his services'—although it is more realistic to say that his services were asked for—to Sir Philip Mitchell, High Commissioner for the Western Pacific.[22] As a member of the British Solomon

---

15   Tigger Wise, *The Self-Made Anthropologist: A life of A. P. Elkin* (Sydney, 1985), p. 138.
16   'I do detest him [Elkin] so.' Hogbin to Mary Turner Shaw, 3 June 1949, HP.
17   For further discussion on morale and the NMC, see John Pomeroy, 'Morale on the Homefront in Australia During the Second World War', PhD thesis, University of Sydney, 1995; and Pomeroy's chapter in this volume.
18   Following Wright's biographer, I have used the nickname 'Pansy', but it is also spelt as 'Panzee', 'Panz' or 'Panzy'. Peter McPhee, *'Pansy': A life of Roy Douglas Wright* (Melbourne, 1999), pp. 25–6.
19   *Civilian Morale in North Queensland* (Report by Dr R. D. Wright, Professor of Physiology in the University Melbourne, and Dr Ian Hogbin, Lecturer in Anthropology in the University of Sydney, to Major A. A. Conlon, Chairman of the Prime Minister's Committee on National Morale), 1 February 1943, National Archives of Australia, Canberra [hereinafter NAA], A5954/1, 328/21.
20   Pomeroy, 'Morale on the Homefront in Australia During the Second World War', p. 263.
21   McPhee, *'Pansy'*, pp. 50–71; H. C. Coombs, *Trial Balance: Issues of my working life* (Melbourne, 1983), pp. 197–8; Geoffrey Gray, '"The next focus of power to fall under the spell of this little gang": Anthropology and Australia's post war policy in Papua New Guinea', *War & Society*, 14:2 (1996), pp. 101–17.
22   High Commissioner from 21 July 1942 to 1 January 1945.

Islands Defence Force, he was set the task, for which he was well qualified, of looking into the question of 'Native courts and Native counsellors', the results of which were published in 1944.[23] All his recommendations were accepted.[24] In 1945 a new set of regulations, 'Instructions to natives', was promulgated. Hogbin approved of these changes, adding that indirect rule was 'beginning to take definite shape'. He hoped that the newly established civil administration in Papua and New Guinea 'will be as fully alive to its responsibilities and follow the example of its enlightened neighbour'.[25] He wrote a confidential report, *Big Gela and Olevuga-Vatilau Sub-districts, Florida. Report to Colonel O. C. Noel, Resident Commissioner, BSIP, October 1943*, which examined a range of matters including the loyalty of Solomon Islanders and reasons for Solomon Islander resentment towards the British. He described the way in which the villagers greeted the incoming Americans and their dissatisfaction with the withdrawal of British officials in the face of imminent Japanese attack. He told Elkin that his main task was to make a month's investigation at the village he worked at in the 1930s (described in *Experiments in Civilization*) and a 'short tour of the more heavily devastated areas where the [British] administration is now experiencing considerable difficulty'.[26] These were also matters that he addressed during and after the war with regard to Papuan and New Guinean people who were caught in the competing and often conflicting demands of wartime allegiance and loyalty.

On his return to Sydney, in early November 1943, Hogbin recalled that 'almost immediately' he was appointed to the rank of Lieutenant Colonel in the AIF. In April that year Conlon had convinced Major-General Victor Stantke, Adjutant-General of Land Headquarters, to form a small research section under his command.[27] Most of those who were part of the NMC were appointed, and it expanded and became the Directorate of Research under Sir Thomas Blamey, Commander-in-Chief of Australian forces.[28] (It was only in April 1945 that it became the Directorate of Research and Civil Affairs.)[29] Hogbin told Jeremy Beckett that he 'went up to New Guinea and did various jobs for Conlon and the administration generally',[30] but this downplayed his work and his role. Elsewhere, Hogbin described himself as 'official adviser on native affairs to

---

23 H. Ian Hogbin, 'Native Councils and Native Courts in the Solomon Islands', *Oceania*, 14:2 (1944), pp. 257–83. Hogbin was awarded the 1944 Royal Anthropological Institute's Wellcome Medal for this essay.
24 Royal Anthropological Institute (RAI) Archives, MS 185, item 204.
25 H. Ian Hogbin, 'Notes and Instructions to Native Administrators in the British Solomon Islands', *Oceania*, 16:1 (1945), pp. 61–9.
26 Hogbin to Elkin, 18 September 1943, HP.
27 For Stantke's memory of his meeting with Conlon, see John Thompson (ed.), *Five to Remember* (Melbourne, 1964), pp. 101–2.
28 Pybus, in this volume.
29 I have referred to the Directorate of Research as the directorate; after April 1945, I have used the acronym DORCA.
30 Jeremy Beckett, *Conversations with Ian Hogbin* (Sydney, 1989), p. 26.

the High Command of the Western Pacific'.[31] In March 1942, the Allied South West Pacific Command was formed and US General Douglas MacArthur was appointed Supreme Allied Commander South West Pacific Area. The South-West Pacific was clearly defined and was one of two theatres of World War II in the Pacific; it included the Philippines, the Netherlands East Indies (excluding Sumatra), British Borneo, Australian-controlled Papua and New Guinea and the British Solomon Islands. Notwithstanding his diverse war work, Hogbin spent most of his time during the war in Papua and New Guinea.

One of Hogbin's first tasks with the Directorate of Research was to study the effects on village life following the Army's use of native labour—that is, the removal of men from the village thus disrupting the social and economic life of people. These men were employed to support actual operations as carriers and stretcher-bearers. They were also engaged in tasks such as road making, clearing, construction of storage sheds and camps, and stevedoring. In bald terms, the number of New Guineans who were employed by ANGAU in June 1944 was 35 958—up from 2033 in June 1942.[32] Hogbin spent short periods at various places as is indicated in the proposed itinerary: 'Depart…April 26 [1944] for a couple of days at Lae: then Benabena: then Gusap…then Wau to collect records of court cases only: then up the coast from here [Finschhafen] to accompany a patrol making first contact with reconquered villages.' He was unable 'to see the whole of New Guinea, [and] confined [himself], except for Port Moresby, to the former Mandated Territory', and, with the exception of Manus and Bougainville, he 'spent a few weeks in every other Administrative district which had been freed of enemy occupation'.[33] He was confident that he would produce a 'report which ought to be of value—though whether it will be acted upon is another matter. Briefly, the stink is appalling: at one place I was so angry that I couldn't sleep (largely, I suppose, because I felt it wise to remain silent).'[34] Another member of the Directorate of Research and Civil Affairs (DORCA) with experience in New Guinea commented that the 'longer the smell of Angau clings to the POs [patrol officers], the less use they will be in their proper administrative functions'.[35] After this survey of labour conditions, Hogbin began, in September, his research at Busama, a village south of Lae, located in an area that was for the better part of 18 months at the 'front line' and

---

31 Hogbin to Wedgwood, 20 April 1944, Wedgwood Papers, NLA, MS 483, box 1.
32 J. D. Legge, *Australian Colonial Policy: A survey of native administration and European development in Papua* (Sydney, 1956), p. 185.
33 See also Diary, Native Labour Survey, March to June 1944. During this trip, he travelled, at various times, with his colleagues from the directorate Camilla Wedgwood, James McAuley and Conlon, as well as E. J. (Eddie) Ward, the Minister for Territories. He also managed to go on a 'bombing mission' (10 June 1944).
34 Hogbin to Wedgwood, 20 April 1944, Wedgwood Papers, NLA, MS 483, box 1.
35 McAuley to Wedgwood, 10 September 1946, Wedgwood Papers, NLA, MS 483, box 1.

for many months under Japanese occupation'[36]—where the native people had been 'accused of treachery' by ANGAU officers.[37] Hogbin's report was critical of ANGAU's recruitment practices.

In his reports and correspondence, Hogbin was critical of ANGAU's leadership and its staff—unlike his estranged colleague W. E. H. Stanner, who was laudatory, particularly of Morris and the Adjutant-General, Donald Cleland. Stanner, a constant critic-from-within of the directorate and particularly critical of Conlon, Kerr and Hogbin ('the triumvirate'), commended Major-General Basil Morris, Commander-in-Chief of ANGAU, and doubted whether 'any other General Officer could do better'.[38] Hogbin thought Morris was not up to the task, later describing him as a 'boofhead'.[39] Hogbin's assessment of the situation was contrary to that contained in an internal ANGAU report—*Report on the activities of Angau in respect of native relief and rehabilitation in the Territory of Papua and the Mandated Territory of New Guinea*—which covered the period from February 1942 to September 1944.[40] It is probable, however, that the ANGAU report was in part a response to Hogbin's *Report of an investigation of native labour in New Guinea*—an investigation conducted between March and mid-June 1944.[41] Hogbin concentrated almost exclusively on the situation in the Territory of New Guinea. He assailed all aspects of ANGAU's labour control and what he saw as the abuse and misuse of New Guinean labour in working for officers in the Army's mess, building and decorating gardens, acting as personal servants and such like and being kept therefore unnecessarily away from their home villages with the effect that village social and economic life was deprived of physically fit men. He was concerned that many New Guineans had suffered 'considerable loss of property and foodstuffs as a result of the war' (p. 4), which would improve once men were returned to their villages. He was also critical of the Native Labour Officers: 'the majority of these men have no real interest in native welfare and [are] chiefly concerned with maintaining or increasing employment figures for the sake of their promotion' (p. 5). Hogbin also produced a report on *The natives of the Salamaua Coast, a preliminary report by Lieutenant-Colonel Ian Hogbin forwarded to Brigadier Cleland for perusal* (7 October 1944), in which he recommended that indentured labourers should be 'freed' to return

---

36 Camilla Wedgwood to Elkin, 9 February 1946, EP, 160/4/1/80.
37 H. Ian Hogbin, *Transformation Scene: The changing culture of a New Guinea village* (London, 1951), p. 10.
38 Appreciation of Current Situation and Problems of ANGAU by 1943, W. E. H. Stanner, Territories Administration, n.d. [c. November 1943], Australian War Memorial [hereinafter AWM] 54, 80/6/17. See the chapter on Stanner in this volume.
39 Interview of H. Ian Hogbin, 25 April 1971, University of Papua New Guinea Library, AC33/10.
40 *Report on the activities of ANGAU in respect to native relief and rehabilitation in the Territory of Papua and the Mandated Territory of New Guinea February 1942 – September 1944*, NAA, AS 13/35, NN ANGAU.
41 *Report of a investigation of native labour in New Guinea carried out on instructions from the Director of Research by Lieutenant-Colonel Ian Hogbin during the period March to June 1944*, n.d. [22 pp.], copy in HP.

to their villages to produce food.[42] He also declared that both the Australian and the American Armies made use of New Guinean labour far beyond operational requirements.

Hogbin was of the opinion that the percentage of indentured labourers was too high, pointing out that anthropologists like himself believed 25–30 per cent of adult males removed from the villages had the potential to undermine the whole social structure. He favoured somewhere about 5 per cent.[43] Powell, in his history of ANGAU, suggests that Hogbin was overstating the situation and that ANGAU did what it could in the circumstances to ensure indentured labour was properly looked after and repatriation of labour to their home villages could commence once the need for their services abated—that is, when '[m]ilitary demands lessened'.[44] But the home villages nonetheless continued to suffer and the demands of the Australian Army took precedence.[45] In fact, patrol reports from the districts visited by Hogbin confirmed the deleterious effects of labour recruitment on village life.

In contrast with Hogbin's harsh assessment—but more in line with that produced by ANGAU—was Stanner's observation of the labour situation. He declared that service with ANGAU had

> definitely improved the native. His control has been firm, but just; his physique has improved from the excellent housing and rations he receives; he has learnt the value of discipline and his added responsibilities; he has a far more extensive appreciation of health and hygiene matters; he has been taught how to produce more and better food within his own village.

Stanner believed this would ensure that 'when the European returns, or decides to settle in New Guinea he should be well-served with efficient and contented labour'. If this proved to be the case then 'most of the credit should go to the

---

42   Copy in HP. Ian Downs comments on these changes in *The Australian Trusteeship in Papua New Guinea, 1945–1975* (Canberra, 1980), pp. 15, 38–9.
43   Hogbin, *Transformation Scene*, p. 9.
44   Alan Powell, *The Third Force. ANGAU's New Guinea war, 1942–1946* (Melbourne, 2003), pp. 194–8; W. E. H. Stanner, *The South Seas in Transition: A study of post-war rehabilitation and reconstruction in three British Pacific dependencies* (Sydney, 1953), p. 82. See also Hank Nelson, 'Payback: Australian compensation to wartime Papua New Guinea', in Yukio Toyoda and Hank Nelson, *The Pacific War in Papua New Guinea* (Tokyo, 2006), pp. 320–48.
45   Peter Ryan, 'The Australian New Guinea Administrative Unit (ANGAU)', in K. S. Inglis (ed.), *The History of Melanesia: Second Waigani Seminar* (Port Moresby/Canberra, 1969), pp. 531–48; also Geoffrey Gray, 'The coming of the war to the territories: forced labour and broken promises', Unpublished paper presented to Remembering the War in New Guinea, 19–21 October 2000, Australian War Memorial, Canberra.

personnel of ANGAU because of his efforts on behalf of the native during the war period'.[46] This was not their first disagreement over the conditions of employment and condition of indentured labourers by ANGAU.

Indentured labour had long been criticised particularly by missionaries and humanitarian groups calling for its reform but preferably its abolition. In December 1944, the Minister, E. J. Ward, convened a conference on the future of 'Native Labour' in a postwar Papua New Guinea. Elkin chaired the conference. Hogbin, the only other anthropologist besides Elkin, represented the directorate. It was at this conference that Ward announced that indentured labour would be phased out.[47] This led to the repatriation of all indentured labour after the war. Downs stated that 'there was no practical alternative that would have stopped the growing unrest of people who had suffered greater privations and disturbance of their lives than any section of the public on the Australian mainland'.[48]

There had been established in February 1942 a War Damage Commission, which covered white residents in the Australian territories of Papua and New Guinea who had been 'unfortunate enough to suffer loss as a result of war operations'.[49] In October 1944, the Commonwealth Government set up the Native War Damage Compensation Committee to recommend a just and practicable plan for compensating natives in Papua and New Guinea for loss of or damage to land and property, or death or injury, arising from military operations, or 'from causes attributable to the existence of a state of war in the Territories'.[50] There is little doubt that Hogbin's report contributed significantly to the establishment of such a committee. Hogbin was appointed to the committee headed by J. V. Barry, a Victorian barrister, and which included Major James (Jim) Taylor of ANGAU—an experienced prewar district services field officer. Barry spent only eight days in Papua New Guinea so that most of the work fell onto Hogbin and Taylor.[51] The committee reported to the Government in August 1945.[52] Hogbin was assisted by K. E. 'Mick' Read[53] whom he had had transferred to the directorate from army duty at Mataranka, Northern Territory, where he was a general clerk in the traffic section of the 8th Australian Army Ordnance Division;[54] he

---

46 W. E. H. Stanner, 'ANGAU', November 1944, AWM, 54/80/2/1; cf. Lucy Mair, *Australia in New Guinea*, Second edn (Melbourne, 1970), pp. 198–218; Neville Robinson, *Villagers at War: Some Papua New Guinea experiences in World War II* (Canberra, 1979); Yukio Toyoda and Hank Nelson (eds), *The Pacific War in Papua New Guinea: Memories and realities* (Tokyo, 2006); Downs, *The Australian Trusteeship in Papua New Guinea*, pp. 38–9.
47 For a report of the conference, see NAA, MP742/1, 274/1/246.
48 Downs, *The Australian Trusteeship in Papua New Guinea*, p. 39.
49 Hiromutsu Iwamoto, 'Patrol Reports: Sources for assessing war damage in Papua New Guinea', in Toyoda and Nelson, *The Pacific War in Papua New Guinea*, p. 349.
50 'Compensation to Natives', NAA, MP742/1-5/3/167.
51 Legge, *Australian Colonial Policy*, pp. 85–7; also Hogbin, *Transformation Scene*, pp. 19–21.
52 Downs, *The Australian Trusteeship in Papua New Guinea*, pp. 40–1.
53 Hogbin to Patience, 14 May 1944, NAA, MP 742/1, 274/1/245.
54 Hogbin to Grand, 30 March 1944, NAA, MP 742/1, 274/1/245.

arranged for Read's promotion from corporal to sergeant.[55] The committee was exceptional 'in its comprehensiveness, in the time and effort demanded by government officials, in expenditure, and in the direction of funds and effort to ordinary villagers it was an extraordinary policy and even more extraordinary application of a policy'.[56] The membership of the committee, especially Taylor and Hogbin, predisposed it to be generous towards Papuan and New Guineans and not make moral judgments about the loyalty or otherwise of Papuans or New Guineans.[57] As a result of the committee's recommendations, the Australian Government introduced a broad scheme providing compensation for deaths, injury and loss of property that were 'directly or indirectly connected with the war'.[58]

Aside from Hogbin's *Transformation Scene*, Read's resulting report on the Markham Valley is the only anthropological publication dealing with the effects of war on New Guineans. Read studied five villages, but concentrated on one: Ngarawapum. There, as a result of contact with Australian soldiers, the locals had come to see the prewar period as a different time, a time when they were not treated as men. Following the war, they looked towards their own new order. Following this research, Read taught at the School of Civil Affairs, and wrote up the results of his research as an MA thesis, under the supervision of Elkin at Sydney University.[59] He then left for London, where he completed his doctorate at the LSE in 1948, and returned to the Australian School of Pacific Administration (ASOPA) where he stayed for 18 months before taking up a position at The Australian National University (ANU).[60] He returned to New Guinea in 1951–52.[61] In 1956, he moved to the University of Washington, Seattle, first as a visiting, then as a permanent, professor. He did not return to Australia.[62]

---

55   Conlon to Camp Comdt, LHQ, 1 November 1944, NAA, MP 742/1, 274/1/245. Hogbin 'fitted' Read for work in New Guinea by advising him to study Malinowski's *Coral Gardens and Their Magic* and *Argonauts of the Western Pacific*; Williams' report on the Vialala Madness; and Father J. Murphy's *Book of Pidgin English*. Hogbin to Grand, 30 March 1944, NAA, MP 742/1, 274/1/245.
56   Nelson, 'Payback', p. 341. See also Hogbin, *Transformation Scene*, pp. 19–22.
57   Nelson, 'Payback', p. 342. The recommendations of the committee can be found in Hogbin, *Transformation Scene*, pp. 20–1.
58   Nelson, 'Payback', p. 342.
59   Kenneth E. Read, 'Native Thought and the War in the Pacific: A study of the effects of the Pacific War on a native community of the Markham Valley, Australian Mandated Territory of New Guinea', MA thesis, University of Sydney, 1946; Read, 'Effects of the War in the Markham Valley, New Guinea', *Oceania*, 18:1 (1946), pp. 95–116. There has been subsequent work done on indigenous people and the Pacific War—most notably, a series of essays in Geoffrey M. White and Lamont Lindstrom (eds), *The Pacific Theater: Island representations of World War II* (Melbourne, 1990).
60   Dorothy Shineberg, 'The Early Years of Pacific History', *Journal of Pacific Studies*, 20 (1996), pp. 3, 14 n. 4.
61   He was awarded the first Research Fellowship in Anthropology at The Australian National University. From his research among the Gahuku Gama in the Highlands of New Guinea, he produced what is now considered a classic ethnography, *The High Valley* (London, 1966).
62   Personal communication, Kenneth E. Read, 15 August 1993.

3. H. Ian Hogbin: 'Official adviser on native affairs'

Post war, Hogbin concentrated his research on one village, Busama, located on the upper part of the west coast of the Huon Gulf, north-eastern New Guinea. Initially, he was asked by the Army to investigate the village of Busama 'to see whether the people had been guilty of treachery'.[63] He argued that such conceptions were irrelevant, no doubt taking his cue from legal advice provided to the Compensation Committee by Justice F. B. Phillips (previously Chief Judge in New Guinea), who 'pointed out that it was impossible for Papuans and New Guineans in war to distinguish between a *de facto* and a *de jure* government, and acts such as leading Japanese soldiers along tracks did not make them collaborators'. His work for the Army enabled Hogbin to pursue his ethnographic interests: culture contact, changing society and enlightened, anthropologically informed colonial administration (already evident in the earlier *Experiments in Civilisation*). Camilla Wedgwood commented on the value of Hogbin's research: 'with his long stay at Busama…[he] has collected invaluable material on pretty well all aspects of the effects of the war on native life in an area which was for a long time in the "front line" and for many months under Japanese occupation'.[64]

At war's end, Hogbin remained attached to DORCA as a member of the School for Civil Affairs (later the ASOPA when it moved its location from Duntroon in Canberra to Mosman in Sydney) and the Pacific Territories Research Council, which, Conlon and his colleagues anticipated, would oversee all research in Papua New Guinea and the South-West Pacific. Hogbin and Wedgwood were consulted extensively during the framing of the Papua New Guinea Provisional Administration Bill, which was adopted in July 1945.[65] Two other members of DORCA, Julius Stone and J. R. Kerr, were directly concerned with its drafting.[66] In a letter to Elkin, Hogbin gloated that he had written Ward's speech—often called a 'New Deal for Papua New Guinea'. He informed Elkin that Ward 'spoke very well indeed, adapting the material he had…from me to the needs of the occasion'.[67] Ward referred to the failure of past governments and invoked the theme of indebtedness and promised New Guinean advancement. In fact, much of this argument can be found in the pamphlet *Development and Welfare in the Western Pacific* (1943) as well as Julius Stone's *Colonial Trusteeship in Transition* (1944).[68] The common element, and one shared by most of the DORCA members who were interested in the colonial question, was that development—economic,

---

63   Beckett, *Conversations with Ian Hogbin*, pp. 32–5. Neville Robinson has produced an oral history of Busama during the war. Robinson, *Villagers at War*, pp. 128–64.
64   Camilla Wedgwood to Elkin, [?] 9 February 1946, EP, 160/4/1/80.
65   Geoffrey Gray, 'The passing of the Papua New Guinea Provisional Administration Bill 1945', in Hank Nelson, Nancy Lutton and Sue Robertson (eds), *Select Topics in the History of Papua and New Guinea* (Boroko, PNG, 1969), pp. 37–42.
66   David Wetherell and Charlotte Carr-Gregg, *Camilla: C. H. Wedgwood, 1901–1955: a life* (Sydney, 1990), p. 181; McPhee, 'Pansy', p. 65.
67   Hogbin to Elkin, 22 July 1945, EP, 197/4/2/573.
68   H. Ian Hogbin and Camilla Wedgwood, *Development and Welfare in the Western Pacific* (Sydney, 1943), pp. 1–31; Julius Stone, *Colonial Trusteeship in Transition* (Sydney, 1944), pp. 1–32.

social and political—was an imperative but that it should occur at a pace to which New Guineans (and colonised peoples generally) could readily adapt. In fact, it could be said that they did anticipate independence movements as had occurred in some African colonies, and possibly might never concern Papua and New Guinea.[69]

In some ways, it can be concluded that Hogbin's career reached an apogee: he was the applied anthropologist *par excellence*, conducting research, providing what we now call evidence-based research informing policy; he provided not only policy advice but also made recommendations on how policy should be implemented.[70] He was an adviser to the minister (Ward) and to the Administrator, J. K. Murray; his opinion was sought on a range of government policies. His optimism and enthusiasm were fired by the appointment of Murray, whom he considered 'first class', to the position of Administrator. With Murray's appointment, of which Hogbin told Firth he 'can claim a big share' as he 'first suggested his name to the Minister and lobbied like hell in Canberra on his behalf', there was the possibility 'we'll get somewhere' in reforming colonial policy and practice.[71] It was, in retrospect, Hogbin's Indian summer.

Hogbin, Wedgwood and Stone were not the only ones who wrote on the need to change and reform colonial policy and practice. A number of interested individuals and groups including missionaries outlined their ideas for a new order in the colonial governance of 'Native Peoples' in Melanesia and the South-West Pacific in general. Included in this is the debate occurring in San Francisco on the matter of colonial governance and the problem of trusteeship.[72] The Australian Institute of International Affairs hosted a small study group that published a number of discussion papers: *Culture contact in the Pacific* by J. W. Burton, *France and the Pacific*, by R. F. Jackson and *Self-determination in Burma*. Elkin published *Wanted—A charter for the native peoples of the South West Pacific* in 1943; the Anglicans George Cranswick and Ian Shevill published *A New Deal for Papua* (1945). Many stressed the sense of indebtedness and moral duty to assist in the development of Papua New Guinea. But it was the group formed by Conlon that had the greatest influence on the development and formulation of colonial policy in Papua New Guinea in the immediate postwar period—a

---

69 It placed colonised people—forever in a state of transition—'in the waiting room of history'. See Dipesh Chakrabarty, *Provincializing Europe: Postcolonial thought and historical difference* (Princeton, NJ, 2000); also Amit Chaudhuri, 'In the Waiting Room of History', *London Review of Books*, 24 June 2004, pp. 3–8.
70 H. I. Hogbin, 'Our Native Policy', *Australian Quarterly*, 15 (1943), pp. 100–8; H. I. Hogbin, 'Developing New Guinea and the Future of the Natives', *Australian Journal of Science*, 5:5 (1953), pp. 133–5.
71 Hogbin to Firth, 22 September 1945, FIRTH, 8/1/52.
72 See, for example, Huntington Gilchrist, 'Trusteeship and the Colonial System', *Proceedings of the Academy of Political Science*, 22:2 (1947), pp. 95–109. See also [H. E. Hurst], *The Pacific Islanders: After the war what?* (Geelong, Vic, 1944); Cyril Belshaw, *Island Administration in the South West Pacific: Government and reconstruction in New Caledonia, the New Hebrides, and the British Solomon Islands* (London, 1950); W. E. H. Stanner, *The South Seas in Transition: A study of post-war rehabilitation and reconstruction in three British Pacific dependencies* (Sydney, 1953).

position well recognised by W. E. H. Stanner. He was critical of the 'new deal', declaring that 'the policy adumbrated was inherently almost unadministrable in the concrete circumstances of application, and there was undoubtedly an initial misconception of the scale, the intricacy and the phasing of the "new deal" task'.[73] Notwithstanding, many commentators and historians observe that there was no formal policy as such; rather it was a policy developed, Downs explains, by J. K. Murray, taking his 'guidelines from Ministerial statements to Parliament and the press'.[74] As indicated in the introduction to this book, this is an area requiring further investigation.

Relations with Elkin

Relations between Hogbin and Elkin worsened during the war and continued to deteriorate thereafter. The appointment to the directorate of Hogbin, Wedgwood and later the British colonial affairs expert Lucy Mair, to advise on colonial policy and teach at the School of Civil Affairs, meant Elkin was bypassed on all matters to do with the South-West Pacific.[75] Elkin's biographer comments that he 'ground his teeth with rage at this reversal of roles'.[76] Elkin wrote 'reprimanding pieces into addresses', which were most likely directed at colleagues such as Hogbin and Wedgwood. He wrote such things as 'some personalities become objectionable when placed suddenly in a position of authority which enables them to put other people in their place. They will have to construct themselves afresh to fit into a team.'[77]

Hogbin's relationship with Elkin, although professional, was often uncomfortable, tense, at times bitchy and vengeful. Hogbin nonetheless could be quick to take offence, as is illustrated in the following exchange between Hogbin and Wedgwood: he wrote to Wedgwood that in the course of the letter he had sent to Elkin he mentioned that the job of investigating the labour situation in Papua and New Guinea was 'so gigantic' that he 'despaired of doing anything at all'. What he expected from Elkin is unclear but he was disappointed. He went on: 'You'd have thought he'd have given a little encouragement in his reply. Not a bit of it. "I realise the job is gigantic", he said, "but you can't really do anything at all unless you sit tight in one place and make a detailed study"'.[78]

---

73 Stanner, *The South Seas in Transition*, p. 118.
74 Downs, *The Australian Trusteeship in Papua New Guinea*, p. 37.
75 See Geoffrey Gray, '"I was not consulted": A. P. Elkin, Papua New Guinea and the politics of anthropology', *Australian Journal of Politics and History*, 40:2 (1994), pp. 195–213.
76 Wise, *The Self-Made Anthropologist*, p. 151.
77 Quoted in ibid., p. 151.
78 Hogbin to Wedgwood, 20 April 1944, Wedgwood Papers, NLA, MS 483, box 1.

Part of Hogbin's postwar work was lecturing in anthropology at the ASOPA when it moved to Mosman. This created administrative problems for Elkin. Elkin had noted the establishment of the School of Civil Affairs, stressing that '[s]everal anthropologists who have trained in, and/or have been on the staff of, the Department of Anthropology, University of Sydney, and have done research under the auspices of the Australian National Research Council, will be assisting the school'.[79] The school, as has been stated previously, was to train candidates for military and postwar civilian government in Papua and New Guinea and other Allied-occupied territories, including Borneo and Morotai, in law, anthropology, government and geography, in courses of three months' duration.[80] Conlon and his advisers intended that the school continue after the war as a civil institution to fill 'the serious gaps in the training of field staff for Papua and New Guinea.'[81] It was a direct challenge to Elkin's department and its prewar function of training officials for the colonial service. The School of Civil Affairs therefore represented an ever-present threat to the authority and hegemony of Elkin and the future of the Sydney University Anthropology Department. It was a contest not only over the training of colonial officials but at its heart also over who would be best positioned to influence the formulation of colonial policy and the research agenda.[82] Elkin did all he could to retain the importance of the Sydney department and his own standing as Australia's sole expert on Aboriginal Australia. It was exacerbated by a lack of funding, as well as being understaffed in a university that was struggling financially.[83] Stanner had already commented on the danger to the survival of the department as result of the ASOPA and the planned national university in Canberra and the possibility of the withdrawal of the Commonwealth Government subsidy for the training of cadets. Camilla Wedgwood offered a more pessimistic prognosis for Elkin's department:

> [T]he condition…of Anthropology at the University…is a tragedy when one remembers that it is the only Anthropology Dept in Australia. But I doubt whether anything can be done to improve things so long as Elkin is in the Chair…It looks at present as though the Dept. might die out during the next five [years], its place being taken by the anthropological section of the planned School of Pacific Studies in the National University of Canberra, but even the success of that section depends upon finding the right man to run it. Hogbin is the obvious person but I don't think

---

79 Elkin, 'Notes on Anthropology and the Future of Australian Territories', *Oceania*, 15:2 (1944), p. 87.
80 McAuley to Wedgwood, 10 September 1946, Wedgwood Papers, NLA, MS 483, box 1.
81 This reflects Murray's assessment. Brian Jinks, Policy, 'Planning and Administration in Papua New Guinea, 1942–52', PhD thesis, University of Sydney, 1976, p. 152.
82 See Geoffrey Gray, *A Cautious Silence: The politics of Australian anthropology* (Canberra, 2007), pp. 173–202.
83 J. A. Barnes, *Humping My Drum: A memoir* (Self-published: <www.lulu.com>, 2006), pp. 249–363; also Gray, '"I was not consulted"'; Gray, *A Cautious Silence*, pp. 203–16.

he would be the right man; he has no qualities or experience as an administrator, and I do not think he has the qualities to inspire younger workers, and encourage them to reach out and think for themselves. His own ideas are so clear cut that he finds it hard to make due allowance for different points of view. We are certainly short of anthropologists of experience and sound training over here [Australia].[84]

Elkin was not due to retire for almost another decade and until then little would change.

After the war there was an increase in the number of students attending university (many of them returned servicemen and women), and presenting for anthropology courses at the university put increased pressure on the small staff of the department as well as ensuring its continuance as a teaching department.[85] As a consequence, Elkin asked Hogbin to resume full-time lecturing duties, but Hogbin resisted, wishing to continue lecturing at the ASOPA. Elkin informed him that it was not possible. Hogbin was undecided as to what he should do. He wrote to Firth:

> My own future is completely in the air. The university is clamouring for my return next year (in part I firmly believe because Elkin dislikes me having a finger in so important a pie). But there are three other problems: the continuance of the School of Civil Affairs at Canberra, the New Guinea Government asking me to inaugurate a Department of Anthropology here [University College, Canberra], and the Commonwealth is toying with the idea of getting me to do a study of the number of labourers who can safely be permitted to leave the villages without destroying the native economy. And in addition I have had a request from the Solomon Islands Govt…to do a job for them.[86]

Notwithstanding, he returned to the university in 1946 but continued lecturing part-time at the ASOPA. His workload had increased dramatically:

> [L]ecturing here at the University (with 3 times the usual number of students), lecturing at the School of [Pacific] Administration, and spending my vacations in New Guinea as adviser to the Government there—I have just returned from 2 weeks up there—is proving far too strenuous for a permanent diet.[87]

---

84   Wedgwood to Firth, 24 November 1946, FIRTH8/1/136, part 2.
85   For further discussion on these matters, see Geoffrey Gray, 'Managing the Impact of War: Australian anthropology and the South West Pacific', in Roy M. McLeod (ed.), *Science and the Pacific War: Science and survival in the Pacific, 1939–1945* (Dordrecht, 2000), pp. 187–210.
86   Hogbin to Firth, 22 September 1945, FIRTH8/1/52.
87   Hogbin to Firth, 19 September 1946, FIRTH8/1/52.

In early 1947, Elkin appointed the linguist and Anglican priest Arthur Capell to a readership in the department, overlooking Hogbin's claims for promotion. (Elkin had appointed Capell to a lecturership in 1944, which he confidently 'anticipated…would advance to Senior Lecturer'.)[88] Hogbin was furious. Hogbin told Firth, one of his confidants, that he needed 'an audience [such as Firth] which knows the fact[s]' about his relations with Elkin. He explained that applications (from Capell and Hogbin) for two readerships were

> considered first by a Committee of the Professorial Board. And after the meeting of the Committee Elkin came & told me that the Committee had turned me down & advised therefore that I withdraw the application before it reached the Board. This I did. The Board was to meet at 2p.m. today [Friday 27 June]. And at 12.30 [Professor] John Anderson came down to know why my application had been withdrawn. So I told him. Whereupon he enquired was I aware that Capell had had an application approved by the Committee. I was dumbfounded. However. I then got my spies to work & found that Elkin had come to the Committee stating that he wanted 2 readerships in anthropology. The rest said don't be silly: so he added, well, if I can only have one, it must be Capell: he is a unique linguistics expert. So Capell gets his Readership over my head.

It was, as Hogbin pointed out, a preposterous situation 'that an outsider would find…beyond belief'. Firth offered him sympathy:

> Not only from what you say in your letter but also from what I gather from Camilla [Wedgwood, a] really scurvy trick has been played upon you. Quite apart from questions of relative seniority and the like. It really is a most unhappy affair, and I understand that the situation in the department has not been too cheerful altogether.[89]

Soon after, the situation with regard to the readership took a new turn but remained unresolved. The Vice-Chancellor appointed a committee to investigate the 'whole question of readerships'. But in Hogbin's mind, Elkin's 'conduct still stands as a monument of duplicity and vindictiveness'.[90] What Hogbin did not know was that at the end of 1945 Elkin had proposed Stanner as a reader, if he could find the funds.[91] (It is, however, unclear whether Elkin was serious as he held ambivalent views on the ability of Stanner and his work ethic; the motive might simply have been to thwart Hogbin.)[92] A result of the board's inquiries was that the question of readerships in the department was addressed

---

88 Elkin to Stanner, 8 December 1944, and Registar to Elkin, 6 March 1945, EP, 197/4/2/573.
89 Firth to Hogbin, 27 June 1947, FIRTH8/1/52.
90 Hogbin to Firth, 5 July 1947, FIRTH8/1/52.
91 Stanner to Firth, 10 September 1945, FIRTH7/7/31.
92 Geoffrey Gray and Doug Munro, Australian Aboriginal anthropology at the crossroads: finding a successor to A. P. Elkin, Unpublished manuscript.

again. Hogbin and Capell were appointed readers in 1948. Elkin begrudgingly accepted the decision but the situation between the two men deteriorated even further. Hogbin told Firth that Elkin

> grows more impossible daily…and I doubt whether I can stick it much longer. His latest move is to take it on himself to establish night courses in Anthropology 1 next year. The announcement was made to me in these words. 'We are to have night courses in Anthropology I next year. You are the one affected as you will have to do the lectures'.[93]

Their disagreements did not end there. In late 1948 Hogbin heard from J. W. Burton, President of the Australian Methodist Church, that Elkin 'has had himself and Capell appointed as consulting anthropologists to the S[outh] Seas Commission'. Hogbin saw it as 'a nasty slap in the eye for me…[Douglas] Copland [Vice-Chancellor of the ANU] was furious about it when I told him'.[94] In recognition of Hogbin's long field experience in Melanesia, Firth had asked him to prepare a report on anthropological research in Melanesia preparatory to outlining a research program for the new Department of Anthropology at the ANU.[95] Firth, in his capacity as Academic Advisor on Pacific Studies to the ANU Interim Council, had written earlier to the South Seas Commission setting out a desire by Pacific Studies to cooperate 'in any way possible with the work' of the Research Council of the commission. This could take the form of undertaking 'responsibility for one or other of the research projects which your Council has not felt able to undertake at the present time'.[96] This offer was ignored. It was only after he read the *Progress Report No. 6* of the South Pacific Commission, and Elkin's report on anthropological research, that Firth expressed his dissatisfaction to Harry Maude, Executive Officer for Social Development, who was responsible for such appointments:

> May I say to you privately that I think [Elkin] underplayed the possible cooperation of the Research School of Pacific Studies…and…it [is] a great pity that he made so little mention of Hogbin…I know the latter is a matter of personal difference, but I think scientific justice would have given more credit. The omission of Hogbin's name from the acknowledgements in the preface is, of course, very marked.[97]

Hogbin, keen to distance himself from Elkin, successfully applied for an ANU (travelling) scholarship, which enabled him to spend six months in England in 1948. It meant considerable financial sacrifice, but it was a welcome respite from

---

93 Hogbin to Firth, 3 December 1947, FIRTH8/1/52.
94 Hogbin to Firth, 19 August 1949, FIRTH7/1/12.
95 Firth to Elkin, 22 March 1948, EP, 174/4/2/178. See Ian Hogbin, 'Anthropological research in the Pacific', n.d., ANU Archives, Series 19, General files, file 6.1.1.0, H. Ian Hogbin.
96 Firth to Maude, 27 October 1949, FIRTH7/7/22.
97 Firth to Maude, 3 March 1951, FIRTH7/7/22.

Elkin.[98] Hogbin continued to seek employment overseas. He told Firth he 'might apply for the advertised' Oxford lectureship and asked if Firth would act as a referee;[99] he did not 'expect to get it as Fortes tells me they don't want anyone senior'; nor did he 'really…want to go to Oxford'.[100] His ambivalence and indecision are characteristic of his approach to other possible academic positions. He told M. Turner Shaw, who did the maps and diagrams for *Transformation Scene*, that he had 'been told I can have the advertised readership to found a dept [department] at Manchester for the asking. I am not asking. Auckland is also advertising for a (new) professorship. But I don't think I am interested in that either.'[101]

The future of ASOPA remained uncertain and discussions on its future had reached an impasse of sorts with a showdown between the minister and the Secretary of the Department of External Territories, J. R. Halligan. Notwithstanding, it seemed the ASOPA would most likely go ahead but a decision about its future absorption by the ANU would not be considered for some time, although this seemed unlikely. Despite these reservations, Hogbin entertained the possibility of accepting a position in the ASOPA, but he was not sure whether he wanted to abandon an established academic institution. He was, however, considered for a position at the ANU. Firth was asked by the ANU Interim Council for advice and an assessment of the potential candidates for the anthropology professorship in the School of Pacific Studies.[102] He dismissed the possibility of Elkin, who was 'an Australian specialist' and not suitable; 'someone rather different is needed at Canberra'. Hogbin, on the other hand, deserved

> very serious consideration…He has put in years of research in New Guinea and the Solomons and is a first rate field worker. His relations with Government also appear to be very good. I know him very well and have a very great respect for his capacity. However, my feeling is that he would not be the best person to occupy the Chair of Anthropology, and be responsible for the ultimate standard of teaching and research. The test which I apply in my own mind to a Professor of Anthropology in the Pacific Studies School is—how would he get on with my best postgraduate students—could he handle them intellectually? Theoretical anthropology of that order is not Hogbin's forte; his capacities lie in other types of analysis. My feeling, then, is that while he is most certainly a person who should be offered a Readership in the new School, a

---

98   Hogbin to Firth, 3 December 1947, FIRTH8/1/52.
99   Hogbin to Firth, 11 January 1947, FIRTH8/1/52.
100 Hogbin to Firth, 31 March 1947, FIRTH8/1/52.
101 Hogbin to Shaw, 18 January 1949, Hogbin to Shaw, 12 February 1949, HP. Stanner applied unsuccessfully for this position. Max Gluckman was awarded the readership, which he had upgraded to a professorship. David Mills, *Difficult Folk? A political history of social anthropology* (New York, 2008), p. 101.
102 Firth nominated Audrey Richards, Meyer Fortes and S. F. Nadel as the only candidates for the position.

Professor should be looked for elsewhere. This, I think, would be the judgement of colleagues here. He would, I think, be interested in such a post and, if he did well, a Chair of Applied Anthropology might be created for him later.[103]

S. F. Nadel was appointed Foundation Professor. Hogbin and Stanner were offered readerships. Firth advised Hogbin to

> write as soon as you can to the Registrar, telling him that you understand from me that a Readership in Anthropology is being established at the University with the title of Readership in Social Anthropology, that you wish to apply for it, and send him if you would a brief indication of your qualifications.[104]

Once positive replies from Hogbin and Stanner had been received, the advertisements could be placed in the newspapers. It was unclear how much notice Sydney needed but Hogbin hoped to be 'technically free from Elkin' as quickly as could be managed. After visiting Copland, Vice-Chancellor of the ANU, Hogbin anticipated starting from 1 January 1950.[105]

There was considerable discussion over remuneration, with Hogbin wanting more than Stanner and Stanner insisting he receive the same as Hogbin. Firth recommended that both Hogbin and Stanner receive the same amount.[106] It might have been dissatisfaction with this decision that led Hogbin to withdraw his application, although he had stated earlier that he would not want to live in Canberra if he had a choice. Other factors might have been a concern about his superannuation and pension, which were tied to the NSW Public Service and were not transferable to the ANU.[107] A permanent position at Sydney in those circumstances far outweighed what was offered at the ANU. There was also potential conflict with Stanner. It might have been personal, as Firth hinted, which stemmed from their time together at DORCA.[108] On the other hand, he might have decided to wait out Elkin's retirement—due in five years—with the hope he could possibly engineer someone who was more congenial to his interests and demands. Hogbin had little interest in the position, as he disliked the administrative side and the responsibilities that went with a professorship. J. A. Barnes, who replaced Elkin, noted that Hogbin 'held fast to his policy of using his position as Reader to steer clear of administrative tasks as much as

---

103 Firth to ANU Vice-Chancellor, 25 January 1949, FIRTH7/5/8.
104 Firth to Hogbin, 22 July 1949, FIRTH7/7/12.
105 Hogbin to Firth, 19 August 1949, FIRTH7/1/12.
106 Firth to Copland, 22 October 1949, FIRTH7/1/12.
107 Hogbin to Hohnen (Registrar), 15 November 1949, FIRTH7/1/12.
108 Firth to Nadel, 3 December 1949, FIRTH7/1/12. See Geoffrey Gray, '"A chance to be of some use to my country": Stanner during World War II', in Melinda Hinkson and Jeremy Beckett (eds), *An Appreciation of Difference: WEH Stanner and Aboriginal Australia* (Canberra, 2008), pp. 33–41.

possible'.¹⁰⁹ To make matters a little more congenial for himself, he ensured he spent most of 1950 and 1953 in London, well away from Sydney. The immediate problem for Firth, however, was what the ANU should do now that Hogbin had declined the readership. There were two consequential matters, one of which was Hogbin's 'projected visit to New Guinea', which was part of his fellowship with the ANU. The other was Hogbin's offer 'to continue to advise on research matters especially the Melanesian field', which Firth advised Nadel to accept. As to readvertising the position, it was decided to 'hold it over for a period'.¹¹⁰ It was not readvertised.

Thwarting Elkin

When Elkin retired in 1955, Hogbin realised that he would not be offered the chair, if only because of serious opposition from Elkin himself. But neither did Hogbin want the chair and the administrative responsibilities inseparable from a professorship. Rather, his purpose was to prevent a continuation of the Elkin legacy by foiling the appointment of Elkin's chosen successor. Elkin lobbied on behalf of Ronald Berndt, his former student, commending him to the university appointment committee. Hogbin counter-lobbied even more strenuously through backstairs intrigue, sending and receiving a stream of letters to and from friends and associates, pressing his case and fuelling the rumour mill. A sense of urgency was imparted when his old foe Stanner declared his interest, leading Hogbin to urge the youthful Maurice Freedman of the LSE to submit an application.¹¹¹ Happily, another strong candidate, John Barnes, also applied: 'In any case, how much better either [Freedman or Barnes] would be than Berndt!'—or Stanner or Cyril Belshaw, who, if appointed, would 'not only [be] a tragedy for Sydney but for the future of anthropology in Australia'.¹¹²

In the event, Barnes was appointed, which foiled Elkins' best-laid plans. It was a satisfactory outcome for Hogbin but the fact remains that Barnes's appointment had nothing to do with his machinations.¹¹³ It was also an opportunity for renewal and reinvigoration and the setting of a new direction for what had become a moribund, narrow and stagnating department. Barnes worked hard in the interests of change and betterment, but without material assistance from Hogbin, who continued to evade administrative responsibility and refused to develop new undergraduate courses, content to continue delivering the same

---

109   Barnes, *Humping My Drum*, p. 273.
110   Firth to Nadel, 3 December 1949, FIRTH7/1/12.
111   Hogbin to Firth, 11 April 1955, FIRTH8/1/52.
112   Hogbin to Firth, 20 April 1955, and Hogbin to Firth, 6 June 1955, both in FIRTH8/1/52.
113   See 'Chair of Anthropology 1955', University of Sydney Archives, G3/190; Gray and Munro, Australian Aboriginal anthropology at the crossroads.

ageing lectures.[114] Dispirited by the under-funding and the general lack of academic achievement at Sydney University, Barnes was appointed to the Chair of Anthropology at the ANU following the sudden and unexpected death of S. F. Nadel in 1956. By then, Berndt was at the University of Western Australia and he decided not to apply on this occasion for the Sydney job. The successful applicant was W. R. (Bill) Geddes, and again Hogbin interfered with the selection process from the sidelines. He opposed the appointment of Geddes and they did not get on.[115] But Geddes did usher in a period of stability, which enabled Hogbin to settle down to teaching—something he enjoyed—and writing. He did not return to Papua New Guinea except for short visits in the 1970s.[116]

Jeremy Beckett, who interviewed Hogbin in the early 1980s, told me that he tried on several occasions to get Hogbin to talk about his war experiences but to little avail. In his interview with Beckett, Hogbin played down his role in the formulation of Ward's 'New Deal' and skirted over his war work including the work of DORCA and his time with them as well as the Barry Compensation Commission. Yet the war can be seen as a high point for an anthropologist who was interested in applied anthropology. He was an advisor to two colonial administrations both during and after the war. It was a time he was most involved at a senior government level in the formulation and implementation of colonial policy—a role he continued after the war: 'for some years I was advising [the Administrator, J. K. Murray] on anthropological matters…after Murray's retirement', he ceased regular trips to Papua New Guinea.[117]

The multiple opportunities offered during and after the war, particularly the ANU readership—all of which he declined—suggest a stalled career and a man who wanted no further adventure or political involvement. This might have been in part due to the impact the Cold War had on Australian political life and thinking. He might have become disillusioned with the Realpolitik of colonial politics. He remained Reader at the University of Sydney until his retirement in 1970. He was, however, productive, publishing a number of monographs on his research in Wogeo and Guadalcanal.[118] On his retirement, he took an adjunct professorial position at Macquarie University, where he taught one day a week.

---

114 Barnes, *Humping My Drum*, p. 262.
115 Beckett, *Conversations with Ian Hogbin*, p. 31.
116 Personal communication, Jeremy Beckett.
117 Beckett, *Conversations with Ian Hogbin*, p. 31.
118 H. Ian Hogbin, *A Guadalcanal Society: The Kaoka speakers* (New York, 1964); H. Ian Hogbin, *Kinship and Marriage in a New Guinea Village* (London, 1964); H. Ian Hogbin, *The Island of Menstruating Men: Religion in Wogeo, New Guinea* (Scranton, Pa, 1980); H. Ian Hogbin, *The Leaders and the Led: Social control in Wogeo, New Guinea* (Melbourne, 1987). There is also a *Festschrift*: L. R. Hiatt and Chandra Jayawardena (eds), *Anthropology in Oceania: Essays in honour of Ian Hogbin* (Sydney), 1971.

4. W. E. H. Stanner: Wasted war years

Geoffrey Gray

William Edward Hanley Stanner (1905–81) came to anthropology as a mature-age student having first worked as a bank clerk and journalist. He was twenty-three when he attended his first anthropology lectures at the University of Sydney, given by A. R. Radcliffe-Brown, Camilla Wedgwood and Raymond Firth. On completion of his degree—in both economics and anthropology—he was sent to Daly River, NT, where he conducted research for his MA, awarded in May 1934. Returning to Daly River in 1934–35, he spent a brief period at the newly founded Catholic mission at Port Keats (now Wadeye), which became his primary field site until he ceased fieldwork in 1959. For the second half of 1935, he tutored at the University of Sydney (as part of his research fellowship obligations). In between completing his degree and leaving for London, he worked also in the NSW Premier's office advising on economic matters and writing speeches.[1] In 1937 and 1938 he attended the London School of Economics (LSE), at his own expense.[2] Raymond Firth assisted him by employing him as his amanuensis for *Human Types*, a general volume on anthropology.[3] Stanner acknowledged this was 'of great assistance to his own [work and]…closely allied with the thesis I am preparing…it has been a great stimulus to me and also a discipline for some of the methods I have been applying to my own work.'[4] He was awarded his doctorate, 'Economic Change in North Australian Tribes', in 1938.[5] As there were no positions for anthropologists in Australian universities, he remained in Britain, finding work with the Oxford Social Studies Research Committee, which saw him in Kenya when war was declared.

Stanner's 'scrupulousness about the quality of his published work' resulted in no published book on the results of his field research in East Africa or Australia.[6] His major publication was a survey of British, New Zealand and Australian colonies in the South-West Pacific, *The South Seas in Transition* (1953). He was

---

1   Stanner to Firth, 6 July 1936, Archive of Sir Raymond Firth, British Library of Political and Economic Science, London School of Economics and Political Science [hereinafter FIRTH], 8/2/3. It was in Bertram Steven's office that Stanner met W. C. Wentworth, who helped found the Australian Institute of Aboriginal Studies in 1964, and was the first Minister for Aboriginal Affairs in the Holt Government.
2   Elkin to Firth, 12 February 1937, Firth to Elkin, 19 March 1937 and Stanner to Elkin, 12 January 1937, all in Elkin Papers [hereinafter EP], University of Sydney Archives, 160/4/1/78; Stanner to Firth, 11 June 1937, FIRTH7/7/31.
3   Raymond Firth, *Human Types: An introduction to social anthropology* (London, 1938).
4   Stanner to Firth, 11 June 1937, FIRTH7/7/31.
5   University of London. Stanner asked Firth if he could change the title of his doctorate to 'A Study of Social and Economic Change in North Australian Tribes'. Firth refused. Stanner to Firth, 11 June 1937, FIRTH7/7/31.
6   Firth to Registrar (ANU), 26 February 1964, FIRTH8/1/121. In Stanner's papers there are several unfinished manuscripts.

a man of essays—a genre of engaged argument, short, polished and aiming at insights about the present. The same could be said of his scholarly work. In fact, his most important writings—those on which his reputation largely stands—were produced between 1956 and 1968, commencing with his essay 'The Dreaming' (1956) and culminating in 1968 with his five-part Boyer Lectures, *After the Dreaming*.[7] In 1979 an eclectic collection of some 19 essays written over his lifetime was published as *White Man Got No Dreaming*. He was a master of crafted essays and his standards of perfection disabled him to complete the writing of books.[8] He restricted access to his MA thesis, for example, because he was concerned that it was incomplete and that it could be misused and misunderstood. Perhaps he was anxious about how his work would be received by his colleagues and others, fearful they might find weaknesses. Perhaps we gain a sense of Stanner from a comment in his wartime security file when he was described as a man of 'cultured and restrained manner', and his point of view 'is never startling rather non-committal if anything'.[9] Raymond Firth, on the other hand, saw a man who was both 'critical and negative', a man who was emotionally and intellectually 'outside', which is revealed most in Stanner's correspondence with Firth and A. P. Elkin.[10] Combined with what I see as a fear of failure—a certain dubiety—was a sense of his own importance and entitlement. It led him to state his objective, particularly his wish to have a chair, but when offered one he found reasons for not accepting it, usually stating he was not ready. That is, he was not content with junior or middle positions nor was he prepared to take on leadership positions, perhaps even fearful of failure.[11] Sometimes he put his failure to obtain a post down to obstacles put in the way by others, which is seen, for example, in his relations with members of the wartime Army's Directorate of Research and Civil Affairs (DORCA). During the war, he made

---

7   For further discussion, see Tim Rowse, 'After the Dreaming: The Boyer lecturer as social critic', in Melinda Hinkson and Jeremy Beckett (eds), *An Appreciation of Difference: WEH Stanner and Aboriginal Australia* (Canberra, 2008), pp. 233–50; Ann Curthoys, 'WEH Stanner and the Historians', in Hinkson and Beckett, *An Appreciation of Difference*, pp. 233–50. For another largely uncritical assessment of Stanner, see Jeremy Beckett and Melinda Hinkson, '"Going more than half way to meet them": On the life and legacy of WEH Stanner', in Hinkson and Beckett, *An Appreciation of Difference*, pp. 1–23.
8   In Stanner's papers there are several unfinished manuscripts, all started in the 1930s or later. As will be seen in this chapter, he confidently informed his sponsors, especially Elkin and Firth, of their completion, near publication or their near completion. Melinda Hinkson offers another explanation, arguing that Stanner had two abiding ambitions: to contribute to public life, which was 'cut across by a deep intellectual interest in the questions of social process'. She goes on to say that while these two ambitions are not incompatible, it was an 'increasing burden of public responsibility in his later life that kept Stanner from writing the books he imagined he might complete'. Hinkson, 'Thinking with Stanner in the Present', *Humanities Research*, 16:2 (2010), p. 92.
9   Report, 8 April 1942, National Archives of Australia, Canberra [hereinafter NAA], C123, item 12630.
10 See Melinda Hinkson, 'Stanner and Makerere: On the "insuperable" challenges of practical anthropology in post-war East Africa', in Hinkson and Beckett, *An Appreciation of Difference*, p. 51; also David Mills, 'How Not to be a "Government House Pet": Audrey Richards and the East African Institute for Social Research', in Mwenda Ntarangwi, David Mills and Mustafa Babiker (eds), *African Anthropologies: History, critique and practice* (London, 2006), pp. 85–6, who offers another viewpoint on Makerere to that of Hinkson.
11 Stanner to Firth, 5 August 1949, FIRTH7/7/31.

powerful enemies and friends and would probably be surprised by the negative assessments of many of his colleagues from that time. He no doubt would be surprised too by various comments and assessments made by Raymond Firth whom he considered a friend and supporter, and, sometimes confidant. For example, in his referee's report for the Sydney University Chair, in 1955, Firth was almost wholly positive. But by 1957, in his report to The Australian National University (ANU), he appears to have lost patience with Stanner's dithering and his lack of direction, which is highlighted by a comparison of Firth's referee's reports. In 1955, Firth knowingly misrepresented Stanner's East African experience as being successful, but in 1957 he stated quite the opposite and was far more reserved and critical in his overall assessment.[12]

Stanner returned to Australia in October 1939 and spent the first few months writing up his East African research. He undertook lecture tours for the University of Sydney Extension Board and prepared scripts on 'political and military matters'—that is, propaganda for broadcast by the Australian Broadcasting Commission (now Corporation: ABC) as part of his duties with the Department of Information.[13] In these, he encouraged Australians to recognise their triumphal past and the heroic men and women who settled the country as models for the coming days of war.[14] He was adviser to Percy Spender, Minister for the Army in the third Menzies Ministry, who, after a change of government, remained a member of the War Cabinet until February 1944.[15] Stanner even contemplated becoming a politician himself, standing for the United Australia Party (UAP) in the federal election of 1940.[16]

At the end of June 1942, Stanner was appointed to the Prime Minister's Committee on National Morale (CNM), chaired by Alfred Austin Conlon, who prepared an interim report on the problem of civilian morale for submission to the Prime Minister, John Curtin.[17] Stanner's appointment came after he had provided a critique of the draft report on the committee.[18] Stanner had a 'gift for simplicity in describing problems of a complex nature', which appealed to Conlon.[19]

---

12 Firth to University of Sydney Registrar, 6 July 1955, University of Sydney Archives G3/190; Firth to ANU Registrar, 25 July 1957, FIRTH8/1/3.
13 Diane E. Barwick, Jeremy Beckett and Marie Reay, 'W. E. H. Stanner: An Australian anthropologist', in Diane E. Barwick, Jeremy Beckett and Marie Reay (eds), *Metaphors of Interpretation: Essays in honour of W. E. H. Stanner* (Canberra, 1985), p. 13.
14 See, for example, 'War Morale: A challenge to Australian youth', ABC Broadcast, 1942. Stanner Collection, Australian Institute of Aboriginal and Torres Strait Islander Studies [hereinafter SC], MS 3572, item 69. For Stanner's broadcast scripts, see also NAA, SP109/3, 318/48.
15 David Horner, *Inside the War Cabinet: Directing Australia's war effort, 1939–1945* (Sydney, 1996), pp. 209–13.
16 Report, 8 April 1942, NAA, C123, item 12630.
17 Conlon to Curtin, 4 April 1942, NAA, A1608/1, AK 29/1/2.
18 'Criticism by Major W. E. Stanner of the draft Interim Report of Committee on National Morale to the Prime Minister', n.d. [probably April 1942], SC, MS 3752, item 68.
19 John Pomeroy, 'Morale on the Homefront in Australia During the Second World War', PhD thesis, University of Sydney, 1995, p. 200.

Conlon, a medical student, was availing himself of the opportunities opened by the exigencies of war; he headed the university's Manpower Section, before heading the CNM. The committee, however, turned out to be more a tool for political networking than an effective organisation to raise national morale. Conlon's strengths were his charisma and vision for the nation; he created groups to deal with specific ideas and issues with the intent of formulating new policies. Stanner's strengths were analysing and critiquing such ideas and policy. Their talents, while on the surface appearing complementary, were not.[20]

In early 1942, the problem of guarding northern Australia against a possible Japanese invasion was raised at a joint meeting of the Australian Navy, Army and Air Force, the US Army and the Flying Doctor Service, which recommended that an observer unit (similar to that of the coast watchers in New Guinea) be formed to communicate all information from observer stations and in particular aircraft sightings and naval and military movements.[21] At the request of Major-General Edmund Herring, Stanner made an appreciation of the requirements for an observer unit in northern Australia. He recommended a highly mobile unit, 'horsed rather than wheeled', capable of operating on their own initiative. An East Africa district officer and ex-army officer Lieutenant Colonel Henderson, who had described the South African Boer commando action to Stanner, inspired the idea for such a unit.[22] On 11 May 1942, the establishment of the North Australia Observer Unit (NAOU) was officially announced and Stanner was made Commanding Officer, with his headquarters at Katherine, NT.[23] In this position, he remained until October 1943 when he was transferred to the Directorate of Research (from April 1945, it was the Directorate of Research and Civil Affairs or DORCA), located at Land Headquarters, Victoria Barracks 'L' Block, Melbourne. He was promoted to Lieutenant Colonel and made Assistant Director of Research (Territories Administration). J. R. Kerr was the other Assistant Director, which dated from the time it was a research section under Stantke. Stanner recalled some time later it was an unsought appointment: 'I was posted (against my will and protest) to the Research Directorate at LHQ.'[24]

---

20   Brian Jinks, 'Alfred Conlon, the Directorate of Research and New Guinea', *Journal of Australian Studies*, 12 (1983), pp. 21–33; H. C. Coombs, *Trial Balance: Issues of my working life* (Melbourne, 1983), p. 197; also Paul Hasluck, *The Government and the People* (Canberra, 1970), p. 399; Pomeroy, 'Morale on the Homefront in Australia During the Second World War'.
21   Report: Joint Services and US Army meeting on the organization of observer and intelligence services, North Australia, 7 March 1942, NAA, MP 729/6, 29/401/618.
22   Richard Walker and Helen Walker, *Curtin's Cowboys: Australia's secret bush commandos* (Sydney, 1986), pp. 6–7.
23   Apart from his 'interest in soldiering', Stanner's only 'military experience was serving in a Militia Signals unit during the early 1930s'. See Geoffrey Gray, '"The army requires anthropologists": Australian anthropologists at war, 1939–1946', *Australian Historical Studies*, 37:127 (2006), pp. 156–80; also Walker and Walker, *Curtin's Cowboys*, pp. 178–82.
24   Quoted in Walker and Walker, *Curtin's Cowboys*, p. 179.

The idea of a research section was first put to the Adjutant-General of Land Headquarters, Major-General Victor P. H. Stantke, by Conlon, who argued that such a section would assist in the development of a strategy that could be implemented in the event of an invasion and occupation of Australia by the Japanese. Stantke had 'put in' the Army Education Service to 'keep the morale of troops up', while the research section focused on civilian morale.[25] In early February 1943, Stantke was replaced with Major-General C. E. M. Lloyd, who saw no value in such a research section and threatened it with closure. Conlon managed to have the section transferred, in February, to the Directorate of Military Intelligence and, by October, had convinced Thomas Blamey, Commander-in-Chief of Australian armed forces, to bring the section under his command and rename it the Directorate of Research. John Kerr, then a close friend of and deputy to Conlon, stated that Blamey needed a group of people who could advise him on what were 'non-military problems, not merely internally, but in relation to Whitehall, the British Army, and also…colonial problems in New Guinea and Borneo and relations with the Americans in Japan and so on'.[26] The directorate developed policies for the colonies in the South-West Pacific from Melanesia to Borneo as well as plans to train colonial officials in a specialist school, a national university, and a universities commission.[27] Conlon proposed that the directorate should become the policy arm of the Australian New Guinea Administrative Unit (ANGAU) so that by the time a civilian administration took over it would be 'in a state of development far ahead of any that had been contemplated previously'.[28]

Richard Hall observed that war provided the opportunity for intellectual talent to play a role in running the country.[29] The new generation—confident that past mistakes would be avoided, sure of their ability to influence the course of events, if not during the war, then certainly in the postwar period—saw themselves as liberal, reform-minded progressives, with a nationalist agenda and a bias for state intervention. They were representative of the new academic and professional elite that emerged during the war and which was to play an influential part in public life during the decades following the war.[30] It was as part of this intellectual and social milieu that members of the directorate

---

25   Stantke, in John Thompson (ed.), *Five to Remember* (Melbourne, 1964), p. 101.
26   Kerr, in ibid., pp. 104–5.
27   L. P. Mair, *Australia in New Guinea* (London, 1948), p. 18; Brian Jinks, 'Policy, Planning and Administration in Papua New Guinea 1942–52, with special reference to the role of Colonel J. K. Murray,' PhD thesis, University of Sydney, 1976; Jinks, 'Alfred Conlon, the Directorate of Research and New Guinea', pp. 21–33; S. G. Foster and Margaret M. Varghese, *The Making of The Australian National University 1946–1950* (Sydney, 1996), pp. 3, 12–13, 20, 22, 26; Cassandra Pybus, *The Devil and James McAuley* (St Lucia, Qld, 1999), pp. 47–73.
28   John Kerr, *Matters for Judgment: An autobiography* (Melbourne, 1978), pp. 101–5. See also Alan Powell, *The Third Force: ANGAU'S New Guinea war, 1942–46* (Melbourne, 2003), especially pp. 92–139.
29   Richard Hall, *The Real John Kerr* (Sydney, 1978), pp. 43–5, 53.
30   Pomeroy, 'Morale on the Homefront in Australia During the Second World War', p. 231; see also Paul Hasluck, *Diplomatic Witness: Australian foreign affairs 1941–1947* (Melbourne, 1980).

found themselves. Stanner did not see himself as part of this new progressive professional elite of which Conlon was a fierce promoter. Peter Ryan, a member of the directorate, recalls that when Stanner left the directorate, he had written a note by hand that was 'a document of private hatred, loathing and contempt, expressed with such articulate venom'. Conlon commented, 'a little sadly: "Poor old Bill. We never really did get him round to our way of thinking, did we?"'[31]

Conlon believed that Stanner's experience in East Africa and knowledge of British colonial policy and practice, as well as his critical and analytical skills, would be useful in formulating postwar colonial policy for Papua and New Guinea in particular, although Stanner had little experience with Papua New Guinea or the South-West Pacific generally. Initially, Stanner was given the task of providing an overview of colonial issues involving the United States and Britain in terms of obligations and commitments, economic capacity, manpower requirements, and policy imperatives and such like. Conlon in a sense misjudged Stanner's lack of practical experience and misread him, judging him to be sympathetic to the enterprise that Conlon was overseeing. Stanner was clear sighted and perceptive in setting out the situation found in British colonies and the failures of colonial governance, and his experience in East Africa only heightened his understanding of these problems—racial, economic and political tensions, the calls for independence—but he was not constructive in the sense of formulating and assisting in implementing policy. Stanner's strength was his ability to identify problems. Stanner was on the side of reforming colonial government rather than arguing for the abolition of colonial rule (decolonisation) and encouraging self-government and eventual independence for colonised states in the Pacific region especially.[32] In fact, he thought independence movements 'might never concern New Guinea and Papua'; nevertheless, he was cognisant that international pressure and attention, plus the changes brought about by war, would result in changed conditions post war.[33] The effect of this pressure and how it would impact on the obligations of small colonial powers such as Australia and New Zealand in the Pacific was hard to predict other than a recognition that there would be change of some sort.

With Kerr and J. D. Patience, his directorate colleagues, Stanner attended the Field Officers' Conference, held in Port Moresby in February 1944.[34] The conference ranged over various administrative and policy matters, such as health, agricultural production, land tenure and 'native' labour and welfare,

---

31 Peter Ryan, *Brief Lives* (Sydney, 2004), p. 45.
32   See David Mills, 'Anthropology at the End of Empire: The rise and fall of the Colonial Social Sciences Research Council, 1944–1962', in Benoit De L'estoile, Federico Neiburg and Lygia Sigaud (eds), *Empires, Nations, and Natives: Anthropology and state-making* (Durham, NC, 2005), pp. 136–9.
33 ANGAU, Conference of Officers of Headquarters and Officers of Districts Staff, Port Moresby, 7–12 February 1944, NAA, MP 742/1, 65/1/435, vol. 3.
34 Ibid., vols 1–3.

as well as discussion on the development and organisation of ANGAU. It was stressed by Major- General Basil Morris, General Officer Commanding ANGAU, that it was a military unit and as such it was not possible to commit to a future civil administration but it was able to lay the foundations for a 'sound progressive policy of betterment'. Lieutenant Colonel Stanner, who was the senior directorate officer, presented a paper: 'Broad Aspects of Colonial Administration.' Majors Kerr and Patience were observers. Stanner concluded that the conference had produced much evidence of 'conflicting opinion as to the objectives which Colonial policy should seek to attain, and the methods which should be adopted to ensure the attainment of these objectives'. Stanner's presentation illustrated, the chair of the meeting noted, 'how many of our [ANGAU] problems were intimately related to the national and international sphere' as well as putting all these matters into perspective.

There were aspects of ANGAU about which Stanner was critical but this did not extend to the treatment of New Guinean labour; on the basis of little research, he declared that service mostly as labourers and carriers with ANGAU has 'definitely improved the native'. Control had

> been firm, but just; his physique has improved from the excellent housing and rations he receives; he has learnt the value of discipline and his added responsibilities; he has a far more extensive appreciation of health and hygiene matters; he has been taught how to produce more and better food within his own village.[35]

In making such a judgment, Stanner in fact 'endorsed the army's policy of placing war needs ahead of native interests'.[36] When the Australian administration returned after the war, Stanner was confident that there would be an 'efficient and contented labour [force], and if such proves the case, most of the credit should go to the personnel [patrol officers] of ANGAU because of his efforts on behalf of the native during the war period'.[37]

Native Labour Officers (often from the prewar civil administration) were responsible for recruiting labour; they handled labour right down to the front line. H. I. Hogbin, who had undertaken research on labour in New Guinea, disagreed with Stanner. He was critical of practices he saw as endemic, particularly the systematic brutality of ANGAU labour overseers.[38] He suggested ANGAU was

---

35   Ibid., vol. 3.
36   Powell, *The Third Force*, p. 196.
37   W. E. H. Stanner, 'ANGAU', November 1944, Australian War Memorial [hereinafter AWM], 54/80/2/1.
38   H. Ian Hogbin, *Report of an investigation of native labour in New Guinea, carried out on instructions from the Director of Research by Lieutenant-Colonel Ian Hogbin during the period March to June 1944*; Hogbin, *The natives of the Salamaua Coast*, A preliminary report by Lieutenant-Colonel Ian Hogbin forwarded to Brigadier Cleland, ANGAU HQ, for perusal and despatch to the Director of Research, LHQ, 7 October 1944 (copies in possession of author).

'losing standing in the people's eyes by itself engaging in any form of recruiting'. Stanner questioned the objectivity of Hogbin's report.[39] Hogbin was supported by James McAuley, also a member of the directorate, who commented to the anthropologist Camilla Wedgwood that 'the longer the smell of Angau clings to the POs [patrol officers], the less use they will be in their proper administrative functions'.[40] At the Native Labour Conference, held in Sydney on 1 December 1944, which examined ways of changing the various laws governing indenture, Hogbin represented the directorate.[41] Stanner was in London. A result of the conference was a decision by the Minister for Territories, E. J. Ward, to phase out indentured labour. Stanner, however, maintained his view that 'working under indenture was agreeable to the natives and had become of some positive social and economic importance to them. An increasing volume of labour offered itself without direct compulsion.' In fact, he was confident that prewar labour legislation 'would more than stand comparison with labour laws in any other country'.[42] Criticism had been levelled at these laws by the League of Nations Mandates Commission, headed by Lord Hailey. The Australian social scientist C. D. Rowley showed that statistical and other data 'drives home the point of [the] unpopularity of working for the Europeans'.[43]

Soon after the Field Officers' Conference in Port Moresby, Stanner and Kerr left to advise Blamey and the Australian Prime Minister at the Imperial Prime Ministers' Conference in London. Kerr, the story goes, was sent to keep watch over Stanner, who was not trusted to represent the views of the directorate fairly or to promote Australian interests as understood by Conlon and the others.[44] Kerr and Stanner attended meetings on Borneo and Hong Kong, which formed the basis of planning for the installation of military, and eventually civilian, government in those locations. Stanner prepared a number of papers on British colonial policy and its application to Australian territories and those parts of the region deemed as Australian interests at the time.[45] Kerr returned to Australia but Stanner remained in London at the request of Conlon who by now was unsure how best to counter the critical and troublesome Stanner.

Increasingly, Stanner was unhappy over the influence the directorate was exercising and the possibility of their ideas becoming government policy.[46] He

---

39 Powell, *The Third Force*, pp. 196, 198.
40 McAuley to Camilla Wedgwood, 10 September 1946, Wedgwood Papers, National Library of Australia [hereinafter NLA], MS 483, box 1.
41 Conference on Native Labour, 1 December 1944, NAA, MP 742/1, 274/1/246.
42 Stanner, *The South Seas in Transition*, p. 81; cf. Powell, *The Third Force*, pp. 196, 200–2, 223–8.
43 C. D. Rowley, *The New Guinea Villager* (Melbourne, 1965), p. 106.
44 Various, NAA, MP729/8, 49/439/73.
45 See various, NAA, A 518, R 815/1/1.
46 Elkin was not in agreement with Stanner; rather he looked upon the 'announced intentions' of Ward as 'indeed promising. I hope there is no retraction.' Elkin to Hogbin, 27 September 1945, Hogbin Papers, University of Sydney Archives.

was concerned that 'Conlon and Co will not long be content to limit themselves to Papua New Guinea'. It was 'not easy to see how or when', but he expected 'some wider penetrations…There are wider fields to buy into' such as Indonesia, the Solomons and other South-West Pacific territories.[47] He dismissed the directorate's plans as illustrating 'the increasing erectility of the Directorate's libido…likely to afford equal assistance to the bounding megalomanias or melancholias between which we now alternate'.[48] He condemned

> the amount of outright nepotism, and the extra-ordinary coincidence that each burst of what purports to be zeal for liberalism and native rights always ends up the same way—higher salaries, expense accounts, positions of power, wider influence for one or other [of the group]—all these [things] sickened me.

It even extended to London to include Audrey Richards and Lucy Mair, whom he described as part of a small, 'self-interested coterie' at the LSE with 'whose views I have disagreed'.[49]

In mid-August 1945, when Japan announced its unconditional surrender, Australian forces were in general control of northern Sarawak, Brunei and North Borneo—all the former territories collectively referred to as British Borneo in the prewar period.[50] The British had sent a civil affairs unit to Australia, led by Brigadier C. F. C. Macaskie, former Chief Justice and Deputy Governor of Borneo. This was unacceptable to Conlon and DORCA, who wanted an Australian-controlled civil administration in British Borneo. J. R. Black, a prewar patrol officer[51] and member of ANGAU as well as being attached to the directorate, was ordered to raise a detachment: the British Borneo Civil Affairs Unit (BBCAU). Stanner was attached to BBCAU as Senior Civil Affairs Officer. He had been 'lifted off the plane from America' where he had been enrolled in a three-month course at the School of Civil Affairs, Virginia, and 'hustled straight to Borneo'.[52] Kerr had been sent back to London, liaising with, and plotting against, the British over the occupation of the returned British territories.[53] Stanner described his Borneo appointment: it 'amounts to a militarized Provisional Commissionership, with a pretty fair staff of District Officers and ADOs, plus all the former civilian employers in the usual string of colonial technical departments. As it grows it will approach the Administratorship.'[54]

---

47 Stanner to Firth, 23 September 1944, FIRTH7/7/31.
48 Quoted in Pybus, *The Devil and James McAuley*, p. 45.
49 Stanner to Elkin, 25 October 1948, EP, 197/4/2/573.
50 Joan Beaumont, *Australia's War 1939–1945* (Sydney, 1996), pp. 45–7.
51 For an example of Black and Taylor on patrol, see Bill Gammage, *Sky Travellers: Journeys in New Guinea, 1938–1939* (Melbourne, 1998).
52 Stanner to Firth, 10 September 1945, FIRTH7/7/31.
53 Pybus, *The Devil and James McAuley*, p. 68.
54 Stanner to Firth, 10 September 1945, FIRTH7/7/31.

Stanner had disagreements with the British occupying forces, which only compounded the difficulties between DORCA officials and the British. Conlon and Kerr were unable to maintain Australian control and the British took over military administration in January 1946.[55] Stanner returned to Australia and was demobbed in the same month.

While in London, Stanner had compiled a series of reports on British colonial policy.[56] It was a further opportunity to lay out his disagreement with Conlon and his colleagues at the directorate. He reiterated his unease over 'the network of power the "boys"…have built up [which] is so strong', but their 'theory is showy [and] confused…using phrases which have long since been shown in Africa, their homeland, to have lost meaning'.[57] Stanner's support for a reformed prewar British colonial system in Africa and its applicability for a postwar Papua New Guinea was unacceptable to his directorate colleagues, especially to Hogbin and Wedgwood.[58] Despite the beginnings of a debate in Britain over the future of the British colonies and arguments about decolonisation, self-government and independence, Stanner remained wedded to the colonial mission: 'I believe that our [British, which included Australian] efforts in any field will be of little value unless we recapture conviction on our own colonial mission.'[59] Stanner was of a view that the basic problem was to 'achieve balanced and progressive social economies'.[60] As in many matters, here he advocated a cautious approach, stressing the need to first establish the forms before formulating and implementing policy.[61] He identified difficulties in achieving a balanced and progressive approach, such as the constitutional arrangements between Papua (an Australian territory) and New Guinea (a League of Nations Trust Territory); political and economic relations between the colonies and the metropolitan power; the development of resources; and a major impediment being the skills and abilities of Papuans and New Guineans. He could not decide which was the most important issue: nutrition, education, technical training, or political development. He did not neglect the strategic importance of Papua and New Guinea and the Pacific in general; it was, he reminded his readers, in Australia's security interests to ensure that Papua New Guinea was viable.[62]

---

55   R. W. Reece, Alf Conlon, the fall of Singapore and British Borneo, Unpublished paper (1993) (copy in possession of author). See also Memo, Hood to Sinclair, 24 May 1945, NAA, A2671, 57/1945.
56   Stanner to Firth, 6 April 1946, LSE, FIRTH7/7/31; Stanner, British Planning in the Pacific, Section I, pp. 3–4; Colonial Policy, Section III; Memo, Pacific Territories Research Council, 6 July 1945, NAA, A 518, R 815/1/1.
57   Stanner to Elkin, 25 October 1948, EP, 197/4/2/573.
58   H. Ian Hogbin and Camilla Wedgwood, *Development and Welfare in the Western Pacific* (Sydney, 1943), pp. 1–31.
59   For a sustained critique of postwar colonial planning in East Africa, see W. E. H. Stanner, 'Observations on Colonial Planning', *International Affairs*, 25:3 (1949), pp. 318–28.
60   W. E. H. Stanner, 'New Guinea Under War Conditions', *International Affairs*, 20:4 (1944), p. 493.
61   Stanner to Firth, 2 June 1946, FIRTH7/7/31.
62   Stanner, 'New Guinea Under War Conditions', pp. 489–94.

After the war, he continued to voice his opposition to the policies being implemented under the administration of J. K. Murray, the Administrator of a recently amalgamated Papua and New Guinea and ex-Principal of the School of Civil Affairs. In mid-1946, Stanner was asked by the American Institute of Pacific Relations to 'undertake a survey of post-war rehabilitation and reconstruction in the south-west Pacific'.[63] It was a further opportunity to not only distance himself from DORCA (and the Labor Government, especially H. V. Evatt, Minister for External Affairs, and E. J. Ward, Minister for Territories) and their views but also to point to their shortcomings and how these had impacted on policy in Papua New Guinea and elsewhere in the South-West Pacific. He did not expect to return to Australia. In a presentation of his research findings to Chatham House in mid-November 1947, Stanner explained his criticism:

> If the New Guinea scene is looked at closely it is difficult to resist the impression that what may well have begun as genuine idealism has now begun to degenerate into futile, piecemeal welfarism which is paying little regard to the limitations of the primitive culture of the natives on the one hand, and on the other of the controlling factors of Australian politics and economics. I do not think the local administration is to be held altogether responsible. A number of factors have made their contribution. The military authorities withdrew before the civil authorities were ready. The devastation and social disturbance…were of great magnitude. A large proportion of the trained staffs were lost in the war…The planning situation was badly mishandled…[T]he Minister [Ward] was given and acted upon some very bad advice. A number of administrative blunders were made. A large proportion of officials have been out of sympathy with the new policy. The present administration is deeply divided. Shortages of staff and material have been a heavy handicap. The natives have been unhelpful and restive. But the underlying mentality of the planners [Conlon, Kerr and Hogbin] has been, or seems to have been if we judge by the outcome, at fault.[64]

So, while there was almost 'nothing good to be said of the…policy…the intentions [of the officials] are of the best'.[65] His opposition had not lessened with time.

Stanner's hostility to Conlon, whom he described as his 'bete noir',[66] and others in the directorate such as Hogbin and Kerr was unrestrained and unrelenting.

---

63   Stanner, *The South Seas in Transition*, p. v.
64   The post war situation in the South-West Pacific, Address given at Chatham House, London, 12 November 1947, SC, MS 3572, item 91.
65   Stanner to Firth, 23 May 1947, FIRTH7/7/31.
66   Stanner to Firth, 6 April 1946, FIRTH7/7/31. He added, with obvious pleasure, that Conlon 'is in obscurity again and has resumed his medical course'. See also Pybus, *The Devil and James McAuley*, p. 49.

It was mutual dislike and distrust. He referred to them as 'the triumvirate' and accused them of being behind his failure to obtain a suitable appointment in Australia. There was no love lost between them, and Stanner never let an opportunity go without criticising the actions and decisions of 'the boys', as Conlon, Kerr and Hogbin described themselves. Stanner commented to Elkin at the end of 1944 that he did not regret his decision to break with 'that group',[67] although he remained with the directorate until he was demobbed in January 1946.

In early 1946, Lucy Mair, a British scholar who was the recognised expert on colonial administration, had been brought out by Conlon (no doubt on the recommendation of Hogbin) to assist in the development of colonial policy and to lecture at the School of Civil Affairs. When reviewing Mair's *Australia in New Guinea* (1948), Stanner was seemingly gracious: 'with the exception of Stephen Read's [sic] *The Making of Modern New Guinea*, [there has been no] systematic examination of the colonial problems of colonial administration in the area [Papua and New Guinea]…This book remedies the deficiency…with one exception.' The 'one exception' was Mair's 'appraisal of the new policy', which in Stanner's opinion was 'in several important aspects defective…There is not merely a loss of objectivity but a flight from it, which mar an otherwise excellent book'. Stanner believed the 'whole experiment conducted in Papua-New Guinea from 1945 to 1948 [the Labor Government was voted out of office in 1949] will be a source of interest and a subject of debate for many years'.[68] On that he was correct!

While 'Conlon and Co.', to use Stanner's expression, largely ignored Stanner's critique of colonial governance, his report on the Colonial Social Sciences Research Council (CSSRC) was of particular interest to Conlon, who attempted to develop an Australian equivalent: the Australian Pacific Territories Research Committee (APTRC). This had the potential, Conlon believed, to provide a process through which progressive policy for Papua and New Guinea and the other Melanesian colonies could be debated and formulated. It also had the potential to influence the type of research undertaken in these areas. Concomitant with the APTRC was the establishment, in December 1944, of a School of Civil Affairs—later the Australian School of Pacific Administration (ASOPA); it was envisaged as taking over from the University of Sydney all the training of field officials and overseeing research in the colonies.[69]

The school and the Pacific Territories Research Committee were, in Stanner's view, a danger to the long-term viability of Elkin's department:

---

67   Stanner to Elkin, 22 September 1944, EP, 197/4/2/573.
68   Stanner, 'Review of *Australia in New Guinea*, by L. P. Mair', *International Affairs*, 25:3 (1949), p. 394.
69   Elkin 'disapproved strongly' of Conlon. Conlon, in turn, 'loathed everything Elkin stood for'. Tigger Wise, *The Self-Made Anthropologist: A life of A. P. Elkin* (Sydney, 1985), pp. 151–2, 155.

You see the position that is shaping; it will be an extraordinary array of personalities with their mingled gifts and weaknesses. If Conlon can mould them into an effective team, they may do good work, but the more I ponder on the long term position of your department, the more I wonder at the final outcome. The position of the Federal grant [the subsidy provided by the Commonwealth to the University of Sydney for the Chair of Anthropology] rather worries me, too.[70]

In early 1946, when it appeared the school was to be wound up, Stanner conceded that 'on the whole it seems to have done good work'.[71] By 1948 he was convinced his earlier prognostication on the establishment of the ASOPA (the successor to the School of Civil Affairs) and the Pacific Territories Research Committee had come to pass and threatened not only the training of colonial officials and the teaching of anthropology at the University of Sydney but also Elkin's control over anthropological research. But worse was in store, he told Elkin:

> [T]he next focus of power to fall under the spell of this little gang will be the South Seas Commission. The next will be your chair, when you go; and when they have that, *all* the research into anthropology, sociology and colonial administration in the S. W. P. will be in the same hands—cocksure, ambitious, politically-minded, and quite unscrupulous.[72]

He blamed Hogbin most of all; in Stanner's opinion, it was he who undermined the integrity of anthropology. What Stanner objected to was the 'indirect effect of ambitious, untrained outsiders [the staff of the ASOPA] being allowed to build up vast showy research projects which will ultimately weaken the University departments, merely to please transient political interests'. He accused Hogbin of

> pursuing consciously a policy which he knew could only weaken the Sydney department, which has a long and honourable tradition. And to please whom? A group of power-hungry thrusters on the one hand, and a political party on the other. This is bad stuff, Elkin. Short-sighted, unscholarly, and in my opinion politically venal.[73]

But he was not necessarily enamoured with the situation at Sydney under Elkin. He was critical of both the journal *Oceania* (under the editorship of Elkin) and the department. Both *Oceania* and the department reflected, in his opinion, a

---

70   Stanner to Elkin, 22 September 1944, EP, 197/4/2/573. See also Stanner to Firth, 23 September 1944, FIRTH7/7/31.
71   Stanner to Firth, 6 April 1946, FIRTH7/7/31.
72   Stanner to Elkin, 25 October 1948, EP, 197/4/2/573.
73   Stanner to Elkin, 25 October 1948, EP, 197/4/2/573. He made similar observations to Firth. Stanner to Firth, 6 April 1946, FIRTH7/7/31.

lack of interest in theory and the 'thin sociological studies of the Middletown type' pursued by the department. He told Firth that 'since you and Radcliffe Brown left I can't find one theoretical gleam'.[74]

The war opened up space for new ideas and new groupings, often bypassing or replacing older institutions, some of which lasted, some of which did not survive the war and the immediate postwar years. Stanner, living through these times, more and more positioned himself on the side of continuity, tradition and stability—what might be seen as his inherent conservatism. He also had to confront his future post war. There were possibilities, such as staying on in London to act as a 'counsellor on colonial and allied matters' on Stanley Melbourne Bruce's staff; Bruce, from Stanner's correspondence, appeared to be negotiating a position with an agency of the United Nations Organisation. This did not eventuate; Bruce retired from public life in 1945. Stanner was optimistic and reasonably sure he would find a position as an anthropologist or economist, either in the academy or in colonial administration either in Australia or in Britain, or a research project in East Africa or Malaya. He even raised the possibility of a colonial governorship. In his view, it was a question of hitting the 'right note' as he realised he had 'an extraordinary range of experiences to capitalize' on.[75]

Before war's end, he told Elkin that he did not

> quite see the lines clearly shaping yet. A Chair is the best solution from every point of view and I will make that a firm ambition from now on. I always knew that I would reach a point of having a lot to say and teach and being ready to do so if the circumstances would do their stuff. I hope…that some opportunity will arise, if not in Australia then abroad.[76]

Two years later, the situation had hardly altered and he now doubted whether the academy was a possibility:

> I was always prepared to scratch along till I was about 40 but it would be ruinous to go on doing it until I am 50! Slowly but surely my hope of perpetual and careless youth fades, at which I get more and more annoyed. So I have ruled out any more academic research at the fellowship level and what I want now is a reasonably well-paid, if possible a well-paid appointment, academic or departmental. There are too many well-

---

74   Stanner to Firth, 6 April 1946, FIRTH7/7/31. At the Australian Institute of Aboriginal Studies conference in May 1961, Mervyn Meggitt voiced similar misgivings about the state of theory in Australia. M. J. Meggitt, 'Social Organization: Morphology and typology', in H. Sheils (ed.), *Australian Aboriginal Studies* (Melbourne, 1963), p. 216.
75   Stanner to Firth, 23 September 1944, FIRTH7/7/31.
76   Stanner to Elkin, 22 September 1944, EP, 197/4/2/573.

experienced people a bit older than I am in line for the academic posts, so I think they're excluded. I am thinking now rather along the lines of a Colonial Office advisorship or even an administrative job.[77]

Stanner was supportive of regional commissions as he anticipated regional bodies, such as the Caribbean Regional Commission, would bode well for the future of colonial rule; thus 'when…the [South Seas] Commission [is established it] should bring the machinery of administration to the Pacific right up into the vanguard of progressive colonial policy'.[78] Stanner was an adviser to the Department of External Affairs on the setting up of the South Seas Regional Commission. John Kerr was the organising secretary for the first South Seas Conference and some of the staff of the ASOPA wrote background papers for the conference held between 28 January and 6 February 1947. An outcome of the Canberra Agreement signed between Australia and New Zealand in 1944, the South Pacific Commission (SPC) was established on 6 February 1946.[79] Its purpose was to promote economic and social development of the indigenous peoples in the Pacific Island territories under the control of the administering powers.[80]

Although supportive of such bodies in principle, Stanner was critical of the way the South Pacific Commission had been established and worried about its future:

> What sickens me is the amount of jockeying going on behind the scenes. As far as I can see there are going to be some terrific struggles departmentally and between various interested personages…It will be several years…before it can free itself from such influences and get down to work.

In addition, there would be staffing difficulties, which he believed would be its main problem 'for years to come'. His 'formal advice had been to go slowly, not to promise much, and make the first target the organization of a first-class technical staff on the lines of the Caribbean Commission'. He did not 'think it is possible to spend a great deal of money in sensible ways for some time to come. But the usual crowd of idea-merchants are coming in guaranteeing that they can do everything overnight.'[81]

Nevertheless, he hoped to be offered 'a very good job' with the commission but this was not to be despite having the support of Sir Frederic Eggleston.[82]

---

77   Stanner to Firth, 6 April 1946, FIRTH7/7/31.
78   The South Seas Commission, ABC Broadcast, 8 May 1946, SC, MS 3752, item 83.
79   'South Pacific Commission', *International Organization*, 1:2 (1947), pp. 368–70.
80   Agreement Establishing the South Pacific Commission, 6 February 1947, NAA, A1838, 346/4/3.
81   Stanner to Firth, 2 June 1946, FIRTH7/7/31.
82   Stanner to Firth, 2 June 1946, Stanner to Firth, 5 November 1946, also Stanner to Firth, 12 May 1947, all in FIRTH. He had also had his name put forward for a senior diplomatic position in Russia; he was opposed,

It was a complicated matter and the hand of his enemies continued to deny him any opportunities in Australia, including a position on the commission.[83] His fears about the continued influence of 'the boys' might have been realised had Kerr accepted the position of Secretary-General when it was offered to him on a permanent basis at the first formal meeting of the commission held at the ASOPA in May 1948.[84] Stanner commented to Firth on realising that he would be overlooked by Evatt for any role in the SPC: 'I am striking bad trouble once again with Evatt, who seems to have been advised against me or just doesn't like the look of my face or something.'[85] Stanner's past, and his negativity towards others, was coming back to haunt him. 'Around each corner', he told Ian Clunies Ross, were those who did 'not like the cut of my jib'.[86] Stanner had a rather inflated view of himself, even a sense of entitlement; added to this was a touch of personal pique. Kerr described Stanner as having 'an ego of terrific size which gets mixed up with the objective problem'.[87] Hogbin thought Stanner's lack of success with Evatt and the others explained why 'his prejudices have run away with him', especially in *The South Seas in Transition*. Hogbin had read the PNG section of the manuscript, which he had severely criticised, as Stanner's facts 'are sadly at fault'.[88]

Once it became clear that Kerr had rejected the position of General Secretary, Conlon asked Eddie Ward to nominate him for the position, as it would, Kerr wrote, 'open the way for him to do the sort of things he had done in the war time years'; with reservations, both Kerr and Evatt supported Conlon's nomination. Certainly, there was concern by the British delegation that Conlon would capture the key position of Secretary-General. They had not forgotten Conlon's role in trying to secure Borneo for Australia. It was not until the next meeting, in Suva, that W. D. Forsyth, a career diplomat from External Affairs, was appointed Secretary-General.[89] This was the end of Kerr's involvement. He returned to the Bar. Conlon, after a brief and disastrous principalship of the ASOPA, also ceased to exercise any influence on returning to university and completing his medical degree, which was awarded in 1951.

---

however, by those in the Department of External Affairs (as well as by Evatt) whom he considered 'not very good, and I could buy and sell most of them for general experience and competence'. Stanner to Firth, 6 April 1946, FIRTH7/7/31.
83   Stanner to Firth, 2 June 1946, FIRTH7/7/31.
84   Kerr, *Matters for Judgment*, pp. 108–9; see also SC, MS 3752, item 63.
85   Stanner to Firth, 2 June 1946, FIRTH7/7/31; Hogbin to Linden A. Mander, 12 May 1948, University of Washington Libraries (Seattle), Mander Papers, Accession No. 730-7-55, box 5, folder 5-12.
86   Stanner to Ian Clunies Ross, 30 September 1948, NAA, A10651, ICR 23/28. Stanner blamed 'the boys' for the late publication of *The South Seas in Transition* (completed in 1947 and published in 1953). The publication of Mair's *Australia in New Guinea* (1948) and Hogbin's *Transformation Scene* (1951) was further evidence.
87   Kerr to Conlon, 19 June 1945, University of Tasmania Archives, Keith Isles Papers (unsorted).
88   Hogbin to Mander, 12 May 1948, University of Washington Libraries (Seattle), Mander Papers, Accession No. 730-7-55, box 5, folder 5-12.
89   Susan Woodburn, *Where Our Hearts Still Lie: A life of Harry and Honor Maude in the Pacific Islands* (Adelaide, 2003), p. 218.

While disappointed that he had missed a job with the commission, Stanner had been offered and accepted the position of Director of the Institute for Social Research at Makerere College in Uganda to undertake research in Tanganyika (now Tanzania), Uganda and Kenya. He confidently informed Firth that the survey of the South-West Pacific had provided him with an opportunity to 'read and think hard' about wider, fundamental issues, and 'the sequence of problems one encounters in moving from New Guinea on the West to the Cooks [Cook Islands] on the East involves just about everything the British colonies have to face up to anywhere'. He was 'sure I shall be able to work much more quickly and surely in Africa as a result'.[90] An initial task was to develop a comprehensive research plan in consultation with the three East African governments of Uganda, Kenya and Tanganyika. As director, Stanner was allowed 'the utmost possible latitude in the planning of research', but it was stipulated by the CSSRC that 'the central interests of…the Institute should lie in the social, economic, political and linguistic problems which now confront the inhabitants of the three territories'.[91]

Stanner's report questioned the 'wisdom of establishing an Institute' and made much of the financial, logistical and political complexities; in all he felt it 'would be a matter of years before either the Institute or Makerere could confer noticeable benefits upon one another'. More damning was Stanner's assessment that he could not see 'the value from an administrative viewpoint of much anthropological material'. In his opinion, the 'yearning for anthropological services in East Africa is as great as the desire in England to send them'. This was not what the CSSRC wanted to hear. Stanner's resignation took effect after he had completed 'the two field tasks which he came out to do'.[92] Audrey Richards, who had initially been convinced by Firth of the suitability of Stanner, was not going to abandon the project and the establishment of the institute. She took over the directorship and placed the institute on a sound footing.[93]

Resigning only contributed to an already difficult situation regarding Stanner's future. Returning to Australia was not an easy option although the political situation was changing and the power of 'the boys' was somewhat diminished. Elkin was a possibility. While it appeared that Elkin would offer him wholehearted support, this was not the case. Elkin was wary of Stanner's ability to complete the task at hand. (Elkin had, before the war, attempted to find positions for Stanner, such as putting his name forward for the new position of Director of the NT Native Affairs Branch, which was given to E. W. P. Chinnery.)

---

90   Stanner to Firth, 23 May 1947, FIRTH7/7/31.
91   Mills, 'How Not to be a "Government House Pet"', pp. 85–6. For a history of the CSSRC, see Mills, 'Anthropology at the End of Empire', pp. 135–66; Stanner to Firth, 5 November 1946, Stanner to Firth, 23 May 1947, both in FIRTH7/7/31.
92   Stanner to Canham, 11 December 1948, and Stanner to Firth, 27 June 1948, both in FIRTH7/7/31.
93   Mills, 'How Not to be a "Government House Pet"', pp. 85–6.

Towards the end of the war, Elkin held out the possibility of a readership should the funds become available. One other factor that militated against Stanner was Elkin's full embrace of his young students Ronald and Catherine Berndt.[94]

Elkin had found a new student who was more to his liking, Ronald Murray Berndt, who with Catherine, his wife, formed the ideal anthropological partnership. Ronald and Catherine were full of energy, enthusiasm and, like Elkin, stuck solidly at a task until it was completed; moreover, they were prolific, publishing paper after paper, book after book. Elkin had also lost some of his enthusiasm for Stanner due in part because Stanner had not fulfilled the expectations of Elkin, who wanted tangible results from the research undertaken between 1932 and 1935. Stanner, aware of this, assured Elkin:

> I have a great deal almost ready for publication, given a little more work upon it…I will make a supreme effort in 1949 to publish my study on aboriginal economics (now 10 yrs old but fairly good), and to bring my Kamba study of government, economics, law and tribal history…up to date…With luck, I might therefore have three books out or in the press by the end of next year. I will also send you that long report on the Warramunga and other tribes for publication in *Oceania* if you think it is still acceptable.[95]

He had made similar undertakings four years earlier; he was confident then that Faber 'will accept my book on Kenya. It's with them now for reading, with a strong recommendation from Oxford. [Lord] Hailey has seen it and seems to think well of it. I am hoping Mannheim will also publish my PhD thesis.'[96]

In his pitch to Elkin, Stanner pointed to his wish to be back in Australia, 'where my roots and home and heart are. But to do what? Every avenue seems closed for reasons which you know as well as I.'[97] He lamented that there was 'nothing for me in the Aust. universities until they found more chairs, or some one does'. And there was nothing in Canberra, 'so long as Evatt and Ward are there. I found my disagreements with them [and their entourages] insuperable.'[98] It had not been easy, he told Elkin; it had 'been a terrific struggle since 1936 to keep going, earning a living before being free to write and publish; even so…I always planned to make my run a bit later than most, but the war and other things have made me later than even I wanted to be'.[99] He retained his ambition for a chair in anthropology, particularly the Sydney University Chair. But after the

---

94   Geoffrey Gray, '"You are…my anthropological children": A. P. Elkin, Ronald Berndt and Catherine Berndt, 1940–1956', *Aboriginal History*, 29:1 (2005), pp. 77–106.
95   Stanner to Elkin, 25 October 1948, EP, 197/4/2/573.
96   Stanner to Elkin, 22 September 1944, EP, 197/4/2/573.
97   Stanner to Elkin, 25 October 1948, EP, 197/4/2/573.
98   Stanner to Clunies Ross, 30 September 1948, NAA, A10651, ICR 23/28.
99   Stanner to Elkin, 25 October 1948, EP, 197/4/2/573.

war he seems to have lost belief in this ambition, seeing himself as not ready for elevation—further illustrated by the range of positions he applied for, many of which he was ill suited for. Ian Hogbin informed Linden A. Mander, Professor of Political Science at the University of Washington (Seattle), that Stanner had applied for the job of Administrator of Papua New Guinea and was 'turned down in favour of Colonel [J. K.] Murray'.[100] He applied unsuccessfully for a position with the International Wool Secretariat as Australian representative in London. He missed out on a position as Reader in Colonial Administration at Oxford University, which he was confident of winning. He applied for a readership at Manchester only to lose out to Max Gluckman.[101] Possibly unknown to Stanner, he was considered as a suitable replacement for Reo Fortune should he reject the offer of Government Anthropologist in Burma.[102] This did not eventuate. Stanner was back to a situation where he was working to keep himself alive with little opportunity to write, once more faced with further interruption to his career and possibly more wasted years.[103]

When the Auckland University College advertised its Chair of Anthropology, Stanner applied.[104] It was a late application and somewhat half-hearted. The London selection committee commented on his apparent lack of interest, but nevertheless this was ignored or overlooked by the Council of Auckland University College, which offered him the Chair. He was also offered, at the same time, the Readership in Comparative Institutions in the Research School of Pacific Studies at the newly established Australian National University. He declined the Auckland Chair. It was a peculiar decision in light of Stanner's often-stated ambition to obtain a chair. 'My aim', he told Firth,

> is a Chair in Anthropology as soon as practicable, if possible in a few years. Whatever I now do must be directed to that end…It is either that or get out of the subject altogether…The six years lost in the war nearly crippled me as it is. I do not know anyone else, who had no job to go back to, who lost as much time.[105]

Notwithstanding his self-pity, his dubiety came to the fore once again. By way of explanation, he told Firth, who had been on the London selection panel along with E. E. Evans-Pritchard and Darryl Forde, that he was 'not mad keen on a Chair for the sake of having one…when one comes I want there to be no doubt

---

100   Hogbin to Mander, 12 May 1948, Mander Papers, University of Washington Libraries (Seattle), Accession No. 730-7-55, box 5, folder 5-12.
101   David Mills, *Difficult Folk? A political history of social anthropology* (New York, 2008), pp. 99–101.
102   J. Hutton to Stallman, 28 May 1946, RAI (Applied Anthropology, 1928–1949), A/43, 15/81.
103   Stanner to Firth, 23 May 1947, FIRTH7/7/31.
104   Firth to Stanner, 7 December 1948, FIRTH7/7/31; Geoffrey Gray and Doug Munro, Establishing anthropology and Maori language (studies), Auckland University College: the appointment of Ralph Piddington, 1949, Unpublished manuscript.
105   Stanner to Firth, 18 May 1949, FIRTH7/6/15.

about my fitness for it'. He did not think he would be ready 'for a couple of years at least'. Had it been Sydney, which he most coveted, it would be the same. He realised it was a decision of

> some importance…I either have to take this chance in New Zealand or prepare myself to win out [on] an independent chair at some later stage… it means if I persist in the idea of a chair, going to Canberra presumably for four or five years, which puts me in the late 40's—a bit late for a first chair. And I cannot count on this chance coming again.[106]

Firth was disappointed that Stanner had turned down the Auckland Chair; it was an opportunity for Stanner to establish his academic credentials, which, on his own admission, were so lacking.

In the years that followed, Stanner's academic reputation steadily declined; he did not take the opportunity, in those early years at ANU, to complete the several manuscripts for publication that had been promised over the years. When Elkin retired in 1955, Stanner applied for the Sydney Chair, expecting support from Elkin.[107] It was not forthcoming. Elkin's assessment of Stanner was anything but supportive and he supported Ronald Berndt. Ignoring this, however, the selection committee ranked Stanner with J. A. Barnes, the eventual appointee. He failed primarily on the grounds that the committee considered he had been out of anthropology doing other work and his anthropology work was not recent. As one member of the committee commented: 'Stanner's past rose up and defeated him.'[108] He believed himself to be in line for the ANU Chair after Nadel's unexpected death in early 1956 but he was overlooked.[109] When Elkin's successor, J. A. Barnes, resigned from the Sydney Chair in 1958 to take up the ANU Chair, Stanner again applied to Sydney—again unsuccessfully. Stanner was eliminated in the first round; W. R. Geddes was appointed ahead of K. E. Read and Bill Epstein. Stanner accused Barnes of 'influencing the electors against him'.[110] It illustrates a tendency in Stanner to blame the circumstances or others for his failures. He had, however, made a late application. When applications were called for, Stanner was away at Port Keats (Wadeye) on a field trip and he hastily put forward his 1955 application, which included two dead referees: Radcliffe-Brown and S. F. Nadel.

The problem remains: why, when he was so close in 1955 for election to the Sydney Chair, was he rebuffed by the ANU in 1957 and again by Sydney in 1958? The explanation lies with Raymond Firth's judgment of his suitability for

---

106   Stanner to Firth, 5 August 1949, FIRTH7/7/31.
107   Gray, *A Cautious Silence*, p. 223.
108   Notes taken at meeting of selection panel, 9 September 1955, University of Sydney Archives, G3/190.
109   See Geoffrey Gray and Doug Munro, 'Your own position is not being overlooked': the politics of choosing a successor to S. F. Nadel, 1957, Unpublished manuscript.
110   J. A. Barnes, *Humping My Drum: A memoir* (Self-published: <www.lulu.com>, 2007), pp. 273, 277–8.

the ANU Chair in 1957. Firth noted Stanner's strengths, especially his training in economics and his interest in politics, his 'intelligence and insight and admired his grasp of broad subjects'. Notwithstanding, the concerns Firth expressed in 1949 and in 1955 remained:

> [I]n a way Stanner's achievement has tended to fall short of expectation and very far short of his own ideal. In some ways he has been his own worst academic enemy. Essentially he has seemed unwilling to face responsibility. His refusal of the Directorship of the East African Institute of Social Research was symptomatic of his tendency to dwell upon the difficulties inherent in the situation rather than the possibilities of what can be made out of it. His desire for a really worth-while achievement sometimes makes him over-elaborate his argument.[111]

Once at the ANU, Stanner reduced his academic and political interest in both East Africa and Papua New Guinea, and turned his attention to Aboriginal Australia, particularly Port Keats (Wadeye). This is not to say that he did not in those early years at ANU retain some interest in East Africa and to a lesser degree Papua New Guinea, as he completed *The South Seas in Transition* and continued to struggle with his Kamba book. He continued to write the occasional paper on both areas. In recognition of his knowledge, the Menzies Government had him appointed as Second Australian Commissioner of the South Pacific Commission in 1953—a position he retained until 1956. (J. R. Halligan, previously Secretary of the Department of External Affairs, was Senior Commissioner.) In the same year, Stanner and Nadel reported on the ASOPA to Paul Hasluck, Minister for Territories. Hasluck wanted ASOPA relocated to the Canberra University College. Stanner, who completed the final report, made a series of recommendations regarding the length and scope of courses provided by ASOPA, but his ideas were opposed by the then Principal, C. D. Rowley. In the end, despite pressure from Hasluck, ASOPA remained at Mosman and the courses were retained.[112]

In the early 1960s Stanner was largely responsible, together with his old friend from Bertram Steven's office William C. Wentworth, MHR, for establishing the Australian Institute of Aboriginal Studies. In 1964 he was awarded the second Chair in Anthropology at the ANU, which, due to his previous experience in 1957 and his firm conviction that he had too many enemies, he believed was not for him.[113] Elkin, somewhat hypocritically congratulating Stanner on his appointment, wrote: 'you have had an unnecessarily long wait—a delay not unconnected with the machinations, which have had no relation with

---

111 Firth to ANU Registrar, 25 July 1957, FIRTH8/1/3.
112 Nadel to Lambert, 27 May 1953, NAA, A518, A114/1/1, part 3; Minutes, ASOPA Council on Tuesday 2 March 1954; Discussion and Recommendations by Subcommittee of the School Council at Port Moresby, 19–26 March 1954, NAA, A518, A114/1/1, part 3.
113 Firth to Stanner, 11 February 1964, Stanner to Firth, 17 February 1964, both in FIRTH8/1/121.

anthropology as an academic discipline.'[114] After the change in the Australian Constitution in 1967 that enabled the Commonwealth to develop programs for Aborigines, Stanner was appointed to the Council for Aboriginal Affairs, which was headed by H. C. Coombs.[115] Their task was to make recommendations regarding Aboriginal policy and its implementation. Stanner resigned from the council in 1976 on the grounds of ill health.

Stanner was a man of many talents and abilities. Although he saw the war years as wasted, he nevertheless gained much from those years. He commented to Firth that '[i]t's extraordinary how productive my wasted years (1940–46) have been in one sense'. And while he had not been able to read much while serving, his 'ideas and theoretical interest sharpened considerably of their own volition almost'.[116] The war years brought a number of these to the fore. It enabled him to demonstrate his administrative skills, especially the establishment of the NAOU and his work for DORCA. He was detached, possessed of a gift for simplicity in describing problems of a complex nature, and he could in his analysis be both 'critical and negative'. These abilities did not always work to his advantage and, coupled with his uncertainty about a professional direction—economist, colonial administrator or anthropologist—saw him seeking a career across disparate fields and regions. It was only at the ANU, where he was sure of a permanent position, that he was able to consolidate, refocus and, to some degree, relax. He died in 1981.

The anthropologist and historian Diane Barwick, who, over more than 20 years, developed a close professional association with Stanner, remarked on his death: 'in his later years he had disproved the Colonel Blimp image he once had and achieved very great stature for his contribution to the reform of Aussie policy and perhaps to a reform of the public image of Aborigines.'[117]

---

114   Elkin to Stanner, 10 June 1964, cited in Hinkson and Beckett (eds), *An Appreciation of Difference*, p. 22.
115   For a discussion of the work of the council, see Tim Rowse, *Obliged to be Difficult: Nugget Coombs' legacy in Indigenous affairs* (Melbourne, 2000).
116   Stanner to Firth, 6 April 1946, FIRTH7/7/31.
117   Diane Barwick to Harvey and Audrey [unknown], 5 January 1982, Barwick Papers (unsorted), State Library of Victoria. An indication of her relationship with Stanner is possibly explained by her comment: 'I felt as if I had lost two fathers in a year.' Her father died the same year as Stanner. Derek Freeman, with a hint of sarcasm, referred to Stanner as 'the Brigadier of Anthropology'. Interview with Freeman, 13 February 1993.

5. Camilla Wedgwood: 'what are you educating natives for'[1]

David Wetherell

Camilla Wedgwood, anthropologist and educationalist (1901–55), spent much of the Pacific War and its immediate aftermath in Papua New Guinea—the scene of her field research in anthropology in the previous decade. Tough yet in some ways timid, mannish yet maternal, intellectually and physically tireless yet oddly dispersed in her enthusiasms, she seemed a paradoxical personality. Born at Newcastle-on-Tyne, UK, Camilla Hildegarde Wedgwood was the fifth of seven children of Josiah Clement Wedgwood, later first Baron Wedgwood (1872–1943), a long-time Member of Parliament, and his first wife, Ethel Kate Bowen (d. 1952), daughter of Charles (Lord) Bowen, a lord of appeal in ordinary. Descended from Josiah Wedgwood the master potter, the Wedgwoods belonged to what Noel Annan called the 'intellectual aristocracy'.[2] The Wedgwood and Darwin families were intertwined. Geoffrey and Maynard Keynes were related to the Wedgwoods by marriage as were the descendants of T. H. Huxley; Dame Veronica Wedgwood OM, the historian, and Ralph Vaughan Williams, the composer, were cousins.[3] After attending the Orme Girls' School not far from the family kilns in Staffordshire, Camilla followed her two brothers to the progressive Bedales School in Hampshire before studying English and Icelandic literature at Bedford College, University of London, from 1918. Here she developed a lifelong interest in Old Norse and in such old-English sagas as *Beowulf*. Her rugged, independent bearing, as well as her sympathy for 'primitive' peoples, earned her the sobriquet of 'The Ancient Briton'.[4] In 1920 she moved to Newnham College, Cambridge. Reading for the tripos in English and Anthropology, she completed each stage with first-class honours, qualifying as MA in 1927 (the university did not award degrees to women until 1948). She was trained as an anthropologist by A. C. Haddon and her lecturers included W. E. Armstrong, former Acting Government Anthropologist in Papua.

---

1   I acknowledge the Hon. Julia Wedgwood's gift of her sister Camilla's correspondence with the Wedgwood family (in my possession), hereinafter cited as WPC (abbreviation for Wedgwood Personal Correspondence). I am also indebted to Dr John Wedgwood for his help during the early stages of research.
2   Noel Annan, 'The Intellectual Aristocracy', in J. H. Plumb (ed.), *Studies in Social History: A tribute to G. M. Trevelyan* (London, 1955), p. 253; Paul Mulvey, *The Political Life of Josiah C. Wedgwood: Land, liberty and empire, 1872–1943* (Woodbridge, UK, 2010).
3   Geoffrey Keynes, Maynard's brother, was married to Camilla's cousin Margaret. Helen Wedgwood's daughter Richenda was the wife of Andrew Huxley, son of Leonard Huxley. For a Wedgwood genealogy, see David Wetherell and Charlotte Carr-Gregg, *Camilla: C. V. Wedgwood, 1901–1955: a life* (Sydney, 1990), p. viii.
4   *Thersites* (Cambridge), 10 March 1923.

Wedgwood was teaching at Bedford College when Bernard Deacon, a young Cambridge-trained anthropologist, died in the New Hebrides in 1927, and she was offered the lectureship in anthropology at the University of Sydney left vacant by his death with the proviso that she undertake the important task of editing Deacon's field notes for publication. In addition, instead of pursuing her own research, she also accepted the self-effacing task of editing her friend and age-mate Raymond Firth's *Primitive Economics of the New Zealand Maori* (1929). The task of immersing herself in Deacon's disorderly notes became an albatross, although she brought them to publication in the book *Malekula* in 1934.

After holding temporary research and teaching posts under Professor A. R. Radcliffe-Brown at the University of Sydney (1928–30), Camilla lectured at Cape Town (1930), then attended Bronislaw Malinowski's seminar at the London School of Economics (LSE). In 1933–34, she conducted field research on Manam, a volcanic island of 4000 inhabitants in New Guinea, helped by an Australian National Research Council (ANRC) grant that had been secured by Firth.[5] In 1935 she conducted methods of reviving native arts and crafts on the island of Nauru. She was in her sixth year as Principal of Women's College at the University of Sydney when the Pacific War began with the Japanese attacks on Pearl Harbor and Malaya. By early 1942, the Japanese had bombed Rabaul, the colonial capital of New Guinea, entered the Australian-controlled Territory of Papua, and by August they were well down the Huon Peninsula and were striking over the terrain of the Owen Stanley Range towards Port Moresby, the capital of Papua.

Camilla felt personally affected by these events. She had lost friends in the fall of Singapore, and wrote to her sister Helen at the beginning of the academic year of 1942 that 'my chief feeling about the war in Malaya, Java & New Guinea is a feeling of the wicked injustice of involving the natives…in this highly organized form of mechanical destruction'.[6] Her convictions about an individual's moral responsibility did not allow her to remain detached for long, and she was rethinking the Quaker's pacifist principles she had long held—a revision due, ironically enough, to what Malinowski had called her 'damned Quaker conscience'.[7] Though President of the Peace Society in Sydney, she felt a growing conviction, in the face of Japanese expansion, that absolute pacifism

---

5   Firth had left Sydney by September 1932. A. P. Elkin was lecturer in charge until he was appointed Professor on 23 December 1933—a position he took up on 1 January 1934. ANRC grants for anthropological research were recommended by a committee chaired by Sydney University's Professor of Anthropology, who made the final decision.
6   Wedgwood to her sister, 1 April 1942, WPC.
7   Wedgwood's views on the individual's moral responsibility and the need for 'some sort of faith and the hope that faith gives' are expressed in 'The Bondage of Despair' [c. 1943], Wedgwood Papers, National Library of Australia [hereinafter NLA], MS 483/7/32.

offered no answer to the emergency. There was a second strand laid bare by her constant reflections on Manam in her letters: she began to feel that her research in New Guinea had been in abeyance too long.[8]

Before 1943 Wedgwood had been a member of the pacifist Sydney Meeting of the Religious Society of Friends (Quakers). Her move from a pacifist's opposition to all warfare into a lieutenant colonel's uniform was part of a religious transition away from the liberal, sceptical environment of her youth, of which she had become highly critical. Originally sharing in her parents' agnosticism (friends of the Wedgwoods said they were atheists), her early life was strongly influenced by the secular Fabian beliefs of her family—an assumption that a social utopia of planned democracy was attainable through enlightened legislation. Her sister Helen was married to the geneticist Michael Pease, son of the Secretary of the British Fabian Society. Inclining with Helen towards militant pacifism by 1918, she had become a Quaker at Cambridge—a move that gave a broader base to her Fabian convictions.[9] As the 1930s wore on, she was increasingly drawn to Anglicanism, much influenced by C. S. Lewis and Dorothy L. Sayers. Already interested in religious drama, her attraction to the ceremonial of the Church of England was closely linked with her understanding of visible symbols and rituals as the binding elements of any culture. As a disciple of Malinowski, she well understood that the vehicle of authentic communal religious experience lay in the rites, artefacts and ceremonial feasting of most societies.

Her conversion from pacifism to an acceptance of the doctrine of a 'just war' was influenced by her reading of *A Conditional Justification of War* (1940) by William Temple, Archbishop of York (later of Canterbury).[10] As the plight of the European refugees became known, and Chamberlain's policy of appeasement all too obvious, her calm optimism that all would be well began to ebb. The Nazi persecution of Jews, the prison camps, the *Dunera* and *Struma* scandals involving the shipboard treatment of internees—against which she publicly protested[11]—and the human beastliness of war all seemed to point to something other than man's upward moral evolution; and her Fabian's confidence in a smooth progress towards a more perfect social order was overshadowed by a newfound belief in original sin. Neither the Fabian Society planners nor the Quakers fancied that doctrine. On 18 January 1944, in the presence of witnesses she had chosen, she was baptised in St James' Church in King Street, Sydney. In the same month, Wedgwood was commissioned in the Australian Army Medical Women's Service, holding the temporary rank of lieutenant colonel—an officer

---

8   Wedgwood to her sister, 18 June 1948, and Dowager Lady Wedgwood to Wedgwood, 3 February 1949, both in WPC.
9   See, generally, Patricia Pugh, *Educate, Agitate, Organize: 100 years of Fabian socialism* (London, 1984).
10 Personal communication, John Garrett, 3 July 1986.
11 The *Dunera* shipped to Australia some 2500 mostly Jewish refugees from *Mitteleuropa* who had escaped to Britain from Nazi persecution.

of field rank that few women ever held. Her appointment to the Australian Army, *The Times* said, was made at General Sir Thomas Blamey's wish to ensure that 'the best anthropological knowledge would be applied to the problem of protecting native society from the disruptive effects of the war'.[12]

As a member also of the Australian Army's Directorate of Research and Civil Affairs (DORCA), Wedgwood was able to combine her beliefs with a non-combatant's position. She was responsible for the first comprehensive research into mission school education in Papua New Guinea as a preparation for postwar government educational planning. Others involved in the directorate were Colonel J. K. Murray, who conducted a detailed survey of the agricultural potential of the region, and H. Ian Hogbin, who recommended reform of the labour system governing employment in businesses and plantations.

The directorate's role in planning for postwar reconstruction has given rise to several conflicting views. All agree that it owed its existence to Alfred Conlon (1908–61) who recruited Camilla with such other talented Australians as the historian J. D. Legge, the jurists J. R. Kerr and Julius Stone, the soldier and agricultural scientist J. K. Murray and the poet James McAuley. A curious figure of bulky outline and somewhat owlish appearance, Conlon possessed an insight that gave some people an impression of having intuitive understanding. An unlit pipe, thrust near his nostrils at significant pauses in a conversation, became his motif: it heightened the air of mystery and authority that surrounded him.[13] It is probable that Alf Conlon and Camilla Wedgwood met at Women's College in his role as university Manpower Officer. Through his contacts in the Army, Conlon was brought to the notice of General Blamey, who from March 1942 had been the Australian Army's Commander-in-Chief. As the Japanese threat receded from the islands, the directorate, established by Blamey in late 1943, was meant to help the Army frame policies that had not previously been handled by the armed forces: what role should Australia seek in the Pacific region? How should the islands cleared of Japanese forces be administered, and how could Australia retain the friendship of Pacific Islanders, particularly the 'Fuzzy Wuzzy Angels' of Papua and New Guinea? Camilla followed the directorate in January 1945 as it moved from Melbourne to Duntroon in Canberra (there called the School of Civil Affairs) and finally in January 1946 to Mosman in Sydney where it was transformed finally into the Australian School of Pacific Administration (ASOPA). Her colleagues during these years included H. Ian Hogbin, Lucy Mair,

---

12 *The Times*, 25 February 1944.
13 See Brian Jinks, 'Alfred Conlon: The Directorate of Research and New Guinea', *Journal of Australian Studies*, 12 (1983), p. 24. See also the chapters by Cassandra Pybus and John Legge in this volume.

C. D. Rowley and Peter Ryan. The Australian New Guinea Administrative Unit (ANGAU) was another field organisation involved in what was called the 'native affairs' of Papua and New Guinea.[14]

In the second week of March 1944, Lieutenant Colonel the Hon. Camilla Wedgwood VF 515041 left by plane from Melbourne. She flew over Port Moresby on the morning of 11 March. There was a coral reef outside the harbour, and a wrecked ship, *Prath*, on it, while the town, abandoned by its citizens, was drab, squalid, hot and sultry. It had been bombed several times, the liquour stores looted, and pieces of twisted corrugated iron left over the main streets. The headquarters of the 8th Military District was dispersed through more than 30 km of dreary scrubland. Camilla went immediately to the 2/5 Australian General Hospital, where she interviewed the General Officer Commanding ANGAU, Major-General Basil M. Morris.

Morris was interested in schooling. He had already expressed dissatisfaction with the record in Papuan development of the long-serving Lieutenant Governor, Sir Hubert Murray, whose government he brusquely described as an 'effete and discredited Administration'. He was, he said, 'appalled by what has been left undone by Sir Hubert in his later years'.[15] Morris spoke to Wedgwood of his hopes for a Central High School for Papuans at Sogeri in the hills behind Port Moresby in order to train agriculturalists, teachers and native medical assistants. Evidently, Morris foresaw a system of education that would need no overall policy, but only the arrival of Australian headmasters and headmistresses of a pioneering bent. (A brother and two sisters had established Church of England grammar schools in Brisbane and Melbourne.)

Wedgwood expressed surprise that Morris and others 'cannot see that the planning of an educational policy is an essential prerequisite for starting a school or appointing headmasters'—a reflection of her attraction to Fabian thinking, with its penchant for centralised planning and administration. She confessed to being shocked at the slow progress of education in the Western Pacific. Perhaps, however, such backwardness provided a way of avoiding the mistakes of the past in Africa. What these mistakes were, she left her readers in no doubt: the main one had been the schools' contribution to the spawning of a landless urban African class adrift from its cultural moorings. This was a judgment only to be expected of an ardent disciple of Malinowski and his

---

14 Alan Powell, *The Third Force: ANGAU's New Guinea war, 1942–46* (Melbourne, 2003).
15 Basil Morris to F. J. Forde, 'Offer to visit Papua—Mr A. G. Rentoul', 28 November 1942 (copy in author's possession).

conservative school of functional anthropology. Referring to a conversation with Morris, she concluded: 'He has never really answered, perhaps not asked himself the question, "What are you educating the natives for?".'[16]

For what future, then, were Melanesian schoolchildren to be educated? The educational wisdom propounded in Camilla's reading on African schools reflected the influence of Malinowski, who held a similar aversion and whose pronouncements on urban Africans in *The Dynamics of Culture Change* (1945) contained similar warnings. Education should not be a tool to aid migration to European towns. Instead it should be adapted to the mentality, aptitude, occupations and traditions of a people's rural environment. She said the 'first essential' was to relate the type of education to a people's traditional ideas and local conditions. 'There are some things which please God will not happen here', she wrote to her sister Helen, 'like the rise of a babu [bureaucrat's assistant] class divorced from the life & needs of their own people, belonging nowhere, "wandering for ever in the hell of make-belief which never is belief"'. Nowhere was her disapproval of rapid Westernisation sharper than in her exchanges with the Seventh-Day Adventist (SDA) missionaries in eastern Papua—'whose principles I detest but whose medical work here is, I believe, very good'.[17] It was also present in a muted form in her conversations at the strongly English-assimilationist Kwato Mission in China Strait. Her later glowing description of the Central High School at Sogeri established by Morris—a school devoted to producing a white-collar group if ever there was one—showed that Sogeri was the single exception she was prepared to make. But her assumption was that Sogeri would produce only teachers and medical assistants, not a Europeanised elite estranged from its cultural roots.

If the 'first essential' was to link educational curricula to local culture, the second educational prerequisite—'to relate it to the general culture of the world'—lacked precision, and its vagueness contrasted with the clarity of her trenchant affirmation about the 'inescapable fact that the natives must lead a rural life'. This was also the central message of the publication *Development and Welfare in the Western Pacific*, which Wedgwood and Hogbin had prepared in 1943. The authors deprecated the use of the English or New Zealand syllabi in Pacific Island schools, deploring the fact that a handful of Pacific Islanders had passed through such schools for further qualifications in New Zealand or Britain, 'more ignorant' than even the average European of the 'point of view of the uneducated native'. The diffusion of 'wholesale Westernization' was the wrong goal for African and Islander education. Instead, schools should help

---

16   Wedgwood to her sister, 7 April 1944, WPC. Another discussion of Wedgwood's educational work in Papua and New Guinea is in Nancy C. Lutkehaus, *Zaria's Fire: Engendered moments in Manam ethnography* (Durham, NC, 1995), pp. 408–9, 420–6.
17   Wedgwood to her sister, 7 April 1944, WPC; also Wedgwood Diary, VIII, 13–17 November 1944, Wedgwood Papers, NLA, MS 483/7/32.

younger people 'to blend what is good in their tradition with what is good in the tradition of western civilization'.[18] Camilla Wedgwood's reading had been supplemented with William C. Groves' reports on education in the Western Pacific. Groves was appointed first Director of Education in Papua and New Guinea in 1946, and the main theme of his major publication *Native Education and Culture-Contact in New Guinea* (1936) was 'cultural adaptation' in the education of indigenous people. But, as Groves admitted, few of his ideas could claim originality; indeed, most of them had long been current.[19] A similar observation can be made of Camilla, a case in point being her insistence that 'native' education blend the best of both cultures.

She believed indigenous vernacular languages should be used in schools for the first five years of infant class—language being 'an expression of a people's culture, of their physical, intellectual and spiritual life'. But F. E. Williams, Papuan Government Anthropologist (1928–42), stated the opposite: 'I would declare…that the curriculum of the infant class should be divided into three parts—English, English, English.'[20] By the time of Wedgwood's wartime inspections, most world literary experts had reached a consensus that agreed with Wedgwood and disagreed with Williams: teaching through the medium of English should begin only after the first few years of schooling in the vernacular.

Camilla was a tireless and meticulous worker who would spend weeks on bush treks, visiting schools, recording information and preparing reports before returning to base in Port Moresby. In the provision of her quarters at base, she perhaps detected a grudging acceptance, as if the Army resented an officer who was a non-combatant, a civilian in khaki and a woman being forced upon it by superior orders. She would have been regarded in the Army as a 'boffin' or intellectual, promoted to the position of lieutenant colonel—three ranks above her substantive rank; and in any case, having a research unit was unusual in an army 'order of battle'. In Wedgwood's letters, however, she never said that her presence was resented. She said simply that it was beneficial for a scholar like herself to be 'pitchforked' into a mixed male group in ANGAU. She liked bustling activity and, like her sisters, was often combative in speech. 'I'm in the mood for a good argument' was one of her favourite openings. She possessed a distinguished voice, heightened by a pronounced speech idiosyncrasy, being unable to differentiate between /r/ and /w/ (thus, addressing young soldiers bound for New Guinea, she would emphasise the need for 'mowal fibre' in dealing with 'pwimitive people'). Her gregariousness made her a companionable

---

18   H. Ian Hogbin and C. M. Wedgwood, *Development and Welfare in the Western Pacific* (Sydney, 1943), p. 27.
19   D. J. Dickson, 'W. C. Groves: Educationist', in James Griffin (ed.), *Papua New Guinea Portraits: The expatriate experience* (Canberra, 1978), pp. 101–25.
20   F. E. Williams, *Native Education: The language of instruction and intellectual education* (Port Moresby, 1928). See also Deirdre J. F. Griffiths, 'The Career of F. E. Williams, Government Anthropologist of Papua, 1922–1943', MA thesis, Australian National University, 1977, pp. 116–17.

guest at mission centres along the south Papuan coast. Most of the few European civilians remaining after evacuation had been drafted into ANGAU. On her visits, she made a point of calling on all she could in villages and missions, joining in the netball competitions, swimming parties and school games; she played cats' cradle with the children, and she visited their parents. She had a strong dash of egalitarianism and encountered no difficulty as the only woman lieutenant colonel in a male army; later in Australia, she led bivouacs of up to 40 young men who had spent an extended period on active warfare in the Middle East, and was able to gain their acceptance. She was a chain smoker, and a characteristic of hers when offered a cigarette by her young cadets was to reply 'No thanks, I roll my own'—from her army ration.[21]

This is to suggest a somewhat 'tough' woman coming into her own, a 'man among men', but the picture needs focusing. She was always gracious, speaking impeccable English without, however, any trace of Oxbridge 'plumminess'. No matter how red her sunburn, how much 'like a swagman' she might look, she always managed to give an impression of smiling good nature and serenity—a serenity of a kind often possessed by English county families with an unquestioning acceptance of their own worth.

It is not surprising that, with such a striking and assertive manner, she was widely regarded as a feminist, a 'blue stocking', an unmarried female academic. Camilla's distinguished women colleagues in Malinowski's class were unkindly known as 'the flat-heeled school of social anthropology', and she appeared to fit well the description of a 'blue stocking', of not being dependent upon marriage and not subordinate to men. She had been the only woman lecturer in anthropology at Sydney University; in wartime, the only Australian woman lieutenant colonel in Papua and New Guinea. In such entirely male institutions, a woman with a fine intellect and unfeminine looks could not realistically hope for an offer of marriage from a suitable mate. It is clear from Wedgwood's publications and wartime reports, however, that she saw gender stratification and marriage as the natural order of society. She believed that women of her own family and class were able to lead full lives within the limitations imposed by a male-dominated society.[22] A woman's proper place was in marriage and the family, tempered by good works and scholarship. She was angry at being described as a 'leading Australian feminist' in her citation for the award of the

---

21   Personal communication, H. W. West, 20 January 1985.
22   Marie Reay, 'Review [of Wetherell and Carr-Gregg, *Camilla*]', *Canberra Anthropology*, 14:2 (1991), pp. 120–3. I am grateful to Dr Reay for pointing out this inconsistency in Wedgwood's attitudes—an inconsistency more apparent than real.

1937 Coronation Medal ('you have no idea how I loathe feminism'), and she remained critical of women who were, as she put it, 'obsessed with women's rights'.[23]

Wedgwood's wartime research consolidated her earlier work on Manam. While she was no feminist, such research made her the pioneer anthropologist of women's social roles in Melanesia. Long before the discipline of anthropology recognised gender relations as essential to social cohesion, Wedgwood had gone to Manam Island to investigate 'the lives of women and children'. Her first article on Manam (1934) was an account of girls' puberty rites, written while still in the field. She obtained an 'inside view' of women's lives by putting into practice her own version of the 'participant-observation' method of fieldwork. As Manam women reportedly said 20 years later:

> [S]he knew how to plant taro. She dug the hole. She cooked the taro just as we do. She cut away the scrub with a bush knife as we do. If a man died she sat in the middle with all the other women and grieved for him. She was not like white people, she was just like us black-skinned folk.[24]

If Wedgwood's first aim in 1944 was to devise an education curriculum suited to Papua New Guinea's rural culture, her second was to persuade the Christian churches to accept secular government control in the place of a shreds-and-patches system of mission schools. The colonial governments of both territories had been happy to hand over education to the missions, and education was almost entirely in the hands of the churches. From the 1920s, missionaries had been nominated to represent Papuan interests on the legislative council; their role was as mediators between the core of the colonial territory and the indigenous periphery. But their activities were severely constrained by chronic shortages of funds. They could not command the financial resources available to the colonial governments and received grants-in-aid in health and education, tied to a government-supervised examination of pupils.

Here Wedgwood's initial expectations were again marked by the directorate's venturesome confidence at the time. In her diary at the Sacred Heart Mission on Yule Island in June, she had commented ominously that the mission 'resents increased control by Government'.[25] The Roman Catholic Church, she wrote, was likely to prove the greatest of the 'awful snags ahead', blocking 'constructive work', by which she meant the creation of a government-controlled education system. She had thought that a postwar administration would quickly take

---

23 Wedgwood to her father, 28 June 1937, and Wedgwood to Dowager Lady Wedgwood, 19 September 1951, both in WPC.
24 H. Ian Hogbin and C. D. Rowley, 'Camilla Hildegarde Wedgwood', *South Pacific*, 8:6 (1955), pp. 110–12. See also Luktehaus, *Zaria's Fire*, especially pp. 73–122, 419–32.
25 Wedgwood, Diary, 15 June [1944], Wedgwood Papers, NLA, MS 483/7/32.

over all the schools and that the non-Roman Catholic churches would facilitate a smooth transfer, but during her second Papuan patrol in August 1944 (she spent a brief interval in Melbourne between patrols), she became aware that the Anglican diocese—one of the major missions in Papua—was not likely to hand over its schools without a fight. Other missions, including the London Missionary Society, were also affronted by Morris creating the government secondary school at Sogeri and enrolling mission students there without consulting the missions.[26]

The Anglican Mission had been deeply involved in the circumstances of the New Guinea campaign. For most of 1942, thousands of Japanese soldiers had occupied the northern third of the mission area in north-eastern coastal Papua, and all but one of its missionary staff had remained at their stations attempting to maintain their spiritual, medical and educational endeavours in the face of increasing threat. In March 1942, its bishop, Philip Strong, and some of his Papuan mission helpers aboard ship were machine-gunned from the air by a Japanese Zero and narrowly escaped death. In July, the northern missionaries at Gona and the inland stations of Sangara and Isivita were caught by the Japanese landing at Gona and advancing on Kokoda. They had tried to escape but were variously led to the Japanese lines and executed. One, Father James Benson—separated from other groups—was captured and made prisoner-of-war until 1945.[27]

The experience of war—particularly the deaths of the northern mission staff in horrifying circumstances—had toughened the attitude of Bishop Strong to the possibility of postwar secular intrusion into the sphere of education, which the mission considered its own. It was church control over the training of teachers that prompted the most unyielding statement of policy: teachers were trained to fulfil the multiple roles of lay readers, teachers and evangelists: 'the maintaining of the Training of our Teachers in our own hands is a matter of fundamental and absolutely vital importance to us and to the life of the Church in this diocese', wrote Strong: '*We will under no circumstances surrender it.*'[28]

How was it possible for Wedgwood to have underestimated Anglican opposition to her educational plans when she herself was already an Anglican? The answer seems to be that, as a recent convert, she was unfamiliar with educational thought within the Church of England. The fact that her own educational background was either secular or nonconformist explains her unpreparedness

---

26 Wedgwood to her sister, 22 October 1944, WPC; Wedgwood, 'Papua Reports on Mission Schools, Anglican Mission (Baniara Sub-Division—visited August–September 1944)', Wedgwood Papers, NLA, MS 483/7/32.
27 See Hank Nelson, 'The Swinging Index: Capital punishment and British and Australian administrations in Papua and New Guinea, 1888–1945', *Journal of Pacific History*, 13:3 (1978), pp. 130–52.
28 'The Bishop of New Guinea's Educational Policy', n.d., 2, cited in *ABM Review*, June 1945.

for church resistance. In addition, her conversion was theological, not social, in nature: a heartfelt acceptance of the doctrine of original sin and the reality of the sacraments. In her moral and social concerns, she remained strongly a Friend and a Fabian all her life, and her Fabian convictions favoured the growth of government bureaucracy over education, as in other areas.

In the event, it was the Anglicans rather than the Roman Catholics who were to become the 'awful snag ahead'. In the days when Colonel Conlon was establishing the basis for a directorate in which 'new deal' policies for postwar education would be hammered out, Bishop Strong was addressing large public meetings in crowded town-hall meetings in Australian capital cities. Ministering to servicemen as senior chaplain to the forces had reinforced Strong's views on education. It had become apparent in 1943 that many servicemen had developed an appreciation of the work of missions which they had not had before. Experience of Papuan carriers and medical orderlies who were kind, courteous, honest and hardworking—the 'Fuzzy Wuzzy Angels' with many of whom they could converse in English—so astonished some servicemen that they wrote to friends and newspapers of their discovery that missions were worthwhile. Strong used this discovery to support his own evaluation of missions: Australians should be aroused to provide a 'new order' for the people of New Guinea.[29] But it was a different 'new order' from that of the directorate's blueprints, and it differed sharply from Camilla Wedgwood's. A theme repeated with many variations was the 'very real danger' of a 'purely secular education'. Strong added: 'if we allow education to pass out of the hands of the missions I believe we shall be selling our trust.' As noted by Donald Dickson, historian of the Anglican educational system, Bishop Strong appeared as apprehensive, distrustful and belligerently defensive.[30]

On the other hand, Wedgwood became more than ever convinced that government control was necessary. It was desirable, first, on grounds of finance and the reluctance of the Australian public to devote large sums to church schools in the territories. Second, the right of freedom of conscience was in her view violated by compulsory education administered in a geographical zone where, under the comity of missions in Papua agreed upon in 1890, a single denomination had a monopoly.

While Camilla completed her plans for a government system, Bishop Strong's fear of secular schools became more pronounced. His rare letters to Lieutenant-Colonel Wedgwood were courtly ('I hope you feel your visit has been profitable';

---

29 *Sydney Morning Herald*, 27 April 1943. See also D. J. Dickson, 'Government and Mission in Education', MEd thesis, University of Papua New Guinea, 1971, p. 15; David Wetherell (ed.), *The New Guinea Diaries of Philip Strong, 1936–1945* (Melbourne, 1981), pp. 161–7 (8–23 March 1943).
30 D. J. Dickson, Transcript of interview with P. N. W. Strong, 1 February 1969, p. 133, University of Papua New Guinea Library.

'I hope it was not too uncomfortable');[31] but he had little doubt that the hand of Jacob lay behind Esau's glove. In his private diary, he wrote that he '[h]ad seen of the appointment of Col. I. Hogbin and Col. Camilla Wedgwood Anthro[pologists] to go up to New Guinea to advise the authorities. [The Bishop of] Melanesia told me of his experiences of Hogbin, and that he is anti-mission and an unbeliever.'[32] Hogbin provided confirmation of his nonconformist missionaries at Kwato in China Strait. In the words of Russell Abel, son of Kwato's founder:

> Hogbin is fed up and bitter about Missions and is very outspoken, said most damaging things and added—'you can quote me—everything I said is for publication!'...[He is] very like Camilla, except that Camilla is a Christian...whereas Hogbin stoutly avers that he is *not*...'I have no faith, little hope, and absolutely no charity!' I can well believe the latter![33]

Among other preoccupations, Wedgwood maintained an interest in 'mixed-race' people who were gathered in the towns and at the Yule Island headquarters of the Sacred Heart and at St Agnes's home at the Anglican headquarters at Dogura. She agreed with the mission heads that an 'English' or European education would continue to be necessary. Most of them had no villages and no land, and their lives would continue to be identified with the whites, most of them as employees. She compiled brief studies of prominent mixed-race families (including Guise, Parascos, Burfitt, Cadogan, Dolla, Evennett)—the first genealogical information about them to have been recorded. At the Yule Island headquarters of the Sacred Heart Mission, she had regarded the future of mixed-race people as 'bound up' by education and marriage with Europeans. But later at Dogura she recorded that the attitude of Papua's Europeans to mixed-race families was such that she felt there was 'no hope of their being absorbed into them'.[34] The consensus among Anglicans was that the gap between mixed-race and Papuan should be reduced and that intermarriage between Papuan men and mixed-race women be encouraged.

With the coming of a state-supervised system and government schools, the missions could concentrate on secondary schools and teachers' colleges while spreading out their informal 'systems' of schools on the other. The effect of dealing with such shreds-and-patches mission systems tended to decentralise,

---

31 See Wetherell and Carr-Gregg, *Camilla*, pp. 175–6.
32 Wetherell, *The New Guinea Diaries of Philip Strong*, p. 194 (28 February 1944).
33 R. W. Abel to S. Abel, 25 March 1945, Abel Papers, New Guinea Collection, University of Papua New Guinea Library.
34 Wedgwood, Diary I, 28 August 1944; and more generally Wedgwood, Diary III, 18 September – 2 October 1944, both in Wedgwood Papers, NLA, MS 483/7/32.

or at least blunt, the centralising tendencies of the state, and this was implicit in Wedgwood's final report, which accepted that replacing mission schools with government schools would not be as easy as initially expected.

In her writing about the Government's assumption of authority over education, Wedgwood's intentions now became drastically modified. She concluded there were cogent arguments against taking native education 'entirely' away from mission hands. These were practical: almost all the educationists in Papua and New Guinea, whether European or Melanesian, were mission teachers. The Europeans were men and women, many of them holding degrees and diplomas in teaching, who had gone to the territories 'not to make a living but with a sense of vocation, and prepared to spend most of their lives there'. No satisfactory development in education could be expected if the European personnel who were to be recruited as government teachers regarded the work only as a 'job' and were prepared to stay in New Guinea for only two or three years.[35]

In short, Camilla Wedgwood realised that, in spite of pipe dreams in the directorate, there was no other body offering the manpower and expertise to replace the mission education systems. 'For the immediate present', she wrote, 'I believe it would be wisest to concentrate educational activities in those areas where education has already been begun with success by the missions'.[36] But the prewar 'bob-a-nob' funds awarded on the basis of an inspector's appraisal of Papuan students' competence in the mission classroom would be replaced with a grant-in-aid system based on a mission teacher's proved competence established by a government-supervised certificate of training.

The first four of Camilla Wedgwood's five reports on aims, problems and suggested policies, based on field research between March and December 1944, were completed in May 1945. The fifth was published three months later. After the first report, *Some problems of native education in the Mandated Territory and Papua* (1944), the reports were: *Summary of native education in Papua*; *The development of native education in New Guinea*; *Some suggestions concerning the organisation of education in the Territory of New Guinea* (all in May 1945); and *The aims of native education and the incentives which lead the natives to desire it* (August 1945).[37]

Wedgwood's writing on education projected the conservative, non-evolutionary functionalism of Malinowski and his disciples who, from the end of World War I, had proposed that among tribal societies, things should be kept as far as possible as they were. Though written from within the functionalist camp, Wedgwood's writing nonetheless recognised that the war had brought irrevocable change

---

35 Wetherell and Carr-Gregg, *Camilla*, pp. 178–9
36 Quoted in ibid., p. 179.
37 The reports are housed in the National Archives of Australia (Melbourne), MP742/1, WOB 274/1247.

in the Western Pacific. Her articles spoke of the application of anthropology to postwar conditions—notably, 'The Contribution of Anthropology to the Education and Development of Colonial Peoples'.[38] Along with F. E. Williams, Ian Hogbin and A. P. Elkin, she was a significant figure in the history of Australia's dealings with indigenous peoples in Australia and Papua New Guinea. Though she did not make a lasting mark on anthropology, the contribution she made through such writing to education and public service was shaped by anthropology.[39] Her advice reveals the intersection between anthropology and colonial administration during and after the Pacific War.

Wedgwood's wartime reports were thorough, informed and confident. Her 30-year plan to provide 'mass education' or primary schooling for all—thus avoiding the social problems flowing from an elitist program for only a few—was consistent with her own deeply held ideological outlook. The optimism about the degree of progress possible in providing primary education reflected the idealism of the Fabian reformer. But Camilla did not visualise the opposition her ideals would have to face from Melanesian parents as well as from international planners. The postwar clamour of indigenous people for schools meant that conditions had changed. Rural education no longer sufficed: the indigenous PNG people were not satisfied with an educational curriculum that fitted them only for village life, but were anxious to 'catch up' with Europeans and be able to migrate to opportunities of taking part in the cash economy.

Camilla Wedgwood had initially proposed replacing mission schools with a universal government system, but she had seriously underestimated the strength of Anglican objections to secularising tendencies. She argued the cause of early vernacular education with vigour and suggested practical policies for organisation. On the basis provided by her detailed plans for educational policies, the Federal Government could be confident that a comprehensive educational program could be devised. Opinions differ on the extent of her influence in the stages leading to the drafting of the Papua New Guinea Provisional Administration Bill of 1945. Those close to her in Melbourne and Canberra, such as Peter Ryan, say she and Hogbin were consulted extensively during its framing.[40] Her surveys—though not explicitly invoked during the debate on the Bill—had led to the first formulation of an education policy for Papua New Guinea by an Australian administration. The Wedgwood reports, however, were only one incident in an unfolding story that included Hogbin, J. R. Kerr, Julius Stone and J. K. Murray, and none of them contributed a share of the planning

---

38 Wedgwood, 'The Contribution of Anthropology to the Education and Development of Colonial Peoples', *South Pacific*, 4:5 (1950), pp. 78–84.
39 Nancy Lutkehaus, 'Review [of Wetherell and Carr-Gregg, *Camilla*]', *Oceania*, 62:2 (1991), pp. 156–7.
40 Interview, Peter Ryan, 11 February 1986. Hogbin told Elkin that he was largely responsible for the content of its framing (see chapter on Hogbin in this volume).

large enough to be able to say, 'Alone, I did it'.[41] Camilla Wedgwood's plans for the structure of formal education made it clear that the Government could not manage, for the time being, a workable education program without the missions' assistance. This represented a considerable modification of the views she had held at the outset of her wartime work for the directorate.

The experiences of some of the other individuals in *Scholars at War* demonstrate that there was no easy road in adjusting to the changed conditions of postwar Australia and New Zealand. For Wedgwood, as well as for others experiencing demobilisation, the lull allowed the freedom for reflection in place of the disciplined activity of the directorate, and with it came the stirrings of discontent. She felt disappointment with the school that had developed with high hopes from the School of Civil Affairs in Canberra; she felt disappointment with W. C. Groves—sent to inaugurate a system of government education in Papua New Guinea—especially since she had recommended his appointment; and she felt uncertain about her own future in Australia. Wartime confidence and camaraderie were evaporating. She expected to be involved as an educational adviser in postwar reconstruction. The opportunity never came her way. Apart from a return visit to finish her surveys in 1946–47, she found it impossible, in the administrative stagnation that beset the territories after the war, to do any more than train *kiaps* and teacher trainees at a distance. At ASOPA, Wedgwood was remembered with affection by *kiaps* as an outstandingly popular lecturer.

She tried to meet her own ebbing certainty by searching for closer relationships with her family during visits to Britain, and saw her mother for the last time in Switzerland in 1952. The reunion was a happy one, marred only by Camilla's failing health. On her return to Sydney, she worked in the office of the South Pacific Commission (SPC) with Harry Maude and his social development research group—'young university folk, full of energy and initiative and gaiety'.[42] During this time, she compiled, on behalf of the SPC, an *Annotated Bibliography of Native Education in the South Pacific* (1956).

In spite of privileged beginnings and influential family connections, Camilla Wedgwood was dogged by professional disappointments. Her painstaking editing of *Malekula*, based on Bernard Deacon's field research, was rewarded with a threat of legal action by another anthropologist. John Layard had threatened the publishers of her edition of *Malekula* with litigation because, faced with Deacon's disorderly field notes, Wedgwood had unwittingly ascribed material in her text to him instead of to Layard. This harrowing experience probably contributed to her failure to produce a full-length book based on her own research on Manam Island, thus placing her in the second rank of

---

41 As is made clear in Lucy Mair, *Australia in New Guinea* (London 1948), pp. 161–73 (ch. 8, 'Education').
42 Wedgwood to her sister, 31 October 1951, WPC.

professional anthropologists after Malinowski's other women students such as Audrey Richards and Lucy Mair.[43] She worked as Malinowski's research assistant on his manuscript about kinship, but the book was ill fated and never appeared. She failed to secure tenured academic positions at Sydney and London—the LSE lectureship was given to Richards instead—and in 1945 she was passed over for the coveted headship of Lady Margaret Hall at Oxford. Her remarkable wartime research on education in Papua New Guinea received little recognition at the time, and she was ill rewarded by seeing the position of first Director of Education given to W. C. Groves—a lesser talent.

A. P. Elkin found that, '[b]eneath her apparent self-confidence', she was 'somewhat retiring and lonely'.[44] After the war, she kept in close touch through correspondence with her distant family, especially her father and her sister Helen, and relied on old Sydney friends, particularly Theresa Britton, her husband and children. Before 1951, she lived in a series of flats in North Sydney before finding herself 'a permanent abode' in Alfred Street overlooking Sydney Harbour. She had few possessions in Australia, having left her furniture and books in her family home at The Ark in Moddershall in Staffordshire in 1927. The main room of the Alfred Street flat was simply furnished with an iron bed at the side. The wall shelves contained some magnificent Wedgwood pottery.

Camilla Wedgwood died of cancer on 17 May 1955 and was cremated. Her friend James McAuley dedicated to her his poem 'Winter Nightfall' (1967). A government girls' high school at Goroka was named after her, and in Port Moresby an annual educational lecture series for international scholars was inaugurated in her honour.[45]

---

43   Michael Young, 'Review [of Wetherell and Carr-Gregg, *Camilla*]', *Journal of Pacific History*, 26:1 (1991), pp. 121–3. See also Nancy Luktehaus, '"She was *very* Cambridge": Camilla Wedgwood and British female anthropologists', *American Ethnologist*, 13:4 (1986), pp. 776–98.
44   A. P. Elkin, 'Camilla Hildegarde Wedgwood, 1901–1955', *Oceania*, 26:3 (1956), p. 177.
45   A list of speakers in the Camilla Wedgwood Memorial Lectures 1959–66 is given in Wetherell and Carr-Gregg, *Camilla*, pp. 231–2.

6. Ronald Murray Berndt: 'Work of national importance'

Geoffrey Gray

A. P. Elkin, who was never slow to seize an opportunity to promote himself and the importance of anthropology, wrote to the Prime Minister, John Curtin, pointing out that problems associated with the administration of 'native peoples' during war could be resolved only through anthropological research. These problems, he added, would increase in number and complexity as a result of the war, especially in northern Australia and Australia's external territories of Papua and New Guinea. Consequently, it was no longer simply a matter of understanding cultural contact, and social organisation, economic life, local customs and religion. It was necessary also to examine the psychological and sociological effects of the war, and of the military administration. The attitudes of the 'natives to the white man and his administration' had to be understood if 'the latter [was] to succeed' once the war had ended. He anticipated an increased role for himself and some of his selected students, two of whom were Ronald Berndt (1916–90) and Catherine Berndt (née Webb) (1918–94). This chapter focuses on the early career of Ronald rather than Catherine; she is no less important at this time but it is Ronald who ends up with a tenured academic career in anthropology. We can say, however, that as their careers took shape Catherine, perhaps putting aside her ambitions, increasingly devoted herself to actively supporting, developing and helping make Ronald's career.

The war enabled Ronald Berndt to develop and establish himself as an anthropologist—something that could not have happened had he not had an exemption from military duty. It was underpinned by his determination and single-mindedness combined with the support of A. P. Elkin. An only child, Ronald was born in Adelaide in 1916. His father was a jeweller and both parents were born in Australia of German descent. His father broke with the Lutheran Church soon after Ronald's birth. Subsequently, Ronald attended Anglican primary schools and did his secondary education at Pulteney Grammar School, Adelaide, leaving at the age of fourteen, and—largely at the request of his father who was concerned that his son might not obtain work during the Depression years—undertook an accountancy course at the South Australian School of Mines and Industry.

At the age of twenty-three, Berndt, Honorary Assistant in Ethnology at the South Australian Museum, was casting round for a way into anthropology. At the urging of T. H. Johnston and J. B. Cleland—both members of the University of Adelaide Board for Anthropological Research—he wrote to Elkin seeking information on enrolment for the Diploma in Anthropology. This was an ideal entry for Berndt as it did not require matriculation.[1] It was while he was at the University of Sydney that he met his future wife and partner in anthropology, Catherine Helen Webb, a New Zealander who completed her BA at Victoria University College, Wellington, in 1938, and a Certificate of Proficiency in Anthropology at the University of Otago in 1939.

In June 1941, Catherine was funded by the Australian National Research Council (ANRC) to undertake research at Ooldea Soak, SA, where Ronald had visited briefly as member of the University of Adelaide Board for Anthropological Research expedition in August 1939. This research formed the basis of Catherine's thesis—a requirement for the diploma. Elkin had hoped Ronald would also be funded for the Ooldea research—Catherine to 'concentrate on the women and on the linguistics while [Ronald] will work through the men'—but his application was rejected.[2] Ronald, who had spent the end of 1939 and early 1940 at the Lower River Murray interviewing 'remnants' of the Jaralde (Ngarrindjeri), planned to write his thesis from this research.

When Catherine applied for a permit from the SA Aborigines' Protection Board (APB) to reside at Ooldea Soak, the Commonwealth Investigation Branch (CIB)—the precursor of the Australian Security Intelligence Organisation (ASIO)—noted that her husband (they were married in April 1941) was already under observation. Being of German descent had brought him to the attention of the authorities following a complaint by his landlord in Sydney. He was visited by the police but they found nothing untoward. It had been alleged that Ronald had stated 'that six of his friends were interned in [South Australia]. Berendt [sic] is supposed to be employed at the University'; that he 'engages himself in his studies in his bedroom and spends a large portion of his time there… He spends all his spare time writing letters in his room'. Berndt denied that he knew any person interned, and informed the officer that both his parents were born in Adelaide, and he would return there at the conclusion of his studies.[3]

One of the CIB informants considered Ronald a security threat and produced a report based on a mixture of truths, half-truths, hearsay and fabrications. The informant recommended that Ronald (there was little interest in the New Zealand-born Catherine) be prevented from going to Ooldea for the following reasons:

---

1   R. M. Berndt, Student Record Card, University of Sydney Archives; Minutes, Professorial Board, Arts Faculty, University of Sydney, 16 June 1948, University of Sydney Archives.
2   Elkin to Hon. Sec., ANRC, 2 May 1941, Elkin Papers, University of Sydney Archives [hereinafter EP], 156/4/1/14.
3   Sergeant 3rd Class (Roadley), No. 6 Police Station, North Sydney to Inspector 1/c (Keefe), MPI Section, 29 May 1940, National Archives of Australia, Canberra [hereinafter NAA], C123, 16553.

6. Ronald Murray Berndt: 'Work of national importance'

1. He is decidedly pro-German.

2. He is not a Scientist.

3. He proposes going by motor car at a big expenditure of petrol [at a time of petrol rationing].

4. The trip has been arranged to avoid Military Service.

5. He told a friend that he would not stay at Ooldea but would go further inland.

This was based on evidence—if it can be so considered—such as: when asked whether he was a conscientious objector, Ronald replied, 'Yes and no'. He declined to qualify this statement. Discussing the war with a friend, Berndt said: 'We should not have interfered and fought against Germany.'[4] He was reported as saying 'that he loathed the Nazis but admired the Hindenburg regime'. It showed that Ronald could be outspoken, indiscreet and inconsistent in his comments about the war. As with most security dossiers, in Ronald's, the often unsubstantiated and unfounded allegations are based on character; in the opinion of an unnamed friend—someone who had known him for a number of years—Ronald Berndt was a

> very irresponsible person, childish in many ways. He seems to have deeply resented the fact that his flat was searched in Sydney and when in that city, boasted that he would not take the Oath to serve in the Militia. However he thought better of it and complied with Defence requirements, but the Authorities granted him exemption…from training.[5]

Nonetheless, a permit was issued, primarily as a result of representations by J. B. Cleland (Chairman of the APB), who assured the CIB and the members of the APB that Ronald was 'being assisted by Elkin', and, mistakenly, that Elkin had obtained cash grants for Ronald to cover the cost of the trip. Some days later, Cleland might have had second thoughts about Ronald's loyalty and sincerity:

> On the Sunday following the issue of the permit, Professor Cleland invited Berndt and his wife out to tea. After the meal, Berndt offended Professor Cleland's women-folk by bragging that he had avoided military

---

[4] Report by No. 17, in A. C. Palmer (Inquiry Officer, Investigation Branch, Adelaide) to The Inspector, Commonwealth Investigation Branch, Adelaide, 20 June 1941, NAA, D1915/0, SA 19248.
[5] Palmer to The Inspector, Commonwealth Investigation Branch, Adelaide, 16 September 1941, NAA, D1915/0, SA 19248. Ronald had enlisted in the Army on 11 September 1940, at the University of Sydney. He had been medically examined and 'found FIT and attested under Part IV of the Defence Act 1903–1939'. He would be 'notified by post of the Unit to which you are allotted and the time, date and place to report for camp'. Certificate of Enrolment, Eastern Command.

training, and would continue to do so. Professor Cleland stated that the female members of his household left the room...Berndt made no disloyal utterances, apart from his statements regarding military training.

After further discussion with Cleland, it was concluded by the Officer-in-Charge of the CIB 'that Berndt will find difficulties in securing further support from the Aborigines' Board'.[6] It had consequences for their future research.

Once Ronald was at Ooldea—rather than being out of sight and out of mind—further allegations were made against him. He was accused of being 'very friendly with a Rlwy Ganger who is suspected of Anti-British feelings'. It had been 'reported to the Police that Natives smashed two locks on Railway property. Natives had nothing to do with it. Berndt and his ganger pal suspected... Gangers name is not known. [The missionary Harrie Green] knows the full facts. If approached secretly...[he] would assist.'[7] This information is unlikely to have originated with Green who had earlier informed Cleland

> that the trouble over the ganger and the Natives here is a nasty affair. But I can assure you that the root of the trouble is...[the] ganger [who] is definitely opposed to the natives and also the policeman is rough and brutal to them...the natives...highly resent it and told me when he [the policeman] first came here that he would not get on with them if he treated them like that. They said he does not understand us.[8]

Perhaps more worrying for Cleland and the APB was Green's allegation that the Berndts were 'having an unsettling effect upon the natives'. Aboriginal people had spoken to Green

> on several occasions and deeply resent [Ronald Berndt's] persistent questioning into matters which concern their tribal life and Secret Customs. Also taking photos of them with no covering at all, representing them to be wild bush Natives in Central Australia and they do not get around like that here at Ooldea.[9]

---

6 Palmer to The Inspector, Commonwealth Investigation Branch, Adelaide, 20 June 1941, NAA, D1915/0, SA 19248.
7 Palmer to The Inspector, Commonwealth Investigation Branch, Adelaide, 20 June 1941, NAA, D1915/0, SA 19248.
8 Green to J. B. Cleland, 17 July 1941, Cleland Papers, South Australian Museum Archives [hereinafter SAMA], AA60/03. For a brief discussion on the ganger and the policemen, see Cameron Raynes, 'Ooldea, Boxing Day, 1941: Part two', *recordSArchives* [official newsletter of the State Records of South Australia], 23 (November 2002), pp. 4–5.
9 Green to Aborigines' Protection Board (APB), 20 September 1941, State Records of South Australia [hereinafter SRSA], Aborigines' Office, GRG52/1/1941/25. Cf. Ronald Berndt and Catherine Berndt, who stated that there was amongst Aboriginal people at the mission a measure of discontent over the scant rations and poor material resources provided. 'A Preliminary Report of Field Work in the Ooldea Region, Western South Australia', *Oceania*, 12:4 (1942), p. 323.

While he was at Ooldea, Ronald's mother died. She had been 'very ill for some time, and was still so when we left'. She had been misdiagnosed with arthritis[10] and Ronald received a telegram 'asking to come home urgently, at once'. Illustrating his determination, it was his intention to return to Ooldea the next day, 'but as his mother is unlikely to recover, the end being expected any day, he did not feel justified in doing so'. So determined was he to continue his work and not lose the support of Elkin that he asked Catherine to write to Elkin assuring him 'that this will cause minimum of hindrance to his work', that he 'has been working with concentrated energy all day without missing a day since we arrived here. And he means to redouble his efforts on his return.'[11] His mother died four days after he returned to Ooldea. He notified Elkin, adding: 'My wife and I are both well, however the weather has been most unpleasant, and now very hot with swarms of flies.'[12] It was a loss that he was unable to discuss in a letter with Elkin.

The Berndts returned to Adelaide at the end of November.[13] The CIB continued its inquiries into Ronald's activities and, to question his loyalty, sought further information from Green,[14] but he appears not to have replied. The CIB was advised by one of its informants that 'Berndt, to avoid Military training, is now going to Western Australia, where he will apply to the Aborigines Department for a permit to continue his studies on the native areas in that State'.[15] The WA Commissioner for Native Affairs, F. I. Bray, was interviewed by security, 'and [after] a résumé of the circumstances personally conveyed to him…decided to… refuse consent to the issue of a permit'.[16]

The Berndts left Adelaide in late December for Dunedin in New Zealand, returning in late March. They used the time to write up their Ooldea research but their future in anthropology was unclear. War service was not out of the question for Ronald but not as a frontline soldier if he could help it. He hoped that, rather than being called up, 'my wife and I would…get to New Guinea in a semi-military capacity…in a position where there would be opportunities to study the natives and carry on anthropological work at the same time'.[17] Once Rabaul was bombed in January 1942, however, the possibility of work in New Guinea ended. Eager to find some anthropologically based war work that

---

10   Ronald's cancer was also misdiagnosed, which led to his early death. John E. Stanton, Tribute to Ronald M. Berndt, viewed 6 November 2010, <http://www.berndt.uwa.edu.au/generic.lasso?token_value=berndt>
11   C. H. Berndt to Elkin, 6 September 1941, EP, 246/613. Catherine's mother had died the previous year.
12   R. M. Berndt to Elkin, 13 September 1941, EP, 246/613.
13   Penhall to R. M. Berndt, 2 October 1941; R. M. Berndt to Penhall, 18 October 1941, SRSA, GRG52/1/1941/25.
14   Notes: 9a 3 October 1941, No. 17, in R. Williams, Inspector, to H. E. Green, 3 October 1941, NAA, D1915/0, SA 19248.
15   A. C. Palmer (Inquiry Officer, Investigation Branch, Adelaide) to The Inspector, CIB (Adelaide), 17 November 1941, NAA, D1915/0, SA 19248.
16   J. Adams, Inspector (Perth) to The Inspector, CIB (Adelaide), 25 November 1941, NAA, D1915/0, SA 19248.
17   R. M. Berndt to Elkin, 4 December 1941, EP, 246/613.

would enable him to pre-empt being called up for military service, he proposed 'some post, in a semi-military capacity or otherwise, dealing with the natives directly or indirectly in Northern Australia…Catherine is willing to join me in this work if there is a possible opportunity'.[18] At the end of January 1942, Elkin warned them not to get 'too hopeful about getting a position connected with the natives in Northern Australia. There is just a chance that Mr [E. W. P.] Chinnery [Director of the NT Native Affairs Branch] might feel that they can deal with native problems without having anthropological specialists.'[19] Ronald persisted: perhaps 'a departmental position in [Native Affairs] in Sydney or Melbourne, would enable me to do something that was helpful, while Catherine continued with her writing up'.[20]

Elkin advised Ronald to write directly to the Prime Minister, John Curtin, offering his services, which he did in April 1942. Elkin also wrote to Curtin telling him that when it came to matters of Aboriginal loyalty, anthropologists were the ones able to assist in the 'best use of Aborigines' in the fight against the Japanese; unless Aborigines 'were told to the contrary by [anthropologists] whom they understood and trusted, [the Aborigines] would not see why they should not guide the Japanese'. It was also an opportunity, by allowing the enlistment of Aborigines, to demonstrate that the citizenship 'we talk about is the real thing and not a species of segregation'. He attached two projects, prepared by a 'researcher [Ronald Berndt] working under his supervision'. One project, 'Voluntary War Service for Aborigines', suggested the employment of 'half-castes' in the war effort, specifically to 'form an Aborigines' Corps'. The other was 'Regarding Closer Co-operation and mutual understanding' between 'the white folk and the natives' as a way of ensuring 'a solid and cohesive front against the Japanese'.[21]

Ronald possessed ambition and determination that enabled him to think that his abilities would be recognised, despite no formal academic qualifications or experience in administering Indigenous people. But his main purpose was finding a way to remain in the field whether it be in Australia or New Guinea and fulfil his ambition to be an anthropologist: 'During the last year [1940] I have studied and attended at the Anthropology Course at the Uni. of Syd. hoping thereby to better fit myself for a *lifetime of work in ethnological fields*.'[22] Should Elkin not obtain a positive response regarding the two projects that

---

18   R. M. Berndt to Elkin, 11 January 1942, EP, 246/613.
19   Elkin to R. M. Berndt, 26 January 1942, EP, 246/613.
20   R. M. Berndt to Elkin, 10 February 1942, EP, 246/613.
21   Elkin to Curtin, 2 April 1942, NAA, MP 508/1, 240/701/217. Ronald Berndt was the researcher.
22   [My emphasis.] Ronald M. Berndt to ANRC, 3 March 1941, EP, 160/4/1/78. There are other factors that possibly came into play but which are outside the scope of this chapter, such as the transformation and remaking of the self when in the field. (Ronald was inspired by the main character in Rider Haggard's novels of exotic adventures.) See various chapters in Jean-Guy A. Goulet and Bruce Granville Miller (eds), *Extraordinary Anthropology: Transformations in the field* (Lincoln, Neb., 2007).

Ronald would oversee, or should Ronald not be offered some war work in a 'semi-military capacity', he proposed to inquire into 'the Warburton track'. Ronald hoped to arrange funding, either through the ANRC or the University of Sydney, for he and Catherine to do a survey of desert culture from Ooldea to Warburton, which would take about 12 months.[23] It was an abandoned research project of the University of Adelaide Board for Anthropological Research (which included Ronald as a researcher) that had been granted permission by the WA authorities; nonetheless, after receiving information from the CIB, the WA authorities withdrew the permit for Ronald to enter reserves.

Elkin did not receive a favourable reply from Curtin. Subsequently, most of the latter half of 1942 was spent at Murray Bridge and Adelaide. Ronald continued his work with Albert Karloan and other Jaralde people at the Lower River Murray while Catherine continued to write up the Ooldea material for her thesis, although it had become a joint thesis.[24] Over the period 1942–45, their thesis, added to and enlarged (including some rewriting by Elkin), was published in instalments in the journal *Oceania* as 'A Preliminary Report of Field Work in the Ooldea Region, Western South Australia'. Some years later, Elkin described it as the 'best complete monograph' of an Australian tribe.[25]

While there had been little research on Aboriginal people living in urban and rural Australia before the Pacific War, limited funding for research shifted the interest of Elkin away from northern Australia to south-east Australia.[26] Elkin supervised a diverse range of projects. Towards the end of the war, Marie Reay, who had recently completed her degree, undertook research among 'mixed-bloods' in north-western New South Wales at the direction of Elkin and under the auspices of the NSW Aborigines' Welfare Board (AWB), 'which not only appreciated the practical value of her work, but in addition assisted in financial and other ways'.[27] Elkin also developed an interest in the assimilation of recent European immigrants to Australia, reflecting Elkin's ambition to include sociology as integral to the department's functions.[28] He facilitated research 'into problems connected with the assimilation of alien groups', which was done 'under the

---

23 R. M. Berndt to Elkin, 17 April 1942, EP, 246/613.
24 Part 1 of their thesis was sent to Elkin in January 1942. R. M. Berndt to Elkin, 28 January 1942, EP, 246/613. It was completed by December 1942, and the Diploma in Anthropology awarded in May 1943.
25 Elkin to Raymond Firth, 13 November 1948, EP, 178/4/2/178.
26 Geoffrey Gray, *A Cautious Silence: The politics of Australian anthropology* (Canberra, 2007), p. 148; Gray, '"[The Sydney School] seem[s] to view the Aborigines as forever unchanging": Southeastern Australia and Australian anthropology', *Aboriginal History*, 24 (2000), pp. 176–200.
27 Marie Reay, 'A Half-Caste Aboriginal Community in North-Western New South Wales', *Oceania*, 15:4 (1945), pp. 296–323.
28 A. P. Elkin, *Our Opinions and the National Effort* (Sydney, 1941) was Elkin's first attempt at writing about non-Aboriginal sociology. It was 'based on a survey and analysis of opinions of individuals of the typical and various sections and ages of the community in which the author was assisted by twenty observers mostly graduates in anthropology. The results of the survey were sent in the first instance to the Commonwealth authorities. Amongst other things the book shows the necessity for basing all appeals and calls to the nation

auspices' of the Department of Post-War Reconstruction, the Department of the Interior and the Sydney University Anthropology Department. This research was carried out by Jean Craig (later Martin) and Caroline Tennant Kelly.[29] Craig also researched problems associated with rural housing for the Department of Post-War Reconstruction,[30] as did Mona Ravenscroft.[31] Kelly did field research on migrants in Victoria and Queensland.[32] Elkin described the work as research of 'a high standard and national importance'.[33]

The Berndts were, however, the main recipients of this limited funding. In early February 1943, Elkin wrote to A. J. Gibson, Honorary Secretary of the ANRC, seeking financial assistance for the Berndts. Most of 1942, he informed the ANRC, had been spent working at their 'own expense…doing very careful research amongst the remaining Aborigines [at the Lower River Murray]—checking and adding to work done there 20 years and more ago of Radcliffe-Brown'. These funds were to enable the writing up of their Murray Bridge research and finalising the writing up of their Ooldea research.[34] It was for six months, or until such time, if earlier, as the Berndts enter the Commonwealth service[35] 'to take charge of a Feeding Station for Aborigines at the Granites, Northn. (sic) Territory'.[36] This did not eventuate.

In August 1943, Elkin presented a further grant application on their behalf to the ANRC to do 'field work in South Australia especially in (1) the Adelaide, (2) the Quorn–Maree [sic], (3) Lower Murray and possibly (4) Koonibba–Port Augusta districts, for (a) research on acculturation of aborigines and (b) recording of tribal knowledge provided by remaining members of former tribes in these districts'. Both projects were 'important scientifically, and the former also practically'.[37] The ANRC approved at the rate of £200 per annum each, plus a limit of £100 for expenses.[38] Elkin also took it upon himself to write to Cleland as Chairman of the APB explaining the Berndts' research project and seeking his as well as the board's support.[39]

---

on a knowledge of the various divisions of opinion and the types of reaction which exist.' 'Notes and News', *Oceania*, 12:2 (1941), p. 187. See also A. P. Elkin, 'The Need for Sociological Research in Australia', *Social Horizons* (July 1943), pp. 5–15. See also John Pomeroy's chapter in this volume.
29   'Notes and News', *Oceania*, 14:2 (1943); 15:3 (1945), p. 276; 16:4 (1946), p. 353; 15:3 (1945), p. 276.
30   'Notes and News', *Oceania*, 15:3 (1945), p. 276.
31   Mona Ravenscroft, 'The Housing Problem', *Social Horizons* (July 1943), pp. 48–53.
32   'Notes and News', *Oceania*, 16:4 (1946), p. 353.
33   'Notes and News', *Oceania*, 15:3 (1945), p. 276.
34   Elkin to Hon. Sec., ANRC, 16 February 1943, Records of the Australian National Research Council, National Library of Australia [hereinafter ANRC Records, NLA], MS 482, folder 840 [hereinafter MS482, 840].
35   Hon. Sec., ANRC, to Elkin, 26 February 1943, ANRC Records, NLA, MS 482, 840.
36   Elkin to Hon. Sec., ANRC, 16 February 1943, ANRC Records, NLA, MS 482, 840.
37   Elkin to Hon. Sec., ANRC, 19 August 1943, ANRC Records, NLA, MS 482, 840.
38   Isabel Houison to R. M. Berndt and C. H. Berndt, 13 September 1943, ANRC Records, NLA, MS 482, 840.
39   Elkin to Cleland, 30 September 1943, Cleland Papers, SAMA, AA60/03.

Between September and November 1943, the Berndts undertook two months' research on 'mixed-race' people at Menindee Government Aboriginal Station, where they investigated, for the NSW AWB and supported by ANRC funding, 'the importance of the attitudes and opinions held by the natives themselves in regard to the persons and institutions with whom they come in contact'.[40] Their aim was to 'supply a general picture of the Aborigines' changing circumstances'. Their research was a mixture of anthropology and sociology focusing on problems of acculturation and relations between 'white folk' and Aboriginal people in urban and rural South Australia. In their opinion, 'the behaviour of white people towards the natives they meet has an inevitable effect on the reactions and attitudes of the natives themselves. Quite often it is the cause of a great deal of trouble.'[41]

Their research in Adelaide was 'interesting but depressing, since most of the natives live in the worst part of the town—the slums here are of course not to be compared with those in Sydney, but are still unpleasant as living quarters'.[42] After Christmas, they planned to travel to Port Augusta immediately,[43] but problems with the APB and the CIB continued to hamper them. The board refused to grant a permit to carry out research at Port Augusta, Point Pearce, Point McLeay and Swan Reach Reserves.[44] On hearing this, Elkin made strong representations on their behalf, informing the board that the Berndts were 'proficient and skilled', 'earnest and sincere' and 'got on very well with the Aborigines'.[45] Elkin stressed that comparative work like the Berndts' on the 'scientific study of acculturation and assimilation is an essential basis for [enlightened] administration' of Aborigines.[46] It was all to no avail. Cleland advised Elkin that 'there are likely to be [further] difficulties…in granting permission for the Berndts to enter the reserves'.[47]

The issue of Ronald's military exemption permeated the discussion between Elkin and Cleland and amongst board members. Cleland raised the possibility that anthropological research was a manoeuvre to avoid military service. Elkin addressed this, assuring Cleland that the ANRC was cognisant of such matters. He again underlined the importance of this type of research, telling Cleland it was of 'national importance':

---

40 R. M. Berndt and C. H. Berndt, A short study of acculturation at Menindee Government Station, Darling River, Typescript, 92 pp + tables and diagrams, maps, Adelaide, 19 November 1943. See also R. M. Berndt, 'Wuradjeri Magic and "clever men"', Oceania, 17:4 (1947), pp. 327–65; and 18:1 (1947), pp. 60–86.
41 C. H. Berndt to Houison, 17 October 1943, ANRC Records, NLA, MS 482, folder 857a [hereinafter MS482, 857a].
42 C. H. Berndt to Houison, 16 January 1944, ANRC Records, NLA, MS 482, 840.
43 C. H. Berndt to Houison, 19 December 1943, ANRC Records, NLA, MS 482, 840, 857a.
44 R. M. Berndt to Penhall, 15 November 1943, SRSA, GRG52/1/1940/97.
45 Elkin to APB, 10 November 1943, Cleland Papers, SAMA, AA60/03.
46 Elkin to Cleland, 13 December 1943, EP, 157/4/1/23.
47 Cleland to Elkin, 30 November 1943, Cleland Papers, SAMA, AA60/03.

> The question as to whether the Berndts should be doing war work has been considered each time the Executive of the Australian National Research Council has made any grant to them, and the Executive is satisfied and so too is scientific manpower, that in doing the present work, they are contributing towards a solution of a very important present and post-war reconstruction problem. I am sure you can understand why [this] work should be done in South Australia, as well as in New South Wales and Queensland and, of course, the obvious persons to do it in South Australia are the Berndts. They have already done work there and Mr Berndt is a native. [Their research] at one of the Government Settlements [Menindee] in this State was welcomed by the [NSW] Welfare Board, and their report...will prove very helpful. The problem with the more or less civilized aborigines is a very difficult one sociologically and psychologically, and the more detailed and deep analysis of all aspects of the problem, the more hope we have of finding a solution...we need work done on the subject all over Australia and, as Mr Berndt had worked to some extent under your guidance and with your blessing, I thought he should continue the research in South Australia...I would like to emphasize the fact too that this work should be done under the special conditions which arise during wartime, for this will affect their future.[48]

At its meeting on 22 December, the APB deferred consideration of the Berndts' application, 'as many of the natives are not accessible, being engaged in work related to the prosecution of the war, and also on the grounds that the applicants have a disturbing influence on the tranquillity of the natives on the Reserves'.[49] (Harrie Green's complaint had become an uncontested fact.) Ronald, as requested by the board, provided extra information on the purpose and potential significance of their research, methods and aims, but, at its January meeting, the APB again refused a permit.[50] Ronald wrote to the board seeking the reasons his application was not approved. Cleland noted that the APB was not required to give reasons for its decisions and directed that Berndt be advised that his letter had been 'received'.[51]

The Berndts—not deterred by the obstinacy of the board—left Adelaide for Murray Bridge to continue their research on the Jaralde (Ngarrindjeri) people, also travelling to other parts of South Australia, including the forbidden reserves, by camping near them. In March, they were in Port Augusta, followed by a visit to the Yorke Peninsula.[52] From there they set out for Ernabella Mission and

---

48   Elkin to Cleland, 10 November 1943, EP, 157/4/1/23.
49   APB Minutes, 22 December 1943, SRSA, GRG52/16.
50   APB Minutes, 19 January 1944, SRSA, GRG52/16.
51   APB Minutes, 2 December 1943, SRSA, GRG52/16.
52   C. H. Berndt to Houison, 22 March 1944, ANRC Records, NLA, MS 482, 857a.

spent some time at Macumba, 'where some ceremonies were being held; it was very cold camping out in the open but it was well worth while'.[53] Overall, the situation in South Australia was untenable, and despite their cheeky forays to the fringes of government and mission reserves, the Berndts were restricted and restrained in their anthropological work in South Australia; they needed to find work outside South Australia. They turned for assistance once more to Elkin, who was approached by the Australian Investment Agency (the Australian arm of Vestey Brothers, a British-based family company), which employed Aboriginal stockmen on its vast tracts of leased pastoral land in northern Australia.[54]

Elkin told J. A. Carrodus, Secretary of the Department of the Interior, that he had 'spent some considerable time with the General Manager of Vesteys [discussing] something of the scheme that [he and Chinnery] are trying to work, namely, to get Vesteys to employ Mr and Mrs Berndt as welfare officers among their Aboriginal employees'. The Berndts would keep an eye on 'conditions of employment, and gradually endeavour to build these up, so that the welfare of the Aborigines and the interests of Vesteys would both be served. Matters of diet and health, increase or decrease of population, and such like would be in their province.' He was pleased that 'after an interview with the Chairman of Directors and the Manager yesterday, the matter seems finalized, at least for the first six months survey'.[55] This matter had been under discussion since early February.[56]

In May 1944, Elkin wrote to the Berndts informing them of the position with Vesteys, detailing the purpose of the survey.[57] The Berndts eagerly accepted the position and were no doubt relieved that their travails in South Australia were at an end. The overall scheme, they were told by Elkin, had been discussed with Chinnery and A. S. Bingle, General Manager of the Australian Investment Agency (commonly referred to as Vesteys): 'each…concerned, from different points of view, with Aboriginal labour problems in that region and with the diminishing Aboriginal population on cattle stations, as well as with the future of the "bush" people and of Aborigines [eventually] released from military employment.'[58]

They were interviewed by Bingle, who decided to give them a six-month trial. Almost from the start, there were problems. Soon after agreeing to employ

---

53   C. H. Berndt to Houison, 22 June 1944, ANRC Records, NLA, MS 482, 857a.
54   Geoffrey Gray, *Abrogating Responsibility: Vesteys, anthropology and the future of Aboriginal people* (Melbourne, 2011 [forthcoming]).
55   Elkin to Carrodus, 9 August 1944, EP, 41/4/2/213.
56   Australian Investment Agency to Chinnery, 22 May 1944, Chinnery Papers [hereinafter CP]. Now in the NLA (MS 766), but I accessed this material when it was in the care of the family.
57   Elkin to R. M. Berndt and C. H. Berndt, 30 May 1944, EP, 246/613.
58   R. M. Berndt and C. H. Berndt, *End of an Era: Aboriginal labour in the Northern Territory* (Canberra, 1987), p. 29; Gray, *Abrogating Responsibility*.

them, Bingle was informed that Ronald had adverse reports emanating from South Australia and that the WA Government had refused to grant the Berndts a permit to visit Aboriginal reserves and of the unfavourable views of Military Intelligence. Initially Bingle had offered to provide the Berndts with a car and full camping equipment 'so they could wander at their convenience over the whole areas and become acquainted with their problem'.[59] This was not possible as Military intelligence imposed restrictions on the movement of the Berndts, forbidding movement north of Alice Springs without supervision. The Berndts were disappointed and believed it would seriously hinder their research. Nevertheless, Bingle and the Berndts decided to go ahead with the survey. Bingle's decision was aided in part by the recommendations of Elkin and Chinnery of the Berndts being the 'right type'.

As the survey progressed, relations between the Berndts and Bingle deteriorated. Vesteys was disappointed with what it saw as hostility towards the problems of running a commercial organisation that needed to show a profit; the Berndts accused Vesteys of not being interested in changing the conditions of employment and treatment of Aboriginal station workers.

When Bingle attempted to terminate their services at the end of December 1944, they refused to move from Birrundudu, an outstation of Gordon Downs, where they were at the time. Bingle relented and the survey continued. On the other hand, almost paradoxically, they occasionally threatened to resign, although not directly to Bingle. They wrote to Chinnery: 'after a period of nearly ten months, we see that Mr Bingle's attitude is quite unchanged, that conditions on the stations are unaltered, and that our position is not only negative but, at times, farcical.' Bingle did not 'wish to utilise us in the capacity of anthropologists, or welfare or liaison officers; he is concerned solely with the possibilities of active recruiting'. They considered resignation but decided to 'not resign for the time being, but will await our dismissal—unless of course you and Professor Elkin would like us to take the initiative in this respect'.[60]

The overriding problem and cause for much of their disagreement with Bingle was the way in which they were expected to recruit new labour; it was anathema, as they saw themselves as 'legitimate anthropologists' who would not violate existing [government] regulations…If there were to be any hint of this, then our future work would be jeopardized, a prospect which causes us considerable apprehension'.[61] They were 'unhappy to think that our association with this firm can prejudice our status as anthropologists, and so severely limit the natural course of our work'.[62] Concern for the treatment, conditions and welfare of

---

59   Bingle to Abbott, 10 August 1944, CP.
60   R. M. Berndt to Chinnery, 24 June 1945, CP.
61   R. M. Berndt to Chinnery, 21 August 1945, CP.
62   R. M. Berndt to Chinnery, 24 June 1945, CP.

Aboriginal pastoral workers was important but their future as anthropologists was equally as important.⁶³ Vesteys might have been hostile and resistant to change but the Berndts' time had not been wasted. They had collected 'a great amount of material, giving a fairly complete picture of the indigenous cultures of 'Gurindgi, 'Mudbara, 'Njining-'Wundgira, and 'Walbiri-'Woneiga people, including language, phonetic text, long song cycles of mythology, camp census, individual genealogies and case histories, etc.', and they were 'carrying out work in which we are deeply interested'.⁶⁴

They completed their report for Vesteys in June 1946. It was, they claimed with some justification, the first applied anthropological study undertaken in Australia.⁶⁵

In the event of either their dismissal or their resignation, they offered their services to Chinnery. They wanted

> to be of greater use to [the Native Affairs] Department and to the natives generally…if there was work available in the department at some time in the future it might be possible for us to carry out anthropological work in co-operation or connection with your Department, so that all the material obtained by us could be presented and utilised for the benefit of the natives.

They could be used to 'study special areas or given situations—e.g. the release of natives from military camps and the question of their ultimate absorption in pastoral or other occupations; or field or patrol work in Arnhem Land'. Most of the information they had collected while working at Vesteys they would make available for use by the Native Affairs Branch—'[f]or instance, data which we have collected in reference to individual natives (their names, case histories, etc.) should by rights be on the files of your Department, to supplement existing information'.⁶⁶ In addition, they had collected 'much information relating to culture contact, in which we were mainly interested' and which would be of use in the administration—that is, the management and control—of Aboriginal people.⁶⁷ Chinnery did not avail himself of their offer.

In September 1946, Elkin arranged funding for them to work at Yirrkala in eastern Arnhem Land, where they spent the next 12 months. They returned to Arnhem Land in 1949 and 1950 and frequently thereafter for the rest of their

---

63 See Geoffrey Gray, 'Abrogating Responsibility? Applied anthropology, Vesteys, Aboriginal labour, 1944–1946', *Australian Aboriginal Studies*, 2 (2000), pp. 27–39.
64 R. M. Berndt to Chinnery, 24 June 1945, CP.
65 R. M. Berndt, 'Aboriginal Fieldwork in South Australia in the 1940s and its Implications for the Present', *Records of the South Australian Museum*, 23:1 (1989), pp. 59–68.
66 Providing such personal material on Aboriginal people to a government agency seems to have presented no ethical problem for the Berndts at the time.
67 R. M. Berndt to Chinnery, 24 June 1945, CP.

lives. Between 1952 and 1953, they worked in the eastern Highlands of New Guinea, which formed the basis of their PhDs, which they completed in 1955. In all they spent almost 15 years in the field. The results of their research during the war—with few exceptions, particularly *From Black to White* (1951)—remained unpublished and unavailable after the war. A revised and edited version of their 1946 *Vesteys Report* was published as *End of an Era* in 1987, and their Lower River Murray research was published as *A World That Was* in 1993.[68]

There is little doubt that anthropological fieldwork absorbed them: they wanted nothing more than to remain in the field, working as anthropologists and collecting ethnographic information including artefacts.[69] Ronald had come to anthropology poorly qualified; he had left school at fourteen and, to enrol in the diploma course at the University of Sydney, he had to fudge his schooling and university entry. He needed not only determination but also patronage to achieve his ambition, unlike Catherine, who had followed what we might think of as a normal academic trajectory.

Ronald and Catherine gained considerable advantage over their contemporaries, many of whom had suspended their studies for the duration of the war. Their work for Vesteys did them no harm; it was after all under the auspices of Elkin, who controlled both funding and research in Australia. The grounds for Ronald's military exemption remain unclear but it benefited him directly in that he was able to conduct unimpeded anthropological research during the war. In the end, it was a combination of happenstance, luck, determination, ambition and strategic advice from, and the patronage of, Elkin that enabled the Berndts to work through the war at their chosen vocation. The war undoubtedly enhanced Ronald's career, providing opportunities and preferment that would never otherwise have arisen. At the war's end, they were described as 'these two most experienced and thorough workers'.[70]

Ronald overcame his poor academic record by initially being awarded a Diploma in Anthropology (in May 1943) but more importantly by obtaining a Bachelor of Arts degree by Research in 1951, followed by an MA in 1954, all based on his (and Catherine's) decade in the field, and the publications arising from that research. He attended the London School of Economics (LSE), with Catherine, where they were both awarded their doctorates in June 1956. He returned to a

---

68   For a list of their publications, see Robert Tonkinson and Michael Howard (eds), *Going It Alone? Prospects for Aboriginal autonomy: essays in honour on Ronald and Catherine Bendt* (Canberra, 1990), pp. 45–63.
69   Geoffrey Gray, '"Cluttering up the department": Ronald Berndt and the distribution of the University of Sydney ethnographic collection', *reCollections: Journal of the National Museum of Australia*, 2:2 (2007), pp. 153–79; Kate Brittlebank, 'Anthropology, Fine Art and Missionaries: The Berndt Kalighat album rediscovered', *Journal of the History of Collections* [e-journal], 2007, pp. 1–16, viewed 24 May 2008, <http://jhc.oxfordjournals.org/cgi/reprint/fhm017v1?ijkey=es6PvCTMKd7t0sK&keytype=ref> For the extent of their collection in the Berndt Museum, see <http://www.berndt.uwa.edu.au/>
70   Elkin, *Report of Committee on Anthropology*, 7 August 1947, EP, 161/4/1/81.

lectureship at the University of Sydney, but on the appointment of J. A. Barnes as Professor and the realisation that Barnes was not favourably disposed to him, Ronald accepted a position as Senior Lecturer in Anthropology at the University of Western Australia.[71] Between 1956 and his retirement in 1984, Ronald built a large and successful department. In 1963, he was made professor.

---

71 Geoffrey Gray and Doug Munro, 'Australian Aboriginal Anthropology at the Crossroads: Finding a successor to A. P. Elkin, 1955', *The Australian Journal of Anthropology*, 22:3 (2011), pp. 351–69.

7. The Road to Conlon's Circus—and Beyond: A personal retrospective

J. D. Legge

I was still a schoolboy when World War II broke out in September 1939. The son of a Presbyterian Minister in a small town to the north of Warrnambool, Victoria, I did most of my secondary schooling at Warrnambool High. After matriculating there, I went on to Geelong College to complete two years of 'Leaving Honours' as a preparation for university studies. From there, I had observed the Munich Agreement, the *Anschluss*, the Czechoslovakia crisis, the German–Soviet agreement of August 1939, and the German invasion of Poland, all leading up to the final outbreak of war. To an Australian schoolboy in his late teens, these events seemed to be essentially European affairs—indeed the war itself appeared almost as a continuation of World War I, and there seemed no reason why I should not embark, as planned, on a university course.

I enrolled at the University of Melbourne in what, in retrospect, seem the golden days of R. M. Crawford's School of History.[1] The emphasis was largely on European and British history: Crawford's modern history course dealing especially with the Renaissance and Reformation, Kathleen Fitzpatrick's course on Tudors and Stuarts, the Civil War, and the Protectorate and the Restoration, and Jessie Webb's ancient history course. This perspective followed naturally from the courses offered in Victorian secondary schooling of the day, leading on to university studies. There too we had studied British history from 1066 to 1914, European history from 1453 to 1848, and accompanying courses in English literature (including four or five plays of Shakespeare between years 9 and 11), English poetry from the fifteenth to the nineteenth centuries, and a foreign language—usually French or German. The result was a firmly Eurocentric view of the past, with Britain and Europe at the centre and Australia and the other dominions very much on the imperial periphery. But the central feature of Crawford's school was less the choice of periods for study than his underlying concern, in all courses, with process and theory.

It was his view that, as scientific explanation depended on underlying natural laws, so historians might discover laws of human behaviour and historical processes, and history might become a science.[2] There were obvious links here

---

1   Fay Anderson, *A Historian's Life: Max Crawford and the politics of academic freedom* (Melbourne, 2005).
2   This view was later developed in R. M. Crawford, 'History as a Science', *Historical Studies: Australia and New Zealand*, 3:11 (1947), pp. 153–75. The issues involved were canvassed by other writers: Carl Hempel, 'The Function of General Laws in History', *Journal of Philosophy*, 39:2 (1942), pp. 35–48; Patrick Gardiner,

with Marxist theory—economic causation, class struggle and the dialectical process towards the ultimate classless society—and in the early 1940s the left wing of the Labour Club and the University Branch of the Australian Communist Party made their own contribution to the arguments of the day.

Over the years these questions formed a matter of continuing debate and criticism. In particular, it was argued that though, formally speaking, historical explanation implied covering law, this did not mean that history bore any close relation to, say, physics or chemistry. The so-called laws were either trivial, or so obvious as to not require explication. They required so many 'fillers' to make them valid that they might be described as laws with only a single case, and therefore were not really laws at all. For these reasons, however logically valid the idea of 'covering laws' might be, they had little bearing on the actual nature of historical inquiry.[3] In later years, Crawford himself withdrew from the confidence of his earlier views.[4]

Crawford's teaching in the early 1940s interacted with philosophy as taught by George Paul. Paul had been a student in Cambridge of Ludwig Wittgenstein and his teaching in Melbourne challenged many of the received views of his colleagues and their students about appearance and reality. His History of Philosophy course was delivered to an audience of maybe 40 or 50, of whom only a small handful was formally enrolled in the subject. The others were students, and also staff, from other disciplines who found in these lectures a critical framework within which their respective disciplines could be set. For historians, Paul's analysis of some of Crawford's theoretical certainties enlivened undergraduate discussion of the central tenets of departmental doctrine, and contributed to Crawford's ultimate rethinking of his earlier position.

In the meantime, Australia's wartime involvement moved on and began to impinge even on the sheltered groves of academe. In my second year—in 1941—students were enrolled in the Melbourne University Rifles (MUR), a militia unit that had, I think, weekly parades in preparation for a training camp scheduled for the 1941–42 vacation. We entered camp—at Bonegilla, Victoria, near Wodonga—on 8 December 1941. This was the day of the Japanese attack on Pearl Harbor. As we gathered that morning on Spencer Street Station, news

---

The Nature of Historical Explanation (Oxford, 1952). For a further brief discussion of these views in Crawford's department, see J. D. Legge, 'Chance and Circumstance: A gradual journey towards Asian studies', in Nicholas Tarling (ed.), *Historians and Their Discipline: The call of Southeast Asian history* (Kuala Lumpur, 2007), pp. 55–71.
3   For example, W. H. Dray, *Laws and Explanation in History* (Oxford, 1960); Douglas Gasking, 'The Historian's Craft and Scientific History', *Historical Studies: Australia and New Zealand*, 4:14 (1950), pp. 112–24.
4   R. M. Crawford, 'The School of Prudence or Inaccuracy and Incoherence in Describing Chaos', *Historical Studies*, 15:57 (1971), pp. 27–42.

of Pearl Harbor spread through the ranks and we realised that the war had entered a new phase. The assumption was that we would now be in the Army for the duration.

There followed three months of intensive infantry training: weapons drill, long marches, night bivouacs and the rest. (Perhaps the most useful contribution we made to the actual war effort was being called on occasion to the Albury Railway Station where there was then a break of gauge between the Victorian railway system with its broad gauge and the NSW system with its standard gauge. Our task was to carry ammunition across the platform and load it on to the NSW carrier.)

At the end of three months, the members of the MUR were dispersed to a variety of operational units. My posting was to an anti-aircraft battalion, and I went into training at Braybrook where I learned to load and fire a 3.7-inch antiaircraft gun—quite an experience in itself. I was also one of the people who saw an unexpected and unusual plane—a float plane—emerge from the clouds for a couple of moments and then disappear into them again. Nobody—even our experienced teachers—could recognise it as one of ours, and the conclusion was that it was, in fact, a Japanese plane operating perhaps from a naval ship or a submarine somewhere off the Victorian coast.[5]

After this training, I was expecting to be posted to New Guinea, Darwin or somewhere else. Before this happened, I was called in by my commanding officer and told (rather scornfully, I think) that I had been nominated as a 'reserved student'. Reserved students were a small number who were exempted from service in order to complete their university courses. This was a policy designed to keep arts faculties in operation. I took a day's leave in order to visit the university and discuss the matter with Crawford, after which I decided to refuse the nomination and remain with my unit. A little later, however, I was again summoned by the CO and informed that the choice was not mine. I was to be drafted back to the university. So I was discharged, and, having at least done what seemed to be the proper thing by electing to remain in the Army, I was happy enough with the outcome.

The year 1942 was an interesting one to be a student. One tackled the demands of the final honours year in the company of a smaller student body, composed essentially of other reserved students, together with a number of close friends who were conscientious objectors awaiting their appearance before the tribunal

---

5 This might indeed have been the case. See the Travel Section of *The Weekend Australian*, 11–12 June 2005, for an article by Nicholas Shakespeare about the east coast of Tasmania. It recounts how a collapsible float plane operated from a submarine moored there in 1942. The date of March 1942 is about right. This might have been the plane seen from Braybrook.

that would consider their case for registration as objectors. (In the end, they were all able to continue with their studies.) Intellectual exchanges were intense and lasting friendships were made.

Final exams came and after the results were announced it was a matter of contemplating my next step. At this point, Max Crawford called me and told me he had been asked to nominate appropriate new graduates for an Army Research Section at Victoria Barracks. Would I go for an interview? I did and was appointed and, though I did not understand it at the time, entered a new phase of my educational process.

What was this Research Section (and later, more grandly, a Directorate)? An esoteric unit. It was vaguely known, within the Army, to be there but no-one quite knew what it did—including, it was said, those who were in it. That shadowy reputation remained even after the war. It was not in any sense an intelligence outfit as some thought, but was engaged in a wide variety of non-military inquiries of which more below. But essentially—at least initially—it was a base for the multifarious activities of its Commanding Officer, Major (later Lieutenant Colonel and Colonel) Alfred Conlon, known to all and sundry, including even his most junior subordinates, simply as Alf.[6]

Alf, stocky, crew cut, pipe smoking, was a familiar and perhaps conspiratorial figure in the corridors of power—that is, the back corridors. Pushing a particular barrow here, arguing a case there, managing to worm his way into the confidence of important people—politicians, bureaucrats, generals—and able to persuade them of the importance of proposals he had to make. He was thought to exercise great power and influence—sometimes correctly, sometimes not. One example was his ability to persuade the Prime Minister, John Curtin, of the need for a special committee to consider questions of national morale. Such a committee—the Prime Minister's Committee on National Morale—was indeed established. It included a number of senior academic figures, including Professor Julius Stone, Professor of Law at Sydney University, Professor R. D. (Pansy) Wright, Professor of Physiology at Melbourne University, and others. In fact, this particular initiative had a fairly short life and had little impact.

One of Alf's characteristics was his attitude to bureaucratic forms and procedures. He loved cutting through red tape and bureaucratic nonsense, partly because it got in the way of things he wanted to do and partly for the sheer enjoyment of doing it, even when it was totally unnecessary. The account given by Peter Ryan of his being plucked from the Leave and Transit Depot at Caulfield Racecourse[7] almost exactly paralleled my own experience in 1943. When appointed to the

---

6   For a lively portrait of Alf, see Peter Ryan, *Brief Lives* (Sydney, 2004), pp. 28–61; also John Thompson (ed.), *Alfred Conlon: A memorial by some of his friends* (Sydney, 1963).
7   Ryan, *Brief Lives*, p. 40.

Research Section, I had to go the LTD at Royal Park to be processed. Having been in the Army already, my papers had to be collected from wherever they were. This took some days and it was clear that my arrival at the section would be delayed. I rang Alf to inform him of the fact. He instructed me to have myself paraded before the CO. I said surely that was not necessary. It would not matter if I was a bit late. He said just do it. So to the Sergeant Major, who strongly resisted my request. I insisted, so he marched me angrily to the CO's door and said, 'I've got this man, Legge, here who insists on being paraded'. The CO was just putting down his phone and said, 'Ah, yes, I've just had a call about him from Victoria Barracks. He's to be out of here in half an hour. Just see to it, Sergeant Major.'

How did Alf achieve the rank of major and become head of the Research Section? Largely, it would seem, by a series of stops and starts. A Sydney man, born in 1908, he became a student at Fort Street High School, but dropped out before matriculating. He completed matriculation a little later by private study and went on to the University of Sydney. He completed an arts degree in 1931 and, like others of his generation, he was much influenced by John Anderson, the Challis Professor of Philosophy.[8] He then started medicine but dropped out after first year and began law. He came back to medicine in 1937 and completed second and third years before again dropping out. In fact, he did not complete the medical degree until after the war, graduating MB.BS in 1951—20 years after his initial enrolment at the University of Sydney. In 1939, he managed to become an undergraduate representative on the University Senate and in 1940–41 became Manpower Officer of the university.

It was in the latter capacity that he met the Adjutant-General, Brigadier General V. H. Stantke. Alf persuaded Stantke that the Army needed some kind of think tank to advise on non-military matters: civil affairs, postwar planning, and so on. Such a unit would provide a place to locate odd bodies—civilian types whom the Army wished to use in a specialist capacity: anthropologists in the Northern Territory to smooth Aboriginal contacts, agricultural scientists in New Guinea. Stantke was persuaded and the Research Section was established in the Adjutant-General's Department.

In my early weeks in the section, I was not at all sure what I was supposed to be doing. Alf would put me on to preparing short papers on matters on which he wanted to be informed, but there was not much system about that, at least at first. One such task was an investigation of German administration of north-eastern New Guinea before World War I. Another was a similar study of Australian administration in prewar Papua. (The latter in fact became rather more than a short paper and in due course was submitted for an MA at the

---

8 Brian Kennedy, *A Passion to Oppose: John Anderson, philosopher* (Melbourne, 1995).

University of Melbourne. I continued to work on this after the war and, after extensive revision, it was eventually published.[9] I am not sure that Alf ever read any of these little essays. He asked for them often on the spur of the moment. By the time I had written something, his interests had shifted to other things.

Shortly after my arrival in the section, General Stantke was transferred to the position of Commander of the Third Military District (Queensland) and was succeeded as Adjutant-General by Brigadier C. E. M. Lloyd. Lloyd knew he had this peculiar outfit under his immediate command, but did not like it or its commanding officer. He knew, however, that Alf had political friends in Canberra, including perhaps Prime Minister Curtin and therefore hesitated to dissolve us. He made a visitation to the section and went round asking each member of staff what he did—in some cases, a rather embarrassing question, given the context of the inquiry. As a mere private, I escaped interrogation. I believe Lloyd could have closed us down by a stroke of his pen, but he spared us that. He did the next best thing: he left us without anything to do.

So it was for some time, until Alf's next move. In typical fashion, he managed to sell himself to the Commander-in-Chief, General Sir Thomas Blamey, as he had once sold himself to Stantke. I remember Alf bustling into the office on the day this was finally arranged and, on bumping into me, saying, 'Well, John, we've had our orgasm'. From then on, we did have things to do of a wide variety of kinds: anything the Commander-in-Chief wanted information on. And in general Alf's knowledge of the Canberra political scene was of use to Blamey, who was not in touch with that world. The pair clearly entered into a close relationship, which lasted until the end of the war.

Our status changed. From having been a 'section', we were now a 'directorate' and later the Directorate of Research and Civil Affairs (DORCA). And amongst the various matters on which Alf gave advice, our major and continuing cluster of functions came to concern New Guinea. It was for this purpose that we acquired the anthropologists, economists, educationalists and others whose expertise was necessary to what became a major enterprise in postwar planning.

They were a remarkable array of people. They included one future Governor-General (John Kerr), one future Ambassador to Moscow, Secretary of Foreign Affairs and Governor of Tasmania (Jim Plimsoll), Australia's most distinguished librarian (Ida Leeson),[10] one of Australia's leading poets (James McAuley; and also Harold Stewart), a number of anthropologists (Camilla Wedgwood and Ian

---

9 J. D. Legge, *Australian Colonial Policy: A survey of native administration and European development in Papua* (Sydney, 1956) was published under the auspices of the Australian Institute of International Affairs.
10 Sylvia Martin, *Ida Leeson: A life* (Sydney, 2006).

Hogbin, both former students of Malinowski), a geographer (future founding Professor of Geography at the University of Melbourne, John Andrews), and a future Director of Melbourne University Press (Peter Ryan).

Some of these deserve further comment. Peter Ryan was a special case. He arrived in the directorate as a young warrant officer in 1944, having come directly from New Guinea where he had been cut off beyond enemy lines in the Huon Peninsula. He was one of a small group who had managed to survive, learn Pidgin, and build up a network of communication amongst the indigenous people. They had been, in effect, patrol officers sometimes in isolation from each other over quite a considerable area.[11] This experience was to be of direct relevance to the work of the directorate over the next few years.

McAuley and Stewart might also seem to be unusual recruits. What were they doing in an outfit of this kind? It was not that the Army needed poets, though it was sometimes suggested amongst the directorate's rank and file that if a cultivated society was what we were fighting for, poets should be prevented from being killed in the process. More seriously, Alf recognised McAuley's exceptional intellectual powers and in due course he did turn his mind to the serious study of New Guinea and became a recognised authority on colonial administration. Before then, of course, he and Stewart organised the famous Ern Malley hoax.[12] The Ern Malley poems were written in the directorate and sent off to Max Harris, editor of the literary journal *Angry Penguins*. They were intended to be meaningless and were constructed by choosing words at random, putting in irrelevant lines from a report on mosquito control, and constantly interrupting each other so that there could be no possibility of unconscious meaning. The intention had been to discover whether the members of the literary movement to which Harris belonged could distinguish between genuine poems and meaningless ones. Harris was taken in, but it could nevertheless be argued that the poems were not as meaningless as their authors claimed. It was reported that George Paul saw them as a hoax but attributed them to 'a' student of John Anderson. There were, in fact, two students but the pair was so much in tune with each other that there could have been more unity than they pretended.

From 1943, New Guinea remained the directorate's main preoccupation. Before the war, Australian New Guinea (the eastern part of the island) consisted of two territories: the Territory of New Guinea, administered by Australia under mandate from the League of Nations, and the Territory of Papua, covering the

---

11 See his account of that experience in his book: Peter Ryan, *Fear Drive My Feet* (Sydney, 1959).
12 Michael Heyward, *The Ern Malley Affair* (St Lucia, Qld, 1993).

south-eastern part of the island. The former was a German colony before World War I.[13] The latter, formerly a British Protectorate, had been passed over to Australia in 1906.

During World War II, the two administrations were brought under military control and were governed by a special unit: the Australian New Guinea Administrative Unit (ANGAU) under the command of Major-General B. Morris. Clearly, this involved a mass of complex and intricate issues and the need for a major non-military, or at least non-operational, input. Here lay the role of the directorate, advising the Army and also the Government about administrative matters. It became, in effect, the liaison body between ANGAU and the Department of External Territories in matters relating to the government of the combined territories. It was involved also at both ends of that liaison in considering the possible direction of postwar policies in New Guinea and in the South-West Pacific in general, and in maintaining contact with E. J. (Eddie) Ward, Minister of External Territories, and with the department.

The specific issues on which the directorate focused included the question of whether the wartime union of the two territories should be continued after the war; the codification of the laws of the new united administration; the question of whether indentured labour, on which the existing plantation system depended, should be abolished; future agricultural policy—cash cropping by the indigenous population, cooperatives, agricultural extension; and the health and education of a native elite. In short, the whole complex of what, in evolving British thinking, was called a development and welfare policy. Included in all this was the possibility of a future transition to independence, though in the context of contemporary thinking, that seemed to be a very long-term matter. Some of these issues were very contentious. The question of indentured labour was one of these. Planters looked with anger at proposals to abolish it, or at least to remove the penal sanction that gave force to contracts with native labourers. To the planter community, these proposals were seen as likely to stand in the way of future development.

In addition to engaging in research on various aspects of future policy, the directorate was made responsible for preparing and then establishing a school for the training of servicemen for appointment as patrol officers under ANGAU. This was done with an eye to the creation of a new territorial administration after the war. It was hoped that some of those who volunteered for training at the school would elect to stay on after the war. Some of them did, though most

---

13   Stewart Firth, *New Guinea under the Germans* (Melbourne, 1982); Charles Rowley, *The Australians in German New Guinea, 1914–1921* (Melbourne, 1958).

were keen to get back to civilian life as soon as the war ended. But it was also intended that the school would continue to exist after the war, to train members of a future reconstructed administrative service.

From then on, my own work lay within the directorate's New Guinea enterprise. In 1944 I transferred to the Australian Infantry Force (AIF) and was posted to New Guinea to serve in ANGAU. Based at Popondetta and Kokoda, I was able to travel in the surrounding area. (Having been involved in a study of prewar administration, this was a kind of continuing fieldwork.) Then, when the School of Civil Affairs opened in Canberra in 1945, I was commissioned and became one of its more junior staff members.

The school was located in some huts in the grounds of the Royal Military College (Duntroon). Duntroon was a somewhat terrifying neighbour—or landlord—for such a way-out institution as ours. We were always very conscious of this elite military college looking, as it were, over our shoulders at this very un-military batch of academics in uniform. But we managed to survive their scrutiny. New staff were added to our existing list. Colonel J. K. Murray (formerly Professor of Agriculture at the University of Queensland) was appointed as Commanding Officer (Chief Instructor, to give his proper title). Ralph Piddington, as second-in-command, joined Wedgwood and Hogbin as an additional anthropologist. Lucy Mair, Reader in Colonial Administration at the London School of Economics (LSE), was brought over from England to provide a different source of expertise. Ted Strehlow, son of a German missionary at Hermannsburg Mission in the Northern Territory and also, we understood, a member of the Arrernte people, filled a gap in our anthropological knowledge. Perhaps the most unusual appointment was that of a philosopher, Douglas Gasking— another student of Wittgenstein—to teach scientific method. We also imported two former members of the administrative staff of the territories, Jim Taylor and Jack McKenna, who provided a practical dimension. And Ida Leeson continued to lay the foundations of a relevant library.

The school was intended not merely to meet the immediate demand for territorial administrative officers but as part of a reshaping of the prewar system. As such it aimed to give a radically changed course of training for those entering the service. Before the war, recruits were given a preliminary period in the field and were then brought back to the University of Sydney where they were given a brief course in anthropology. But for the most part they learned on the job, and in so doing they tended to acquire the conservative outlook of the old territory hands. In contrast, the school sought to provide a broader educational experience that would give them a framework into which their practical experience could be fitted, and that would include long-term perceptions of administrative policy.

So, some imperial history, including late-nineteenth-century imperialism, the partition of Africa, and competing principles of what was then called 'native administration' (themes developed by Lucy Mair), plus some anthropology—not merely as an introduction to New Guinea societies as the Sydney course did, but setting that in the context of broader anthropological theory—plus some elementary legal training since the patrol officers would be magistrates. And Gasking's scientific method course was in effect an introduction to philosophy, which did capture the interest of the brighter students.

It was a grand—if not grandiose—plan, and it was intended as a new start. The Sydney University Anthropology Department was not a party to the planning for the school but was simply ignored—a fact that was humiliating for its head, Professor A. P. Elkin.[14] It was clearly exciting for the students who had been specially selected and who were taught, university style, by lectures and tutorials. It was also an exciting experience for staff, who felt that they were participating in an important and innovative enterprise. And for me, it launched me into the field of imperial history en route to the study of the Western Pacific and then South-East Asia. Intellectually, I enjoyed the stimulus of the (for me) new discipline of social anthropology and the introduction to social theory of a kind that I had not had in the Melbourne School of History.

The education of these embryonic patrol officers was seen as part of a dramatic departure in postwar policy towards New Guinea, which in turn reflected new perceptions of Australia's possible future role in the region as a whole. Alf and other senior members of the directorate had a warm rapport with the Minister for External Territories, Eddie Ward. In July 1945, Ward made a policy statement in his Second Reading speech to the House of Representatives on the PNG Provisional Administration Bill, setting out the broad lines of a new policy of development 'having regard to the moral and material welfare of the native inhabitants'. This 'new deal' for New Guinea, as it came to be called, was based on the principle of trusteeship, which replaced the League of Nations term—mandates—in all discussions of the government of dependent territories.

In my earlier study of prewar Australian administration of Papua, my emphasis had been on a perception of a continuing tension between European development based on a plantation system on the one hand, and welfare policies (health, education, agricultural extension) for the subject population on the other. Prewar administrators—Sir William MacGregor and Sir Hubert Murray[15]—were seen by me as having managed to moderate this tension and to have been more sensitive to the need to protect the native population than were their

---

14 Geoffrey Gray, '"I was not consulted": A. P. Elkin, Papua New Guinea and the politics of anthropology', *Australian Journal of Politics and History*, 40:2 (1994), pp. 195–213.
15 R. B. Joyce, *Sir William MacGregor* (Melbourne, 1971); Francis West, *Hubert Murray: The Australian Pro-Consul* (Melbourne, 1968).

counterparts in the neighbouring mandated Territory of New Guinea. Ward's speech (which certainly reflected the views of the directorate) addressed some of these questions.

The speech foreshadowed the continuance of what had already happened during the war: the creation of a single administration of the two territories, which were to become the Territory of Papua and New Guinea. The existing plantation system would remain, but with important changes to the indentured labour system that sustained it. The central feature of that system was the penal sanction imposed for breaches of contract—a feature that had a sniff of slavery about it. Ward's speech envisaged the abolition of the system within five years. As already indicated, this aroused great opposition amongst the planter community, which complained that policy was being influenced by 'long-haired anthropologists'—no doubt a reference to the school. In addition, extra funds were to be made available to enable a greater provision of educational facilities, medical services and support for native agriculture. Behind this thinking was the idea that Papua New Guinea would gradually move towards independence though, even in the directorate, it was not thought that this could come about in the near future.

And shortly after this speech, the Chief Instructor of the school, Colonel J. K. Murray, was appointed as the Administrator of the combined territories, which seemed an earnest indication of the influence of the directorate in planning postwar policy. Murray, too, had developed a good relationship with Ward—possibly an unlikely rapport, given Murray's stern military bearing and Ward's tougher, more larrikin style! But there it was. Undoubtedly, Murray saw himself as specifically selected to implement the new deal. And so, more or less, it came about. Policy changes formed a foundation for ultimate independence some 30 years later.

It remains a question, however, how far the directorate really could take credit for this. Its period of influence was not to last. The defeat of Japan meant that the Army had less time to prepare for the implementation of its new policies, and responsibility for these reverted to the department. When Blamey stepped down at the end of 1945, Alf's power base was gone, and officers of the department—perhaps more conservatively inclined—began to reassert their influence. And Ward himself appeared to lose interest as he was caught up in the pressures of postwar politics. The school continued. It moved to Sydney to quarters at Middle Head, and became the Australian School of Pacific Administration (ASOPA)—a civilian organisation that carried on with the task of educating PNG administrative staff. Many of the wartime staff began to disperse, going back to prewar occupations or to new jobs. McAuley stayed on for some time and so did Ida Leeson. Before the move from Canberra, I had been offered, and accepted, a lectureship in history at the University of Western

Australia. And new appointments were made. John Kerr stayed for a while as Principal in succession to Murray, and later that job went to Charles Rowley. Alf—desperately seeking a new power base—hoped that the school would become part of The Australian National University (ANU), which was about to be formed, and that its responsibility would extend to a role in the newly formed South Pacific Commission, but that was not to be.

For all that there is no doubt that the role of the directorate and the school had been considerable. Lucy Mair, having been brought from the LSE to teach in the school, observed in her subsequent study, *Australia in New Guinea* (1948), that it was no secret that many of the initiatives shaping future policy came from the directorate—a view echoed later by Brian Jinks, who, in a 1983 article, allowed that the directorate had created a climate of reform of a kind that had simply not been there before, and its ideas had acquired a momentum that enabled them to carry on after the war.[16] When a Liberal Government succeeded Labor in 1949, new ministers broadly accepted policies that had been hammered out during the war.

The most distinguished of these, Paul Hasluck (1951–63), would not have admitted that. In his account of his work as Minister for Territories, he mentioned the work of the directorate in a dismissive footnote, and, in the same work, he spoke contemptuously of 'a circle of confident people' at the school 'who were glowing with ideas about the proper way to administer the Territory and how to shape the world'.[17] He referred to J. K. Murray as 'a tired and disappointed man' who believed that he had been chosen by Ward 'to inaugurate and carry out vigorously an enlightened policy'. He also referred to the 'Ward–Murray policy' and spoke of Murray's 'misgivings about anything that came from Canberra'.

Certainly, Hasluck did not get on with Murray. He spoke of him as a 'good and devoted man' but found him uncooperative. For his part, Murray appeared stiff in manner and was suspicious, no doubt, that Hasluck would be in the hands of departmental officers and might betray the Conlon vision. Be that as it may, Murray was removed after a year and replaced with Donald Cleland, who had also had wartime experience in New Guinea as head of the Production Control Board, but who had not been part of the directorate's range of influence.

Much of this was made clear in Hasluck's account of his work as minister in *A Time for Building*. And he takes credit for laying the foundations of the new Papua New Guinea. He did deserve much of that. He was an able and scholarly person who already had an interest in the administering of indigenous people—

---

16   L. P. Mair, *Australia in New Guinea* (Melbourne, 1948), pp. 19–23; Brian Jinks, 'A. A. Conlon, the Directorate of Research and New Guinea', *Journal of Australian Studies*, 12 (1983), pp. 21–33.
17   Paul Hasluck, *A Time for Building: Australian administration in Papua and New Guinea, 1951–1963* (Melbourne, 1976), pp. 38, 15, respectively.

demonstrated in his study of Aboriginal policy in Western Australia, *Black Australians*. And he did propel Papua New Guinea a considerable distance along the road to eventual independence. At the same time, he had faults of his own. I was to get to know him well in the late 1940s when I was Lecturer in History at the University of Western Australia. After Hasluck had fallen out with External Affairs Minister, H. V. Evatt, and resigned from the department, Fred Alexander, Professor of History, managed to get Paul a readership in the department so that he could work on the volume he had been assigned to write in the official war history. For that period, we were close colleagues. We got on well together but I felt he had some odd limitations. He had a streak of arrogance and considerable intellectual stubbornness. His intellectual powers were not always matched by receptivity to alternative ideas. These characteristics, in my view, might be seen in his handling of the directorate in *A Time for Building*. It is my assessment that he was less than fair in his judgments about the directorate and the school.

But at the end of the war, and with the transfer of the school to Sydney, these arguments lay in the future. For me, my participation ended in 1945 with my move to Perth. Nevertheless, the influence of the directorate and the school over the previous three years remained. The experience had turned my attention away from the preoccupations of my undergraduate days and directed them rather to Western Pacific history. As a lecturer in the Department of History at the University of Western Australia, I found myself teaching a broad survey course on East and South-East Asia, and another on Australian history, but at the same time I was beginning to revise the work on the prewar administration of Papua. That was not finished until the early 1950s, but when, in 1948, I was the recipient of an ANU scholarship, I continued to work on other aspects of Western Pacific history in Oxford.

The ANU at that time was just coming into existence. There were to be no undergraduates. It was to be a graduate institution with, initially, four research schools: Medicine, Physics, Social Sciences and Pacific Studies. The Interim Council established the new scholarships in 1948 in order to provide a small body of graduate students in advance of the completion of the initial buildings, the appointment of academic staff and the recruitment of graduate students to study in Canberra. The Interim Council had also formed a committee in England of senior academic advisors to assist in the planning of the research schools. Two of these were Raymond Firth (Pacific Studies) and W. K. Hancock (Social Sciences). Hancock was Professor of Economic History at Oxford, and it was he to whom I reported on my arrival. He took me for a long walk across Port Meadow to Wytham and back, in the course of which I indicated the kind of study I had in mind. My plan was to focus on changes in British policy in the mid-nineteenth century, taking Fiji as a case study, using the Colonial Office records available in the Public Records Office, and examining especially the work of Sir Arthur Gordon, first Governor of Fiji after its cession to Britain. At the end of our walk, Hancock said, as he bade me farewell at his front door, 'Well, one thing is clear. You've come to the wrong place. You ought to be at Cambridge with [Jim] Davidson', who at the time was a Fellow of St John's College and University Lecturer in Colonial Studies.

It was a bit late for that. I, of course, knew of Jim Davidson—shortly to take up the Chair of Pacific History at the ANU—and had already planned to get in touch with him. Thereafter we met occasionally and he was a kind of unofficial supervisor. My official supervisor, V. T. Harlow, was a Caribbean historian with only a slight interest in the Pacific, but he was a firm critic of whatever I wrote. And there were others at Oxford who had an interest in my subject: A. F. Madden, of Rhodes House, E. T. (Bill) Williams, later Warden of Rhodes House, not to mention, amongst the student body, Fijian student Ratu Kamisese Mara, later to become his country's Prime Minister (and later President) after independence. And in London, Sir Arthur Gordon's son, Lord Stanmore, who made available his father's correspondence from his Fijian days.

In embarking on this topic, I was taking some of the African themes that had been developed by Lucy Mair at the School of Civil Affairs: Lord Lugard and his ideas of indirect rule in Nigeria, later notions of a development and welfare policy for colonial peoples, and so forth. In effect, I was taking these ideas back in time and using them as a framework for the study of Fiji. The thesis was eventually completed, after a resubmission, and was published as *Britain in Fiji, 1858–1880* (1958). On my return to Perth in 1951, it was my intention to pursue Western Pacific issues further. I had in mind a study of alternative missionary preconceptions in different territories; however, the main centre for such work in Australia was the ANU—a long way from Western Australia. There was a possibility for a time that there might be an opening in Jim Davidson's Department of Pacific History. This did not eventuate, however, and in 1954 I made a sharp decision to change course, and to switch my focus from the Pacific to South-East Asia. I began to learn Indonesian, and then, in 1956, with the aid of a Carnegie Fellowship, I made my way to Cornell University for a semester, followed by my first spell of fieldwork in Indonesia.[18]

Thereafter it was South-East Asia rather than the Pacific, but no doubt with intellectual influences carried over from the directorate and the Australian School of Pacific Administration.

---

18 For an account of that, see Legge, 'Chance and Circumstance', pp. 55–71.

Part II: The New Zealanders

Doug Munro

The experiences of the New Zealand scholars reveal a different pattern to those of their Australian counterparts. The depiction in the previous section is one of cohesiveness, because almost all the dramatis personae were involved in some way or another with the Directorate of Research and Civil Affairs (DORCA); the Army needed anthropologists. In Australia, and in Britain, the state mobilised scholarship as well as brawn, if the distinction might be allowed. But it was different in New Zealand, which was too small and too far from the theatres of war for scholarship to be pressed into the war effort on any scale. There were no New Zealand equivalents to the Committee on National Morale (CNM) or DORCA; there was no Bletchley Park (the British codebreaking facility to intercept high-level German intelligence); there was nothing akin to the British Naval Intelligence project, which provided wide-ranging information to naval operations in a series of 'Admiralty Handbooks'; there was nothing in the nature of British 'Civil Histories' of the domestic war effort.[1] More noticeable was an exodus of young New Zealanders to enlist in the Royal Air Force, including the historian-to-be Brian Dalton, who became Foundation Professor of History at the James Cook University of North Queensland.[2]

There was, however, some mobilisation of New Zealand scientists during World War II—notably, the Radio Development Laboratory. So named to disguise its real purpose, the laboratory developed types of radar for local defence and ultimately for use in the Pacific War.[3] Once it was evident—after the Battle of Midway in June 1942—that the Japanese would not be invading New Zealand,[4] there was a conscious dispersal of New Zealand's scientific talent abroad. Robin

---

1   F. H. Hinsley and John Stripp (eds), *Codebreakers: The inside story of Bletchley Park* (Oxford, 1992); Hugh Clout and Cyril Gosme, 'The Naval Intelligence Handbooks: A monument to geographical writing', *Progress in Human Geography*, 27:2 (2003), pp. 153–73; Denys Hay, 'British Historians and the Beginnings of the Civil History of the Second World War', in M. R. D. Foot (ed.), *War and Society: Essays in honour and memory of J. R. Weston, 1928–1971* (London, 1973), pp. 39–57; J. H. Davidson, *A Three-Cornered Life: The historian W. K. Hancock* (Sydney, 2010), ch. 6 ('The Civil Histories').
2   L. H. Thompson, *New Zealanders with the Royal Air Force. Volume 1: European theatre* (Wellington, 1953); Kett Kennedy, 'Foreword: Brian James Dalton, 1924–1996', in Anne Smith and B. J. Dalton (eds), *Doctor on the Landsborough: The memoirs of Joseph Arratta* (Townsville, Qld, 1997), pp. v–vii. Dalton's major work is *War and Politics in New Zealand, 1855–1879* (Sydney, 1967).
3   Ross Galbreath, 'New Zealand Scientists in Action: The Radio Development Laboratory and the Pacific War', in Roy MacLeod (ed.), *Science and the Pacific War: Science and survival in the Pacific, 1939–1945* (Dordrecht, 2000), pp. 211–27; Ross Galbreath, 'Dr Marsden and Admiral Halsey: New Zealand radar scientists in the Pacific War', in John Crawford (ed.), *Kia Kaha: New Zealand in the Second World War* (Melbourne, 2002), pp. 252–63.
4   The widespread fear of invasion was unfounded because Japan never seriously entertained occupying the isolated outpost that New Zealand strategically was. An invasion would have tied up troops and naval vessels

Williams, for example, became a member of the British Group in the Manhatten Project to develop the atomic bomb.[5] If New Zealand scholars of whatever stripe were going to be mobilised for the war efforts, it would overwhelmingly be overseas and not necessarily in their capacity as scholars.

Hence, two themes of the present section are dispersal and expatriation. The historians Jim Davidson and Neville Phillips, the anthropologist Derek Freeman, and the polymath Dan Davin went to England for basically three reasons: the colonial cringe—the idea that all things British were superior; the associated yearning of people in a small and isolated country, if not to see that wider world then at least to visit the 'old country'; and the lack of postgraduate training in New Zealand. As Davin later remarked, New Zealand society in the 1930s was so discouraging that 'we got out in droves'.[6] A common (and autobiographical) theme in the fiction of the time was the discouraging, even hostile, environment that New Zealand writers had to endure.[7] Thus, Davidson, Phillips and Davin took the colonial high road, enrolling at Oxbridge on one or other of the few postgraduate scholarships that were available in the mid to late 1930s—in Davin's case, a Rhodes Scholarship.

Davin, Davidson and Phillips all went to England before 1939 and were then caught up in the war mobilisation. There were basically two paths for young scholars in wartime Britain. There was service of one kind or another in the domestic war machine, such as Bletchley Park, or in one of the government ministries. Such was Davidson's revulsion of war and his even greater revulsion against killing another human being—not to mention a reluctance to disrupt his studies—that he took all possible steps to avoid being swept into the armed forces. He was, instead, able to finish his PhD thesis and only then was he drawn into war work—as a researcher, writer and editor for the Admiralty's 'Naval Intelligence Handbooks' relating to the Pacific Islands. In contrast, many younger British-based scholars, including Davin and Phillips, saw it as their duty to enlist—as, for example, did John Mulgan, another young New Zealander at Oxford, although he had no 'illusions about the stupidity of military life'.[8]

---

needed elsewhere. Gerald Hensley, *Beyond the Battlefield: New Zealand and its Allies, 1939–45* (Auckland, 2009), pp. 178–9; see also F. L. W. Wood, *The New Zealand People at War: Political and external affairs* (Wellington, 1958), pp. 244–5.

5   Robin Williams, Telephone interview, 31 May 2010 (Wellington, NZ). Williams embarked on postgraduate research at Cambridge after the war, was successively Vice-Chancellor of Otago University and The Australian National University. Now in retirement, Williams ended his career as Chairman of the New Zealand Public Service Commission. See also Owen Wilkes, 'New Zealand and the Atomic Bomb', in Crawford, *Kia Kaha*, pp. 264–75.

6   Quoted in Paul Millar, *No Fretful Sleeper: A life of Bill Pearson* (Auckland, 2010), p. 200.

7   See Patrick Evans, *The Penguin History of New Zealand Literature* (Auckland, 1990), *passim*.

8   Quoted in Vincent O'Sullivan, *Long Journey to the Border: A life of John Mulgan* (Auckland, 2003), p. 207.

With the approach of war, and correctly foreseeing what the rise of fascism would entail, he joined the territorials in 1938 and thence to postings in Northern Ireland, the Middle East and Greece.

Derek Freeman's war service was different again. He had gone to Western Samoa in 1940 as a schoolteacher, ostensibly to earn a living but really as a means to conduct fieldwork on the side. He shared Davidson's distaste for war and got himself offside with both the administration and the expatriate community as 'a man of peculiar ideas (and undoubtedly a pacifist)'. But the attack on Pearl Harbor (in December 1941) made such a stance untenable; eventually returning to New Zealand, Freeman enlisted in the Navy's Scheme B for an officers' training course in Britain. Arriving in England in 1944, he pursued what anthropological study he could, built up a network of associates in the discipline, and set himself up for postgraduate work in immediate postwar Britain. He made the most of his limited opportunities.

With the end of the war, our scholars had to decide whether or not to return to New Zealand—and from this consideration emerges the nebulous question of identity. Was one still an expatriate, who feels positively about New Zealand from afar, or had one become an exile, nurturing a sense of alienation or even betrayal?[9] It is not difficult to see why some scholars were reluctant to return to New Zealand. As well as being a conformist and generally philistine environment, and inimical to a life of the mind, there was not much on offer by way of suitable employment. New Zealand was simply unable to absorb all the talent it produced—what James Belich has described as 'cultural overproduction'.[10]

Davin noted the double bind: 'the staffs of the New Zealand universities were so small that there were no jobs for the expatriate scholars to return to…And where, in New Zealand in 1945, could I have found a job at all equivalent in interest or emolument to my job at the Clarendon Press?'[11] Davin exaggerates in saying that there were *no* academic openings in New Zealand, but they were certainly scarce. Moreover, there were few other employment outlets for returning scholars, unless they could be absorbed into the public service or schoolteaching. During the 1930s and 1940s, the University of New Zealand had four constituent colleges. The individual departments were small: typically a male professor, usually from overseas, and a sole lecturer or tutor, often a female. In the late 1940s, there was some expansion to cater for an influx of

---

9   The distinction is that of Richard Ellmann, 'Becoming Exiles', in *A Long the Riverrun: Selected essays* (London, 1988), p. 33.
10 James Belich, *Paradise Reforged: A history of the New Zealanders from the 1880s to the year 2000* (Auckland, 2001), pp. 341–5.
11 Dan Davin, 'Correspondence', *New Zealand Journal of History*, 13:1 (1979), p. 105.

returned servicemen on rehabilitation scholarships, but the numbers of social scientists, particularly historians, in each university department could still be counted on the fingers of one hand.

At the very time that more university places were becoming available for historians, however, their employment opportunities were contracting on other fronts. The government-sponsored centennial celebrations had created openings in the late 1930s and early 1940s with the commissioning of a number of Historical Surveys, a separate series of Pictorial Surveys and an Historical Atlas.[12] Davidson was employed on the last while he anxiously scanned the horizon for the scholarship that would take him to England. Following the Centennial celebrations in 1940, the Surveys and Atlas were reconstituted as separate branches within the Department of Internal Affairs. Even that was a chimera; both were put to the sword after the 1949 election with the advent of a new government, for whom scholarship and the arts meant nothing. The War History Branch, for which Davin and Phillips wrote volumes on Crete and Italy respectively, did manage to survive but with diminished funding.[13]

Phillips was the only one of the quartet of New Zealanders who returned to New Zealand, and only because he had to. Ironically, Phillips was the one least suited to go back. He embraced all that England had to offer—what his son Jock Phillips (in this volume) refers to as 'the excitement and stimulus of living in a place with real culture, tradition and history'. But in 1946 he had a family to support, so he wrote to J. H. E. Schroder, his former boss at the Christchurch *Press*, asking for a job. Schroder, who was on the Council of Canterbury University College, mentioned his name to the History Professor, James Hight, and Phillips was offered a lectureship. He slid in with a deceptive ease when, in fact, he was very lucky indeed. He was luckier still in succeeding Hight as professor three years later, being placed ahead of a more experienced and better published candidate.[14] Phillips eventually became Vice-Chancellor, so his interrupted war years did not retard his career. What, at the time, appeared to be a lost opportunity did not turn out so bad in terms of its lasting consequences. But his heart lay in England, and upon retirement he resettled in his country of choice. Davin presents the obvious contrast. For all his self-conscious New Zealandness,

---

12 William Renwick (ed.), *Creating a National Spirit: Celebrating New Zealand's Centennial* (Wellington, 2004). The Centennial Branch was the watershed in New Zealand historiography between the old style of 'amateur' historians and the hard-nosed 'professionals'. See Rachel Barrowman, '"Culture-organising": Joe Heenan and the beginnings of state patronage of the arts', *New Zealand Studies*, 6:2 (1996), pp. 3–10; Chris Hilliard, *The Bookmen's Dominion: Cultural life in New Zealand, 1920–1950* (Auckland, 2006), pp. 84, 106.
13 Michael Bassett, *The Mother of All Departments: The history of the Department of Internal Affairs* (Auckland, 1997), pp. 158–60; Ian McGibbon, '"Something of them is here recorded": Official history in New Zealand', in Jeffrey Grey (ed.), *The Last Word? Essays on official history in the United States and British Commonwealth* (New York, 2003), pp. 53–68; Dan Davin, *Crete* (Wellington, 1953); N. C. Phillips, *Italy. Volume 1: The Sangro to Cassino* (Wellington, 1957).
14 See Edmund Bohan, 'McLintock, Alexander Hare, 1903–1968', *Dictionary of New Zealand Biography*, updated 22 June 2007, <http://www.dnzb.govt.nz/>

Davin lived in Oxford by preference, although he had to make adjustments in order to come to grips with the peculiarities of the English. Of the other two, Davidson completed his degree and was able to contribute to the war effort by continuing with historical research whilst Freeman used his scaled-down opportunities as the springboard to a future career in anthropology.

The New Zealand scholars who were in Britain at the outbreak of World War II had very different experiences to those who remained behind—unsurprisingly, because the country did not have to defend its shores or endure bombing attacks. Davidson's mentor, J. C. Beaglehole, almost had a non-war. Too young to have been involved in the First World War and just too old to be liable for call-up in the Second, he sat it out for the duration. Only two of his relatives, whom he did not know very well, were killed on active service. There was the inconvenience of petrol rationing, the relative austerity and the uncertainty of it all. He chafed under the restrictions of wartime censorship and made unsuccessful representations to have it moderated. Otherwise, he was largely unaffected.[15]

Our four New Zealand scholars, in contrast, were closer to the fray and in no way can they be said to have had non-wars. But their experience of war was not entirely negative, unpleasant though it was at the time. Davidson's work for the Naval Intelligence Division was the springboard to a future academic career at Cambridge and The Australian National University. Freeman's naval service took him to England where he made the necessary contacts and arrangements for postgraduate work. Davin's and Phillips' lengthy army service did not impede their careers, and might even have provided impetus in the sense that their combat experiences resulted in publications they would not otherwise have written. War is not usually thought of as an enabler, but in these cases it was.

---

15   Tim Beaglehole, *A Life of J. C. Beaglehole: New Zealand scholar* (Wellington, 2006), pp. 239, 245, 310–11.

8. Derek Freeman at War

Peter Hempenstall

When one thinks of Derek Freeman (1915–2001) at war, World War II does not come automatically to mind. Rather one remembers the long, drawn-out war of attack, counterattack and exhausting attrition that immersed Freeman through the 1980s over Margaret Mead and her Samoan researches. Freeman's campaign to demonstrate the shoddiness of Mead's research and the error in her findings about the nature of adolescent sexual freedom among Samoans stretched from the 1960s to virtually the end of his life in 2001.[1] This is not the place to rehearse the attacks and vilification that Freeman endured from the North American anthropology establishment, but they seared themselves into his soul. And he fought back relentlessly, on the principle that error could be gradually eliminated when all the evidence was revealed, debated and synthesised.

Derek Freeman was perennially at war with others, and they with him. If it was not over Margaret Mead and the nature of Samoan society it was over his later conversion to what he called an 'interactionist anthropology model', in which anthropologists would learn to absorb the neuroscientists' discoveries about brain functions and their evolution and apply them to the study of behaviour in culture. This would produce a more holistic study of humankind, according to Freeman. But it had him (mis)cast as a crude sociobiologist and ethologist, a follower of Konrad Lorenz, E. O. Wilson and others, and therefore dangerously close to racial theories of human evolution.[2]

War and rumours of war swirled endlessly round Freeman. His tenure as Professor of Anthropology at The Australian National University's Research School of Pacific and Asian Studies was marked by controversies over his acerbic relationship with some of his postgraduate students and with colleagues. His acute intellect and passionate mission to eliminate error led him to adopt a seminar debating style that was intimidating, ruthless and, to many observers, hostile to the conventions of academic discourse.[3] He was involved in several

---
1 See Derek Freeman, *Margaret Mead and Samoa: The making and unmaking of an anthropological myth* (Cambridge, Mass., 1983); Derek Freeman, *The Fatal Hoaxing of Margaret Mead: An historical analysis of her Samoan work* (Boulder, Colo., 1999).
2 See Derek Freeman, 'Sociobiology: The "antidiscipline" of anthropology', in Ashley Montagu (ed.), *Sociobiology Examined* (New York, 1980), pp. 198–219; Derek Freeman, 'Choice, Values and the Solution of Human Problems', in John B. Calhoun (ed.), *Environment and Population: Problems of adaptation* (New York, 1983); Derek Freeman, *Dilthey's Dream: Essays on human nature and culture* (Canberra, 2001), pp. 63–4.
3 The ghost of Derek Freeman patrols the pages of the book of reminiscences about the Coombs Building at the ANU, where his Department of Anthropology was housed: Brij V. Lal and Allison Ley (eds), *The Coombs: A house of memories* (Canberra, 2006), pp. 45, 65–6, 75–6, 85, 121, 237; and in John Barnes, *Humping My Drum: A memoir* (Self-published: <www.lulu.com>, 2008), pp. 270–2, 274, 278, 337–8, 345–58, 363, 425, 432.

controversial incidents that drew his name and eccentricity to the attention of the wider community. One of these involved his own private 'war' against the donation of an Aztec calendar stone to The Australian National University (ANU) by the Mexican Ambassador in Canberra, which involved lurid stories of blood throwing and assaults.[4]

But even Freeman's death in July 2001 did not lead to an armistice. He continues to excite ill feeling among some colleagues and the war against his name runs on, seemingly unabated, even as this piece is being written.[5] In March 2008, a new theatre of war was opened in the web pages of the Association for Social Anthropology in Oceania (ASAO). An innocent request on the ASAO Bulletin Board about the whereabouts of Freeman's 1940s ethnographic study of the village of Sa'anapu, which he wrote as a thesis for his Diploma in Anthropology at the University of London, elicited an outpouring of agonised correspondence about Freeman among anthropologists in America, Europe and the Pacific. Many of the mailings retailed rumours and gossip about this larger-than-life figure, even the rumour that Derek had stolen and burnt all library copies of the thesis to prevent anyone investigating his conventional structuralist ideas of the time, which ran counter to his later thinking. Others wondered whether he had ever written a *real* thesis, for he seemed to hide away any evidence of his earliest forays into Samoan research. In fact, a thread of commonsense ultimately prevailed in the postings: one of his former students confirmed Derek's readiness to lend his thesis to those studying Samoa and the correspondence winkled out its eventual provenance and fate.[6]

But before this 'truce' was reached, the armies of anti-Freemanites repeated allegations that in life Freeman was clearly 'mad' and guilty of bullying, damaging behaviour in his relations with colleagues and students. The irony was that Freeman was in this instance himself a victim of posthumous cyber-bullying—a form of warfare that some correspondents were notably uneasy about for it seemed to rival Freeman's own reputation and presented as acts of revenge. 'Derek Freeman is our Other', wrote one contributor. 'He is constructed out of all the things that our mentors should never do'.[7]

---

4   This incident can be followed in Freeman's own correspondence with university authorities. His extensive papers are held in the Mandeville Special Collections of the Geisel Library at the University of California, San Diego [hereinafter Freeman UCSD]. See box 150, folders 12–13.
5   The latest of numerous rebuttals of Freeman's attacks on Mead is Paul Shankman, *The Trashing of Margaret Mead: Anatomy of an anthropological controversy* (Madison, Wis., 2009).
6   The present author edited and annotated Freeman's thesis, presented for the Academic Diploma in Postgraduate Anthropology at the University of London in 1948. Freeman never finished his undergraduate degree at Victoria University College in Wellington in the 1930s and was therefore not allowed to pursue a PhD using his Samoan work. His diploma thesis was published as Derek Freeman, *The Social Structure of a Samoan Village Community*, Peter Hempenstall (ed.) (Canberra, 2006). Freeman later wrote his PhD thesis on the Iban people of Sarawak, a version of which was published as *Iban Agriculture: A report on the shifting cultivation of hill rice by the Iban of Sarawak* (London, 1955).
7   Posting, <asaonet@listserv.uci.edu>, 4 March 2008.

By a roundabout way, World War II did figure in this latest campaign. A story was posted quoting an unnamed informant who remembered talking to Freeman in the 1960s about his presence in Singapore in 1945 when the Japanese surrender was taken. Freeman allegedly remembered an Australian Navy admiral announcing that the sailors could rape and loot, but they must not disturb or destroy any official records. The informant claims this had a profound effect on Freeman, as did the behaviour of Allied sailors on the island.[8] To explore where Freeman was during World War II, and how war laid the foundations for his later career and feelings, it is necessary to begin in his homeland, New Zealand, and investigate the origins of his various quests.

John Derek Freeman was born in Wellington on 16 August 1916. His Australian-born father was a hairdresser with an elegant salon in the city. Derek's mother, also born in Australia but resident in New Zealand since she was a child, was the daughter of a prominent Presbyterian family. She possessed undoubted influence over the young Derek. She wanted him to be a missionary (which, eventually, in a way, he became). Family members were formidable Christian characters and the house was suffused with a religious atmosphere. A constant tension reigned between his mother, who was accustomed to high culture and good music, and his father, who was no intellectual and simply wished Derek to join him in the business. Their relationship was the crucible in which Freeman's personality was formed—Derek admitting late in life that he was perhaps turned against his father by his mother: the 'good' mother and the 'ineffectual' father who did not understand the higher values and was condescending and negative towards him.[9] His sister, Margaret, remembered him as strong, argumentative and fearsome in his strength: 'you always were going to be a "Great Man".'[10] Yet Freeman suffered from self-doubt at school over his inability to spell.

He went on to Wellington Technical College—another blow from the wrong side of the street, allegedly because his father refused to pay his fees to university. But he worked to earn the money and in 1934 enrolled at Victoria University College (one of the four colleges within the University of New Zealand) to study psychology, philosophy and education.[11] The college was small—no more than 700–1000 students during the 1930s—and suffered from the financial sacrifices

---

8   Posting, <asaonet@listserv.uci.edu>, 5 March 2008.
9   Personal communication, Don Tuzin, 31 August 2006.
10 Margaret Brock to Freeman, 8 August 1992, Freeman UCSD, box 153, folder 5.
11 The material on Freeman's early life, when not separately documented, comes from interviews with Freeman's wife, Monica Freeman, in October and November 2002, December 2003, and December 2005; discussions with Don Tuzin, who before his death in 2007 was working on a biography of Freeman; from Don Tuzin, 'Derek Freeman (1916–2001)', *American Anthropologist*, 104:3 (2002), pp. 1013–15; and Derek Freeman, 'Notes Towards an Intellectual Biography', which became the opening chapter in G. N. Appell and T. N. Madan (eds), *Choice and Morality in Anthropological Perspective: Essays in honour of Derek Freeman* (Albany, NY, 1988), pp. 3–27. I have used Freeman's annotated copy of this manuscript chapter, loaned by Mrs Freeman, since it presumably represents his 'authorised' version.

forced on all educational institutions by the Great Depression. Nonetheless, the 1930s was the beginning of an age of social-science initiatives at Victoria, with modernist trends in educational development filtering through and appointments of young intellectuals in psychology, history, English and education to take over from a tiring professoriate of an older generation.[12] Two Beagleholes were at the centre of the renaissance: John, as a lecturer in history, later the pre-eminent editor of James Cook's journals and his biographer, and his younger brother, Ernest, in psychology, student of Ginsburg at London and Sapir at Yale and a researcher alongside Peter Buck at the Bishop Museum in Hawai'i. Ernest Beaglehole eventually rose to the Chair of Psychology and produced anthropological studies as well.[13] Under his teaching, Derek Freeman began to imagine the possibility of doing anthropological fieldwork with a psychological edge somewhere in Polynesia (though there was as yet no formal course in anthropology at Victoria).

The 1930s also of course witnessed the crisis of capitalism in the Depression, alongside the rise of fascism, socialist resistance by communists throughout Europe, and the slide towards world war again. These had their bitter impacts on the college where academic freedom became an issue in the establishment's opposition to socialist and pacifist tendencies. Indeed in 1940, with war broken out, the College Council terminated the appointment of a tutor who had published a pacifist pamphlet, and New Zealand descended into an era of censorship and internment harsher even than Britain's.[14]

Derek Freeman was to fall foul of this approach to war himself (though he was never a Marxist or communist fellow traveller), but as a student in the 1930s he took a full and active part in the life of Victoria College, whose student body was reputed to be the most radical in New Zealand.[15] He was secretary of the anti-war movement, ran a Free Discussions Club, produced and acted in plays, and was on the editorial staff of the students' annual magazine, *Spike*, from 1936 and was literary editor then editor of the weekly students' newspaper, *Salient*, in 1938–39. In 1937 he took out first prize in *Spike*'s literary competition with three poems that were judged 'intricate and difficult', though he showed 'a greater poetic sensibility and a wider range of knowledge and experience than any of the others'.[16] One of his winning poems, '(lovE)ution', suggested a growing disillusionment with New Zealand:

---

12   Rachel Barrowman, *Victoria University of Wellington 1899–1999: A history* (Wellington, 1999), pp. 50–75 ('The Hunter Years').
13   Ibid., p. 57.
14   See Jonathan Scott, *Harry's Absence: Looking for my father on the mountain* (Wellington, 1997); also J. E. Cookson, 'Appeal Boards and Conscientious Objectors', in John Crawford (ed.), *Kia Kaha: New Zealand in the Second World War* (Auckland, 2002), pp. 173–98.
15   Barrowman, *Victoria University of Wellington*, p. 53.
16   *Spike*, 36:65 (1937), p. 49.

> ONCE   I would have said—
> > 'There is nothing of confining here
> > no hemming in
> > between the deliberate dissonance of walls
> > naught but the full quick-flowing beauty
> > of water curving round a stone'.
>
> AND NOW 'Empty—
> > Empty are the ways of this land,
> > As empty as a Lord mayor's laugh.
> > Empty—yes and bitter
> > — bitter as the unvintageable sea.'

Another poem, 'Bishop', also published in *Spike*, reveals his distaste for militarism in unambiguous terms:

> I watched him stand
> By the Military Band
> With scroll in hand,
> And with syrupy tongue
> Sing songs long sung
> Of 'heroes young'
> (who by some mischance
> made excellent dung
> for the farmers of France)
> Of 'rearming fast,'
> And 'things that last,'
> And 'all the glories of the past.'
> For such as he that stand and vent
> The old men's fetid sacrament,
> For such as he, and none exempt
> The virulence of my contempt.[17]

The same year, he was prominent in a public talk by the German Consul, Dr Hellenthal, at the Free Discussions Club. After a lengthy attempt by Hellenthal to praise the accomplishments of Hitler and the Nazi Party, glossing over questions of rearmament and persecution of the Jews, Freeman and others challenged him to confront the evidence of violence by the Nazi regime. Freeman quoted a British report that documented 447 murders committed by Nazis and wanted to produce photos of people showing injuries from beatings. Hellenthal declared himself insulted and, amid cries for him to justify himself, he walked out.[18]

---

17 Ibid., p. 30.
18 'Free Discussions Club. Unofficial report on the meeting held on the 8th April 1937' (copy from Mrs Freeman, in author's possession); also Tim Beaglehole, *A Life of J. C. Beaglehole: New Zealand scholar* (Wellington, 2006), p. 230.

War was already in the air, and, in 1938, the year of Munich and appeasement, Derek entered the Plunket Medal for Oratory. He did not win the medal but he did win acclaim for his speech on the English poet John Cornford, grandson of Charles Darwin, killed in the Spanish Civil War; Freeman's speech was a semi-political appeal to the audience to get involved. Spain's agonies more and more provoked Freeman's anger and passion; he won 'best speaker' arguing against Franco's cause in a debate in July 1938.[19] Freeman much later told his student Don Tuzin that the Spanish Civil War seemed to him the end of civilisation and he resolved to 'get out' of the increasingly tight social and moral atmosphere of New Zealand.[20] He might also have been moved by a personal tragedy. Climbing—Freeman's favourite pastime—on the flank of Mt Evans in the Southern Alps, he fell with two companions he was roped to: Norman Dowling and Stan Davis. Dowling was killed; Freeman and Davis survived, but Freeman had to carry Davis off the mountain and leave Dowling's body behind.[21] Freeman's lifelong fascination with mountains was shadowed by this youthful trauma.

The year World War II broke out, Freeman became a disciple of the Indian divine Jiddu Krishnamurti and his radical scepticism about all dogmatisms. Krishnamurti planted in the young student a seed of belief that worldly enlightenment was possible through critical inquiry and 'the primacy of the individual'.[22] That seed was at odds with the current doctrines of cultural and social anthropology and 'remained a private reserve in his thinking until he began the systematic study of choice in human behaviour' two decades later.[23] But Krishnamurti released Freeman from many of his earlier passions for politics and engagement and strengthened his questioning.

In 1938, Derek joined Ernest Beaglehole's graduate seminar after studying under Sir Thomas Hunter, the Professor. Hunter was an experimental psychologist but one who taught courses that linked a biological understanding of humans with an appreciation of cultural formation. Beaglehole first interested Freeman in Mead. Both Hunter and Beaglehole had become friends with Margaret Mead and Freeman later admitted he was fed a diet of Mead during these years,

---

19 *Salient*, 6 July 1938, p. 1.
20 Don Tuzin, Interview with the author, 8 August 2006; also James Belich, *Paradise Reforged: A history of the New Zealanders from the 1880s to the year 2000* (Auckland, 2001), pp. 121–5.
21 The full story is in Frank Heiman's recorded interview with Derek Freeman, 12 February 2001, National Library of Australia [hereinafter NLA], Oral History Collection, TRC 4660, pp. 5–7. Freeman's 'Poem for a Friend Killed on Mt. Evans' is in *Spike*, 37:66 (1938), p. 22. The loss of a climbing companion in the Southern Alps has inspired other creative art in New Zealand—notably, Alistair Campbell's poem 'Elegy', which was set to music by Douglas Lilburn in 1951 as a substantial song cycle for baritone and piano. Alistair Campbell, 'Elegy', *Landfall: A New Zealand quarterly*, 3:3 (1949), pp. 223–8; Philip Norman, *Douglas Lilburn: His life and music* (Christchurch, 2006), pp. 175–6. Likewise, Scott's *Harry's Absence* centres on the death of his father on Mt Cook in 1960.
22 Freeman to David Mackay, 21 November 1997 (letter loaned by Mrs Freeman); Tuzin, 'Derek Freeman (1916–2001)', p. 5.
23 Appell and Madan, *Choice and Morality in Anthropological Perspective*, p. 4.

imbibing a general sense of the dominance of culture. In 1938, he wrote for *Salient* an article entitled 'Anatomy of Mind' in which he declared that the social environment determined the aims and desires that set human behaviour. Freeman remembered standing on a street corner in Wellington watching the flow of humankind, wondering what their behaviour was all about. He accepted that culture was the determinant.[24] From Beaglehole, Freeman also learned of Freud and psychoanalysis, and carried out some psychological research on the super-ego in young children as a student teacher in several Wellington schools.[25]

Freeman had spent two years training at Wellington Teachers' College when his parents could not, or would not, pay his fees after the first year of university study.[26] As a student teacher, he proved a gifted guide for small children. One of his former pupils, Heather Morrison, who, as a ten-year-old, encountered Freeman at Ridgeway School in Wellington, remembered how his teaching style was different and emphasised drama, free expression and the making of puppets. He turned 'the worst class in the school' into the best and pointed many students towards later learning. Morrison's memory had lingered for 50 years on the small bag of cherries that Freeman gave each child on the last day of school.[27]

But it was anthropology and the Pacific Islands—specifically Western Samoa—that Beaglehole turned Freeman towards as his disillusionment with New Zealand mounted. Here events and influences came together. One of Derek's climbing companions (and fellow activist at Victoria College) was Wolfgang Rosenberg, a young German and a socialist who had left Germany with his wife because of anti-Semitism, had seen the film *Moana* in Europe, and resolved to get to Samoa from New Zealand, which had obtained the mandate over Western Samoa from the League of Nations. Rosenberg never did get there. But he and Freeman both remembered sitting on Mt Hector in the Tararua Ranges behind Wellington in 1939, with Freeman wondering whether to go to Samoa. Rosenberg encouraged him.[28] Beaglehole was also promoting Samoa to Derek as a field for study at the same moment the New Zealand Education Department advertised for teachers.

---

24 Heiman's interview, NLA, Oral History Collection, TRC 4660, pp. 5–7, 10.
25 Freeman to Meyer Fortes, 20 September 1962, Freeman UCSD, box 8, folder 9. On Hunter's approach, see Ernest Beaglehole's 1964 Hudson Lecture to the Royal Society of New Zealand, 'The Third Culture in New Zealand: Human nature and conduct', copy in Freeman UCSD, box 118, folder 27; also Freeman to John Money, 13 August 1986, Freeman UCSD, box 15, folder 2, and Kathleen Ross Papers, Alexander Turnbull Library, Wellington, MS-Papers-6963-18. Ross, a playwright, was at Victoria with Freeman.
26 The story that Derek told in old age was that his anti-intellectual father refused to pay his fees and wanted him to get 'real' employment. Freeman tried his hand at a succession of dull jobs before enrolling at Teachers' College, but he kept up his literary and social activities at the university.
27 Heather Packer (née Morrison) to Freeman, n.d. [1998], Freeman UCSD, box 157, folder 32.
28 Freeman to Rosenberg, 7 January 2001, Rosenberg Collection (Copy of letter in author's possession). Wolfgang and Ann Rosenberg, Interview with author, Christchurch, 31 January 2002. Rosenberg became

Western Samoa—a colony of Imperial Germany since 1899—had fallen into New Zealand hands on the outbreak of the Great War. A small naval force had forced the surrender of the German Governor and his officials, and proceeded to install a military regime, which became a civilian administration with the issue of the league's mandate in 1920. New Zealand's administration of the islands was not a happy experience during the inter-war years. Under the Germans, Samoan factions had stirred up political turmoil; a resistance movement based on Savai'i was put down with a mixture of threats and deportations. New Zealand's military regime experienced some economic resistance but it was the flu pandemic of 1919 that caused major resentment—the flu carrying off 20 per cent of the population after a failure in New Zealand quarantine, decimating the ranks of older, experienced chiefs and orators. The 1920s was a period of escalating tension, culminating in a violent confrontation in Apia on 28 December 1929 between marching Samoans and New Zealand police: 11 Samoans and a New Zealand policeman died, among them Samoa's highest-ranking chief, Tupua Tamasese.[29]

By the outbreak of World War II, Western Samoa was much quieter. The Samoan resistance movement, the *Mau*—both a proto-nationalist movement and one split between churches and major families—had been harassed into sullen, passive resistance, but the election of a Labour government in New Zealand in 1935 brought a new era of reconciliation and some cooperation. War meant a marking of time till peace returned and a new future might be constructed under different conditions.

The New Zealand Education Department had advertised in February 1940 for a male assistant teacher for Leifiifi School in Apia to take the place of a teacher about to join the armed forces overseas. The war was beginning to bite into available staff. The conditions were not particularly inviting. A state education was not compulsory for native Samoans and pupils came and went in a school week of just 16 hours. Class sizes were large—about 70 pupils in each room. Teaching resources, especially materials printed in Samoan, were lacking, libraries were non-existent and the buildings and furniture were poor.[30] Pastor or mission schools dominated the villages, though the Administration also ran

---

an economist and academic at Canterbury University. See Gerhard Träbing, 'Wolfgang Rosenberg', in James N. Bade (ed.), *Out of the Shadow of War: The German connection with New Zealand in the twentieth century* (Melbourne, 1998), pp. 162–8.

29 See Peter Hempenstall and Noel Rutherford, *Protest and Dissent in the Colonial Pacific* (Suva, 1984), pp. 18–43; Michael Field, *Mau: Samoa's struggle for freedom* (Auckland, 1991); I. C. Campbell, 'Resistance and Colonial Government: A comparative study of Samoa', *Journal of Pacific History*, 40:1 (2005), pp. 45–69.

30 These details are taken from a report, *Education in Samoa*, written after the war, based on a visit to Samoa by the Director of Education in New Zealand, C. E. Beeby, in June 1945 to report on the state of affairs that prevailed during the war. See Beeby to Secretary External Affairs, 18 July 1947, IT1, EX13/1 Part 2: Education: Samoa General File, 1926–49, Archives New Zealand [hereinafter ArchivesNZ]; C. E. Beeby, *The Biography of an Idea: Beeby on education* (Wellington, 1992), pp. 212–18.

village schools staffed by Samoan teachers. Leifiifi was the government school in Apia, with 600 pupils, attended mainly by part-Samoan, part-European children. Most staff were also of mixed descent, though the senior staff were New Zealanders. The salary structure was poorer than in New Zealand and housing was not provided, though a 'tropical allowance' was included.

It was into this atmosphere—of a rather ramshackle New Zealand colonialism seeking an accommodation with a Polynesian people similar to, yet unlike 'their' Maori—that Derek Freeman arrived onboard a banana boat, the *Maui Pomare*, in April 1940. White prestige and distance from the 'natives' were still the gold standard among civil servants. Samoans were still largely dispersed among their myriad villages strung along the coasts of both Upolu and Savai'i, practising their social and political arts, hardly touched by New Zealand's policies, or the war, the further from Apia one lived.

Freeman had left New Zealand without finishing his degree[31] but with good references from the Education Department. The Inspector for Schools described him as a young man with 'any amount of ideas, very thoughtful and intelligent, with a great capacity for work and [he] has no difficulty in maintaining discipline'.[32] He was appointed an Assistant Master at Leifiifi School.

In later life, as the nemesis of Margaret Mead and the North American anthropological establishment, Freeman's sense of his time in wartime Samoa was that it was the beginning of his own war against Meadian error. But there is no evidence of a sudden epiphany—more of a drawn-out and cumulative process. Rather like Robert Louis Stevenson and Rupert Brooke, Freeman found Samoa's lushness, its handsome people and the romance of the islands' past arresting and galvanising. The relaxed teaching regime from 8 am till midday afforded him plenty of time to pursue his own interests. He quickly picked up Samoan, studied it formally and sat the Government exam to prove his proficiency; it added a welcome £25 a year to his salary.

He also began archaeological explorations of caves and earth mounds that he was told about inland from the northern and southern coasts of Upolu. He took precise measurements of the Falemaunga caves 8 km inland from Malie on the north coast and researched the history of their finding by German planters. On one occasion in 1943, Freeman took 17 Samoans from the Teachers' Training School to clear the site around a large megalithic circle of stone columns, which

---

31 And his grades were not particularly good in the subjects he did complete—achieving only a third class for logic and ethics. See Doug Munro, *The Ivory Tower and Beyond: Participant historians of the Pacific* (Newcastle upon Tyne, 2009), p. 83. Freeman spent too much time on student activities. For example, the Dramatic Club staged *The Royal Inn* and Freeman, 'as the American sailor, gave a splendid performance, keeping in character throughout in a perfectly natural manner'. *Salient*, 29 June 1938, p. 1.

32 Memo for Secretary of External Affairs from Permanent Head Education Dept, n.d., IT1, EX89/3, Part 3, ArchivesNZ.

John Macmillan Brown had in earlier days likened to Stonehenge and which Samoans rumoured was of godly origin. Freeman searched for grave sites, collected traditions and read all the authorities he could find on Samoan myths, from Percy Smith through Augustin Krämer to Margaret Mead. He concluded that Peter Buck was correct that the blocks were natural and the site manipulated through history by the Samoans. Freeman collected all the traditions he could from local talking chiefs (*tulafale*) and sacred chiefs (*ali'i*) and wrote up his findings for a series of articles—his first major academic pieces—for the *Journal of the Polynesian Society* back in New Zealand.[33] In breaking with older European opinions about the origins of these sites and exploring with Samoans themselves the meaning of traditions surrounding them, Freeman began his oppositional stance on things Samoan—a position he later saw as the start of his 'heretic' reputation.[34]

It was the exploration of Seuao Cave in Safata on the south coast, where he found his first stone adze, that led Freeman to the village of Sa'anapu.[35] The village lay on a small isthmus facing the sea and to get there one had to walk or ride for more than four hours across Upolu from the administrative centre, Apia, climbing to more than 900 m before dropping down to the coast. Sa'anapu became his home for the remainder of Freeman's investigations of Samoan culture and the centre of his emotional relations with Samoans. This is where Freeman claimed he began to see through Margaret Mead.[36] He had probably read Mead under Beaglehole's tutelage in Wellington and he sent away for her *Coming of Age in Samoa*, which arrived along with her *Growing Up in New Guinea* and *Sex and Temperament in Three Primitive Societies*.

Freeman became friendly during his visits to the Seauo Cave with a senior talking chief and village mayor, Lauvi Vainu'u. Having decided to make Sa'anapu his base for detailed ethnographic research alongside his teaching tasks, Freeman discovered that Lauvi regarded him as reparation for the death of his youngest son, Fa'imoto, also known as Loani, or John. John Derek Freeman now became the adopted son of Lauvi Vainu'u—a privileged position that granted him intimate access to the family circle. His good fortune increased when the assembled chiefs conferred on him the title of Logona-i-taga ('heard at the tree felling')—a title belonging to the *manaia* or son of the leading chief of the lineage 'Anapu, and thus the leader of the young men of the village. This enabled Freeman to attend

---

33 'The Falemaunga Caves', *Journal of the Polynesian Society* [hereinafter *JPS*], 53:3 (1944), pp. 86–104; 'O le Fele o le Fe'e', *JPS*, 53:4 (1944), pp. 121–44; 'The Vailele Earthmounds', *JPS*, 53:4 (1944), pp. 145–62.
34 Heiman's interview, NLA, Oral History Collection, TRC 4660, 14. Freeman was partly projecting back in the shadow of David Williamson's play about him and Margaret Mead: *Heretic: Based on the life of Derek Freeman* (Melbourne, 1996).
35 'The Seuao Cave', *JPS*, 52:3 (1943), pp. 101–9.
36 Freeman, *Margaret Mead and Samoa*, pp. xiii–xiv.

all *fono*, or village councils, and, with his fluent Samoan, to understand their oratory and observe at first hand the behaviour of chiefs from the perspective of the young men.[37]

Freeman's notes from 1942–43 document his meticulous approach as an ethnographer. He observed the daily routine of his family and listed their comings and goings, and their periods of rest and sleep. He collected instances of the intrigues of the *matai* (title-holders) who made up the village council, noting how disputes were not allowed to be referred beyond village boundaries to the Administration, even though this was illegal. Neat plans of the village square (*malae*) were filed, along with seating arrangements at *fono*, lists of *matai* titles and their holders, and kinship charts. He researched the history of Sa'anapu during the conflicts of the nineteenth century that preceded the annexation of Western Samoa to Germany and discovered the village was split between followers of Tamasese and the eventual victor as paramount title-holder, Mata'afa Iosefo. He began to recognise the fluidity in Samoan cultural behaviour, the series of precedents and rights and gracious deferrals that qualified the ideal seating arrangements and speaking rights among *matai*. His stories about ghosts, or *aitu*, which were treated carefully by Samoans, and the religious implications for current religious practices, became a seminar paper to colleagues at the London School of Economics (LSE) after the war.[38] Freeman was also capable of a poetic, sensual feel for his surroundings and beautiful line drawings of the village and its equipment. He might have been an amateur academic-in-training at this stage in wartime Samoa, but his methods sowed the seeds of his later reputation as a superior ethnographer.

Freeman spent some five months living and working in Sa'anapu during 1942–43, but he had to maintain his work as a teacher and continued to visit the area on weekends from Apia; Sa'anapu people also visited him in town, the chiefs sometimes staying as his guests. In all Freeman had the village and its surroundings under fairly close scrutiny for 19 months.[39] He was now living in the lavish home of an Austrian doctor, a refugee from Nazi Germany, Hans Neumann, opposite the hospital. Freeman became very friendly with a Samoan nurse, Sisi, after a fall from his horse. Though it became a passionate, serious affair, Sisi would not allow sexual intercourse for she informed Derek that Samoan culture required her to guard her virginity until after marriage. Freeman later argued this revelation, which he checked with other nurses, along with his

---

37 Information supplied to the author by Serge Tcherkezoff, January 2006, from his own correspondence with Freeman. The account of Freeman's activities in Sa'anapu is based largely on Heiman's interview, NLA, Oral History Collection, TRC 4660, 14–18; and Freeman's own ethnographic notes in his papers: Freeman, UCSD, box 50.
38 See Peter Hempenstall, '"On Missionaries and Cultural Change in Samoa": Derek Freeman preparing for a "heretical" life', *Journal of Pacific History*, 39:2 (2004), pp. 241–50.
39 Details in Freeman's December 1946 seminar paper at LSE: 'On Samoan Social Organization' (in possession of the Freeman family).

experience in Sa'anapu of witnessing an *ifoga*, or ceremonial abasement by a *matai* on account of a rape of a fifteen-year-old girl by a youth, and other similar incidents, persuaded him that Mead had Samoan adolescent sexual behaviour totally wrong.[40] This is difficult to prove, but Freeman's much more intensive relationship with Samoan culture was certainly moving him to be more sceptical of Mead's picture of a society of free love.

Though Freeman received assistance in his quests from a variety of other Europeans stationed in Samoa, his relations with the Administration turned sour soon after his arrival. On the eve of the Japanese entry into the war, the Acting Administrator in Samoa, A. C. Turnbull, argued to Wellington that Freeman should be sent home for he would not assist the war effort by joining the local defence force or volunteering for overseas service: 'he is a man of peculiar ideas (and undoubtedly a pacifist).'[41] Pacifism is perhaps too simple a term for the complex of feelings Derek Freeman was carrying. Anti-war sentiments had been part of the education of the children of the Great War—Freeman's generation. It seeped down into school textbooks and journals. By the early 1930s, it had become almost conventional to speak sceptically of modern warfare and its toll on lives and ideals. A religiously inspired pacifism was undoubtedly part of the mix but it was not the only case for resisting state pressures on men to march again to war. Freeman's anti-militarism was partly driven by the kind of disillusionment manifested in the anti-war novels of the 1920s and 1930s, refined by his experiences at university and his contact with Krishnamurti's views. Once war broke out, uncertainty over war aims and the terms of any postwar peace led to opposition to war in all its forms in New Zealand.[42]

Freeman had deliberately escaped the confines of New Zealand's highly regulated society, which endured even greater constraints on freedom of expression and communication once wartime censorship regulations were introduced. New Zealand was the earliest country in the Empire outside Britain to reintroduce conscription. Conscientious objectors to war were brought before Appeals Boards dotted around the country, which determined the genuineness of their cases, without further appeal, and condemned those who refused to accept their decisions to defaulters' concentration camps for the duration of the war.[43]

---

40   Heiman's interview, NLA, Oral History Collection, TRC 4660, 18. Also Don Tuzin, Interview with Freeman, 25–30 June 2000, set IV, 23–32 (in possession of Tuzin family); Tcherkezoff, Information to author, January 2006.
41   Turnbull to Secretary External Affairs, 2 October 1941, IT1, EX89/3, Part 4, ArchivesNZ.
42   For a detailed examination of this aspect of New Zealand history, see F. L. W. Wood, *The New Zealand People at War: Political and external affairs* (Wellington, 1958), especially pp. 25–7, 111; also Cookson, 'Appeal Boards and Conscientious Objectors', p. 181.
43   Cookson, 'Appeal Boards and Conscientious Objectors', pp. 173–98; Wood, *The New Zealand People at War*, pp. 123–50; also Srinjoy Bose, 'Students or Soldiers? Conscientious objection during World War II', in The Time Keepers (eds), *Tower Turmoil: Characters and controversies at the University of Otago* (Dunedin, 2005), pp. 81–94.

Derek Freeman's opposition to war sprang from his frustration with the decay and breakdown of international order and his wish to be free of it all. It saw him ostracised by the expatriate community in Samoa—reinforced by his difference from ordinary Kiwis, his academic pursuits and his open fraternisation with Samoans in their villages.[44] But the Japanese attack on Pearl Harbor and the dire implications for the defence of New Zealand and the islands to her north brought Freeman up short. Since 1938 the New Zealand Labour Government had been aware that they were to all intents and purposes on their own for an indefinite period if Japan attacked the United States or South-East Asia and Britain was caught in a European conflict. At the Pacific Defence Conference in Wellington, in April 1939, New Zealand took the lead in agreeing to defend Fiji against Japanese aggression but leaving other islands in the South-West Pacific, including Samoa, to be defended by local militia. With the Pearl Harbor attack, conscription was also extended into civilian life and industry.[45]

Freeman joined the local defence force and began patrolling the islands, reaching parts of the group he had never visited. His term as a teacher was due to expire on 9 April 1943, and Freeman initially indicated he was prepared to stay for a further term with the Education Department.[46] But in November 1943, on furlough, he decided to return to New Zealand and join the Navy. Freeman was a keen yachtsman and had been secretary of the local sailing club in Samoa. He volunteered for Scheme B, a scheme for ratings of the Royal New Zealand Naval Volunteer Reserve who had the potential to become officers after training in Britain; under the *Naval Defence Act* of 1913, New Zealand warships passed to the control of the British Admiralty in wartime. Some 1100 Scheme B personnel were sent overseas.[47]

Freeman sailed from Wellington for England on a battered tramp steamer, the *Themistocles*, in company with other aspiring ratings, among whom was Keith Sinclair, the later *enfant terrible* of New Zealand letters, nationalist poet, commentator and academic historian.[48] Before he left, Freeman visited Ernest Beaglehole and told him he thought Mead had been in error over her Samoan conclusions; Beaglehole 'sort of just laughed'.[49] If this was a declaration of hostilities on Freeman's part then it would have to wait, for a larger and more existential war claimed his attention for the next two years.

---

44   Freeman to Michael Field, 22 November 1984, Freeman UCSD, box 8, folder 1. Jim Davidson encountered the same problems with expatriates in Samoa in the late 1940s and early 1950s. See Doug Munro, 'J. W. Davidson—The making of a participant historian', in Brij V. Lal and Peter Hempenstall (eds), *Pacific Lives, Pacific Places: Bursting boundaries in Pacific history* (Canberra, 2001), pp. 107–8.
45   Wood, *The New Zealand People at War*, pp. 67–89, 215.
46   D. McCulloch (Secretary Administration) to Secretary External Affairs, 31 August 1942, IT1, EX89/3, Part 4, ArchivesNZ.
47   Peter Dennerley, 'The Royal New Zealand Navy', in Crawford, *Kia Kaha*, pp. 110–11.
48   The following account of Freeman's time overseas is taken largely from Sinclair's robust autobiography: *Halfway Round the Harbour: An autobiography* (Auckland, 1993), ch. 6 ('To See the World').
49   Heiman's interview, NLA, Oral History Collection, TRC 4660, 19.

They sailed west to Europe via Australia, the Indian Ocean and South Africa. In Melbourne, both Freeman and Sinclair headed for the Melbourne University Library—Freeman to follow-up translations of Samoan songs, Sinclair to read for exams he still had to sit for his degree. Sinclair's retrospective views on Freeman, who was older than the men he sailed with, present an eccentric figure from the beginning: 'a big man, with a big voice. He was an intellectual extremist or fanatic.'[50] (Freeman later disputed Sinclair's description of him as a 'fanatic'—'a heretic, yes'—but agreed his work against the Meadites might have him accurately described as an intellectual extremist.)[51] After a stopover in a very hot Perth, the *Themistocles* limped across the Indian Ocean to Durban, keeping well to the south to avoid Japanese submarines. They spent a month in South Africa observing at close quarters the tightening tentacles of the embryonic apartheid state. One night Freeman stole a South African flag with other sailors and slept on the flag in a gutter. It was a rare instance of high jinks by someone less socially adventurous than Keith Sinclair. The two of them—with their intellectual pursuits and un-nautical appearance—were unlike most of the ratings they trained with.

Once in England from September 1944, their time was taken up with courses of training in signals, weapons, officer leadership, navigation and sailing. There were personality tests, in one of which they had to write about themselves from the standpoint of a severe critic. Freeman recognised in himself the stern disciplinarian (Keith Sinclair admitted he talked too much). But he was emotional and passionate, too. While he was drilling on the parade ground at HMS *Raleigh*, near Plymouth, in 1945, he received mail informing him that his Samoan lover, Sisi, had died of yellow fever. He wept unashamedly.[52] They were constantly interviewed by boards and sat exams. Freeman and Sinclair stood out for their unusual verbal and literary skills but were weak at mechanical tests. Nevertheless, at the end of the classes, the drilling, the training on small ships and the induction into rigid Royal Navy behaviour, Freeman placed third and Sinclair fourth and they were commissioned as temporary sublieutenants. Many sailors fell by the wayside; only 11 of 50 Kiwis—four from their draft—passed, with a handful of Englishmen.[53]

The war against the Axis powers was only one of Derek Freeman's campaigns while he was in England. The other was to set up networks and make contacts with scholars in anthropology against the day when the war was over and he could think about a different kind of professional training. The trainee officers had ample leave during their courses and London was the obvious centre for

---

50 Sinclair, *Halfway Round the Harbour*, p. 85.
51 Freeman to Sinclair, 15 October 1993, Freeman UCSD, box 21, folder 9.
52 Tuzin, Interview with Freeman, Tuzin family, set V, 29.
53 Sinclair, *Halfway Round the Harbour*, p. 100.

their attention, though the city was still being targeted by German V1 and V2 rockets. Freeman used the time to approach Raymond Firth, himself a Kiwi and the successor to Malinowski as Professor at the LSE within the University of London. Freeman sent Firth testimonials about his studies in both New Zealand and Samoa. It appears that he hoped to be allowed to register for a PhD under Firth. Firth encouraged him, setting his sights on Freeman working in either the Gilbert and Ellice Islands or the Solomons after the war. Firth put a case to the Higher Degree Committee and approached the Rehabilitation Board in New Zealand on Freeman's behalf. In May 1945, as the European war was ending, they hit a snag. The University of London regulations would not allow a student to register for a PhD who had not completed his Bachelor's degree; Freeman was one unit shy. The university would not budge, despite Firth's willingness to take Freeman on, given the research work he had already carried out in Samoa. The confusion seems to have been Firth's fault, but compensation came in the form of a favourable decision by New Zealand's Rehabilitation Board to support Freeman to study in London for a Postgraduate Academic Diploma.[54]

These matters were literally academic while the war ground on. After graduation as an officer, Freeman applied to Naval Intelligence and was sent to study Japanese at the School of Oriental and African Studies as a prelude to the postwar occupation. Keith Sinclair later claimed Freeman had gone over the heads of his superior officers to persuade Naval Intelligence he was a linguist, and was subsequently taken off the course and posted to a dangerous assignment in the Far East.[55] The sequence of events was both more pedestrian and typically Freemanesque. He became impatient at the prospect of months spent studying a new language and approached the Professor of Japanese, a New Zealander, successfully persuading her that he was unsuited to the course, which she duly reported to the Navy. Freeman was assigned to a far more hazardous undertaking: watch officer onboard a landing ship tank (LST) joining the Eastern Fleet—later the British Pacific Fleet—to participate in the last stages of the advance against Japan.[56]

He never reached Japan, or even the Malayan Peninsula that was the invasion target for his LST 9 and crew. When the atomic bomb was dropped on Hiroshima, Freeman and his crew were preparing in Trincomalee Harbour, Ceylon (now Sri Lanka). They were dispatched instead to Hong Kong and thence to the coast of Borneo to take the Japanese surrender. Travelling up and down the coast, Freeman apparently accumulated an impressive collection of Japanese

---

54 This set of circumstances can be traced in Firth's correspondence in Freeman's papers: Firth to Freeman, 22 February 1945, 28 May 1945, 1 July 1946; and Dean Postgraduate Studies to Firth, 11 April 1945, Freeman UCSD, box 8, folder 4.
55 Sinclair, *Halfway Round the Harbour*, p. 86.
56 See Freeman to Sinclair, 15 October 1993, Freeman UCSD, box 21, folder 9; also Dennerley, 'The Royal New Zealand Navy', pp. 118–20.

officers' swords, and, more significantly, had his first encounter with the Iban, an imperious proto-Malay people—headhunters—who lived in large family groups in riverside long houses. Freeman remembered his first sight of them:

> When I was on this LST we were beached at the mouth of a river and these Iban tribesmen came swaggering on. They wear little loincloths and had long hair and spears in their hands and they walked straight into the captain's cabin, you know, as if they owned the place. I was enormously impressed by these people, the first really wild people I had seen.[57]

War's end saw his ship carrying troops back to Australia (this is possibly the point at which the story about his presence in Singapore, and shock at the instructions of an admiral to his men, originated). In Brisbane, Derek was put into the tropical diseases hospital, for his skin had erupted into sores that required treatment; it was later determined he was allergic to the anti-malarial drug Atebrin. In Sydney while convalescing, Freeman took the opportunity to refresh and enhance his historical research on Samoa in preparation for further postwar studies. He examined early missionary records in the Mitchell Library and did the same when he reached the Turnbull Library in Wellington. Keith Sinclair bumped into him there as he collected material for his Masters thesis on the Aborigines' Protection Society and New Zealand.[58] In 1946, Freeman returned briefly to Western Samoa as research assistant for the Irish writer Robert Gibbings, but he already perceived himself as a 'kind of an academic'[59] and, by 1947, he was back in London on his rehabilitation bursary, enrolled with Firth to study anthropology.

The rest of Freeman's postwar career is a different history, resonant with controversies, not all of them about Margaret Mead and her anthropology. But Freeman did submit successfully in 1948 his diploma thesis, 'The Social Structure of a Samoan Village Community', on Sa'anapu, which was Freeman's main ethnographic contribution to Pacific studies—a conventional structuralist analysis, but one brimming with the dynamism, fluidity and flexible adaptations engineered by Samoans in their everyday lives.[60] He went on to do fieldwork with his new wife, Monica, as partner and assistant among the Iban of Borneo between 1949 and 1951, as a project under Edmund Leach's sponsorship with the Colonial Social Science Research Council. On their return to London,

---

57 Heiman's interview, NLA, Oral History Collection, TRC 4660, 24.
58 Sinclair, *Halfway Round the Harbour*, p. 114.
59 Heiman's interview, NLA, Oral History Collection, TRC 4660, 24. The last stages of Freeman's wartime experiences and the immediate years thereafter are covered here (pp. 24–8).
60 See author's introduction to Freeman's *The Social Structure of a Samoan Village Community*, pp. 9–13.

Freeman joined Meyer Fortes at Cambridge to write up his materials for his PhD. He was awarded the degree in 1953 and sallied forth on a distinguished, albeit sometimes noisy and acrimonious, academic career.

Derek Freeman's presence in wartime Samoa was not the beginning of his war with Margaret Mead. At best, his stay was part of his own 'phoney' war of gradual revelation and training before the real conflict was joined from the 1960s onwards. His tussles during the 1940s were with the New Zealand colonial establishment and they had nothing to do with the classic suspicion of activist anthropologists by colonial governments.[61] Rather they were over his standing out from the conventional expectations of a colonial public servant and his initial refusal to join the war effort. Freeman's real war was with himself over his duty of citizenship in a world gone mad and of which he deeply disapproved. In the event, he met and resolved these tensions in favour of fighting for his country and joining the naval arm of the forces arrayed against the Japanese. Though he served in the Royal Navy, he did so as a Kiwi, and he remained a Kiwi till his dying days. Living most of his life in Canberra, Australia, he planted his and Monica's garden with typical New Zealand shrubs and trees. They visited New Zealand several times and Freeman continued to correspond with relatives there. On his coffin at the memorial service after his death in 2001 lay his ice axe—an expression of his abiding love for New Zealand's mountains.

The axe was also a symbol for the rough violence needed to conquer ideas and people in error as well as mountains. It is possible to see World War II as part of the evolutionary curve in Derek Freeman's own formation as a crusader in the moral pursuit of the truth he came to believe it was the duty of scholars to aim for. Questions still hang heavily around the humaneness and the hypocrisies of his methods in prosecuting error and banishing it from scholarship. Perhaps that is why almost no room was found for Freeman in the written history of the ANU.[62]

Freeman's contribution to anthropology is also still in dispute. His considerable work on the Iban is often swamped in estimation by the tidal wave of clamour and dissent over his Samoan 'war' with Margaret Mead's followers. This is not the place to follow that campaign. Samoa remained special in Freeman's life. In 1983, the year his book about Margaret Mead came out, he told his old friend Wolf Rosenberg that he was making arrangements to have his ashes scattered on the south coast of Upolu—'a place that I have loved like I used to love the Tararuas and the Southern Alps, for over 40 years'.[63]

---

61   Such as bedevilled Ralph Piddington on the Aboriginal frontier in Australia. See Geoffrey Gray, *A Cautious Silence: The politics of Australian anthropology* (Canberra, 2007), pp. 102–8.
62   See S. G. Foster and Margaret M. Varghese, *The Making of The Australian National University, 1946–1996* (Sydney, 1996), p. 110; also correspondence between Freeman and Foster, Freeman UCSD, box 154, folder 29.
63   Freeman to Rosenberg, 15 August 1983, Freeman UCSD, box 19, folder 11.

9. J. W. Davidson on the Home Front[1]

Doug Munro

James (Jim) Wightman Davidson (1915–73) died young. He was then the foundation Professor of Pacific History at The Australian National University (ANU). The first step in that direction was an MA degree (with first-class honours) from Victoria University College, in 1938, on the strength of a thesis on Scandinavian settlement in New Zealand. In those days, the royal road to academic success was a second degree from Oxbridge or London, and Davidson applied for one of the two postgraduate travelling scholarships that were allocated to New Zealand. He had done well in his studies but not well enough and one of the scholarships went to a history student from Christchurch, Neville Phillips (see Chapter 10 in this volume), a Christchurch journalist who was a complete unknown to Davidson and his lecturers at Victoria College. The setback shook Davidson to the core and he was more than happy, in the circumstances, to be appointed to the Centennial Atlas Project and assigned to tracing Maori tracks and waterways.[2] But his heart's desire was postgraduate study abroad and an eventual lectureship at a university. His persistence in applying for overseas scholarships paid off some four months later with the award of a Strathcona Research Studentship to St John's College, Cambridge; he sailed for England in late August on the *Tainui* on two years' leave of absence from the New Zealand Public Service. Neville Phillips was a fellow passenger and the two became friends.

Ever a dutiful son, Davidson sent regular letters to his parents. Within days of the *Tainui* berthing in Southampton, Chamberlain appeased Hitler at Munich, and Davidson wrote that

> the last half of the voyage has left us even more unsettled than the first. The news from Europe seems to be getting steadily worse. Once or twice, however, we have thought that all was well. One night last week I had an argument lasting long into the night because I had said that I thought Chamberlain was justified in saving peace by making concessions to Germany; & then the next day we found that things were

---

[1] I am grateful to Malcolm Underwood, the Archivist at St John's College, Cambridge, for facilitating access to Davidson material at the college; to Caroline Greenwood for donating the papers of her uncle (Miles Greenwood) to the National Library of Australia; and to Jill Palmer for facilitating access to the Lilburn Papers, Alexander Turnbull Library. Niel Gunson, Barrie Macdonald, Gerald Hensley and David Hilliard, all of whom knew Davidson, usefully commented on this chapter, as did Malcolm McKinnon, John Crawford and Ian McGibbon.
[2] Malcolm McKinnon, 'The Uncompleted Centennial Atlas', in William Renwick (ed.), *Creating the National Spirit: Celebrating New Zealand's centennial* (Wellington, 2004), pp. 149–60.

worse than instead of better. I still feel there is hope of averting war, but even in that I do not get much support. However it will be satisfactory to be on land & at least have more news of what is actually happening.[3]

Two days later, he admitted that he left New Zealand never expecting 'so soon to have to regard war as such a matter of fact possibility'. British destroyers were everywhere in the English Channel and further surprises were in store in London where a war seemed to be almost in full swing: trenches in St James Park and Hyde Park, men in khaki wherever one looked, preparations for the evacuation of children to the countryside, gas masks issued to one and all ('[e]ven animals are remembered & gasproof kennels have been devised'); and by night 'the ceaseless raking of the skies by searchlight looking out for enemy planes', and people on air-raid duty. It crossed his mind that leaving New Zealand might have been the height of folly.

When World War II arrived, it complicated his life and caused anguish. But the war also provided opportunities: it was the 'making' of Jim Davidson in providing the springboard to his future career, and brings to mind the words of another New Zealander, John Mulgan, who remarked that '[i]t is a sad commentary on human values that war which has accustomed us to death should have brought with it so full and rich a sense of life'.[4] Davidson's anti-war and anti-militarist convictions, which translated into appeasement, might have got him into trouble, yet he greatly benefited from being where he was and doing what he did during World War II. Not least he was eternally grateful to have avoided being called up for combat duty.

The immediate problem was homesickness, despite being met at the railway station in London by his former New Zealand school mates Miles Greenwood and Douglas (Gordon) Lilburn. (Greenwood was studying drama at the Old Vic and Lilburn was studying composition at the Royal College of Music under Vaughan Williams.) But Davidson soon settled into his new life. He enrolled as a PhD student at St John's College, Cambridge (on his twenty-third birthday: 1 October 1938), decided upon his thesis topic ('Trade and Settlement in the South Pacific, 1788–1840')[5] and got on with his research, mostly in London archival repositories. He also joined in the round of college life and made lasting friendships. Such was Davidson's conviviality and yearning for intelligent company that at one stage he lamented that it would be better for his work 'if I were among people I shunned & disliked'.[6] But he made steady enough progress

---

3 Davidson to his parents, 25 September 1938 (addendum of 27 September), Davidson Papers, National Library of Australia [hereinafter NLA], MS 5105, box 64. There are two sets of Davidson Papers; the other is in the ANU Archives, Series 57 [hereinafter ANUA 57].
4 John Mulgan, *Report on Experience* (Oxford, 1947), p. 148.
5 The topic transformed into: 'European Penetration of the South Pacific, 1779–1842', PhD thesis, Cambridge University, 1942.
6 Davidson to Greenwood, 4 November 1939, Greenwood Papers, NLA, MS 9805.

and had a reminder of his potential when a revised version of his earlier thesis on Scandinavian settlement in New Zealand won the Walter Frewen Lord Prize of the Royal Empire Society for 1938.[7] He did the usual student things of going to the theatre, cinema and art galleries (often in the company of Greenwood or Lilburn), having afternoon tea with his supervisor, overseas travel to France and Ireland, and looking up his British relatives. He was leading a fulfilling life, as he told Greenwood:

> This week I have walked; on Thursday I heard a most brilliant lecture by Eileen Power, of London Univ., on the 'Eve of the Dark Ages'; last night the history club had a sherry party to which I went to meet delightful people & duly met several; in the coming week we have the Pro Arte Quartet [of Brussels] playing Beethoven's Sonatas. My work is equally entertaining, & the time for dinner rapidly approaches. My nostalgia [for New Zealand] is but slight.[8]

Nonetheless, Davidson maintained his connections with New Zealand, above all sending regular letters to his father, mother and sister in Wellington. They, in return, provided family and local news (almost none of their letters survives, unfortunately—only his to them), including a steady flow of newspaper clippings. From time to time, too, his father sent locally published books necessary for Davidson's thesis work but unobtainable in England.

All the while the clouds were gathering over Europe and the prospect of hostilities was more real. Davidson's letters home are largely silent about Hitler's aggression, apart from concerns immediately following the Munich Agreement. Perhaps he did not want to unduly alarm his parents but more probably he did not wish to alarm himself. He had

> a tremendous revulsion against volunteering for any service which involves the destruction of human life. I would volunteer for hospital work, ambulance work, stretcher bearing, or something of that sort, which was concerned with saving life. — But as I say I don't expect war. However, you now know how I feel, & how I would act if anything did happen.[9]

---

7 J. A. Williamson, Report on the essays submitted for the Walter Frewen Lord Prize, 1938, enclosed in the 'Minutes of the Imperial Studies Committee, Royal Empire Society' (Cambridge University Library). Davidson's successes were trumpeted back in New Zealand: 'Honours at Cambridge', *New Zealand Free Lance*, 28 August 1940, p. 6.
8 Davidson to Greenwood, 27 November 1938, Greenwood Papers, NLA, MS 9805; also Maxine Berg, *A Woman in History: Eileen Power, 1889–1940* (Cambridge, 1996).
9 Davidson to his mother, 3 May 1939, Davidson Papers, NLA, MS 5105, box 64. The reluctance of many soldiers during World War II to shoot to kill is perhaps not generally realised. After 1945, the US Army broke down such qualms, with target practice at bullseyes being replaced with simulated battle conditions and shooting at human-like pop-up targets. S. L. A. Marshall, *Men Against Fire* [1947] (Norman, Okla., 2000), ch. 6 ('Fire as the Cure').

Davidson's refrain is that he expected the continuation of peace and he steers clear of such disagreeable realities as the German occupation of the Sudetenland, *Kristallnacht* (the 'Night of the Broken Glass'), Hitler's Reichstag speech against the Jews, the German invasion of Czechoslovakia, and the German 'Pact of Steel' with Italy. There is not simply a disbelief that war might happen but also a definite sense that if one wished hard enough it would go away. He stuck to his guns to the very end. Even with the Russo–German Pact in August 1939 and with war just around the corner, like many people, he continued to hold out hope that hostilities might still be averted. Having experienced one major war in their lifetimes there was an emphatic sense in some quarters that another had to be avoided at almost any price. A case in point is the pacifist and feminist Vera Brittain, whose fiancé, beloved younger brother and numerous friends had been killed in World War I, resulting in her authorship of *Testament of Youth* (1933), a classic memoir of the human sufferings of World War I on soldiers and civilians alike. During World War II, she suffered again—this time for her pacifism and anti-war publications, which affected both friendships and her literary standing.[10] It is easy to see why many people were anti-war, just as it is easy with hindsight to be scornful of appeasement. But as M. D. R. Foot argues, anti-war sentiments of whatever stripe failed

> to tackle the argument that there are some kinds of armed villain who can only be stopped by brute force. Once the Nazis had tricked their way into power in highly industrialised Germany, and bluffed their way into re-creating armed forces that they had been banned from having by treaty, there was bound to be war.[11]

The dreadful sense of foreboding following the Russo–German Pact was realised on 3 September when Britain and France declared war on Germany following the Nazi invasion of Poland. Davidson was staying in London at the time on a research visit and immediately volunteered as an Air Raid Warden. He reassured his parents that he had sufficient funds and asked them to 'try to worry as little as possible, because I know that worrying & feeling you can do nothing about things can be much worse than…any of our experiences will be'.[12] Even then there was guarded, if quixotic, optimism that the German people would rise in revolution against their Nazi overlords—a view shared by many Britons[13]—and

---

10   Paul Berry and Mark Bostridge, *Vera Brittain: A life* (London, 2001); also Jill Ker Conway, *When Memory Speaks: Reflections on autobiography* (New York, 1998), pp. 82–3. Richard Overy, *The Morbid Age: Britain and the crisis of civilization, 1919–1939* (London, 2009), pp. 345–56, analyses popular pacifism and anti-war campaigners in Britain and their varying responses to the advent of World War II. Anti-war attitudes generally are discussed by Peter Calvocoressi, *A Time for Peace: Pacificism, internationalism, and protest forces in the reduction of war* (London, 1987), ch. 8.
11   M. D. R. Foot, '"War is a condition, like peace…"', *Literary Review*, (June 2008), p. 28.
12   Davidson to his mother, 3 September 1939, Davidson Papers, NLA, MS 5105, box 64.
13   Ian Kershaw, *Making Friends with Hitler: Lord Londonderry and Britain's road to war* (London, 2004), p. 299. Indeed, two days after the declaration of war, the RAF dropped leaflets urging Germans to rise against

his assurance of a widespread belief 'in our capacity to wear [Germany] down if revolution does not come; & most people are inclined to imagine war will not be too long'.[14] Two months later, he told Lilburn: 'The Communists are fools, but as they are for the moment right one must support them. They are the only section in England which would give us another Munich.'[15] At the other end of the spectrum was the Australian historian W. K. Hancock, at the time professor at Birmingham and later one of Davidson's academic sponsors, who was staunch in his opposition to Nazism. Recognising that 'a Nazi-dominated Europe…would soon extinguish the values he cared about', Hancock found abhorrent the 'intellectual quietism' (his biographer's words) of the sort that Davidson embraced.[16]

The obvious disruptions to civilian life, the 'Phony War' notwithstanding, were rationing, conscription, industry being geared to armaments manufacture, the dispersal of many civil servants and their files to remoter areas, the evacuation of children to the countryside, and the layers of restriction, regulation and surveillance that all this entailed. For historical researchers, the blackout and later the Blitz created impediments of their own. There was initial talk of the Public Record Office in London being closed for the duration; in the event, some of the material that Davidson needed was transferred to Canterbury and available for consultation—which put these archives in the flight path of German bombers during the Blitz. Another inconvenience was the early closing times of the British Museum Reading Room and the Cambridge University Library (3.30 pm and 4 pm respectively) because the big windows of the former and the glass dome of the latter could not be effectively blacked out. On one occasion, Davidson was nearly refused admission to the British Museum Reading Room because he had not brought along his gas mask. As well, parts of St John's College were requisitioned by the state to accommodate people directly associated with the war effort. Then there were the miscellaneous dangers of being at war: in a memorable episode, the house in which Davidson was staying in London came uncomfortably close to receiving a direct hit from a German bomb.

Meanwhile, the logistics of conducting thesis research in scattered repositories had its ups and downs:

> I left Cambridge on Tuesday…favoured with fog, I dashed about—B.M., R.E.S. [British Museum and Royal Empire Society]—& then went to Oxford. The first siren didn't sound till I was in the train at Paddington. I had arranged to meet that evening a Wellingtonian, son of a friend

---

the Nazis.
14   Davidson to his father, 6 September 1939, Davidson Papers, NLA, MS 5105, box 64.
15   Davidson to Lilburn, 5 November 1939, Lilburn Papers, Alexander Turnbull Library [hereinafter ATL], MS-Papers-2483-052.
16   J. H. Davidson, *A Three-Cornered Life: The historian W. K. Hancock* (Sydney, 2010), pp. 135, 140.

of Mother's, now in the R.A.F. Wednesday and Thursday were mainly spent in Rhodes House Library which proved even more useful than I expected—I hope to return a few days next vacation…Then, as on Tuesday, there was an early train on Friday morning, & a day in the BM. Sirens sounded soon after I arrived, but unexpectedly we were allowed to continue working. Then, two bombs dropped only a mile or so away (1.45 PM) & we were hustled into a shelter where we remained till almost closing time, without books, without even chairs on which to sit. And so to RES, NZ House, & the train. Four exhilarating days, they were much enjoyed.[17]

Occasional excitement or not, it was a grim time. The expectation that able-bodied men would enlist for the armed forces weighed heavily, especially on someone like Davidson whose anti-war outlook made him a staunch appeaser, even if he had little time for Chamberlain as a politician. His decided reluctance to enlist was endorsed by his tutor at St John's College: 'he said any application at present to the Recruiting Board by me would be "an act of unnecessary magnanimity"—so authority backs up one's inclinations towards passivity. He was very insistent that I should continue with my work.'[18] Davidson's supervisor, Professor Eric Walker, was equally adamant that he continue with his thesis rather than enlist. Moral support was also in abundance from his New Zealand friends and kindred spirits Miles Greenwood and Douglas Lilburn.[19] At their respective boarding schools they had been in a minority of 'aesthetics', interested in artistic pursuits and creating their own little haven amongst a philistine environment of 'hearties' for whom rugby and physical prowess were the defining qualities. Lilburn later condemned 'this arena of bullying little bastards—oh God, I hated them, and they hated me'.[20] Greenwood, Lilburn and Davidson were part of a small support group of expatriate New Zealanders, united in their leftist leanings, aesthetic interests and revulsion to war (as distinct from pacifism) that strongly inclined them towards what one historian has termed 'the [British] Labour Party's doctrinaire antimilitarism'.[21] Greenwood expressed his feelings in verse:

---

17 Davidson to Greenwood, 3 November 1940, Greenwood Papers, NLA, MS 9805.
18 Davidson to his mother, 10 October 1939 (addendum of 11 October), Davidson Papers, NLA, MS 5105, box 64.
19 Greenwood (1913–92) was with Davidson at the Hereworth School in Havelock North, which was a feeder for the elite New Zealand secondary schools, such as Wanganui Collegiate and Waitaki Boys' High School. Greenwood went on to Collegiate and Davidson to Waitaki, where he was in the same year as Lilburn (1915–2001).
20 Douglas Lilburn, 'Notes towards "Memories of Early Years"', Lilburn Papers, ATL, MS-Papers-7623-025.
21 Phillip Norman, *Douglas Lilburn: His life and music* (Christchurch, 2005), pp. 78–9; Ernest R. May, *Strange Victory: Hitler's conquest of France* (New York, 2000), p. 172.

> Then die, but die in vain, for slaughtering
> Has never yet eradicated wrong.
> Watch, if you will, the ocean waves that bring
> Their watery legions, endless and strong,
> To pound & battle with the myriad miles
> of our earthly litteral [sic]: and wonder.
> See not the waves, but visualise vast files
> of soldiers, time's players in war's plunder
> of life. They fight a foe not of their race,
> A thing inhuman, drear & oversized
> In might. They fight an understood disgrace,
> And in their dying scorn what once they prized.
> The earth is no man's, & man has unity
> as has the ocean to eternity
>
> 20th October 1939[22]

Davidson made his views known to his parents, telling them that although he expected sooner or later to formally contribute to the war effort, he was 'quite unable to offer my services for any job requiring the taking of human life'; he was relieved to receive his father's approval.[23] Whatever George Davidson's views on the war itself, he was doubtless relieved that his son was removed, for the moment at least, from active combat. Certainly, the gangly Davidson was neither robust nor physically coordinated, and he lacked any inclination for frontline duties. Asthmatic and prone to catarrh, he would have made a hopeless soldier and was no doubt aware of it.[24] His other concern was that his eventual contribution to the war effort would be in accord with his 'capacity & character'.[25] There were other matters of temperament—notably, his disdain for mindless authority, as he saw it. Typical of this was his disparagement of the intelligence section of the War Office for being infested with

> nonentities punishing criticism whenever it shows its head, sticking to all the old notions of button-polishing and floor scrubbing because it is easier to keep men employed that way than to think out intelligent training for them, and trying to create round them an atmosphere of

---

22 Untitled poem, Greenwood Papers, NLA, MS 9805.
23 Davidson to his mother, 30 October 1939, Davidson Papers, NLA, MS 5105, box 64.
24 As was the American historian J. H. Hexter, 'who never learned to march in step, and while he was attempting to negotiate an obstacle course, he blew out a knee'. William Palmer, *Engagement with the Past: The lives and works of the World War II generation of historians* (Lexington, Ky, 2001), p. 72.
25 What could happen to people who were unsuited to army life during wartime is indicated by Julian McLaren-Ross's autobiographical story 'I Had to Go Absent (with commentary by Paul Willetts)', *Times Literary Supplement*, 27 June 2008, pp. 13–15. On the other hand, many artistic types and 'aspirant economists' from Central Europe were initially assigned to the Pioneer Corps as unskilled labourers in wartime Britain and only later were 'more rationally employed in the armed forces'. Eric Hobsbawm, *Interesting Times: A twentieth-century life* (London, 2002), p. 167.

Prussian respect for discipline combined with unbridled Hun-hating. The only hope seems to be that the rank & file wait for the revolution—almost.[26]

Of course, Davidson's wish to avoid, or at least to delay, becoming involved in the war machine was widely shared. Peter Calvocoressi, who became an intelligence officer at Bletchley Park, recalls:

> In the autumn of 1939, twenty-six years old and recently married, I had even less wish than most people to rush off and risk my life. I was content to evade the conflict between family happiness and a wider duty by accepting the current orthodoxy which said that one should wait one's turn to be called up in an orderly manner and when required.[27]

For the moment, it was a matter of Davidson getting on with life the best he could, of pursuing his thesis work in the face of restricted library hours and the dispersal of documents, and waiting for a better day. His views on war remained unchanged, and he told his father:

> I cannot help sticking to my original viewpoint that our making [war]—in the attempt to save Poland—was a tragic mistake. How much does it seem at the moment we are likely to be able to help Poland, or Czechoslovakia, or the rest of Europe? And even if in the end we do so how much greater even than our highest estimates is the cost going to be? If we win freedom for a continent of starved mothers, war-shattered fathers, & stunted & ricketty [sic] children, was it worth it? I cannot for a minute believe it was, but now there is no retreat. We can only continue. The most tragic part of it is apart from the suffering at the moment & in the years to come that if in the end we succeed as fully as we hope & the Nazi government is destroyed even then, I believe all over Europe the leaderless & unfed multitudes whose freedom we desire will probably hate us more than they hate the Germans. Not quite normal because of their suffering they will not be able to see beyond & to recognize the greater oppressor, Germany, the ultimate cause (apart from human folly & selfishness) of their suffering…I wish I could believe, as I think you do in many things, that suffering refines & purifies, acts as a beneficial discipline; but I can't.[28]

The war, in Davidson's view, would result in senseless slaughter and achieve no positive results. Very likely, Davidson's anti-fascist attitudes, which he embraced in the politicised ambience of Victoria University College, were overridden by

---

26 Davidson to Lilburn, 14 June 1942, Lilburn Papers, ATL, MS-Papers-2483-052.
27 Peter Calvocoressi, *Top Secret Ultra* (Sphere edn, 1981), pp. 7–8.
28 Davidson to his father, 5 July 1940, Davidson Papers, NLA, MS 5105, box 64.

his anti-war sensibilities, and probably reinforcing this was a lingering belief from his Wellington student days in the ideals of the League of Nations as arbiter of the global order.[29] One cannot have it both ways—being both anti-fascist and anti-war. But at no point did Davidson find that his senses were dulled by the seemingly interminable condition of war, leading to feelings of fatalism and a 'desire to put off making decisions as long as possible in case something or other turns up'.[30]

It would get worse before it got better, not simply with the ending of the Phony War and the onset of the Blitz, but in Davidson's personal fortunes. A recurring source of uncertainty was his two years' leave from the New Zealand Public Service, which was insufficient time to complete a PhD thesis even without wartime distractions. More ominous was his father's declining health, which Davidson first knew about in January 1940. George Davidson was a staid and genteel manufacturer's representative and his son was already anxious that recent tariff restrictions in New Zealand were hurting his father's business. Now there were health concerns, which made Davidson feel apprehensive because Lilburn's father had died after a long illness in July 1939 while his son was abroad. As 1940 progressed, George Davidson's health remained an underlying worry and in October there was a scare when he was diagnosed as having a blood clot near the heart. Jim Davidson went frantic with worry at the news and wanted to return to New Zealand. The danger seemingly passed but George Davidson died suddenly on 6 February 1941.

It was such a sad letter that Davidson wrote home. Distraught and disconsolate, he tried to gather his thoughts and express his emotions:

> It is now evening (9.30) & the cable still seems as bleak as it did when I first looked at it this morning. I don't seem to be much nearer [a] fuller understanding of it, or nearer an answer to the incessant questions—why, why had it to happen? Only gradually I seem to be relating to the past, & remembering how even in the darkest moments when I knew fully Dad's condition I thought of how both our Grandfathers had lived to be well over 80, and hoped & felt sure there were many happy—if enforcedly quiet—years ahead for Dad. And then came the happy day when I received my first letter from him again—with a few typing mistakes. Then they came regularly & seemed no different to those he had written before he was ill. The mistakes in typing had disappeared. The news always seemed to be getting brighter…

---

29 See J. C. Beaglehole, *Victoria University College: An essay towards a history* (Wellington, 1949), ch. 8; Stephen Hamilton, *A Radical Tradition: A history of the Victoria University of Wellington Students' Association, 1899–1999* (Wellington, 2002), pp. 77–8.
30 Frances Partridge, *A Pacifist's War* (London, 1978), p. 148 (entry for 27 October 1942).

Somehow I can't altogether regard death as a tragedy for those who die, though I am so fond of life. Yet I did so want to bring a little more happiness to Dad before death came to him—to be with him again, & to show him by my work here & afterwards that I had made some use of the opportunities which he had laboured so hard that I might have, and to make him feel able to be fairly sure that come what may I ought to be able to see that you & Ruth would not suffer too much, materially, if he should die.[31] But it has come too soon and too suddenly; there is a war on, & in the turmoil in which we live I couldn't be with him before he died or with you in the sad days that follow...I do wish I was with you tonight.'[32]

Part of Davidson's devastation was that he had not been close to his father in recent years, nor had their relations been entirely cordial (which might explain why Davidson usually wrote separate letters to his mother and father). Like the spent arrow, there were now feelings of unassuaged guilt that he had not done more to mend fences following the rejection of his father's intellectual and parental authority. It only made matters worse when his father's letters continued to arrive for some weeks afterwards, and these coincided with the worse bombing raid to date in the vicinity of Cambridge.

To further disturb Davidson's peace of mind was the matter of his leave from the New Zealand Public Service. He wrote to Joe (later Sir Joseph) Heenan, the Under-Secretary for the Department of Internal Affairs, asking for six months' extension. When it became clear that this was insufficient, Heenan made the extraordinarily generous gesture of extending Davidson's leave-of-absence 'for the duration of the war and, you may take it, such further period as may be necessary to enable you to make up your mind whether you will be coming back to New Zealand'. He went on to say 'the more I see of the work you are doing in England, the more I realise the improbability of your ever coming back to us. The British people have a habit of knowing a good man when they see one and not letting him go.'[33]

Had Davidson returned to New Zealand after two years, he would almost certainly not have completed his PhD thesis and in likelihood he would have had to settle for a lower degree, either an MA or an MLitt.[34] He would have

---

31 The late Ruth Davidson told me that her father did not much like his job but did so uncomplainingly to provide his family with a decent standard of living. Interview, 13 January 1999, Canberra.
32 Davidson to his mother and sister, 7 February 1941, Davidson Papers, NLA, MS 5105, box 64. Davidson refers to a letter he wrote to Miles Greenwood earlier in the day, which unfortunately is not among the Greenwood Papers ('The letter to Miles was, in a way, an effort to see whether I could trust myself with a pen'). An obituary to George Davidson appeared in the *Evening Post* [Wellington], 8 February 1941, p. 11.
33 Heenan to Davidson, 13 April 1942, Heenan Papers, ATL, MS-Papers-1132-048.
34 The Australian historian Manning Clark, who returned home from Oxford in the face of impending war, had great difficulty in finishing his MA thesis, on Alexis de Tocqueville, while holding down teaching

returned to the New Zealand Public Service and he might well have been appointed to a lectureship at his alma mater when an opening occurred in 1948.[35] He would certainly not have become the Professor of Pacific History at the ANU but he might, had he remained in the Public Service and ended up in the Department of Island Territories, have been involved in the decolonisation of Western Samoa—upon which his reputation largely rests. With greater certainty, we can say that he would have chafed under the prevailing wartime restrictions, for New Zealand displayed greater severity towards dissent and disaffection than other outposts of the British Empire.[36] Davidson had already experienced from afar this environment of compulsion and intolerance. When the war broke out, he wrote an article for the New Zealand current affairs magazine *Tomorrow*, saying that planning for postwar reconstruction should start right away in order to avoid the mistakes that beset the aftermath of World War I.[37] The following year, the provocative *Tomorrow* became a casualty of wartime censorship. When the censors opened his parents' mail and cut out the 'offending' portions, he complained to the Wellington morning newspaper that the excisions seemed to relate not to sensitive wartime information but to what might be construed as being critical of the Government.[38] He flattered himself that his intervention would make a difference but the Prime Minister felt that the generally conservative press never gave the Labour Party a fair hearing and he was not about to restrain the censors.[39]

Meanwhile, Davidson had to survive in wartime England. His immediate concern was 'to avoid combat service without declaring himself a conscientious objector': by this time he had 'become too skeptical of the nature of conscience'.[40] His father's death created financial as well as emotional difficulties, and took him down a road he might otherwise not have ventured. As well as his scholarships, Davidson had relied on an irregular allowance from his father, which now dried up. As he explained to his college tutor, he was reluctant to impose financially on his mother in the circumstances. The point was that his mother would need

---

positions, despite having completed sufficient documentary research. Mark McKenna, *An Eye for Posterity: The life of Manning Clark* (Melbourne, 2011), p. 219. The scope and complexity of Davidson's work, together with his research being incomplete and the unavailability of source material in New Zealand, would likely have precluded the completion of the thesis had he returned home beforehand.

35 See Davidson to his mother, 17 June 1948, Davidson Papers, NLA, MS 5105, box 65.
36 Nancy M. Taylor, *The New Zealand People at War: The home front* (Wellington, 1986), chs 5–7, 18–19; David Grant, *Out in the Cold: Pacifists and conscientious objectors in New Zealand during World War II* (Auckland, 1986); J. E. Cookson, 'Appeal Boards and Conscientious Objectors', in John Crawford, (ed.), *Kia Kaha: New Zealand in the Second World War* (Auckland, 2002), pp. 173–98.
37 J. W. Davidson, 'The Present War and the Future Peace', *Tomorrow*, 5:25 (1939), pp. 778–80.
38 *Dominion*, 3 February 1940, p. 16; 5 February 1940, p. 6; 6 February 1940, p. 6 [Editorial]. The matter was also raised in the *Evening Post*.
39 Nan Taylor, 'Human Rights in World War II in New Zealand', *New Zealand Journal of History*, 23:2 (1989), especially pp. 116–19; Andrew Cutler, '*Tomorrow* Magazine and New Zealand Politics, 1934–1940', *New Zealand Journal of History*, 24:1 (1990), pp. 22–44.
40 Davidson to Lilburn, 5 June 1941, Lilburn Papers, ATL, MS-Papers-2483-052.

every penny from his father's estate, and while he was provided for in the will by way of an insurance policy, it would not mature for a number of years.[41] Thus he applied in early 1941 for a British Council-sponsored teaching position in Africa. His College tutor wrote a favourable testimonial, and provided Davidson with a copy. The following day, the tutor wrote a private and confidential follow-up to the effect that Davidson lacked 'the appearance of forcefulness and drive which you might wish your lecturers to show'—to which the British Council expressed its gratitude, saying that such confidential letters 'are particularly helpful'.[42]

Blessing in disguise or not, Davidson remained in England for the duration. His mood was not improved by what he regarded as the brazen deceit of British propaganda, writing to Lilburn about the 'melancholy triumph of being proved right in disbelieving' but in terms that show some false impressions:

> There is much more I should like to say on many things—the propagandist lies, for instance; and one doesn't have to come in very close contact with people in the forces to know how considerable they sometimes are...it is absurd, & might be catastrophic, to try and delude ourselves that there is a big split in the Nazi party or even that Hess believes Germany will lose the war. He believes, I imagine, that she can win only at great cost—but that is very different. Again those suggestions by intelligent people—dons & such like—that Germany is brutally reckless of human life: where is the evidence? To fling Churchill's words, or something like them, back to him, has ever so much been won with the loss of so few? What do we gain by refusing to see that the German forces are being used with magnificent skill, with daring and imagination, certainly, but quiet without recklessness? War is brutal—you won't expect me to deny that—but is efficiently conducted war more brutal than inefficient.[43]

Davidson was seemingly purblind, almost wilfully ignorant, to what one historian has described as 'the new Germany created by will, force, and genocide'.[44]

His immediate financial predicament was resolved by a renewal of the next instalment of his scholarship. To the rescue came his supervisor, Eric Walker (the

---

41 George Davidson's estate realised £7015 15s 11d. He also had an insurance policy (for an undisclosed amount) with two-thirds of this going to Jim Davidson, presumably when it matured in 1951. George Wightman Davidson's probate papers, Archives New Zealand (Wellington), AAOM 6030, 1941/2779. Until then it appears that Davidson received nothing from his father's estate. See also Davidson to his mother, 12 April, 22 September, 21 October 1953, Davidson Papers, NLA, MS 5105, box 66.
42 Bailey to British Council, 19 February and 20 February 1942; British Council to Bailey, 24 February 1942, Davidson's Tutorial File, St John's College, Cambridge. Bailey was Bull Professor of Law at Cambridge University.
43 Davidson to Lilburn, 5 June 1941, Lilburn Papers, ATL, MS-Papers-2483-052.
44 Reba N. Soffer, *History, Historians, and Conservatism in Britain and America* (Oxford, 2009), p. 181.

Vere Harmsworth Professor of Naval and Imperial History at Cambridge), who recommended him to Margery (later Dame Margery) Perham of Nuffield College, Oxford. 'Miss Perham', as Davidson always called her, was directing a major project on colonial legislatures in Africa and Davidson was recruited to write the volume on the Northern Rhodesian Legislative Council.[45] He effectively went part-time on his thesis and alternated between Oxford and Cambridge. Working in another area was a useful comparative exercise but he found it taxing to be constantly shifting mental gears between Africa and the Pacific.

Davidson spent the first half of 1942 completing his PhD thesis whilst maintaining the pretence that the Northern Rhodesian project was ticking along. The thesis, on the 'European Penetration of the South Pacific, 1779–1842', was submitted in May and Davidson satisfied his examiners the following month at the *viva*. Being called up for active service was again in the air and he viewed the prospect of joining the 'arrogant' Army, even in a non-combat role, with unconcealed dismay. Then it emerged that he was still technically a student until actually graduating in October. In other words, he had a four-month reprieve to find alternative work that would be counted as contributing to the war effort. The immediate worry, however, was that Davidson no longer had income from scholarships. Margery Perham wanted him in her stable and made strenuous efforts to get the necessary funding. Uncertain that Miss Perham could do so, he committed himself to a job with the Admiralty—and no sooner had this happened than Miss Perham did find the money.

She was very disappointed, but Davidson was 'overjoyed'. The Admiralty position not only removed 'the gloomy prospect of service in the ranks of the army'.[46] It meant that Davidson was right-hand man to Raymond Firth, the author of *The Primitive Economics of the New Zealand Maori* (1929) and *We, the Tikopia* (1936), who had been seconded from the Department of Anthropology at the London School of Economics (LSE). Davidson and Firth were soul mates. They had met the previous year and Firth was highly impressed with Davidson's ability and potential. Mutual regard deepened into a lifelong friendship that was very evident to me during the Firths' stay at the ANU in 1972–73. The Admiralty work was based at the Scott Polar Institute in Cambridge and involved the compilation of a series of volumes (variously known as the 'Admiralty Handbooks' or the 'Naval Intelligence Handbooks'), which would provide

---

45 Margery Perham's 'Studies in Colonial Legislatures' project is discussed by Richard Symonds, *Oxford and Empire: The last lost cause?* (Basingstoke, UK, 1986), pp. 284–5.
46 Davidson to his mother, 13 July 1942, Davidson Papers, NLA, MS 5105, box 65. Davidson's delight was soon tempered by delays in the confirmation of his appointment and questions over the scope of his duties, which turned out to be onerous.

broad-ranging information for British naval operations. Firth was in charge of the small team responsible for the Handbooks relating to the Pacific Islands,[47] and he recalled Davidson's contribution in terms of high praise:

> Jim was my right-hand man as editorial assistant. As well as his almost encyclopedic knowledge of the field, he was meticulous in his control of detail, with the keenest eye for error—the best proof-reader I have ever known. He was also a pleasure to work with, as you will know from his skeptical, humorous, witty approach to people.[48]

But it was arduous work. As well as authoring or co-authoring some 600 pages for the Handbooks,[49] Davidson was in charge during Firth's frequent illnesses and there were times when he wilted. In reply to Miles Greenwood's inquiries, he wrote:

> 'Burdens of work', you say, do they multiply? Well, yes. For I was not quite out of bed [with illness] when Firth went down with bronchitis, for the fourth time in as many months…[and] he has thrown over the editing of our current volume. I do it, in addition to as much of my own writing as I can't farm out (& I can farm out very little). Of the remaining two members of our team, who were formerly kept up to the mark by Firth & now have to be by me, one is about 35, temperamental, & extremely sensitive to criticism of work which he knows, but hates to admit, is frequently inaccurate & inadequate. So there are difficulties…
>
> All this, I can see, is not very lucid; but I don't feel lucid—garrulous, rather. Perhaps it is a reaction against the inescapable pedantries of editing.[50]

Nor did it help that he had his own health problems. The frequent fogs affected his throat and lungs and there were recurrences of his asthma and catarrh. But at least he had the satisfaction of referring to the 'unmilitary ways' of the Naval Intelligence Division, just as he delighted in the informal manner that his Home Guard contingent carried on. The real problem, however, was his continuing commitment to the Nuffield project. The Northern Rhodesia book became a monkey on his back and his peace of mind was not improved by Miss Perham's suggestion that he write a short history of Northern Rhodesia as well. On one occasion, he lamented that every spare moment of his time was being spent finishing his manuscript for Miss Perham; on another he confessed that it was

---

47   Naval Intelligence Division [of the British Admiralty], *Pacific Islands* (Geographical Handbook Series), 4 vols, [no place of publication], 1943–45.
48   Personal communication, Raymond Firth, 30 September 1997.
49   R. Gerard Ward, 'Davidson's Contribution to the "Admiralty Handbooks"', *Journal of Pacific History*, 29:2 (1994), pp. 238–40.
50   Davidson to Greenwood, 26 February 1944, Greenwood Papers, NLA, MS 9805.

[r]egrettable that one should attempt two things at once, but really [the] activity is unceasing. I have been trying to find a moment to write for long, but without avail. Daytime & evening I am either at the Polar Inst. or else [at my lodgings] writing (I refuse to do that without solitude).[51]

This 'seemingly unending problem', as he described the Northern Rhodesia work, persisted into the following year and in the same breath he heartily hoped that Miss Perham would be off to Jamaica so that her letters of inquiry would become less frequent. It was just as well, he wryly commented, that the authors of other volumes in the Nuffield project were as tardy as him.[52]

Davidson was clearly overworked, as was almost everyone else serving on the home front. It is true there was no invasion but the strains of everyday life included rationing and too much to do on not enough sleep. As well as having joined the Signal and Intelligence Platoon of the Home Guard, Davidson at one point was marking Oxford and Cambridge School Certificate papers to augment his income. To cap it off, Firth urged him to collaborate in an official civil history of World War II, under the general editorship of W. K. Hancock.[53] The offer was attractive but his workload was too much as it was and he pulled out, telling his mother that he simply 'hate[d] the thought of going on & every minute of my time having to be allocated to one job or another'—but also telling Lilburn that, despite the loss of income, persisting with the project meant that 'the majority of my time would [have gone] into doing work useful but not entirely of my own choosing'.[54] Another way of looking at it is that he had ample employment in areas that suited his skills and temperament and which led to professional advancement, whereas in the early days of the war it did cross his mind that he might 'be forced into doing [something] stupidly out of accord with my inclinations'.[55] Nor was Davidson alone in such attitudes. The historian A. J. P. Taylor also knew that he was not soldier material; he too joined the Home Guard, as well as lecturing for the Ministry of Information, broadcasting for the BBC and writing guidebooks for future British occupying forces.[56]

They were indeed a strenuous four years. His father's death impelled a search for paid employment that, in turn, opened up opportunities. One of those

---

51   Davidson to his mother, 27 November 1943, Davidson Papers, NLA, MS 5105, box 65; Davidson to Greenwood, 19 April 1944, Greenwood Papers, NLA, MS 9805.
52   *The Northern Rhodesian Legislative Council* was finally published in 1947 and favourably reviewed in academic journals. It was the first of Davidson's three books.
53   J. M. Lee and Martin Petter, *The Colonial Office, War and Development Policy: Organisation and the planning of a metropolitan initiative, 1939–1945* (London, 1982), p. 257 n. 1; Jim Davidson, *A Three-Cornered Life*, ch. 6 ('The Civil Histories').
54   Davidson to his mother, 26 September 1945, Davidson Papers, NLA, MS 5105, box 65; Davidson to Lilburn, 11 October 1945, Lilburn Papers, ATL, MS-Papers-2483-052.
55   Davidson to his mother, 6 September 1939, Davidson Papers, NLA, MS 5105, box 65.
56   Kathleen Burk, *Troublemaker: The life and history of A. J. P. Taylor* (New Haven, Conn./London, 2000), pp. 170–1.

opportunities was the ambiance of Oxbridge and especially the 'quite remarkable chances of meeting people' as varied as visiting missionaries from the Melanesian Mission, scientists who had worked in the Pacific and colonial administrators from Africa, in addition to other academics, such as Margaret Mead and Reo Fortune on separate occasions. In 1943, he applied for a Fellowship at St John's College with Hancock as one of his sponsors. He had never been so nervous about anything since waiting for his MA results, and was shocked to miss out. The disappointment gnawed at him for months afterwards.[57] He was successful the following year but lecturing duties to army cadets and colonial service probationers only increased his workload. On VE Day, the twenty-nine-year-old Jim Davidson had come a long way since entering the war as a PhD student of less than one year's standing. He probably would have agreed, given the rigours and privations of the home front, that he had lived among a 'brave and stalwart people who suffer[ed] from what their leaders [had] set in motion; it makes one realize how lucky Britain was to have got through the Second World War and how much was owed by so few to so many'.[58]

Even so, Davidson had a 'good war'. Whereas the war was an impediment to budding academics who saw active service (such as Neville Phillips), Davidson was able to find work within the domestic war machine that was directly relevant to his craft and calling. His work was highly regarded and it resulted in a fellowship at St John's College in 1945, a lectureship in the Cambridge History Faculty in 1947, then being shortlisted for the Beit Professorship of the History of the British Empire at Oxford in 1948, and finally recommended by Hancock and Firth for the Foundation Chair of Pacific History at the nascent ANU, an appointment he took up in December 1950.[59] One of the reasons he was appointed was because he had practical as well as scholarly credentials. That is, in 1947 and again in 1949–50, he had been assigned by the New Zealand Government to help prepare the trusteeship of Western Samoa for eventual self-government: 'we wanted someone who would go and make a report on Samoa... You see we had no people of any academic qualifications ourselves'.[60] Although the Western Samoan assignments had nothing directly to do with Davidson's wartime experiences—and he hardly mentions the place in his PhD thesis— his work for Margery Perham imparted a scholarly interest in the problems of

---

57 Doug Munro, 'J. W. Davidson and W. K. Hancock: Patronage, preferment, privilege', *Journal of New Zealand Studies*, 4–5 (2005–06), pp. 39–63 (especially pp. 42–8).
58 Lindsay Duguid, 'Stop to Dress', *Times Literary Supplement*, 18 July 2008, p. 26.
59 Firth to Oxford University Registrar, 21 May 1948, Firth Archive, British Library of Political and Economic Science, London School of Economics and Political Science [hereinafter FIRTH], 8/1/18; Firth to ANU Vice-Chancellor, 25 January 1949, and 6 July 1949, both in FIRTH7/5/1; Davidson to his mother, 23 May 1948 and 6 July 1948, Davidson Papers, NLA, MS 5105, box 65; Davidson to W. K. Hancock, 19 March 1949, Hancock Papers, ANUA 77/12; Davidson to Firth, 21 March 1949, FIRTH8/1/18; Firth to Hancock, 25 March 1949, Hancock Papers, ANUA 77/15.
60 Sir Alister McIntosh (interviewed by F. L. W. Wood and Mary Boyd, 2 December 1975), ATL, OHColl-0163/1 (typescript: ATL, 80-413).

colonial government, provided a disciplined focus for his sympathy towards indigenous self-determination and gave intellectual reasoning for his conversion to a 'participant historian'. By kindling an interest in *contemporary* colonial affairs, his African research provided the springboard to becoming an academic who sought a life of action as much as of the mind. The numbers of scholars who came to, or returned to, Cambridge after their war service—whether at the front or at home—also had a bearing. They were greatly influenced by their war service and frequently enough studied related subjects or wrote about their wartime vocation (Harry Hinsley's work on Bletchley Park, for example), and they almost invariably had an altered outlook on life. They influenced Davidson in a more general sense by providing confirmation that his growing notion of the scholar-in-action had merit. Then it transmuted—or as Ronald Hyam has suggested, Davidson 'represented the apotheosis of "participant history"…for in his case it came to displace the primacy of the academic role'.[61]

Indeed, it did: the only book Davidson published during his tenure at the ANU was *Samoa mo Samoa*, his classic account of Western Samoa's long road to sovereign independence, in which he himself played a part.[62] His departmental colleague Harry Maude thought this unremarkable because he 'always felt that the Samoans came first in [Jim's] affections'.[63] Although Davidson established a pioneering school of Pacific History at the ANU, many colleagues regretted his slender publication record—or what one described as 'the extreme difficulty of getting anything out of him in the research way'.[64] Nor did it help that his love of fast cars, his disregard of the University House dress code and a general exuberance encouraged detractors to mark him off as ANU's senior *enfant terrible* and to doubt his seriousness of purpose. Those closer to him usually begged to differ, not least his PhD students, who found him a superb thesis supervisor.

Despite numerous publication casualties, there is a sense that Davidson developed in a quite different respect—from a position of indifference to one of principled concern. Before the outbreak of war, he expressed no moral outrage at Hitler's activities, in contrast with the Oxford historian Hugh Trevor-Roper. Then a student, Trevor-Roper had visited Germany in 1935 and, in the words of his biographer, was 'nauseated by what he witnessed, revolted by the inflammatory

---

61 Ronald Hyam, *Understanding the British Empire* (Cambridge, 2010), p. 495; also Doug Munro, 'J. W. Davidson—The making of a participant historian', in Brij V. Lal and Peter Hempenstall (eds), *Pacific Lives, Pacific Places: Bursting boundaries in Pacific history* (Canberra, 2001), pp. 98–116 (especially pp. 104–5). Davidson's major statement on participant history is 'Understanding Pacific History: The participant as historian', in Peter Munz (ed.), *The Feel of Truth* (Wellington, 1969), pp. 25–40.
62 J. W. Davidson, *Samoa mo Samoa: The emergence of the Independent State of Western Samoa* (Melbourne, 1967).
63 H. E. Maude to Derek Freeman, 9 January 1982, Maude Papers, Barr Smith Library, University of Adelaide, MSS 0003, series J.
64 John Passmore (interviewed by Stephen Foster, 17 May 1991), ANUA 44/20. Passmore was Professor of Social Philosophy at the ANU.

rhetoric and appalled by what he saw as the abject conformity of the German people'. Three years later, he was 'ashamed of his country's spinelessness in the face of blackmail' over Czechoslovakia.[65] Davidson, in contrast, seemed unconcerned that the Munich Agreement meant a 'grave injustice' towards Czechoslovakia that 'deeply sullied Britain's name and moral standing'.[66] At no point does Davidson seem to have acknowledged that massive erosions of civil liberties and assaults on human rights were integral to the Nazis achieving and maintaining power—although he would probably have seen things in a quite different light had he, like Trevor-Roper, actually visited Germany. Neither did Davidson engage with the prevailing view in 1939 of his own generation in Britain—that an expectation of getting killed in the upcoming war did not prevent the thought 'that war would have to be fought, would be won and could lead to a better society'.[67] Seemingly, Davidson's only concern was that war did not eventuate—in contrast, say, with the Oxford historian A. L. Rowse, who, in the 1930s,

> saw the folly of pacifism and disarmament and the self-deceiving feebleness of appeasement. Contemptuous of the lazy indifference of Baldwin and the National Government, [Rowse] was enraged by the idiocy of Left Wing intellectuals such as G. D. H. Cole and R. H. S. Crossman, whose gifts made idiocy a sin.[68]

Davidson would feel unease were he still alive to read the present chapter, but would probably say that he was reacting to the situation as it seemed to him at the time.

Soon after the inevitable declaration of war, he wrote to Miles Greenwood:

> I find very few who do not share my opinion that we stand little chance of coming out of this war—or of bringing Europe out of it—any better than we & they went in, or even thou [sic] they could come out of it now. To-night Mr Chamberlain speaks, but with the best intentions in the world he will express a decision which—with ever increasing certainty—I believe is mistaken & wrong. *One does not fight because one sees injustice, but because one believes one can put it right: if one can't… well one doesn't*.[69]

---

65 Adam Sisman, *Hugh Trevor-Roper: The biography* (London, 2010), pp. 40, 68.
66 Kershaw, *Making Friends with Hitler*, p. 252.
67 Eric Hobsbawm, 'C (for Crisis)', *London Review of Books*, 6 August 2009, pp. 12–13.
68 Richard Ollard, *A Man of Contradictions: A life of A. L. Rowse* (London, 2000), p. 103.
69 Emphasis added. Davidson to Greenwood, 13 October 1939, Greenwood Papers, NLA, MS 9805. This is remarkably similar to what Chamberlain said to his sister on 20 March 1938, a good six months before Davidson arrived in Britain: 'You only have to look at the map to see that nothing that France or we could do could possibly save Czechoslovakia from being over-run by the Germans if they wanted to do it…Therefore, we should not help Czechoslovakia—she would simply be the pretext for going to war with Germany. That

The last sentence entails a stance at variance with Davidson's later words and deeds, and his wartime attitudes themselves are out of character with everything else about Davidson—for the one thing that he could be counted upon as an ANU professor (and as a constitutional adviser in the Pacific Islands) was to fight hard for what he believed, whether it be upholding academic freedom, criticising government foreign policy, standing watch over humane liberal values or advancing the rights of Pacific Islanders. One might say that Davidson's comment on Chamberlain on the one hand, and, on the other, his view of the futility of war, is hardly to be compared with fighting against injustice in a colonial setting or standing up for academic freedom; and it is worth remembering that the New Zealand Government initially took an appeasing stance towards Nazi Germany.[70] But the sense remains that the younger Jim Davidson transformed into a sturdier older version. No-one at the ANU would have questioned Spate's observation that the older Davidson was 'a bonny fighter' who took 'delight in combat for a cause'.[71] Some would say that he was too abrasive for his own good, although others realised 'that behind a combative facade he was the kindliest of colleagues'.[72] Not surprisingly, his pro-appeasement stance was not something he talked about in later years and those who knew Davidson at the ANU had no idea that he embraced such attitudes—as well they might not because they contradict other aspects of his life and thought.

Perhaps, then, the greatest single influence of the war on Davidson—even more so than giving intellectual reasoning to his notion of participant historian—was to impress upon him that you fight because you *do* see an injustice, whether or not you believe you can put it right. In that sense, Davidson repudiated his wartime stance.

---

we could not think of, unless we had a reasonable prospect of being able to beat her to her knees and of that I see no sign. I have therefore abandoned any idea of giving guarantees to Czechoslovakia or the French in connection with her obligations to that country.' Quoted in Kershaw, *Making Friends with Hitler*, p. 221.

70   John Crawford and James Watson, '"A Most Appeasing Line": New Zealand and Nazi Germany, 1935–1940', *Journal of Imperial and Commonwealth History*, 38:1 (2010), pp. 175–97.

71   O. H. K. Spate, 'And Now There Will Be A Void: A tribute to J. W. Davidson', *Journal of Pacific Studies*, 20 (1996), p. 22; also Spate to A. J. S. Reid, 11 April 1973, Spate Papers, NLA, MS 7886/7/4/2. Spate was Foundation Professor of Geography at the ANU.

72   Geoffrey Sawer (Professor of Law, ANU) to D. A. Low (Director, Research School of Pacific Studies, ANU), 10 April 1973, Davidson Papers, ANUA 57/96.

10. Neville Phillips and the Mother Country

Jock Phillips

Neville Crompton Phillips (1916–2001), later Professor of History at the University of Canterbury, served in the Royal Artillery from 1939 to 1946. He served from the ages of twenty-three to thirty—years of young adulthood that are usually thought of as among the defining period of a person's life, when attitudes are shaped and life courses chosen. This was a time spent in military service witnessing traumatic events, so the expectation might be that the war years would shape his world view and approach to history for the rest of his life. But this is not really a story of change, so much as one of affirmation. The effect of participation in World War II was not to alter radically Neville Phillips' view of the past, but to confirm his views. It gave new content to his historical work, but not a fundamentally different approach.

Essentially, Neville Phillips' world view was already firmly in place by 1939. To explain this we must explore a little of his family background. His father, Samuel Phillips, was born and brought up in the Jewish East End of London.[1] The name suggests that the family was one of the long line of English Jews, but Samuel's mother was a German immigrant and presumably part of that large influx of Ashkenazi Jews who flooded into the East End at the end of the nineteenth century. The Phillips family lived on Mile End and Sam's father pursued the classic Jewish line of work as a 'clother's cutter'. It was an area of poverty and overcrowding, and in the first years of the twentieth century there was growing anti-Jewish feeling, spearheaded especially by the British Brothers' League, set up in 1902 to restrict Jewish immigration. Whether these were the reasons for young Sam Phillips' departure for New Zealand aged seventeen in 1904 we do not know. Certainly, seven years after his arrival, he married a non-Jewish woman, Clara (known as Claire) Bird, so he had clearly broken with orthodox Jewish traditions of marrying within the race; but Neville Phillips did remember being taken to the synagogue as a young boy,[2] and in New Zealand Sam continued in the clothing trade by becoming a travelling salesman of women's clothing. Whether this was what attracted Clara Bird to him is unclear, but certainly her niece remembers that Clara, who was tall and elegant, had an eye for fashion and enjoyed displaying Sam's samples.[3] The family moved about New Zealand as Sam

---

1 Death certificate of Samuel Phillips, 1891 UK Census.
2 Neville Phillips, Interview with author, 12 February 1997.
3 Notes written by Elizabeth Winifred Rathgen, 1987.

pursued his vocation, and, in 1923, when Neville was aged seven, the family was living in Wanganui. Then occurred the traumatic event of my father's life. Sam had taken Neville and some of his friends for a picnic in the December sun at Hipango Park. This was a bush reserve 25 km up the Whanganui River and accessible only by boat. It is said that Neville told his friends to watch his father dive into the river. He did so, but sadly could not swim and Neville apparently saw his father's legs go round and round. The coroner decided that he was accidentally drowned, although teetotal members of Clara's family were convinced that 'strong drink was involved'.[4]

So, at the age of seven, Neville Phillips was left fatherless. His mother, Clara Bird, daughter of a policeman born in India and a mother, Helen Stewart, originally from Maidenhead in Berkshire (near Windsor), earned her living by working as a receptionist in pubs across the lower part of the North Island. She was given accommodation in the pubs, so Neville and his older brother, David, had to find other accommodation. At one stage, Neville certainly lived with his grandmother in Christchurch, but more often he boarded with families in the lower North Island. He was an able child, and managed to win a gold medal as dux at a primary school in Dannevirke and he also won a scholarship that provided a few pounds to help him go on to high school. So in 1928, not yet aged twelve, he went to Dannevirke High School in the same third-form class as his brother, David, who was more than three years older. At Dannevirke, he remembered especially his first classes in Latin and being encouraged in his academic interests by a master called Hogben, the son of the great Secretary of Education (1899–1915), George Hogben. Neville remembered Hogben because he apparently favoured Neville over a girl who had actually done much better in the scholarship examination. At the end of the year, Neville's mother shifted from a Dannevirke pub to a Palmerston North pub, so Neville was transferred to Palmerston North to board with another family and went to the local boys' high school. His brother started work as a mechanic in a local garage.[5]

Neville was at Palmerston North Boys' High from 1929 to 1931—from the ages of thirteen to fifteen. Most of the boys were middle class, and Neville remembered all his life his excruciating shame that when the headmaster invited his form to a party he was the only one who did not have a suit. He was acutely aware of his difference from his peers: he was not only much poorer and lived as a boarder in a strange house, but he was Jewish and considerably younger than most of his classmates. His position as an outsider might have turned him into a social and even political rebel, especially since there were others at the school with a left-wing persuasion such as Jack and Ernie Lewin.[6] It did not. Instead,

---

4 Death certificate of Samuel Phillips, 9 December 1923; Rathgen notes; Coronial Inquest file for Samuel Phillips, Archives New Zealand (Wellington), Records of the Department of Justice, J46, 1923/1146.
5 Rathgen notes; Neville Phillips, Interview with author, 12 February 1997.
6 Bruce Hamilton, *Palmerston North Boys' High School, 1902–2001* (Palmerston North, NZ, 2002), p. 137.

Neville found solace in two activities. The first was cricket. He had always been interested in sport, and in his younger years had followed closely the success of the Hawkes Bay Ranfurly Shield-winning rugby team. At Dannevirke, he had distinguished himself as a long-distance runner. At Palmerston North, he continued to run and play rugby, but his passion became cricket. Cricket was the 'big thing' at Palmerston North Boys' and the classics master, W. P. Anderson, took a special interest in Neville and encouraged his ability to bowl leg-breaks. The other focus of his life became English poetry. The English teacher was A. C. Zohrab. In his history of the school, Bruce Hamilton writes of Zohrab:

> In a school devoted to the Spartan and the sporting he had opened new windows in his teaching of English and his production of plays. Boys felt a strong affection for this gentle man who hated the thought of war, but when Hitler unleashed war on the world he believed it was his duty to go, and he was killed in action in Italy in 1944.[7]

He took a shine to Neville, would invite him home, and directed his attention to the great body of English literature. He became a particular enthusiast for English pastoral poetry such as A. E. Housman's *A Shropshire Lad*. So, feeling a degree of isolation because of his poverty, family situation and Jewishness, Neville came to identify with English culture—both its literary productions and its great game. History was not at this stage determinative in moving him in this direction, but in his last year he did remember studying nineteenth-century British history with a good teacher. This Anglophilia was not unusual among the Jewish community. The great Jewish American lawyer Felix Frankfurter also had a passionate love of England (he also 'grew up in less than prosperous circumstances').[8] What is also of interest is that despite his deprived childhood, Neville aspired to the respectable middle, even upper, class England, not its working-class traditions. It seemed he could escape reminders of his disrupted childhood by adopting a different class persona.[9]

In 1932, not yet sixteen, Neville decided to go to the Canterbury University College. Without any support from the school, and still in the lower sixth form, he had entered the university scholarship examination and won a senior scholarship. It gave him a few pounds to assist his time at university. His favourite teacher, A. C. Zohrab, had wanted him to get a job with the Palmerston North daily paper, but Neville had remembered walking with his father in Christchurch on the way to the synagogue, and as they passed the university grounds, his father said 'one day you should go to university'. Neville recalled thinking that this would become his aim. So he set off for Christchurch, lived

---

7   Ibid., p. 120. Interestingly, Neville paid a special visit to Zohrab's grave at Cassino in 1955.
8   See Michael E. Parrish, *Felix Frankfurter and His Times: The reform years* (New York, 1982), pp. 5, 6–7, 240–1.
9   Neville Phillips, Interview with author, 12 February 1997.

with his grandmother and got a job as a messenger for the *Sun* newspaper. Intending to study law, he enrolled in Latin and constitutional law.[10] In the latter, he came across James Hight who enticed him from law to history. It also made a difference that the history lectures were after 4 pm, which allowed him time to go to work. Hight was at the time Professor of History and Political Science and also Rector of Canterbury University College. Canterbury-born and educated, Hight set out to establish the career of serious academic historian. His standards were rigorous. Although he had researched and written on New Zealand history, especially *The Constitutional History and Law of New Zealand* with H. D. Bamford (1914), he always believed in the central importance of European history. Neville Phillips wrote of him in the *Dictionary of New Zealand Biography*:

> He did not see the Old World until advanced middle age, but throughout his life he was the dauntless foe of insularity and saw his own country as immovably founded on Western civilisation. It would be only a little fanciful to say that he held Richelieu and Mazarin barely less significant for New Zealand than the Maori seafarers and Edward Gibbon Wakefield.[11]

Hight's very first publication was an introduction and notes to Carlyle's *Sartor Resartus*. His second was a 300-page book, *The English as a Colonising Nation* (1903). So where Zohrab had led Neville Phillips to English poetry, Hight led to his appreciation of English imperial history. The interest in poetry did not die. At the *Sun*, Neville had at first been a messenger, then he worked in the reading room as a copy-holder. But on the side he began writing a regular weekly column of light verse, 'Sunspots', which, modelled on A. P. Herbert's light verse, made witty rhyming commentary on current events. It was a fashionable style. When the *Sun* closed, he was offered a position with the *Press*; and he sat next to Allen Curnow, who, as well as becoming a major New Zealand poet, would himself establish a reputation as writer of light topical verse under the pseudonym 'Whim Wham'.[12] At the *Press*, Neville became a subeditor on the cable page, which further developed his interest in overseas politics and news.[13] This was the mid-1930s, a time when the Labour Government was introducing a series of progressive social and political initiatives; Christchurch was also a place where interesting social and cultural activity was happening. Denis Glover had started the Caxton Press and was surrounded by a group of young

---

10 Neville Phillips, Interview with author, 13 February 1997.
11 N. C. Phillips, 'Hight, James, 1870–1958', *Dictionary of New Zealand Biography*, updated 22 June 2007, <http://www.dnzb.govt.nz/>
12 The first selection of Whim Wham verse to be published as a book was *A Present for Hitler and Other Verse* (Christchurch, 1941). Several other selections have since been published, most recently Terry Sturm (ed.), *Whim Wham's New Zealand: The best of Whim Wham, 1937–1988* (Auckland, 2005).
13 Neville Phillips, Interviews with author, 12 and 13 February 1997.

10. Neville Phillips and the Mother Country

poets and intellectuals; Kennaway Henderson had established the left-wing monthly *Tomorrow*.[14] But Neville was not really interested in these local cultural developments; his eyes were on the Old World.

Neville did history honours and wrote a thesis under Hight entitled, 'New Zealand and the Mother Country'. It provides us with an excellent sense of Neville Phillips, the historian, in 1937. For a start, one might ask why the subject was New Zealand history, not British or European history. This was entirely understandable. As Chris Hilliard explains, a thesis in history did require a student to work in primary materials and almost no primary materials were available in non-New Zealand history at that stage. So of 363 history theses completed in New Zealand universities from 1920 to 1940, only 18 were not on New Zealand subjects.[15] There were some British *Parliamentary Papers* in the General Assembly Library in Wellington, but Neville continued to hold down a part-time job so travel to Wellington for research was out of the question. In the event, the primary sources he used were those available in Christchurch: the Parliamentary debates, what he called Parliamentary papers (also known as the *Appendices to the Journals of the House of Representatives*) and two Christchurch newspapers, the *Press* and *Lyttelton Times*. As for the subject matter, it was about New Zealand political history, but the focus was very much on New Zealand as part of the British Empire. The thesis (which is called on the spine 'New Zealand and the Mother Country, 1868–1901' and on the title page 'New Zealand's Relations with Great Britain, 1868–1901') had a subtitle 'A study in Empire unionism' and the title page also includes a quote from Alfred Lord Tennyson:

> May we find, as ages run,
> The mother featured in the son.

The theme of the thesis is the move from colonial hostility towards the mother country to filial devotion. It begins at the end of the New Zealand Wars. Debate over the withdrawal of British troops and forced colonial self-reliance in defence had created a situation when, in Phillips' words: 'Never before or after was mutual regard between imperial and colonial governments at so low an ebb.'[16] The thesis ended at the turn of the century when New Zealand was keenly involved in providing services to the mother country in the South African War and deeply committed to membership of the Empire. It is a triumphant story of what Phillips calls 'Empire unionism'. He sees this as the voluntary commitment

---

14 Gordon Ogilvie, *Denis Glover: His life* (Auckland, 1999), ch. 7; Andrew Cutler, '"Tomorrow" Magazine: The case of the cultural shadow', in Pat Moloney and Kerry Taylor (eds), *Culture and the Labour Movement: Essays in New Zealand labour history* (Palmerston North, NZ, 1991), pp. 209–24.
15 Chris Hilliard, *The Bookmen's Dominion: Cultural life in New Zealand, 1920–1950* (Auckland, 2006), p. 87.
16 Neville Phillips, 'New Zealand's Relations with Great Britain, 1868–1901: A study in Empire unionism', MA thesis, Canterbury University College, Christchurch, 1937, p. 34.

of colonies to the Empire, creating a situation where the Empire acted as one; and he contrasted it with other forms of imperialism that were essentially rule by force. He sees the British Empire as the exemplar of international government where the colonies are allowed to develop their own identity yet remain forever British. In the first chapter of the thesis, he tries to explain this unique form of imperialism. He sees it as partly the fact that these were colonies of settlement, not exploitation, and that they were based in temperate, not tropical, areas of the world. He sees agriculture as crucial to creating happy British colonies, and he also sees the policy of laissez faire in both its economic guise and its political guise (encouraging self-government) as crucial. But he also points to something about the racial characteristic of the British: they were descended from Anglo-Saxons and '[i]n their veins ran the blood of these pioneers, strongly built men, self-reliant, democratic in instinct, and laborious as well as courageous in battle'.[17] It is interesting that in discussing these characteristics he always uses the adjective 'our': 'our success' in the Empire, 'our prowess as seamen', and so on. His identification with Britain is clear; and he also expresses his sense of the importance of British cultural hegemony to the working of the Empire.

> In the arts and literature, London is still the Mecca of all Britons, and the writers of Britain are the writers of the Empire. Colonials make their pilgrimage to the Old land, Oxford admits sons of the dominions, British statesmen meet in conference every four years and there are many British conferences of interest other than political.[18]

Interestingly, in light of Neville Phillips' future writings, the first chapter includes several quotations from the eighteenth-century political theorist of enlightened conservatism Edmund Burke.

Three points are worth making about the thesis. First, the thesis is written with considerable literary grace and without a grammatical or spelling error in sight. It is a fine work of literature of the conventional imperial style. Second, it is not really surprising that Neville Phillips praised the British Empire and British culture. New Zealand in the 1930s was a small, provincial society. As John Beaglehole wrote when he was travelling to London in 1926, it was excellent to be in 'a part of the earth that has really some history behind it & not just a few tuppeny-ha'penny scraps and tenth-rate politics'.[19] Expatriation was a well-recognised cultural phenomenon of the time and anyone who aspired to serious engagement with great minds was likely to go offshore.[20] On the other hand—and this is our third point—Neville Phillips showed some interest in

---

17 Ibid., p. 10.
18 Ibid., p. 30.
19 Quoted in Tim Beaglehole, *A Life of J. C. Beaglehole: New Zealand scholar* (Wellington, 2006), p. 84.
20 See Doug Munro, 'Becoming an Expatriate: J. W. Davidson and the brain drain', *Journal of New Zealand Studies*, 2–3 (2003–04), pp. 19–43.

New Zealand nationalism. The thesis concludes with a portrait of some of the leading political lights of colonial New Zealand. Among these, he describes Richard Seddon (Prime Minister from 1893 to 1906), whom he recognises as stimulating national pride. But he also emphasises the limits of this national spirit: 'Seddon was the chief of those who fostered the "mother complex", the tradition of filial respect, and he, more than any other, created for New Zealand the role of the spoiled child of Britain.'[21] There is a hint here that, perhaps, if only briefly, Phillips was being affected by those stronger currents of nationalism in New Zealand of the 1930s. This, after all, was a time when there was some anger at New Zealand's economic dependence on the United Kingdom and there were clear signs of cultural nationalism—not only writers outside the academy such as James Cowan but also those who had been students just before Neville Phillips and aspired to a richer cultural life within New Zealand that would confront distinctive New Zealand issues. There were intellectuals emerging such as John Mulgan, Denis Glover, Allen Curnow, Frank Sargeson, Douglas Lilburn and, not long to appear, the historian Keith Sinclair. If so, then Phillips was paying but a brief nod in that direction. For the dominant impulse of the thesis is that acceptance of Britain's culture was but the logical response for a provincial culture and that the political reconciliation with the mother country by 1900 was a triumph, not a tragedy. In his personal circumstances, Neville Phillips had suffered economically in the 1930s and experienced a sense of being marginal. This might perhaps have turned his anger against the Empire. Instead, the reverse happened and the Empire beckoned.

So, in 1938, he applied for and—on the strength of the overseas examiner's report—was awarded a postgraduate scholarship to study in Britain, beating out other talented historians such as Jim Davidson.[22] He had long aspired to go to Oxford University—the high academy of imperial values. But the postgraduate award was only sufficient to pay for him to go to London. He would have headed there, but in 1937, the year he wrote his thesis, he had met and fallen in love with another member of the history honours class, Pauline Palmer, whom he married three years later.[23] The granddaughter of a Christchurch banker and daughter of a Hawkes Bay farmer, she was educated at Woodford House for girls. She too was educated in a love of England and she brought with her the values of the rural squattocracy. Her sister, Patricia, had married Jim Nelson, a descendant of the Williams family. Following his schooling at Christ's College, where he was head prefect, Jim went off to Merton College, Oxford, in the early 1920s. There

---

21   Phillips, 'New Zealand's Relations with Great Britain', p. 264.
22   'Degree Results, 1937, Honours etc.' (uncatalogued), J. C. Beaglehole Room, Victoria University of Wellington Library.
23   At the time, postgraduate history students in New Zealand were identified in their theses and sat their examinations under code names rather than their real names. It is a prescient coincidence that Pauline's and Neville's code names were alphabetically contiguous: 'Also' and 'Alter', respectively. W. J. Gardner, E. T. Beardsley and T. E. Carter, *A History of the University of Canterbury, 1873–1973* (Christchurch, 1973), p. 242n.

he studied forestry and also rowed in the college's boat. Jim looked on those years with real affection, and was determined that Neville should experience Oxford college life, too. So he offered to lend sufficient money to Neville to allow him to go to Oxford. In gratitude for this support, Neville wrote every few months back to Jim and Patricia, and it is thanks to this correspondence that we know something about the Oxford and war years.

Neville applied to Jim's old college and in September 1938 he entered Merton College. At the time, he did not see himself as a future historian. His intention was to continue his journalistic career, so he decided to enrol as an undergraduate in philosophy, politics and economics (PPE). He recalled later that while at Oxford he wrote to the *Manchester Guardian* inquiring about a job as a leader writer.[24] But for the next year it was Oxford that fulfilled all his dreams. 'Dreams'—because the reality of Oxford study was not all that he had hoped. Neville was academically ambitious but he did not enjoy his relations with his tutors and found difficult the strain of writing two long essays a week. At least in describing the life to his future brother-in-law and fellow Merton man, Neville's enthusiasm was fired by the wider Oxford environment. It gave him the chance to escape his colonial and socially deprived past and live out a dream of English aristocratic culture. He rapidly became a passionate Merton loyalist, and was delighted when in the second term he was able to move into college with a view over the fellows' garden to the fields. His letters are full of the politics of the junior common room. By the end of the year, he had been appointed college correspondent for the magazine *Isis*, and tasked with penning a witty record of college doings every fortnight.[25] He went punting on the Cherwell and took a header into the river.[26] He became a devoted college sportsman, playing on the wing for the college rugby team and reporting at length (partly for Jim's benefit) on the college's rowing crew's efforts to 'bump' their way up river. Pauline Palmer had followed Neville to England and was training as a teacher in London. She came up and watched one 'division of toggers'[27]; she apparently thought 'it all savoured too much of the Old School Tie',[28] but Neville thought it was exciting when there was a personal stake in the outcome.

At Christmas, Pauline and Neville went off to Paris, which Neville regarded as 'infinitely more beautiful' than London—'a wretched place'.[29] Together, they went to four plays—a practice Neville continued in Oxford. With Pauline, he also discovered the 'beautiful' English countryside. They managed to meet for

---

24 Neville Phillips, Interview with author, 13 February 1997.
25 Neville Phillips to Patricia and Jim Nelson, 11 July 1939.
26 Neville Phillips to Patricia and Jim Nelson, 30 May 1939.
27 Toggers were the so-called 'Torpid' races among college rowing crews but excluding those who had been in the college eight the previous year.
28 Neville Phillips to Patricia and Jim Nelson, 5 March 1939.
29 Neville Phillips to Patricia and Jim Nelson, 29 January 1939.

weekends and there would be walks around Oxford such as along the Thames with tea at 'the Trout Inn'. As warm weather arrived, he became ecstatic at how 'the spring simply changes the face of the earth in England' and he savoured 'the old James II mulberry tree in the garden' where the dons played bowls.[30] There were cycling trips to villages in Berkshire and the Cotswolds; and when Pauline's parents arrived in early summer, they visited gardens and, under Pauline's tutelage, Neville began to learn about English cathedrals and the 'differences between Norm. and E.E. and Dec. and Perp'.[31] Pauline's father took Neville off to a day's test cricket at Lords. Neville looked forward to a vacation to be spent in a small village in Shropshire (no doubt inspired by A. E. Housman) where he could catch up on work. At Oxford there were also the clubs and lectures. Neville was elected (thanks to James Hight's influence) to the Ralegh Club—an exclusive group of 36 who discussed Empire affairs. Before long, he had been made secretary and was marked out as the next president, and the club heard 'fighting imperialist speeches' from assorted aristocrats. He was less enthusiastic about another club: 'The inevitable New Zealanders' club has been formed and I hang my head to think that I've been roped in.'[32] It was called the Pakeha Club. At the first annual dinner in the Merton Senior Common room, the High Commissioner, W. K. Jordan, spoke. The event ended in true Kiwi style when a Balliol man let off a fire extinguisher, and the club president was summoned to the 'Principal of the postmasters' to explain.[33]

So for all his adoration of things imperial and English, Neville could not escape his New Zealand origins. On more than one occasion he acknowledged the presence of other New Zealanders at Oxford and admitted having to vote against one in Merton College politics. He also commented on New Zealand political events. He wrote the day after Walter Nash, the New Zealand Minister of Finance, arrived in England in May 1939 on 'a distasteful mission' of renewing a loan and placating the British and commented: 'Frankly, I'm sorry that New Zealand is so dependent on this country.'[34] There were also some signs of a slight change in his political views. He admitted to attending on one evening a meeting of the Labour Club to hear G. D. H. Cole speak on trade unionism and the need for more militancy. Phillips admired his 'beautifully clear mind', but could not empathise with his outlook and expressed great amusement at the 'common vocative, "Comrades", on the grounds that "Mr" is so beastly bourgeois'.[35] There was also in late February a meeting at the Oxford Town Hall where Stafford Cripps spoke in favour of the Popular Front. Neville especially

---

30 Neville Phillips to Patricia and Jim Nelson, 30 May 1939.
31 Neville Phillips to Patricia and Jim Nelson, 11 July 1939.
32 Neville Phillips to Patricia and Jim Nelson, 20 May 1939.
33 Neville Phillips to Patricia and Jim Nelson, 11 July 1939.
34 Neville Phillips to Patricia and Jim Nelson, 30 May 1939. See also Keith Sinclair, *Walter Nash* (Auckland, 1976), ch. 14.
35 Neville Phillips to Patricia and Jim Nelson, 29 January 1939.

applauded his attacks on Chamberlain, for he agreed that 'in international dealings this present government has neither honour nor acumen'. The shadows of war were lengthening, and Neville concluded his account: 'British foreign "policy" has drifted for so long that it is now next to impossible for us to get out of the present mess without dishonour or without war.'[36]

The year in Oxford had confirmed for Neville Phillips the excitement and stimulus of living in a place with real culture, tradition and history. The reality of England confirmed the dream he had had since his days as a Palmerston North schoolboy, but the outbreak of war confronted him with a tough choice. There was never much doubt where he would stand. In November 1939, he wrote to Jim Nelson that he had left Oxford and was waiting in London to be called up. He admitted that it was not an enjoyable decision and at times he considered himself 'an utter fool'. He did not relish fighting, but it was a just war, and 'it seemed unfair that, after sharing the privileges of Englishmen, as I have done at Oxford, I should shirk their responsibilities'—apart from the fact that 'New Zealand is as closely interested as England in unseating Hitler'.[37] So the loyal imperialist, the man who had always dreamed of the wonders of English culture, was forced to pay for his beliefs and he did not shirk from the responsibilities. Later he was quite frank that war scared him. But he decided that he could serve in as safe a way as possible. As an Oxford student, he was fairly certain of being awarded a commission as an officer, and was promised this when interviewed at Oxford within the first month of war. Further, he quickly decided to choose the artillery because this would place him far from the front and therefore in a less exposed situation.[38] So he chose his war service—an officer in the artillery it would be.[39]

After a couple of weeks waiting round, which he used learning German and brushing up on trigonometry for range-finding, he was formally called up in mid-November 1939. Two weeks later, he decided that army life was 'much overrated'. He had been sent to spend three months as a private learning the basics at Gosforth on the Hampshire coast. The food, he noted, would do for 'Lord Bledisloe's pigs',[40] but was inadequate for adult men and he expressed jealousy of the rations allowed New Zealand soldiers as reported in the *Weekly News*. The bathing arrangements were primitive—two baths, no showers, very

---

36 Neville Phillips to Patricia and Jim Nelson, 5 March 1939.
37 Neville Phillips to Patricia and Jim Nelson, 3 November 1939.
38 Neville Phillips, Interview with author, 15 February 1997.
39 Interestingly, Pauline Phillips claims that Neville's old mentor James Hight was furious that he had abandoned Oxford to become a soldier.
40 Charles Bathurst, First Viscount Bledisloe, was Governor-General of New Zealand, 1930–35.

little hot water—and all for 200 men.⁴¹ On the other hand, after working from 6 am to 4 pm every day, they could then unwind, which is perhaps why Neville remembered the period later as 'the most relaxed period of his life'.⁴²

He found 'many barbarians' among his fellows, but also some who were congenial, including, to his delight, a Fellow of King's College, Cambridge, next door. There was also a chance for some leave, which included tea with the former New Zealand Labour MP Ormond Wilson, who, to Neville's approval, had 'come back from Russia very disgruntled with the Communistic experiment there',⁴³ and also a week in Devon close to where Pauline was teaching and where he enjoyed cycling to attractive villages. Then followed five months at an officer cadet training unit at Larkhill on the Salisbury Plains. He worked hard doing papers on gunnery, map reading and, to his discomfort, learning about the insides of a motorcar. The food and bathing conditions were much improved.⁴⁴ Neville was quite pleased with the marks he received for the various tests. But he was disappointed at his final grade (C) and others suggested that this was because the grading officer had discriminated against him on the basis of his Jewish background.⁴⁵ The upshot was that he was not appointed to a divisional field regiment, but to a position of lesser status with an army field regiment (the 140th) based at Bournemouth. This experience did not lead to any radical alienation, nor were his class aspirations disturbed by his observation that the greatest strain in his life was the behaviour of certain cadets: 'bad cases of arrested development, due, I fear, to the curbing influence of the English public school. They still get adolescent enjoyment out of drinking excessively and still more out of talking about it.'⁴⁶ On the other hand, he wrote of his enjoyment of the regimental sports when the cadets all sipped tea under a marquee that savoured of a 'parish garden party';⁴⁷ and he continued to find solace in the cultural traditions around him. There were visits to nearby Stonehenge and Salisbury with its cathedral, and a weekend at Winchester where the cathedral was explored, and he also took an approving look at Winchester College—the oldest of the public schools.⁴⁸

Then followed some two years of training at various places in the United Kingdom—at Lincolnshire, Berkshire, Motherwell in Scotland, the Isle of Wight, Winchester, Sway in Hampshire and periodically back at Bournemouth. In November 1940, he married Pauline and in August the following year she gave birth to their first child, Elizabeth. How training and fatherhood changed his

---

41 Neville Phillips to Patricia and Jim Nelson, 4 December 1939.
42 Neville Phillips, Interview with author, 15 February 1997.
43 Ormond Wilson, *An Outsider Looks Back: Reflections on experience* (Wellington, 1982), ch. 6.
44 Neville Phillips to Patricia and Jim Nelson, 18 February 1940.
45 Neville Phillips, Interview with author, 15 February 1997.
46 Neville Phillips to Patricia and Jim Nelson, 3 May 1940.
47 Neville Phillips to Patricia and Jim Nelson, 3 May 1940.
48 Neville Phillips to Patricia and Jim Nelson, 13 March 1940.

world view is not very clear. The letters to Patricia and Jim become spasmodic and his memory of those years was not strong, so there are only isolated hints. He achieved steady promotion and by 1941 had reached the heights of being a captain. He became conscious that being an officer was certainly affecting him. He wrote: 'One has to be somewhat of a bully—or more than somewhat—in order to force all the necessary knowledge down eight men's throats and it's good for the cultivation of that quality which the C.O. never tires of demonstrating—"the aggressive spirit".'[49] We also get some hint of his character in those years from another interesting source: a reminiscence written by a signalman in the regiment who reported to Neville. In Joe Berry's account, *Unwillingly to War*, 'Captain Phillips' comes across as quite a demanding officer with high standards. He was described as 'a scholarly man who did not smile readily'[50] and who was in his element poring over maps. Yet there was another side. Joe Berry tells a lovely story that concerned Gunner Jonah who was in Neville's troop. He came from south Wales where he had worked in his parents' café, and he endured much ribbing about the affinity between chips and his chunky figure. One day Neville was teaching a course in which his 'academic bent was given full rein'. But it was after lunch, it was warm, and most of the class was asleep. 'Captain Phillips' asked a question that no-one answered. He called on Jonah, who managed only a few mutterings. 'Gradually the captain's pose relaxed and a hint of a smile flickered at the corners of his mouth. In a voice with just the right amount of mock disbelief he asked, "Is this the face that launched a thousand *chips*?" There were roars of laughter.'[51]

Neville's letters also suggest that he became increasingly intolerant of the Nazis; and interestingly, in a reversal of his earlier comfort about being in the artillery, he saw as one advantage of becoming a troop commander that he would then be positioned up front in a forward observation post directing the guns, 'where you can see what havoc you're working among the swine on the other side. And they are swine, have no doubt about it, especially the insolent, fanatical young Nazis. They have been schooled in evil and they must be destroyed.'[52] Eventually, after a nostalgic night and morning wandering around Oxford, where he found the view of Merton Fields 'the same as ever—the best in England', he heard in November 1942 that he was off to North Africa to join the First Army. The real war was to begin.

Neville landed at Bone in Tunisia in late January 1943. Two weeks later, he went into the line with the Hermann Göring regiment opposite. It was a 'touchy sector' and there were mines and Stuka bombers to be aware of. Joe Berry's

---

49   Neville Phillips to Patricia and Jim Nelson, 2 January 1941.
50   Joe Berry, *Unwillingly to War* (Hull, UK, 1996), p. 8.
51   Ibid., pp. 17–18.
52   Neville Phillips to Patricia and Jim Nelson, 1 June 1941.

account presented the sector as rather more dangerous than Neville recalled, and Berry remembers one occasion when the troop slept in and he woke up to a torrent of abuse from Captain Phillips 'for our damned slackness'.[53] But they had marked artillery dominance, and Neville was lucky to be saved from a potentially fatal moment. On the third day of action, he was returning on a motorbike from serving on a court-martial panel and was thrown. He hurt his leg, and this meant that he was unable to go forward with the infantry to serve in the observation post (OP) directing the guns. A replacement served instead and two days later the Germans surrounded the farmhouse where the OP was positioned. The officer and his two signalmen were found dead. Neville recalled this incident repeatedly and in a letter several months later he described it as a 'bad day' not only because of the deaths but also because he and the gunners were sprayed with machine-gun fire.[54] After a month of wet weather, he was involved in an attack on 23 April 1943. This time, Neville was up front as OP and, with some exhilaration, he watched the infantry move forward.

It was the beginning of the end in North Africa. Following the fall of Tunis and Bizerta, the Germans decided enough was enough. Neville was impressed with them. He described them even in retreat as a 'tidy race' and 'a fine lot…fit, well fed and well clothed'. The Italians impressed him less. Neville was pleased at his booty: a nice sniper's rifle and three machine guns. By 21 May, when he wrote to Patricia and Jim, he was enjoying a bivouac in an olive grove 180 m from the sea. He looked out on 'ruins ancient and modern'—the ancient ruins of Carthage and the modern wrecks of 'Boche and Wop planes' at the airport. He found prices exorbitant and, interestingly, apart from two glasses of vermouth and muscat, all he had been able to buy was a fountain pen for 15 shillings so that he could write, and a volume of *Horace* with a translation in French—a bargain at two bob because no-one else was interested in the classics at this point.[55]

In late 1943, probably in November, Neville came with the 140 field regiment to Italy as part of the Fifth Army. There he shared the Allied line with the New Zealanders. The British Army was located at the waist of Italy, just north of Naples, with the route north blocked on the east by the Sangro River and on the west by high hills with the monastery of Monte Cassino overlooking the major route. We know little about Neville's experiences there. He wrote one very brief and highly censored letter to Patricia and Jim in March 1944 in which he describes the rain and the mud and the accompaniment of his men singing *Drink to Me Only*. He writes of seeing many ruined villages. Although his unit

---

53 Berry, *Unwillingly to War*, p. 40.
54 Neville Phillips, Interview with author, 15 February 1997; Neville Phillips to Patricia and Jim Nelson, 21 May 1943. The incident is also recalled by Berry, *Unwillingly to War*, pp. 42–3.
55 Neville Phillips to Patricia and Jim Nelson, 21 May 1943.

was based at Venafro, about 16 km east of Cassino, he would talk in later years of the terrible psychological effect of the Monte Cassino monastery watching over all their doings, and when he came 10 years later to write about the New Zealanders' experiences in the crossing of the Sangro and the battle for Cassino, official records were supplemented with personal memory. But of the details of his experiences in Italy, we know only isolated bits. He would often speak of the capture of the Umbrian town of Perugia, which is recalled in Joe Berry's book, *Unwillingly to War*.[56] He was clearly impressed by the beauty of the Umbrian and Tuscan countryside, which he would remember fondly in later years. He learned to speak Italian and developed a taste for the local vino; and during those hard months of war he grew closer to the men around him, especially two who would become lifelong friends: Roland Foxwell (later a wine merchant in the south of England) and Edward Chadwyck-Healey. Chadwyck-Healey, the grandson of a distinguished lawyer who became a baronet, was educated at Eton, decorated in World War I, and became the Prime Warden of the Fishmongers Company and the Third Baronet of Wyphurst.[57] Neville's association with Sir Edward Chadwyck-Healey was the closest he came to the English aristocracy. But most of his Italian sojourn is largely a blank. He did write to Patricia and Jim again in November 1944. By that time, Cassino had fallen and it was a steady march northwards against stubborn German resistance. In his letter, Neville notes that he had had two week-long holidays: one in Florence and one in Rome. Sadly, he notes that his rambles about Rome have left no paper for 'that much more worthy city, Florence. I shall only say it is quite equal to its fame.' This comment is confirmed by the fact that he did send Pauline a book about Florence. Of Rome, he describes piazzas, great churches, fountains, statues, columns and obelisks 'by the score'. But he found the city 'impresses without charming'. He visited St Peter's and saw the Pope, but the highlight was undoubtedly a visit to a palazzo where he was shown through rooms full of paintings of the Italian Renaissance placed there for safe-keeping. 'The paintings', he wrote, 'certainly opened my eyes. I don't expect ever to see such a collection again.'[58]

The dénouement can be quickly told. The march up Italy and the end of the war saw Neville briefly at Cremona in charge of a camp of Polish evacuees, which he always described as one of the least pleasant periods of his life, which confirmed in him a hostility to Russian communism. Eventually, he was demobbed, and the choice came as to what he should do. He was a husband with a four-year-old daughter, so returning to Oxford was never an option. There was a possible job in the West Indies, which did not appeal. Pauline was eager to get home, so when his old mentor James Hight offered him a position lecturing in history at his alma mater in Christchurch it seemed a heaven-sent opportunity. He

---

56 Berry, *Unwillingly to War*, pp. 141–50.
57 <http://www.thepeerage.com/p21302.htm#i213019>
58 Neville Phillips to Jim and Patricia Nelson, 26 November 1944.

accepted and returned to Canterbury University College. Within three years, he was appointed to the Chair of History—at the age of thirty-two—so war service had not held up his career despite his having returned without an Oxford, or a higher, degree.

So how had the war affected Neville as a person and a historian? More than five years in the British Army fighting Nazism had confirmed, not upset, his essentially conservative political values and his belief in the value of British civilisation. He had come to like his fellow soldiers and his friendships provided a long-term pull back to England. His experience as a successful soldier reaffirmed his sense of the legitimacy of armed conflict and a pride in his own service. In later years, he would often judge a man by his war record. His experience as an officer in command of troops for five years had given him greater personal confidence and an authoritarian style of command. It is revealing that in his account, Joe Berry recalled meeting the New Zealanders when the regiment reached Cassino in February 1944. Berry was impressed with two things about the Kiwis: 'The divide between officer and other rank was much less pronounced in their army than in ours and they had an easy friendliness which, in my experience, none of our other allies were quite able to match.'[59] So Neville developed a way of directing others that was rather different from the style that might have evolved from five years as an officer in the New Zealand forces. That style was later used effectively when he became Professor of History and later Vice-Chancellor at Canterbury.[60] He had come to believe that social structures had a necessary hierarchy that should be respected and supported. In this way, too, the war strengthened, rather than disrupted, his values.

In terms of his historical interests, the war had two effects. First, when in the early 1950s he was looking for additional income to support a growing family, Neville was offered the chance to write the official history of the New Zealand forces in Italy. He readily accepted and the result was an outstanding book. The book has a fine architecture, beginning with the difficult crossing of the Sangro River and ending with the battle for Cassino. It is beautifully written (the last paragraph is a particularly fine example of English prose),[61] clearly structured and it is

---

59   Berry, *Unwillingly to War*, p. 100.
60   Yet we might also note that Joe Berry (*Unwillingly to War*, p. 178) writes with real affection of Neville and he was impressed when, on the occasion of the regiment being disbanded, Neville summoned him to his office to wish him well even though Berry had not served directly with him since North Africa. Later, he asked Neville to write a foreword to his book.
61   N. C. Phillips, *Italy. Volume 1: The Sangro to Cassino* (Wellington, 1957), pp. 353–4. 'The historian of the battles of Cassino who revisits the scene finds no relief from the difficulty of commemorating them in a way that will do justice to the New Zealanders who fought there, but he is impressed anew by the need for making the attempt. For except in its boldest features, the face of the land has changed even in so short a time. To stand on the summit of Point 593 on the tenth anniversary of the peace was to be engulfed in a tranquillity made the more immense by the emphasis of a few simple sounds—the chime of a cowbell, a skylark's glee and, far below beside the new white abbey, the shouts of black-robed novices as they skirmished with a football. Earth heals her own wounds, and the husbandry of a thousand peasants has tended the growth of twelve

always informed with his own experience. In the Preface, he acknowledges that he 'shared this experience with friends from the British homeland' and that 'there are things that only soldiers know'. The book confronts two contentious political issues. The first was the question as to whether, once the North African campaign was won, the New Zealand forces should have returned home like the Australians to defend the South Pacific in company with the Americans. Neville had no doubts of the answer. He denied that in choosing to remain in the Mediterranean theatre 'New Zealand acted not boldly but traditionally', and he also denied that the act represented 'New Zealand as still the satellite of Britain'. Rather, he saw the decision as 'one of the great maturing moments of the national life...never did a New Zealand parliament make a more difficult, a more adult or a less insular decision'.[62] Yet it is interesting that while pointing out the practical factors—the lack of available shipping, the difficulties of transferring men from North Africa into the jungles of the Pacific—Phillips also emphasises the effect of pleas from General Freyberg, President Roosevelt and above all Winston Churchill, who 'addressed sentences resonant with the cadences of Gibbon and ornamented by a reminiscence of Tennyson'. Churchill's message, which Phillips quoted in extensor, began with a tribute to the New Zealand division ('There could not be any more glorious expression of the links which bind together the hearts of the people of the British and New Zealand isles') and concluded that the New Zealanders should remain in the Mediterranean on the grounds that '[i]t is the symbolic and historic value of our continued comradeship in arms that moves me'. Phillips, author of 'New Zealand and the Mother Country', fully approved the sentiments.[63]

Second, he discusses at length the justification for the bombing of the historical abbey of Monte Cassino. He certainly considers the argument that the bombing was a 'wanton act of terror and vandalism', and he concedes that the evidence of German use of the monastery before the bombing for military reasons is weak.[64] But what sways him is the duty of the commanders to their troops. The men believed, rightly or wrongly, 'that "Jerry" was sitting in the "wee white house"...it was a constant intruding presence: it looked into everything, it nagged at their nerves and became a phobia and an obsession'.[65] Here his personal memories of the monastery watching over everything below clearly had an effect on his view. But it was the strategic arguments that won him

---

successive springs. Ruins are dismantled and new buildings arise on the sites of the old. Men remember but their memories fade and finally die with them. And of the deeds bravely done and the hardships bravely borne, soon nothing will remain but the imperfect record itself.'
62 Phillips, *Italy*, pp. 24–5.
63 Ibid., p. 30.
64 Ibid., p. 211.
65 Ibid., p. 217.

over. When it came to the hard task of breaking through the Cassino front then heritage and history had to give way. Neville showed himself a soldier first, a defender of heritage second.

Italy, Volume 1 was well received.[66] Yet Neville told New Zealand acquaintances that the task of writing the history was not enjoyable and he gave up writing the second volume when the task became too onerous. He wanted to get back to the English history that he loved. On research leave to Britain in 1955, which was designed to allow him to visit the Italian battlefields, he also spent time in Sheffield working on the papers of Edmund Burke. He also collected books on eighteenth-century English politics so that he could continue his real historical love when he got home.[67]

The other long-term effect of his war experience on Phillips' history was to leave him with an enduring love of Italy and the Italian Renaissance. After the 1955 trip, he began to teach a course on the Italian Renaissance, which he illustrated with slides of Renaissance painting and architecture. There were few occasions when Neville lit up with greater enthusiasm than when talking about this subject, and it was my very great privilege to accompany him on a tour of Renaissance art sites in 1963. He never published on the subject, but it always remained a passion and his lectures on the subject are still remembered fondly by his former students.

After 1956, his historical research and publications concerned the history of the British ruling class. Edmund Burke, quoted with affection in his thesis, remained an enduring interest, and, drawing on his researches in 1955, he published about Burke.[68] He became deeply interested in Namierite political history and before long was counting division lists from the eighteenth-century House of Commons.[69] As head of department, he was forced occasionally to show an interest in New Zealand history, overseeing the history of Canterbury and helping young historians such as Philip Ross May.[70] But this was always a distraction and former members of the department recall it being a discouraging place to undertake serious research on New Zealand history. Neville's primary love remained the British ruling class. It was no surprise when, after retiring

---

66   For example, 'Review by Francis West', *Landfall: A New Zealand quarterly*, 11:1 (1958), pp. 84–7.
67   As well as *Italy*, Phillips wrote occasional pieces on contemporary affairs—for example, 'Collectivism and the British Commonwealth', *Landfall*, 1:3 (1947), pp. 174–85; 'The Referendum: A retrospect', *Landfall*, 3:3 (1949), pp. 307–20.
68   N. C. Phillips, 'Burke and Paine: The conservative and radical minds', *Landfall*, 29 (1954), pp. 36–46; N. C. Phillips, 'Edmund Burke and the County Movement, 1779–1780', *English Historical Review*, 76:254 (1961), pp. 254–78.
69   N. C. Phillips, *Yorkshire and English National Politics, 1783–1784* (Christchurch, 1961); Phillips, 'The British General Election of 1780: A vortex of politics', *Political Science*, 11:2 (1959), pp. 3–22; Phillips, 'Namier and His Method', *Political Science*, 14:2 (1962), pp. 16–26.
70   Philip Ross May, *The West Coast Gold Rushes* (Christchurch, 1957, 2nd edn 1962). *A History of Canterbury* was published in three substantial volumes between 1957 and 1965.

from his role as Vice-Chancellor, he decided with Pauline to move to England. There they lived just outside Canterbury, enjoying regular walks in the 'garden of England' until his death in 2001.[71]

Neville Phillips as historian was little affected by the war; a chronicler and admirer of the British Empire was how he entered the war, and, for all the personal torments of those six years, that remained essentially his role as a writer of history.

---

71 See obituaries in *Independent* [London], 11 July 2001; *Press* [Christchurch], 12 July 2001; *New Zealand Herald*, 14 July 2001.

11. Dan Davin: The literary legacy of war[1]

Janet Wilson

'How long will the War last'? 'For the rest of our lives'.

— Dan Davin, *For the Rest of Our Lives* (1947)

Davin's Writing About War

The New Zealander Daniel Marcus Davin (1913–90) had a varied, fulfilling and, by most standards, very successful war. Yet his considerable achievements during these years—three times Mentioned in Dispatches, promoted to captain in 1942, to major in 1943, and the MBE (Military Division) in 1944—are perhaps less important today than his scholarly and literary legacy, which covers writing in different genres and includes unpublished poems, diaries and letters.[2] Davin's prodigious output covering his experiences and those of other New Zealanders in the 2nd New Zealand Expeditionary Force (2NZEF) whom he worked alongside in the Mediterranean and Northern African campaigns confirms that writing about war while he was in the midst of it engaged him as much as the business of fighting. For Davin, more than most, the war exerted a powerful influence over his life and work, often emerging in unexpected ways and so always a vital presence. These six years retained their tenacious hold on his memory and imagination, because the firsthand experiences of war provided unparalleled opportunities for him as a writer, offering a rich resource. His impressions and responses are depicted memorably and vividly in the stories published in *The Gorse Blooms Pale* (1947) and in *Breathing Spaces* (1975), later collected in *The Salamander and the Fire: Collected war stories* (1986); they also form the basis of his war novel, *For the Rest of Our Lives* (1947), and the background to the later novel *The Sullen Bell* (1956).

After the war, this engagement continued and brought him back into closer contact with New Zealand and the provincial society from which he had departed,

---

1 I would like to thank Doug Munro for his valuable editorial assistance, for undertaking some research in New Zealand, and for suggesting sources; also Denis Lenihan, James McNeish and Kevin Ireland for commenting on a draft of this chapter; and to Delia Davin for a careful reading of the final draft.
2 These are available in the Daniel Marcus Davin Literary Papers, Alexander Turnbull Library [hereinafter ATL], MS-Group-0319. Davin's service record with the 2NZEF from June 1940 to July 1945 is in the archive of the New Zealand Defence Force.

in 1936, as a Rhodes Scholar to Oxford. Davin became the official historian of the Crete campaign. As an eyewitness of the German airborne assault on Maleme airport on 20 May 1941, he had written an account for British GHQ while in a hospital in Cairo recovering from wounds received during the attack. General Howard Kippenberger commissioned him to write the volume on Crete in the 'Official History of New Zealand in the Second World War' series.[3] In 1948, he returned to New Zealand for the first time in 12 years, to undertake archival research and discussions with historians in the War History Branch of Internal Affairs, and senior figures in the armed services. The 700-page account was laboriously completed after several years of working at nights and on weekends while he held down a day job as academic publisher for Oxford University Press. *Crete* takes its place as a 'classic', as Kippenberger called it, among official war histories anywhere, such as W. G. McClymont's *To Greece*.[4] It was praised by one reviewer as 'a first class piece of military scholarship' and as 'far and away the most comprehensive' of the official war histories.[5] It immediately became the definitive account—one which, points out his biographer, could not be overlooked in the writing of any subsequent military history of the Crete campaign or of the Mediterranean theatre of war in general.[6] The *Crete* volume has received justifiably high praise from other quarters: 'To write lucidly about war, without falling into the heroic simplicities that trivialize war's tragic chaos, is extremely difficult. Davin succeeds'.[7] But writing the history was time-consuming, painstaking work and it exacerbated the tensions Davin experienced by working in different genres between ascertaining the truth of any matter as far as was possible and the greater freedoms that invention allowed.[8] History as his primary discipline led him to have an 'excessive respect for those facts that can be established at the expense of the power to create';[9] but working with facts slowed the creative processes and he preferred 'writing with

---

3 Dan Davin, *Crete* (Wellington, 1953). For background on the series, see Michael Bassett, *An Overview of the War History Branch* (<http://michaelbassett.co.nz/article_war.htm>, 1997). The War History Branch files relating to the Crete volume are in Archives New Zealand (Wellington), IA1, 3388, 181/32/2, parts 1 and 2.
4 See Nancy M. Taylor, *The New Zealand People at War: The home front* (Wellington, 1986), vol. 1, p. ix.
5 The first quotation comes from *The Economist*, 23 January 1954—quoted in Keith Ovenden, *A Fighting Withdrawal: The life of Dan Davin, writer, soldier, publisher* (Oxford, 1996), p. 247—in a review probably written by Bill Williams. W. E. Murphy praised *Crete* as 'far and away the most comprehensive of the official war histories'. W. E. Murphy, 'Crete', *Comment: A New Zealand quarterly review*, 33 (1967), pp. 28–30. In fact, Murphy was responsible for preparing the narrative of the battle, which was sent to Dan in Oxford in 1948 (Ovenden, *A Fighting Withdrawal*, pp. 237–38, 246; Davin, *Crete*, p. viii). Other reviews of *Crete* include L. S. Hart, 'Disputed Island', *New Zealand Listener*, 6 November 1953, pp. 12–13.
6 Ovenden, *A Fighting Withdrawal*, p. 249.
7 Donald Harman Akenson, *Half the World from Home: Perspectives on the Irish in New Zealand, 1860–1950* (Wellington, 1990), p. 90 (ch. 4: 'Dan Davin, Irish Catholic Historian').
8 Davin's comments on the writing of fiction confirm this 'troublesome…quandary': he 'preferred to set my stories within real battles, or real situations out of battle', because his training as a historian left him 'unable to name a place or even cite a map reference which was not at least hypothetically compatible with the topographical reality'. Dan Davin, 'Introduction', *The Salamander and the Fire* (Oxford, 1986), p. xiii.
9 Ovenden, *A Fighting Withdrawal*, p. 366.

the brakes off', as he confided to the historian Angus Ross, himself the author of an official New Zealand war history.[10] After *Crete*, he never really recovered his momentum in writing fiction.

Alongside the historical assessment of the war in Crete, and the imaginative encounter with war informing his fiction and poetry, Davin also helped get into print the works of others who were writing about the war. His role as an academic publisher at the nerve centre of publishing in Oxford for more than three decades, his historical research and reputation as an authority on the New Zealand Division's presence in the Mediterranean and North Africa, and his considerable output as a fiction writer, made him a reference point for those who needed advice and guidance. He assisted with the finalising and publishing of other histories and memoirs—for example, the draft chapters on the Greek and Crete campaigns for Angus Ross who wrote on the history of 23 Battalion (1959) and Kippenberger's war memoirs, *Infantry Brigadier* (1949).[11]

This chapter, then, will focus on Davin's writing about the war pre-eminently as fiction writer, and will locate his experiences of the war as background to his stories. Both his experiences and the writing about them illustrate the truth of the epigraph, which is also the title of Davin's war novel: the war was *the* formative, unforgettable experience—one that would remain with him for the rest of his life.

Davin's War Experience

At different times, Davin served in both the British and the New Zealand Armies, moving through the ranks from front-line soldier to become Divisional Intelligence Officer for General Freyberg. He first saw action in 1940 with the 2NZEF (of which the main fighting component was known as the 'Div.') as Second Lieutenant with 23 Battalion (Otago and Southland) and Commander of 13 Platoon C Company, while he spent the last year of the war working for the Control Commission for Germany in the War Office in London. During his five years of service, Davin experienced action as an infantryman in the Mediterranean campaign and then as Battalion Intelligence Officer in the German aerial bombardments of Maleme airport in Crete in 1941; he worked

---

10 Margot Ross and Angus Ross, 'Writing About the War', in Janet Wilson (ed.), *Intimate Stranger: Reminiscences of Dan Davin* (Wellington, 2000), p. 64. Davin's output peaked in the years between 1945 and 1953. He published three novels: *Cliffs of Fall* (London, 1945); *For the Rest of Our Lives* (London, 1947); and *Roads from Home* (London, 1949); and a collection of short stories, *The Gorse Blooms Pale* (London, 1947). He completed John Mulgan's *An Introduction to English Literature* (London, 1947) and edited two volumes for the Oxford University Press World's Classics Series—*New Zealand Short Stories* and *Katherine Mansfield: Selected stories* (both in 1953)—as well as writing numerous reviews and articles.
11 Howard Kippenberger, *Infantry Brigadier* (London, 1949); Angus Ross, *23 Battalion* (Wellington, 1959); Ovenden, *A Fighting Withdrawal*, pp. 227, 238; Ross and Ross, 'Writing About the War', p. 63.

for the intelligence staff of the Eighth Army GHQ in Cairo from August 1941 to September 1942; he took part in the Northern African desert campaign against Rommel in 1942, in the employment of the British Army J Staff Information Service; and after El Alamein he served with General Freyberg in the Italian campaign for six months in 1944 as Chief Intelligence Officer (in army terminology, GSO 3 [1]) for the Div., at the time the New Zealand Corps (the special unit that existed from 3 February to 26 March 1944) was formed to bomb Monte Cassino.[12] Serving in these different posts and discharging their duties meant that Davin participated in front-line action, intelligence gathering and decision-making processes, and became familiar with the operational and tactical aspects of war from the top down as well as the bottom up.

His own trajectory through the ranks, therefore, is reflected in the range of military types he introduces into his fiction, and their different attitudes, perspectives and values according to rank and experience. The relationship he had with General Freyberg when working in intelligence, for example, emerges in the portrait of the Staff Intelligence Officer in 'North of the Sangro' who is obliged to dampen his general's bursts of enthusiasm and obsession with the superior might of the Russian forces—his 'visions of dislodging the Germans from the more hideous bits of high ground like the Majella Massif itself and to fantasies of moving at the same pace as the Russian[s] were now moving in one sector after another of their enormous front'—by 'present[ing] him with an accurate but tough assessment of the situation from the enemy point of view'.[13] He is equally preoccupied with the other extreme of the military hierarchy: with the batman or driver—minor figures usually overlooked in narratives of conquest and defeat, but whom Davin idealised as epitomising the commonsensical, egalitarian Kiwi soldier, distinguished by a flair for the vernacular. His batmen are dependable, likeable characters who are also fluent storytellers, and their colourful nicknames epitomise the intimacy of the officer/soldier relationship (in contrast with the menace suggested by nicknames of officers such as Sabretooth in 'Psychological Warfare at Cassino'): Chaffcutter in 'Finders and Losers', so-called because he is clumsy, treats the narrator gently when he contracts yellow jaundice;[14] Jumbo Jordan in 'North of the Sangro' has an ear for nuance and speaks the Kiwi soldier's creative slang;[15] while Smithy in 'Psychological Warfare at Cassino' is a 'rough diamond' who could 'spin endless yarns of heroic behaviour'.[16] In one of Davin's best-loved stories, 'The General and the Nightingale', the military extremes of the servant–master hierarchy

---

12 See Davin, *The Salamander and the Fire*, p. 134.
13 Davin, *The Salamander and the Fire*, p. 101.
14 Ibid., pp. 75–6.
15 Ibid., p. 109.
16 Ibid., p. 125.

emerge in the voices of the three batmen who slyly caricature the idiom, manner and authority of their masters, reduplicating the structure of command as they settle down to gossip among themselves:

> 'Billy's boiling, GI,' he [Plugger Holmes] announced. 'Make the tea, will you? And, AQ, I like my fritters well done on both sides. You'd better turn them over, hadn't you?' It was the General's voice and manner, exactly mimicked but with asperity slightly exaggerated. And there was something of the original's authority.[17]

These years marked formative events in Davin's private life—mostly happy but some unexpected, despite or because of the inevitable separations that war brings about. Davin had married his New Zealand fiancée, Winifred ('Winnie') Gonley, after completing his three-year Rhodes Scholarship tenure in Oxford in May 1939, just before war was declared. Two of their three children were born while he was on active service: Anna Deirdre, in September 1940, Delia (called Helen until the age of seven, then Delia) in June 1944, while the third, Katharine Brigid (known as Brigid), was born just after war ended, in November 1945.[18] There was another child, Patricia Katarina (called 'Patty'), born out of wedlock in December 1943 to Elisabeth Berndt, an expatriate German with whom Davin had a love affair in Cairo in 1942–43. He and Winnie—once her anger had subsided—welcomed Elisabeth and Patty into the family home in Southmoor Road in Oxford. On the other hand, there were losses: his mother died suddenly of a coronary thrombosis at a mental hospital in 1944—a death that Davin heard about only some time later via a letter from his older brother, Tom.[19]

There was also the shock of witnessing sudden death and facing the moral implications of apparently controlling the fates of others under one's command—both unavoidable in war. Mortality and the transience of life are major war stories. Early on, he was faced with the deaths of three men and the capture of another three with whom he served in the Greek campaign of April 1941—soldiers whom he commanded as leader of 13 Platoon and whose lives he felt keenly responsible for.[20] Davin's platoon was ordered to hold one end of the line on a ridge running parallel with the main Olympus Range and then when it was clear that the German advance could not be halted, they pulled out; the men retreated with the remnants of the Central Macedonian Army from Salonika over Mount Olympus, the eastern seaboard of Greece, to Athens, in a 'fighting withdrawal'. The difficulties of this operation in which his men

---

17   Ibid., p. 173.
18   Winnie Davin's wartime experiences are recounted in 'A Soldier's Wife', in Lauris Edmond (ed.), *Women in Wartime: New Zealand women tell their story* (Wellington, 1986), pp. 65–75; and in 'Memories of Wartime Experiences', ATL, MS-Papers-3839.
19   The coronial inquest file relating to Mary Davin is held at Archives New Zealand (Wellington), J46, 1944/1116.
20   Ovenden, *A Fighting Withdrawal*, p. 140.

were dangerously exposed, magnified by the wet, muddy conditions caused by melting snow after a blizzard on Mount Olympus, are recounted in 'Below the Heavens', the opening story in *The Salamander and the Fire*. Three men from Platoon 13, emerging from their slit trenches, manage to attack a group of advancing Germans in their first close-up engagement: the story turns on the reactions of one of them to a mortally wounded Jerry who begs for a mercy killing; one of the trio did finally put the 'poor bastard' out of his misery.[21]

The upheavals of war threw up new opportunities for meeting people, and during these crucial years the gregarious Davin forged many new friendships—some of them brief, as with Lieutenant W. H. (Wattie) McKay, a journalist in civilian life who died of wounds in August 1941.[22] Others were lifelong—most importantly, with the brilliant linguist from Auckland Desmond (Paddy) Costello, who, like Davin, was Irish-Catholic by descent and a classicist (he studied Greek at Trinity College, Cambridge, and had been a Lecturer in Classics at the University of Exeter). So intense was this friendship that they have been described as 'blood brothers'.[23] Costello's reputation for the feat of guiding the remnants of 21 Battalion out of Greece across the sea to Crete, due to his ability to speak Greek, had preceded him by the time they met at the National Hotel in Cairo where Davin was training for Intelligence in Eighth Army GHQ. They became fast friends, and this was to be cemented through their positions as General Freyberg's Intelligence Officers.[24] War also threw Davin into new relationships with his contemporaries—notably, Geoffrey Cox who had also studied at Otago University and at Oxford, and with whom he briefly shared a flat in Cairo. It was Cox who introduced Davin to Costello.[25] All three men—Cox, Costello and Davin—were at different times Chief Intelligence Officers for the Div.: Cox in 1942, Costello in 1943, then Davin in 1944, before he was transferred to the Ministry of War in London. This was largely due to General Freyberg being attracted to intellectual and artistic types, clever young men whose opinions he listened to.[26] The way that Freyberg snatched his officers from the Eighth Army GHQ training school as soon as they were ready in 1942–43 is pointed out in 'Psychological Warfare at Cassino'.[27] The relationship was one of mutual suspicion mixed with admiration and trust as Freyberg, despite his powerful influence, came to depend on his Intelligence Officers for their company, as well

---

21 Davin, *The Salamander and the Fire*, pp. 1–11.
22 Ovenden, *A Fighting Withdrawal*, p. 135.
23 James McNeish, *The Sixth Man: The extraordinary life of Paddy Costello* (Auckland, 2007), p. 381.
24 Ibid., pp. 106–7; Ovenden, *A Fighting Withdrawal*, pp. 153–4.
25 James McNeish, *Dance of the Peacocks: New Zealanders in exile in the time of Hitler and Mao Tse-tung* (Auckland, 2003), pp. 199–200. See also McNeish, *The Sixth Man*, pp. 111–12; Ovenden, *Fighting Withdrawal*, p. 177.
26 Ovenden, *A Fighting Withdrawal*, p. 177.
27 Davin, *The Salamander and the Fire*, p. 123.

as advice. Davin recalls him affectionately in three stories all based on fact—notably, 'North of the Sangro', in which, brooding over the good men he has lost so far, the General says to his Intelligence Officer:

> I care about our men. And so many of them whatever I do or say will be dead…Another few years, just to make it worse and the historians who have never heard a bullet whisper who weren't even out of their cradles in 1939 will be explaining to the next generation how it was all my fault.[28]

In 'Psychological Warfare at Casino', the narrator (that is, Davin) dwells on the General's increasing attachment to Des Cassidy (that is, Costello) during the period when he was on leave in England: 'the General had become devoted to him and refused at first to let him take his period of allotted leave. Des was supposed to go on leave as soon as I got back but the General had found one pretext after another for hanging onto him.'[29]

Other wartime friendships included the history don from Merton College, E. T. (Bill) Williams (later Master of Rhodes House), head of Montgomery's intelligence in 1944, whom Davin met at GHQ in Cairo and remained a loyal friend and ally during the war, and then during Davin's years as academic editor for the Clarendon Press.[30] John Willett, a modern languages graduate from Oxford, was another good friend, and so was Reggie Smith, who had been working for the British Council in Bucharest, and married the novelist Olivia Manning. Davin met them briefly at the house of Walter and Amy Smart in Cairo—Smart was Oriental Counsellor at the British Embassy—where he also met Elisabeth Berndt, who was the Smarts' nanny.[31] There was also Noel ('Wig') Gardiner, whom Davin met in 1943 at the staff training college in Sarafand, Palestine, a machine gunner who won a Distinguished Service Order (DSO) on Miteiriya Ridge during the battle of El Alamein, and who, according to Ovenden, 'opened Dan's ear to the vernacular in the New Zealand language, and taught him how to hear it, copy it and use it in his fiction'.[32]

The variety of friendships, love affairs and acquaintances was one consequence of the haphazardness of war, which threw people together in unexpected ways, as occurred in Cairo in the early 1940s—then a melting pot of many nationalities and creeds, described as 'the cosmopolitan capital of the old world, everything that Berlin and Paris had been between the wars'.[33] The apparent randomness

---

28   Ibid., p. 112.
29   Ibid., p. 119; McNeish, *The Sixth Man*, pp. 128–33.
30   Williams had a New Zealand connection, studying there in the late 1930s on a Harmsworth Scholarship. Tim Beaglehole, *A Life of J. C. Beaglehole: New Zealand scholar* (Wellington, 2006), pp. 255–6.
31   Ovenden, *A Fighting Withdrawal*, p. 157.
32   Ibid., p. 166.
33   Ibid., pp. 152–3.

of movement was also magnified by military command's habit of moving men about in the Div. as the war wore on, bringing in younger men as the senior military officers became fewer either 'because of casualties or relegation to duties in the rear'.[34] Davin's charisma and innate egalitarianism flourished under such circumstances—moreover, he soon found that he could put to good use his intellectual talents and resources, not unlike other scholars with classical backgrounds and a gift for languages, such as Sir Ronald Syme (who was present at Dan's *viva* in Oxford) and Enoch Powell (whom Davin met on an officers' training course in England and again at GHQ in Cairo).[35] War, therefore, was a theatre of action in which Davin applied his academic skills to the demands of intelligence, defined himself as a man among men, and, on more than one occasion, romantically in relation to women.

Dan Davin epitomised the wartime scholar-soldier in that he combined the gifts of scholarship—to assess, analyse and to write succinctly—with courage and an ability to work both independently and with others. He was a verbal tactician, no doubt taking his cues from his extensive reading in Caesar and the classics; he famously spent his spare time reading the *Aeneid* in the original during the battle of El Alamein.[36] He excelled in writing dispatches, at making inferences from information and reports about the enemy, and at providing concise intelligence summaries. There seems little doubt, for example, that his report on the German parachute assault in Crete, written at the request of Colonel Quilliam in Army Intelligence, led to the decision to recruit Davin from the infantry into the intelligence staff at GHQ.[37] The excellence of his reports for J Squadron, the British Army group of mobile units that reported directly on the conduct of operations to Army HQ from the forward positions, led Geoffrey Cox, news reporter, journalist and later founder of *News at Ten*, to comment:

> Dan's capacity for assessing and marshalling information quickly, an invaluable by-product of his years of rigorous scholastic training, and his willingness to draw deductions and stand by them gave his reports in J Squadron an outstanding quality. The Merton Don, Bill Williams, then as Colonel Williams, the head of intelligence at Montgomery's HQ, told me many years later that he quickly realised he could place firm reliance on any report that came in with the signature 'DM Davin, Capt.'[38]

Costello, Cox and Davin were a formidable team in intelligence. According to McNeish, the 'trio of scholars' provided the general with 'a flow of intelligence summaries and reports that would be the envy of rival Allied commanders for

---

34 Davin, *The Salamander and the Fire*, p. ix.
35 Ovenden, *A Fighting Withdrawal*, pp. 123, 128; McNeish, *Dance of the Peacocks*, pp. 196–7.
36 McNeish, *Dance of the Peacocks*, pp. 218–19.
37 Ovenden, *A Fighting Withdrawal*, pp. 150–1; McNeish, *Dance of the Peacocks*, pp. 192, 196.
38 Sir Geoffrey Cox, 'Dan Davin: Soldier', in Wilson, *Intimate Stranger*, p. 54.

11. Dan Davin: The literary legacy of war

the duration of the war'.[39] The respect that all three won from the New Zealand military command led to other careers: Cox, after working for Freyberg, served as First Secretary of the New Zealand legation in Washington, DC, in 1942–43; Costello became a diplomat and First Secretary of the newly established New Zealand Embassy in Moscow in 1944; Kippenberger, even before his return to New Zealand in 1946 as Editor-in-Chief of the New Zealand war histories, had asked Davin to write the volume on the Crete campaign, while Freyberg, when about to take up the position of Governor-General of New Zealand, gave Davin access to his personal archives.[40]

For Davin, then, in both the professional and the personal realms of his life, war was more than a testing ground: it was a crucial axis round which his life perspectives, personal ambitions and values came to be shaped, particularly in relation to New Zealand, creating pride in the society he had come from; writing the short stories and the novel kept alive his name in connection with the war, while *Crete* gave him status among military historians, and authority among other New Zealand senior officers of staff. Most significantly, the war was the crucible for his writing of fiction—the activity for which at that time of his life he cared most passionately.[41] These years retained a tenacious hold on his memory and imagination, and their influence on Davin's later life exceeded their tangible achievements, relationships and experiences: the firsthand encounter with fighting, the acquaintance with suffering and death, and the mechanics and operations of war provided unparalleled material for his literary endeavours. Geoffrey Cox summarises the way that these intense experiences developed Davin's writing abilities:

> The war years were of deep importance in Dan's development as a novelist. They provided him with topics and scenes and characters in abundance for his later writings. But also they were years in which he lived deeply and fully, and in which he undoubtedly gained an added confidence in himself and his talent.[42]

War, Writing and New Zealand

When war was declared on 3 September 1939, Davin had just completed Greats at Balliol College, Oxford (gaining a first). He was in Paris on his honeymoon with Winnie (née Gonley), also of Irish-Catholic descent and from Otautau,

---

39   McNeish, *The Sixth Man*, p. 112.
40   Ovenden, *A Fighting Withdrawal*, p. 236.
41   Davin had already written one novel, *Cliffs of Fall* (1945), and lost the manuscript of a second novel in the retreat over Salonika.
42   Cox, 'Dan Davin', p. 56.

near Invercargill. They had met while students at Otago University in 1931. Davin's biographer paints a vivid picture of their departure from Paris following Germany's invasion of Poland on 1 September (coincidentally Davin's twenty-sixth birthday): the tears of the concierge in the flat they were staying at in the rue Delambre; their farewell to Geoffrey Cox, then a war correspondent, at his office in the *France Soir* building:

> When they had last seen him, the office was busy, Geoffrey constantly on the phone to Berlin, London or Rome. [Now] he was alone, his feet on a desk, the telephones silent. There was nothing more to say. Diplomacy was finished. [His] suitcase was in the corner of the room packed and ready.[43]

After returning to England, Davin enlisted, vowing to ensure his mortality by fathering a child and completing a novel before he was killed. Unaware of the options available for scholars such as himself with knowledge of languages—in areas such as supply, economic warfare or intelligence—he went before the Military and Government Recruitment Board at Oxford, was recruited for the British Infantry and assigned to the Royal Warwickshire Regiment in January 1940. But after training in Aldershot for some months, he requested a transfer to the 2NZEF, and in July took up his commission as a second lieutenant with 23 Battalion (Canterbury and Otago), at Mytchett, Surrey.[44] He thus found himself back in the company of men from Southland and the West Coast where he had grown up—people whom the Catholic, university-educated Davin had not encountered since he left Invercargill in 1930 for his final year at Sacred Heart College in Auckland, and then for the University of Otago on a National Scholarship.[45] Being in the midst of familiar accents and characters made him rediscover his roots after five years away, with a renewed sense of identity—that of being a New Zealander after all. He saw that he was working within a microcosm of the society he had left, writing: 'In parts this battalion is a travelling Invercargill, a peregrinating small town impregnable...in the complacencies of its provincialism.'[46] The Div. then came to act as a bridge, linking Davin's life back to New Zealand origins. Geoffrey Cox describes his impressions of the men of 13 Platoon C Company in the summer of 1940, with Dan as their commander, in Mytchett:

> Dan came past, marching at the head of his platoon. Under the high peaked hats which we still wore at that stage of the war, before they were abandoned for forage caps and berets, Dan's face was dour and set. The

---

43 Ovenden, *A Fighting Withdrawal*, p. 125.
44 Ibid., p. 127.
45 Father John Pound, 'The Marist Brothers, Invercargill', in Wilson, *Intimate Stranger*, p. 26; Ovenden, *A Fighting Withdrawal*, pp. 42–3.
46 Quoted in Ovenden, *A Fighting Withdrawal*, p. 137.

faces of the men behind him, mostly West Coast miners, farm workers and road makers from Southland, were typical of those early 2NZEF… volunteers, alert, hard-bitten, sardonic, the faces of men hardened and shaped by the rigours of the Great Slump, of the 30s. They were men who matched the hour as Dan too showed that he could do so in the testing years that lay ahead.[47]

Working within the ranks of the New Zealand Division awakened a complex sense of national pride that had been dormant at the time he departed from New Zealand at the age of twenty-three, frustrated by its provincialism and keen to explore wider horizons. Davin's understanding of national identity was male oriented, based on comradeship and a discovery of the ordinary, as McNeish puts it, in speaking of both Costello and Davin—of 'something outside themselves that was not intellectual'.[48] It was inevitably informed by values that war tested, such as the egalitarian belief that courage and proven ability in warfare should rank higher than training, hierarchy or privilege. As Davin says in the introduction to *The Salamander and the Fire*: after the 'initial sorting into officers, men and NCOs which was originally based up on the degree of education, obvious qualities of leadership and aptitude, everything depended, if the links of confidence were to be preserved, on merit as proved in battle.'[49] The imputation of physical cowardice to soldiers who held positions of leadership, and the exploration of its effects on the subject, is the focus of at least two stories. Davin's working-class affinities come out in the way he associates fear and its dire consequences with men from privileged backgrounds, or of officer class: in 'Coming and Going', Major Reading, whom the narrator encounters in the mess of the base camp at Maadi, comes from Christchurch, took an interest in territorials and is not the sort of person the narrator would know outside the Army: 'Chaps like him had got off to a flying start when the war broke out',[50] the narrator notes; but on the occasion of a counterattack, Reading had '[c]leared out, Ratted, Buggered off. Said he had to report back to battalion.'[51] Reading finally shoots himself rather than face the disgrace of repatriation. Equally chilling in its exploration of the psychology of the coward is 'East is West': the narrator, a sergeant, is picked up by Captain Curtis in his truck after his tank is blown up and his friend George killed; but the truck then becomes separated from the convoy in the desert and runs into a minefield. Curtis's miscalculations and fears, which he covers up by pulling rank, set up tensions with the others,

---

47 Cox, 'Dan Davin', p. 53.
48 McNeish, *The Sixth Man*, p. 117.
49 Davin, *The Salamander and the Fire*, p. ix.
50 Ibid., p. 48.
51 Ibid., p. 50.

and when his legs are blown off by a mine the sergeant waits for him to die instead of shooting him as he begs him to, saying later to himself: 'I'd have known it was all right [to shoot him] if it'd been a pal like George.'[52]

Davin's nationalist leanings hinged on his confidence in the New Zealanders as a fighting force, because in other ways he became restless in their company. Costello had invented the Div.'s slogan—'Hooray fuck'—and this summarised their anti-authoritarian bravado. Davin's diary confirms this impression: 'I just could not believe the Germans would get past our line at Alamein, past Paddy, past Freyberg, and those high New Zealand voices, full of confidence and courage, I had heard passing through the Cairo night.'[53] Serving with the Div. throughout most of the war, writing about it in fiction, reinforced by the research for *Crete*, anchored Davin in his New Zealand identity in ways that would not otherwise have been possible. It remained with him for the rest of his life although coupled with the growing recognition with time that by remaining on the other side of the world, he was also cutting himself off. As he wrote to the New Zealand novelist Frank Sargeson almost a decade after the end of the war: 'I feel no wish to write about anyone but NZers—indeed don't feel or don't feel in the same way about anything else—and all the time the old navel cord is getting more shriveled.'[54]

All but two of the 19 stories in *The Salamander and the Fire* are about New Zealanders at war. Male comradeship—its expectations and betrayals—is a leitmotif; women are absent but influential, invoked indirectly through memory and dream, and they are addressed in their absence through letter writing, as in the comical but sad story in 'Finders and Losers' of the narrator's friend Herbie, from Southland Boys' High School and Otago University days. Herbie, now a fellow soldier, had married, above his class, the daughter of a Canterbury sheep farmer: he persuades the narrator to compose letters to convince his wife that he is staying out of danger by taking on a safe camp job, although in the end he dies before he receives the 'Dear John' letter he had been anticipating. Davin's narratives about the adjudication of friendships and carefully negotiated relationships between men who are not equals in rank can be compared with Frank Sargeson's stories and anecdotes about male friendship, permeated by hidden tensions and jealousies, marked by their homosexually loaded subtexts, which were published in the 1930s, stemming from that other great social crisis, the Depression. Davin's concept of mateship relies on shared action and common

---

52 Davin, 'East is West', *Breathing Spaces* (London, 1975), p. 119.
53 McNeish, *The Sixth Man*, pp. 114–15.
54 Quoted in Wilson, *Intimate Stranger*, p. 101. A broader discussion of fictional writing about World War II by New Zealanders, including Davin, is provided by Jock Phillips, *A Man's Country?: The image of the Pakeha male: a history* (Auckland, 1987), pp. 198–215.

goals and, as with Sargeson's values, it thrives because it is underpinned by a code of loyalty. The protagonist in *For the Rest of Our Lives*, Frank Fahy, sums it up:

> For the first time in his life, Frank, impervious to the self-conscious esprit de corps of school and university, found himself deep in a group loyalty which he unequivocally shared. Here were men associated with a common purpose, who had built up in their two years campaigning a tradition of boldness, efficiency and resource.[55]

In Davin's stories, male bonding occurs through verbal, intellectual encounters: playing chess, trading ideas through wit and repartee, and conversations involving gossip, rumour and stories. 'Bourbons', for example, focuses on an off-duty English major and two captains in the western desert luxuriating over bourbon and cheroots, enjoying their conversation about 'home' and their guaranteed postwar futures, who wander over to the wireless truck—the men's resort of an evening—where they 'felt the loss of home', to listen to the news.[56] This emphasis reflects the convivial atmosphere that Dan thrived on, in which his conversational skills and aptitude to listen to others as well came into their own. During 1942–43, he and Paddy would hold court each night in the 'I' (Intelligence) truck known as the 'Café' or the 'Bistro', in contrast with the regular staff officers' Armoured Carrying Vehicle, the 'Tin Chapel' (so-called because the officers carried their training manuals like prayer books);[57] in this 'home of amateur intellectuals', intelligence was gathered, troop movements on different fronts were discussed, there were singing, joking and yarning. The telling of stories is an innate part of such entertainment and such gatherings were a fecund source of Davin's tales, many of which are anecdotal, displaying oral storytelling mannerisms, passed down from one narrator to another.

Davin wrote many of his stories—both about the war and about his Southland childhood—in periods of inaction during the war when he had time to write, reflect and concentrate on ways of representing events. The stories in *The Salamander and the Fire* are grouped so as to form an image of his own trajectory in moving from Greece to Crete, Cairo, North Africa, Palestine and Italy.[58] This does not reflect the order in which they were written, but gives a thematic coherence to the collection, as the opening stories that dwell on initiation into war contrast with the sombre, meditative tone of the final stories, in which Davin's narrators brood on the fate of his generation in what becomes a virtual 'anthem for doomed youth'. There is a world of difference from the more subjective, impressionistic mood of early stories such as 'Under the Bridge', in

---

55 Davin, *For the Rest of Our Lives*, p. 55.
56 Davin, *The Salamander and the Fire*, pp. 54–8.
57 Ibid., p. 199.
58 Ovenden, *A Fighting Withdrawal*, p. 383.

which the narrator forces himself to look down at the mass of bodies of those who had been sheltering under a bridge that has been bombed, and experiences an existential moment of ontological denial:

> I listened again. Not a groan or sigh…I hesitated. In sudden horror, I knew there was something else dragging me to the edge. Appetite for frightfulness as well as revulsion. Death squatted within the hollow like a presence, its emanation came up grisly, dragging at me. I felt the hair on the back of my head stiffen, I took two steps forward. My eyes saw but my brain would not see, I turned and ran.[59]

The subjective response to war experiences—significantly correlated to Davin's own—is at the centre of these fictions; but Davin's technique is often to develop its narrative potential. 'Danger's Flower'[60] takes place after the German airborne offensive at Maleme airport in Crete in 1941 where Davin was wounded. It probes the consciousness of a wounded man who, along with others, has been shifted to a cathedral because the hospital is full. During the night a girl comes round and offers each of the wounded a flower, giving Alan a carnation: 'He blushed and tears came into his eyes. There was a lump at his throat. He took the flower in his left hand and looked at it…They used to grow in the front garden at home when he was a boy. They were the first flowers he remembered.'[61] These details are recorded in Davin's diary for 12 September 1940.[62] But onto this setting he attaches an incident of greater consequence that is either invented or based on an anecdote: Alan moves out of the cathedral with the other walking wounded in order to be evacuated from Suda Bay on a warship; with him is a young man who cannot speak English. The boy is hit by an anti-personnel bomb as they walk together; Alan, although exhausted from his own wounds, covers up the boy's wound and helps him to safety.

In contrast, the final story, 'Not Substantial Things', is evaluative and reflective, and the narrator speaks for his generation, summarising the war's meaning for the survivors, no doubt drawing on personal impressions: they had given war the best of their lives, they had burnt up their youth in its service.[63] War had

---

59   Davin, *The Salamander and the Fire*, p. 15.
60   An allusion to Shakespeare, *Henry IV*, part 1 (1597): 'out of this nettle, Danger we pluck this flower, safety.'
61   Davin, *The Salamander and the Fire*, p. 19.
62   Ovenden, *A Fighting Withdrawal*, p. 149.
63   Ovenden (ibid., pp. 355–6) quotes from a letter from Anthony Stones, the sculptor, of how Davin in 1978 at a gathering organised by Wig Gardiner at the Auckland Returned Servicemen's Association spoke extempore: 'It was just as in his stories, he gave their memories and sentiments a form of which they were incapable. He spoke for the men there and the men who weren't there. It was a privileged thing to have seen and heard.'

taken the flower of their manhood, yet it had also yielded riches in the forms of new friendships, company, and ways of dying as well as of living; nothing would be the same again.

> We'd never give anything again what we'd given to the Div. We'd never bring the same energy to anything that we'd brought to things like the break-through at Minqar Quaim or the assault on Cassino. And we'd never be able to make friends again the same way or drink and laugh and die the same way. We'd used up what we had and we'd spend *the rest of our lives* looking over our shoulders.[64]

This seminal statement not only gives the phrase that would become the title of his war novel, it also hints at Davin's philosophy of life, articulated in the short stories and novels, as well as in non-fiction such as the memoirs in *Closing Times* (1975)—a volume that shows his affection for and sympathy with the thinking of Samuel Johnson: life is inextricable from death, we are ruled by transience, and exist in an indifferent, godless universe from which we are estranged.[65]

Davin's war novel, *For the Rest of Our Lives,* written in the last stages of the war when he was living and working in London, moves one step further away from the realm of action to consider the qualities of the Div. as a fighting unit. It also hints at the relationship between the men's bravery and military effectiveness and the land that had nourished them. This patriotic accolade, which embraces both the discipline imposed by the general and the inner calibrations imposed by the threat of death, suggests how the war had brought Davin back emotionally into the centre of the world, which he thought he had left:

> So that in that summer of 1942 no army in the world had a division so free from incompetence, so close to perfect, with so high a percentage of men in their right places from general to private.
>
> Yet there was more than the general and death to thank for this. There was the hard, self-reliant, democratic subsoil of life from which the men had grown, and the pride in body and brain it had given them.[66]

Conclusion: The final years

In retirement from Oxford University Press (1978–90), Davin found more time to pursue the legacy of the war years; but, regretfully, lengthy projects he had planned for his years of greater leisure—such as writing another novel or a

---

64   Davin, *The Salamander and the Fire*, p. 207.
65   Lawrence Jones, *Barbed Wire and Mirrors: Essays on New Zealand prose* (Dunedin, 1987), p. 86.
66   Davin, *For the Rest of Our Lives*, p. 320.

memoir of his friend Paddy Costello as part of a series to be called 'Scholars and Soldiers'—were started but not completed.[67] Suffering from ill health, writer's block and depression, Davin turned to less taxing forms: the short story, the brief memoir and the literary essay. Writing on the war and reflecting on those years loomed large among these activities. He typed up his war diaries for the period 1940–44, and, as Chairman from 1980 to 1983 of the Salamander Oasis Trust—a charity that aimed to publish the work of servicemen from the North African campaigns of 1940–43—he revived his earlier interest in publishing about the war; he assisted in the finalising of many manuscripts and saw into print a second anthology, *From Oasis into Italy* (1983).[68] Time and attention were devoted to the editing of his friend Wig Gardiner's book about his war years, *Freyberg's Circus* (1981); and, for Oxford University Press, he compiled *Night Attack: Short stories from the Second World War* (1982), which included stories by Kingsley Amis, Elizabeth Bowen, V. S. Pritchett, Graham Greene and Julian McLaren Ross, as well as two of his own. Most importantly, he wrote a further six stories about the war—mainly on the Italian campaign—deepening them with reflections about his Southland childhood as in 'When Mum Died', or by using reflections of war to introduce an episode from his early years as in 'Black Diamond'. These were first published in New Zealand journals and collections—the *New Zealand Listener* and *Islands*—and are among the 19 stories collected in *The Salamander and the Fire* (1986).[69]

Davin's social habits had become entrenched due to the evenings spent with Costello and others in the 'I Café' and in Soho pubs subsequently. With Winnie, he maintained a social circle in various local pubs near where they lived in Jericho, Oxford; old and new friends, and members of the press would drop in, as would local and visiting academics including New Zealanders who were either visiting or domiciled in England. In this way, they kept up those ties with New Zealand that Dan also sustained through literary and scholarly avenues: through correspondence with authors such as Sargeson, through reviewing recent New Zealand writing for the *Times Literary Supplement*, writing stories about his childhood, writing memoirs and obituaries of academic colleagues such as Norman Davis and Jack Bennett (both Professors of Medieval English at Oxford), as well as critical essays. There were also return visits with Winnie in which they reconnected with family and friends: in September 1978, the year of his retirement, and again in December 1984 to receive an honorary Doctorate of Literature from the University of Otago. In 1987, on New Year's Day, Dan Davin was appointed CBE in the New Zealand lists.

---

67 Ovenden (*A Fighting Withdrawal*, pp. 364–6) suggests that Davin's frustration at the inability to complete this project—partly due to lack of access to Costello's papers, and his desire to clear Paddy of charges of espionage—overshadowed his later years.
68 He included his own works: the diary extract 'Eavesdropping at Alamein' and a poem, 'Lybian Epitaph'.
69 With the exception of 'East is West' and 'Black Diamond'. The latter is published in Janet Wilson (ed.), *The Gorse Blooms Pale: Dan Davin's Southland stories* (Dunedin, 2007), pp. 255–65.

Davin ended his life already a figure of legend. Long before his death on 28 September 1990, he was known in New Zealand literary circles for his contribution to the short story tradition, perhaps misleadingly as one of the 'sons of Sargeson', and to a lesser extent for his novels. His reputation as one of New Zealand's best and most prolific writers about World War II has until recently been overshadowed by these achievements in fiction, despite the range of his war publications: fiction, official history, radio broadcast (for example, with Leonard Cottrell about the fall of Crete in July 1953), and literary criticism (for example, reviewing works such as John Mulgan's posthumous account, *Report on Experience*).[70] Since his death this has been partly overturned with the publication of Keith Ovenden's indispensable biography, *A Fighting Withdrawal: The life of Dan Davin*, and with a revival of interest in the war years generated partly by James McNeish's two studies of a number of brilliant figures in Davin's generation, several of whom lived out their lives in Europe.[71] Davin's war writings are unique amongst historical and political evaluations because of their generic diversity, and the way they reveal a growing national sentiment and identity and represent the collective presence of members of the Div. The future publication of his war dairies and correspondence will go some way to complete the picture of World War II that these recent biographies and studies have reconstructed, based as they are on Davin's *Crete*, his imaginative fiction, his poetry and his non-fictional and autobiographical writings.

---

70 *Landfall: A New Zealand quarterly*, 2:1 (1948), pp. 50–5.
71 Ovenden, *A Fighting Withdrawal*; McNeish, *The Dance of the Peacocks*; McNeish, *The Sixth Man*.

Consolidated Bibliography

Personal Papers

Abel Papers: Papers of C. W. Abel, New Guinea Collection, University of Papua New Guinea Library, Port Moresby.

Barwick Papers: Papers of Diane E. Barwick, State Library of Victoria [unsorted], Melbourne.

Chinnery Papers: Papers of E. W. P. Chinnery, National Library of Australia, MS 766, Canberra.

Cleland Papers: Papers of J. B. Cleland, South Australian Museum Archives, Series AA60/03, Adelaide.

Davidson Papers: Papers of J. W. Davidson, National Library of Australia, MS 5105, Canberra; and Papers of J. W. Davidson, Australian National University Archives, Series 57, Canberra.

D. M. Davin Papers: Literary Papers of Daniel Marcus Davin, Alexander Turnbull Library, MS-Group-0319, Wellington.

Winnie Davin Papers: 'Memories of Wartime Experiences', Alexander Turnbull Library, MS-Papers-3839, Wellington.

Elkin Papers: Papers of A. P. Elkin, University of Sydney Archives, P.130, Sydney.

Firth Archive: Archive of Sir Raymond Firth, British Library of Political and Economic Science, London School of Economics and Political Science, London.

Florey Papers: Papers of Sir Howard Florey, Australian National University Library, Canberra.

Freeman Papers: Papers of Derek Freeman, Mandeville Special Collections of the Geisel Library at the University of California, San Diego, MSS 0522.

Greenwood Papers: Papers of Miles Greenwood, National Library of Australia, MS 9805, Canberra.

Hancock Papers: Papers of Sir Keith Hancock, Australian National University Archives, Series 77, Canberra.

Hasluck Papers: Papers of Sir Paul Hasluck, in the possession of Nicholas Hasluck.

Hogbin Papers: Papers of H. Ian Hogbin, University of Sydney Archives, P.105, Sydney.

Isles Papers: Papers of Keith Isles, University of Tasmania Archives [unsorted], Hobart.

Lilburn Papers: Papers of Douglas Lilburn, Alexander Turnbull Library, MS-Group-0009, Wellington.

Mander Papers: Papers of Linden A. Mander, University of Washington Libraries, 730-7-55, Seattle.

Maude Papers: Papers of H. C. and H. E. Maude, Special Collections, Barr Smith Library, University of Adelaide, MSS 0003, Adelaide.

Phillips Correspondence: Neville Phillips' letters to Patricia and Jim Nelson, 1939–44, in private possession.

Rosenberg Collection: Rosenberg Family Collection, in private possession.

Ross Papers: Kathleen Ross Papers, Alexander Turnbull Library, MS-6963-18, Wellington.

Spate Papers: Papers of O. H. K. Spate, National Library of Australia, MS 7886, Canberra.

Stanner Collection: W. E. H. Stanner Collection, Australian Institute of Aboriginal and Torres Strait Islander Studies, Canberra.

Stone Papers, Papers of Julius Stone, National Library of Australia, MS 5516, Canberra.

Stout Papers: Papers of Alan Stout, University of Sydney Archives, P.180, Sydney.

Wedgwood Papers: Papers of Camilla Wedgwood, National Library of Australia, MS 483, Canberra.

Wedgwood Personal Correspondence: Personal Correspondence of Camilla Wedgwood, in private possession.

Wright Papers: Papers of R. D. Wright, University of Melbourne Archives, A.1968.0003, Melbourne.

Unpublished Papers and Theses

ALOMES, Stephen, '"Reasonable Men": Middle class reformism in Australia 1928–1939', PhD thesis, Australian National University, Canberra, 1980.

BEAGLEHOLE, Ernest, 'The Third Culture in New Zealand: Human nature and conduct', 1964 Hudson Lecture to the Royal Society of New Zealand, Wellington. Copy in Papers of Derek Freeman, Mandeville Special Collections of the Geisel Library at the University of California, San Diego, MSS 0522, box 118, folder 27.

BERNDT, Catherine H., 'Mythology in the Eastern Central Highlands of New Guinea', PhD thesis, London School of Economics and Political Science, London, 1955.

BERNDT, Ronald M., 'Social Control among Central Highlanders of New Guinea', PhD thesis, London School of Economics and Political Science, London, 1955.

BERNDT, Ronald M. and Catherine H. BERNDT, 'A Preliminary Report of Field Work in the Ooldea Region, Western South Australia', Joint Diploma of Anthropology thesis, University of Sydney, NSW, 1943.

BOLTON, Geoffrey, Dr Evatt and Mr Hasluck at the United Nations, Unpublished paper.

CLOHESY, Lachlan Clohesy, 'Australian Cold Warrior: The anti-communism of W. C. Wentworth', PhD thesis, Victoria University, Melbourne, 2010.

CRAIG, Jean, 'Some Aspects of Life in Selected Areas of Rural New South Wales', MA thesis, University of Sydney, NSW, 1945.

CRAIG, Jean, 'Assimilation of European Immigrants: A study in role assumption and fulfilment', PhD thesis, Australian National University, Canberra, 1954.

DAVIDSON, J. W., 'Scandinavian Settlement in New Zealand', MA thesis, University of New Zealand, Wellington, 1937.

DAVIDSON, J. W., 'European Penetration of the South Pacific, 1779–1842', PhD thesis, Cambridge University, UK, 1942.

DICKSON, D. J., 'Government and Mission in Education', MEd thesis, University of Papua New Guinea, Port Moresby, 1971.

ELKIN, A. P., 'Australia's National Consciousness', BA Honours thesis, University of Sydney, NSW, 1914.

FREEMAN, J. D., 'On Samoan Social Organization', Seminar paper presented to the London School of Economics and Political Science, London, December 1946 [in possession of the Freeman family].

GRAY, Geoffrey, The coming of the war to the territories: forced labour and broken promises, Unpublished paper presented to Remembering the War in New Guinea, 19–21 October 2000, Australian War Memorial, Canberra, <http://ajrp.awm.gov.au/AJRP/remember.nsf/Web-Printer/2BA56E46D717A652CA256A99001D9F10?OpenDocument>

GRAY, Geoffrey and Doug MUNRO, 'Your own position is not being overlooked': the politics of choosing a successor to S. F. Nadel, 1957, Unpublished manuscript.

GRIFFITHS, Deirdre J. F., 'The Career of F. E. Williams, Government Anthropologist of Papua, 1922–1943', MA thesis, Australian National University, Canberra, 1977.

JINKS, Brian, 'Policy, Planning and Administration in Papua New Guinea, 1942–52, with special reference to the role of Colonel J. K. Murray', PhD thesis, University of Sydney, NSW, 1976.

LANE, Jonathan, 'Anchorage in Aboriginal Affairs: A. P. Elkin on religious continuity and civic obligation', PhD thesis, University of Sydney, NSW, 2008.

NADEL, S. F., *Report on activities in 1952, Department of Anthropology and Sociology, ANU*, Copy in authors' possession.

NIXON, Pamela, 'The Integration of a Half-caste Community at La Perouse, NSW', MA thesis, University of Sydney, NSW, 1947.

PHILLIPS, Neville, 'New Zealand's Relations with Great Britain, 1868–1901: A study in Empire unionism', MA thesis, Canterbury University College, Christchurch, 1937.

POMEROY, John, 'Morale on the Homefront in Australia During the Second World War', PhD thesis, University of Sydney, NSW, 1995.

READ, Kenneth E., 'Native Thought and the War in the Pacific: A study of the effects of the Pacific War on a native community of the Markham Valley, Australian Mandated Territory of New Guinea', MA thesis, University of Sydney, NSW, 1946.

REECE, R. W., Alf Conlon, the fall of Singapore and British Borneo, Unpublished paper, 1993.

RISEMAN, Noah J., 'Colonising Yolngu Defence: Arnhem Land in the Second World War and transnational uses of Indigenous people in the Second World War', PhD thesis, University of Melbourne, Vic., 2008.

STANNER, W. E. H., 'Economic Change in North Australian Tribes', PhD thesis, London School of Economics and Political Science, London, 1938.

THOMAS, Caroline, 'Professional Amateurs and Colonial Academics: Steps towards academic anthropology in New Zealand, 1860–1920', MA thesis, University of Auckland, NZ, 1995.

Secondary Sources (excluding theses)

AKENSEN, Donald Harman, *Half the World from Home: Perspectives on the Irish in New Zealand, 1860–1950*. Wellington: Victoria University Press, 1990.

ALLEN, Nessy, 'Test Tubes and White Jackets: The careers of two Australian women scientists', *Journal of Australian Studies*, 52 (1997), pp. 126–34.

ANDERSON, Fay, *An Historian's Life: Max Crawford and the politics of academic freedom*. Melbourne: Melbourne University Press, 2005.

ANDERSON, John, *The Servile State*. Sydney: Angus & Robertson, 1943; republished Sydney: The Centre for Independent Studies, 2009.

ANNAN, Noel, 'The Intellectual Aristocracy', in J. H. Plumb (ed.), *Studies in Social History: A tribute to G. M. Trevelyan*. London: Longmans, Green, 1955, 241–87. Republished in Noel Annan, *The Dons: Mentors, eccentrics and geniuses*. London: Harper Collins, 2000, 304–41.

[ANON.], 'South Pacific Commission', *International Organization*, 1:2 (1947), pp. 368–70.

BACRACH, Paul (ed.), *Political Elites in a Democracy*. New York: Atherton Press, 1971.

BANNER, Lois W., *Intertwined Lives: Margaret Mead, Ruth Benedict, and their circle*. New York: Knopf, 2003.

BANNER, Lois W., 'History as Biography', *American Historical Review*, 114:3 (2009), pp. 579–86.

BARCAN, Alan, *Radical Students: The Old Left at Sydney University*. Melbourne: Melbourne University Press, 2002.

BARNES, J. A., *Humping My Drum: A memoir*. Self-published: <www.lulu.com>, 2007.

BARNETT, Michael, *Empire of Humanity: A history of humanitarianism*. Ithaca, NY, and London: Cornell University Press, 2011.

BARROWMAN, Rachel, '"Culture-organising": Joe Heenan and the beginnings of state patronage of the arts', *New Zealand Studies*, 6:2 (1996), pp. 3–10.

BARROWMAN, Rachel, *Victoria University of Wellington 1899–1999: A history*. Wellington: Victoria University Press, 1999.

BARWICK, Diane E., Jeremy BECKETT and Marie REAY (eds), *Metaphors of Interpretation: Essays in honour of W. E. H. Stanner*. Canberra: Aboriginal Studies Press, 1985.

BASSETT, Michael, *The Mother of All Departments: The history of the Department of Internal Affairs*. Auckland: Auckland University Press, 1977.

BASSETT, Michael, *An Overview of the War History Branch*. <http://michaelbassett.co.nz/article_war.htm>, 1997.

BEAGLEHOLE, Ernest, 'The South Seas Regional Commission', *Journal of the Polynesian Society*, 53:2 (1944), pp. 59–71.

BEAGLEHOLE, J. C., *Victoria University College: An essay towards a history*. Wellington: New Zealand University Press, 1949.

BEAGLEHOLE, Tim, *A Life of J. C. Beaglehole: New Zealand scholar*. Wellington: Victoria University Press, 2006, <http://www.nzetc.org/tm/scholarly/tei-BeaLife.html>

BEAUMONT, Joan, *Australia's War, 1939–1945*. Sydney: Heinemann, 1996.

BECKETT, Jeremy, *Conversations with Ian Hogbin*. Sydney: Oceania Monographs No. 35, 1989.

BECKETT, Jeremy and Geoffrey GRAY, 'Hogbin, Herbert Ian Priestley (1904–1989)', *Australian Dictionary of Biography. Volume 17*. Melbourne: Melbourne University Press, 2007, p. 539, <http://adbonline.anu.edu.au/biogs/A170540b.htm>

BECKETT, Jeremy and Melinda HINKSON, '"Going more than half way to meet them": On the life and legacy of WEH Stanner', in Melinda Hinkson and Jeremy Beckett (eds), *An Appreciation of Difference: WEH Stanner and Aboriginal Australia*. Canberra: Aboriginal Studies Press, 2008, pp. 1–23.

BEEBY, C. E., *The Biography of An Idea: Beeby on education*. Wellington: New Zealand Council for Educational Research, 1992.

BELICH, James, *Paradise Reforged: A history of the New Zealanders from the 1880s to the year 2000*. Auckland: Penguin Books, 2001.

BELSHAW, Cyril, *Island Administration in the South West Pacific: Government and reconstruction in New Caledonia, the New Hebrides, and the British Solomon Islands*. London: Royal Institute of International Affairs, 1950.

BELSHAW, Cyril, *The Great Village: The economic and social welfare of Hanubada, an urban community in Papua*. London: Routledge & Kegan Paul, 1957.

BELSHAW, Cyril, *Bumps on a Long Road*. Self-published: <www.lulu.com>, 2009.

BENNETT, Wendell C., 'The Ethnographic Board', *Smithsonian Miscellaneous Collections*, 107:1 (1947), pp. 1–135.

BERG, Maxine, *A Woman in History: Eileen Power, 1889–1940*. Cambridge: Cambridge University Press, 1996.

BERNDT, Ronald M., 'Wuradjeri Magic and "Clever Men"', *Oceania*, 17:4 (1947), pp. 327–65; 18:1 (1947), pp. 60–86.

BERNDT, Ronald M., *Love Songs of Arnhem Land*. Chicago: University of Chicago Press, 1978.

BERNDT, Ronald M., 'Aboriginal Fieldwork in South Australia in the 1940s and its Implications for the Present', *Records of the South Australian Museum*, 23:1 (1989), pp. 59–68.

BERNDT, Ronald M. and Catherine H. BERNDT, 'A Preliminary Report of Field Work in the Ooldea Region, Western South Australia', *Oceania*, 12:4 (1942), pp. 305–30.

BERNDT, Ronald M. and Catherine H. BERNDT, *End of an Era: Aboriginal labour in the Northern Territory*. Canberra: Australian Institute of Aboriginal Studies, 1987.

BERRY, Joe, *Unwillingly to War*. Hull, UK: Privately published, 1996.

BERRY, Paul and Mark BOSTRIDGE, *Vera Brittain: A life*. London: Virago, 2001.

BOHAN, Edmund, 'McLintock, Alexander Hare, 1903–1968', *Dictionary of New Zealand Biography. Volume 3*. Auckland and Wellington: Auckland University Press with Bridget Williams Books and Department of Internal Affairs, 1996, pp. 321–2, updated 22 June 2007, <http://www.dnzb.govt.nz/>

BOLTON, G. C., 'Foreword', in John A. Moses, *Prussian-German Militarism, 1914–18, in Australian Perspective: The thought of George Arnold Wood*. Bern/New York: P. Lang, 1991, 5-12

BOSE, Srinjoy, 'Students or Soldiers? Conscientious objection during World War II', in The Time Keepers (eds), *Tower Turmoil: Characters and controversies at the University of Otago*. Dunedin: Department of History, University of Otago, 2005, pp. 81–94.

BREMEN, Jan van, 'Comments on David Price', *Anthropology Today*, 18:4 (2002), pp. 21–2.

BREMEN, Jan van, 'Wartime Anthropology: A global perspective', in Akitoshi Shimizu and Jan van Bremen (eds), *Wartime Japanese Anthropology in Asia and the Pacific*. Osaka: National Museum of Ethnology, 2003, pp. 13–48.

BREMEN, Jan van and Akitoshi SHIMIZU (eds), *Anthropology and Colonialism in Asia and Oceania*. Richmond, Surrey: Curzon, 1999.

BRIDGE, Carl Bridge and Kent FEDOROWICH, 'Mapping the British World', *Journal of Imperial and Commonwealth History*, 31:2 2003, pp. 1–15.

BRITTLEBANK, Kate, 'Anthropology, Fine Art and Missionaries: The Berndt Kalighat album rediscovered', *Journal of the History of Collections*, 17:1 (2007), pp. 1–16.

BROWN, Paula, *The Chimbu: A study of cultural change in the New Guinea Highlands*. London: Routledge & Kegan Paul, 1973.

BUCKLEY-MORAN, Jean, 'Australian Scientists and the Cold War', in Brian Martin, C. M. Ann Baker, Clyde Manwell and Cedric Pugh (eds), *Intellectual Suppression: Australian case histories—analysis and responses*. Sydney: Angus & Robertson, 1986, pp. 11–23.

BURK, Kathleen, *Troublemaker: The life and history of A. J. P. Taylor*. New Haven, Conn./London, UK, 2000.

BURTON, J. W., *The Atlantic Charter and the Pacific Races*. Sydney: Department of Methodist Overseas Missions, 1943.

CALDER, Angus and Dorothy SHERIDAN (eds), *Speak for Yourself: A mass-observation anthology, 1937–1949*. London: Jonathan Cape, 1984.

CALLAHAN, Michael D., *A Sacred Trust: The League of Nations and Africa, 1929–1946*. Sussex: Academic Press, 2004.

CALVOCORESSI, Peter, *Top Secret Ultra*. London: Sphere edn, 1981 [1980].

CALVOCORESSI, Peter, *A Time for Peace*. London: Hutchinson, 1987.

CAMPBELL, Alistair, 'Elegy', *Landfall*, 3:3 (1949), pp. 223–8.

CAMPBELL, I. C., 'Anthropology and the Professionalisation of Colonial Administration in Papua and New Guinea', *Journal of Pacific History*, 33:1 (1998), pp. 69–90.

CAMPBELL, I. C., 'Resistance and Colonial Government: A comparative study of Samoa', *Journal of Pacific History*, 40:1 (2005), pp. 45–69.

CHAKRABARTY, Dipesh, *Provincializing Europe: Postcolonial thought and historical difference*. Princeton, NJ: Princeton University Press, 2000.

CHAUDHURI, Amit, 'In the Waiting Room of History', *London Review of Books*, 24 June 2004, pp. 3–8.

CLOUT, Hugh and Cyril GOSME, 'The Naval Intelligence Handbooks: A monument to geographical writing', *Progress in Human Geography*, 27:2 (2003), pp. 153–73.

COLLINI, Stefan, *Public Moralists: Political thought and intellectual life in Britain, 1850–1930*. Oxford: Clarendon Press, 1991.

CONNORS, Libby, Lynette FINCH, Kay SAUNDERS and Helen TAYLOR, *Australia's Frontline: Remembering the 1939–45 war*. St Lucia: University of Queensland Press, 1992.

CONWAY, Jill Ker, *When Memory Speaks: Reflections on autobiography*. New York: Knopf, 1998.

COOKSON, J. E., 'Appeal Boards and Conscientious Objectors', in John Crawford (ed.), *Kia Kaha: New Zealand in the Second World War*. Melbourne: Oxford University Press, 2002, pp. 173–98.

COOMBS, H. C., *Trial Balance: Issues of my working life*. Melbourne: Sun Papermac, 1983 [1981].

COTTLE, Drew, 'A New Order for the Old Disorder: The state, class struggle and social order, 1941–1945', in Richard Kennedy (ed.), *Australian Welfare History: Critical essays*. Melbourne: Macmillan, 1982, pp. 256–80.

COX, Sir Geoffrey, 'Dan Davin: Soldier', in Janet Wilson (ed.), *Intimate Stranger: Reminiscences of Dan Davin*. Wellington: Steele Roberts, 2000, pp. 52–7.

CRANSWICK, G. H. and I. W. A. SHEVILL, *A New Deal for Papua*. Melbourne: Cheshire, [1949].

CRAWFORD, John (ed.), *Kia Kaha: New Zealand in the Second World War*. Melbourne: Oxford University Press, 2002.

CRAWFORD, John and James WATSON, '"A most appeasing line": New Zealand and Nazi Germany, 1935–1940', *Journal of Imperial and Commonwealth History*, 38:1 (2010), pp. 175–97.

CRAWFORD, Patricia and Myrna TONKINSON, *The Missing Chapters: Women staff at the University of Western Australia, 1963–1987*. Perth: Centre for Western Australian History, University of Western Australia, 1988.

CRAWFORD, R. M., 'History as a Science', *Historical Studies: Australia and New Zealand*, 3:11 (1947), pp. 153–75.

CRAWFORD, R. M., 'The School of Prudence or Inaccuracy and Incoherence in Describing Chaos', *Historical Studies*, 15:57 (1971), pp. 27–42.

CUNNINGHAM, K. S., *The Social Science Research Council of Australia, 1942–1952*. Canberra: Social Science Research Council of Australia, 1967.

CURTHOYS, Ann, 'WEH Stanner and the Historians', in Melinda Hinkson and Jeremy Beckett (eds), *An Appreciation of Difference: WEH Stanner and Aboriginal Australia*. Canberra: Aboriginal Studies Press, 2008, pp. 233–50.

CUTLER, Andrew, '*Tomorrow* Magazine and New Zealand Politics, 1934–1940', *New Zealand Journal of History*, 24:1 (1990), pp. 22–44.

CUTLER, Andrew, '"Tomorrow" Magazine: The case of the cultural shadow', in Pat Moloney and Kerry Taylor (eds), *Culture and the Labour Movement: Essays in New Zealand labour history*. Palmerston North, NZ: Dunmore Press, 1991, pp. 209–24.

DALTON, B. J., *War and Politics in New Zealand, 1855–1879*. Sydney: Sydney University Press, 1967.

DARNELL, Regna, *Invisible Genealogies: A history of Americanist anthropology*. Lincoln: University of Nebraska Press, 2001.

DAVIDSON, Jim, *A Three-Cornered Life: The historian W. K. Hancock*. Sydney: University of New South Wales Press, 2010.

DAVIDSON, J. W., 'The Present War and the Future Peace', *Tomorrow*, 5:25 (1939), pp. 778–80.

DAVIDSON, J. W., *The Northern Rhodesian Legislative Council*. London: Faber & Faber, 1947.

DAVIDSON, J. W., *Samoa mo Samoa: The emergence of the Independent State of Western Samoa*. Melbourne: Oxford University Press, 1967.

DAVIDSON, J. W., 'Understanding Pacific History: The participant as historian', in Peter Munz (ed.), *The Feel of Truth: Essays in New Zealand and Pacific history in honour of F. L. W. Wood and J. C. Beaglehole*. Wellington: A. W. & A. H. Reed, 1969, pp. 25–40.

DAVIN, Dan, *Cliffs of Fall*. London: Nicholson & Watson, 1945.

DAVIN, Dan, *For the Rest of Our Lives*. London: Nicholson & Watson, 1947.

DAVIN, Dan, *The Gorse Blooms Pale*. London: Nicholson & Watson, 1947.

DAVIN, Dan, 'Review [of *Report on Experience*, by John Mulgan]', *Landfall*, 2:1 (1948), pp. 50–5.

DAVIN, Dan, *Roads from Home*. London: Michael Joseph, 1949.

DAVIN, Dan, *Crete. Official History of New Zealand in the Second World War, 1939–1945*. Wellington: War History Branch, Department of Internal Affairs, 1953, <http://www.nzetc.org/tm/scholarly/tei-WH2Cret.html>

DAVIN, Dan (ed.), *New Zealand Short Stories*. London: Oxford University Press, 1953.

DAVIN, Dan (ed.), *Katherine Mansfield: Selected stories*. London: Oxford University Press, 1953.

DAVIN, Dan, *Breathing Spaces*. London: Hale, 1975.

DAVIN, Dan, 'Correspondence', *New Zealand Journal of History*, 13:1 (1979), pp. 104–5.

DAVIN, Dan, *The Salamander and the Fire*. Oxford: Oxford University Press, 1986.

[DAVIN, Winnie], 'A Soldier's Wife', in Lauris Edmond with Carolyn Milward (eds), *Women in Wartime: New Zealand women tell their story*. Wellington: Government Printing Office, 1986, pp. 65–75.

DEACON, Desley, Penny RUSSELL and Angela WOOLACOTT (eds), *Transnational Ties: Australian lives in the world*. Canberra: ANU E Press, 2008.

DEERY, Phillip, 'Scientific Freedom and Postwar Politics: Australia, 1945–55', *Historical Records of Australian Science*, 13:1 (1986), pp. 1–18.

DENNERLEY, Peter, 'The Royal New Zealand Navy', in John Crawford (ed.), *Kia Kaha: New Zealand in the Second World War*. Melbourne: Oxford University Press, 2000, pp. 107–22.

DENOON, Donald (ed.), *Emerging from Empire? Decolonisation in the Pacific*. Canberra: Division of Pacific and Asian History, Australian National University, 1997.

DIAMOND, Sigmund, *Compromised Campus: The collaboration of universities with the intelligence community, 1945–1955*. London: Oxford University Press, 1992.

DICKSON, D. J., 'W. C. Groves: Educationist', in James Griffin (ed.), *Papua New Guinea Portraits: The expatriate experience*. Canberra: Australian National University Press, 1978, pp. 101–25.

DOWNS, Ian, *The Australian Trusteeship in Papua New Guinea, 1945–1975*. Canberra: Australian Government Publishing Service, 1980.

DRAKE, David and Debra KELLY, 'Editorial: Intellectuals and war', *Journal of War and Culture Studies*, 2:1 (2009), pp. 1–16.

DRAY, W. H., *Laws and Explanation in History*. Oxford: Oxford University Press, 1960.

DUGUID, Lindsay, 'Stop to Dress', *Times Literary Supplement*, 18 July 2008, p. 26.

ELKIN, A. P., *Our Opinions and the National Effort*. Sydney: Australasian Medical Publishing Company, 1941.

ELKIN, A. P., *Society, the Individual and Change with Special Reference to War and Other Present-Day Problems. The Livingstone Lectures*. Sydney: Camden College, 1941.

ELKIN, A. P., 'Study of Public Opinion', *Australian Journal of Science*, 5:1 (1942), pp. 16–18.

ELKIN, A. P., *Wanted—A charter for the native peoples of the South-West Pacific*. Sydney: Australasian Publishing, 1943.

ELKIN, A. P., 'The Need for Sociological Research in Australia', *Social Horizons* (July 1943), pp. 5–15.

ELKIN, A. P., 'Notes on Anthropology and the Future of Australian Territories', *Oceania*, 15:2 (1944), pp. 85–8.

ELKIN, A. P., 'Foreword', in Ronald M. Berndt and Catherine H. Berndt, *Sexual Behaviour in Arnhem Land*. New York: The Viking Fund, 1958 [1951], pp. 9–10.

ELKIN, A. P., 'The Emergence of Psychology, Anthropology and Education', in *One Hundred Years of the Faculty of Arts: A series of commemorative lectures given in the Great Hall, University of Sydney, during April and May, 1952*. Sydney: Angus & Robertson, 1952, pp. 21–41.

ELKIN, A. P., 'The Australian National Research Council', *Australian Journal of Science*, 16:6 (1954), pp. 203–11.

ELKIN, A. P., 'A. R. Radcliffe-Brown, 1880–1955', *Oceania*, 26:1 (1956), pp. 239–51.

ELKIN, A. P., 'Camilla Hildegarde Wedgwood, 1901–1955', *Oceania*, 26:3 (1956), pp. 174–80.

ELKIN, A. P., 'The Journal *Oceania*: 1930–1970', *Oceania*, 40:4 (1970), pp. 245–79.

ELLMANN, Richard, *Along the Riverrun: Selected essays*. London: Vintage Books, 1988.

EVANS, Patrick, *The Penguin History of New Zealand Literature*. Auckland: Penguin, 1990.

FARISH, Matthew, 'Archiving Areas: The Ethnogeographic Board and the Second World War', *Annals of the Association of American Geographers*, 95:3 (2005), pp. 663–79.

FARISH, Matthew, *The Contours of America's Cold War*. Minneapolis: University of Minnesota Press, 2010.

FIELD, Michael, *Mau: Samoa's struggle for freedom*. Auckland: Polynesian Press, 1991.

FIRTH, Raymond, *Primitive Economics of the New Zealand Maori*. London: George Routledge & Sons, 1929.

FIRTH, Raymond, *We, the Tikopia: A sociological study of kinship in primitive Polynesia*. London: George Allen & Unwin, 1936.

FIRTH, Raymond, *Human Types: An introduction to social anthropology*. London: Thomas Nelson & Sons, 1938.

FIRTH, Raymond, 'An Anthropologist's View of Mass-Observation', *Sociological Review*, 31:1 (1939), pp. 166–93.

FIRTH, Stewart, *New Guinea under the Germans*. Melbourne: Melbourne University Press, 1982.

FIRTH, Stewart, 'The War in the Pacific', in Donald Denoon et al. (eds), *The Cambridge History of the Pacific Islanders*. Cambridge: Cambridge University Press, 1997, pp. 291–323.

FOOT, M. D. R., '"War is a condition, like peace..."', *Literary Review*, (June 2008), p. 28.

FOSTER, S. G. and Margaret M. VARGHESE, *The Making of The Australian National University, 1946–1996*. Sydney: Allen & Unwin, 1996.

FREEMAN, J. D., 'Poem for a Friend Killed on Mt. Evans', *Spike*, [Wellington], 37:66 (1938), p. 22.

FREEMAN, J. D., 'The Seuao Cave', *Journal of the Polynesian Society*, 52:3 (1943), pp. 101–9.

FREEMAN, J. D., 'The Falemaunga Caves', *Journal of the Polynesian Society*, 53:3 (1944), pp. 86–104.

FREEMAN, J. D., 'O le Fele o le Fe'e', *Journal of the Polynesian Society*, 53:4 (1944), pp. 121–44.

FREEMAN, J. D., 'The Vailele Earthmounds', *Journal of the Polynesian Society*, 53:4 (1944), pp. 145–62.

FREEMAN, J. D., *Iban Agriculture: A report on the shifting cultivation of hill rice by the Iban of Sarawak*. London: Her Majesty's Stationery Office, 1955.

FREEMAN, Derek, 'Sociobiology: The "antidiscipline" of anthropology', in Ashley Montagu (ed.), *Sociobiology Examined*. New York: Oxford University Press, 1980, pp. 198–219.

FREEMAN, Derek, *Margaret Mead and Samoa: The making and unmaking of an anthropological myth*. Cambridge, Mass.: Harvard University Press, 1983.

FREEMAN, Derek, 'Choice, Values and the Solution of Human Problems', in John B. Calhoun (ed.), *Environment and Population: Problems of adaptation*. New York: Praeger, 1983, pp. 63–4.

FREEMAN, Derek, 'Notes Towards an Intellectual Biography', in G. N. Appell and T. N. Madan (eds), *Choice and Morality in Anthropological Perspective: Essays in honour of Derek Freeman*. Albany, NY: State University of New York Press, 1988, pp. 3–27.

FREEMAN, Derek, *The Fateful Hoaxing of Margaret Mead: An historical analysis of her Samoan work*. Boulder, Colo.: Westview Press, 1999.

FREEMAN, Derek, *Dilthey's Dream: Essays on human nature and culture*. Canberra: Pandanus Books, 2001.

FREEMAN, Derek, *The Social Structure of a Samoan Village Community*, Peter Hempenstall (ed.). Canberra: Target Oceania, 2006.

FREEMAN, Michelle, 'Australian Universities at War: The mobilsation of universities in the battle for the Pacific', in Roy M. MacLeod (ed.), *Science and the Pacific War: Science and survival in the Pacific, 1939–1945*. Dordrecht: Kluwer, 2000, pp. 119–38.

GALBREATH, Ross, 'New Zealand Scientists in Action: The Radio Development Laboratory and the Pacific War', in Roy MacLeod (ed.), *Science and the Pacific War: Science and survival in the Pacific, 1939–1945*. Dordrecht: Kluwer, 2000, 211–27.

GALBREATH, Ross, 'Dr Marsden and Admiral Halsey: New Zealand radar scientists in the Pacific War', in John Crawford (ed.), *Kia Kaha: New Zealand in the Second World War*. Melbourne: Oxford University Press, 2002, pp. 252–63.

GAMMAGE, Bill, *Sky Travellers: Journeys in New Guinea, 1938–1939*. Melbourne: Miegunyah Press of Melbourne University Press, 1998.

GARDINER, Patrick, *The Nature of Historical Explanation*. Oxford: Oxford University Press, 1952.

GARDNER, W. J., E. T. BEARDSLEY and T. E. CARTER, *A History of the University of Canterbury, 1873–1973*. Christchurch: University of Canterbury, 1973.

GASKING, Douglas, 'The Historian's Craft and Scientific History', *Historical Studies: Australia and New Zealand*, 4:14 (1950), pp. 112–24.

GILCHRIST, Huntington, 'Trusteeship and the Colonial System', *Proceedings of the Academy of Social Science*, 22:2 (1947), pp. 95–109.

GILLESPIE, Oliver, *The Pacific. Official History of New Zealand in the Second World War, 1939–1945*. Wellington: War History Branch, Department of Internal Affairs, 1952.

GOLLAN, Robin, *The Coalminers of New South Wales: A history of the union, 1860–1960*. Melbourne: Melbourne University Press, 1963.

GOULET, Jean-Guy A. and Bruce Granville MILLER (eds), *Extraordinary Anthropology: Transformations in the field*. Lincoln: University of Nebraska Press, 2007.

GRANT, David, *Out in the Cold: Pacifists and conscientious objectors in New Zealand during World War II*. Auckland: Reed Methuen, 1986.

GRAY, Geoffrey, 'The Passing of the Papua New Guinea Provisional Administration Bill 1945', in Hank Nelson, Nancy Lutton and Sue Robertson (eds), *Select Topics in the History of Papua and New Guinea*. Boroko, PNG: History Department, University of Papua New Guinea, 1969, pp. 37–42.

GRAY, Geoffrey, '"Piddington's Indiscretion": Ralph Piddington, the Australian National Research Council and academic freedom', *Oceania*, 64:3 (1994), pp. 217–45.

GRAY, Geoffrey, '"I was not consulted": A. P. Elkin, Papua New Guinea and the politics of anthropology', *Australian Journal of Politics and History*, 40:2 (1994), pp. 195–213.

GRAY, Geoffrey, '(This Often) Sympathetic Collaboration: Anthropologists, academic freedom and government', *Humanities Research*, 2 (1998), pp. 37–61.

GRAY, Geoffrey, '"The next focus of power to fall under the spell of this little gang": Anthropology and Australia's postwar policy in Papua New Guinea', *War & Society*, 14:2 (1996), pp. 101–17.

GRAY, Geoffrey, 'Managing the Impact of War: Australian anthropology and the South West Pacific', in Roy MacLeod (ed.), *Science and the Pacific War: Science and survival in the Pacific, 1939–1945*. Dordrecht: Kluwer, 2000, pp. 187–210.

GRAY, Geoffrey, '"[The Sydney School] seem[s] to view the Aborigines as forever unchanging": Southeastern Australia and Australian anthropology', *Aboriginal History*, 24 (2000), pp. 176–200.

GRAY, Geoffrey, 'Abrogating Responsibility? Applied anthropology, Vesteys, Aboriginal labour, 1944–1946', *Australian Aboriginal Studies*, 2 (2000), pp. 27–39.

GRAY, Geoffrey, 'There are Many Difficult Problems: Ernest William Pearson Chinnery—government anthropologist', *Journal of Pacific History*, 38:3 (2003), pp. 313–30.

GRAY, Geoffrey, 'Australian Anthropologists and WWII', *Anthropology Today*, 21:3 (2005), pp. 18–21.

GRAY, Geoffrey, '"You are…my anthropological children": A. P. Elkin, Ronald Berndt and Catherine Berndt, 1940–1956', *Aboriginal History*, 29:1 (2005), pp. 77–106.

GRAY, Geoffrey, 'Stanner's War: W. E. H. Stanner, the Pacific War and its aftermath', *Journal of Pacific History*, 41:2 (2006), pp. 145–63.

GRAY, Geoffrey, '"The Army requires anthropologists": Australian anthropologists at war, 1939–1946', *Australian Historical Studies*, 37:127 (2006), pp. 156–80.

GRAY, Geoffrey, *A Cautious Silence: The politics of Australian anthropology*. Canberra: Aboriginal Studies Press, 2007.

GRAY, Geoffrey, '"Cluttering up the department": Ronald Berndt and the distribution of the University of Sydney ethnographic collection', *reCollections: Journal of the National Museum of Australia*, 2:2 (2007), pp. 153–79, <http://recollections.nma.gov.au/issues/vol_2_no2/papers/cluttering_up_the_department/>

GRAY, Geoffrey, '"A chance to be of some use to my country": Stanner during World War II', in Melinda Hinkson and Jeremy Beckett (eds), *Breaking the Silence: WEH Stanner and the Australian Aborigines*. Canberra: Aboriginal Studies Press, 2008, pp. 27–43.

GRAY, Geoffrey, 'E. W. P. Chinnery: A self-made anthropologist', in Brij V. Lal and Vicki Luker (eds), *Telling Pacific Lives: Prisms of process*, Canberra: ANU E Press, 2008, pp. 227–42.

GRAY, Geoffrey, *Abrogating Responsibility: Vesteys, anthropology and the future of Aboriginal people*. Melbourne: Australian Scholarly Publishing, 2011 (forthcoming).

GRAY, Geoffrey and Doug MUNRO, 'Australian Aboriginal Anthropology at the Crossroads: Finding a successor to A. P. Elkin, 1955', *The Australian Journal of Anthropology*, 22:3 (2011), pp. 351–369.

GRAY, Geoffrey and Doug MUNRO, 'Establishing Anthropology and Maori Language (Studies), Auckland University College: The appointment of Ralph Piddington, 1949', in Regna Darnell and Frederic W. Gleach (eds), *Histories of Anthropology Annual*. Lincoln: University of Nebraska Press, (forthcoming).

GUSTAFSON, Barry, *From the Cradle to the Grave: A biography of Michael Joseph Savage*. Auckland: Reed Methuen, 1986.

HALL, Richard, *The Real John Kerr: His brilliant career*. Sydney: Angus & Robertson, 1978.

HALL, Robert A., *The Black Diggers: Aborigines and Torres Strait Islanders in the Second World War*. Sydney: Allen & Unwin, 1979.

HALL, Robert A., 'Aborigines and Torres Strait Islanders in the Second World War', in Desmond Ball (ed.), *Aborigines in the Defence of Australia*. Sydney: Australian National University Press, 1991, pp. 32–63.

HALL, Robert A., *Fighters from the Fringe: Aborigines and Torres Strait Islanders recall the Second World War*. Canberra: Aboriginal Studies Press, 1995.

HALL, Timothy, *Darwin 1942: Australia's darkest hour*. Sydney: Methuen Australia, 1980.

HAMILTON, Bruce, *Palmerston North Boys' High School, 1902–2001*. Palmerston North, NZ: Palmerston North Boys' High School, 2002.

HAMILTON, Stephen, *A Radical Tradition: A history of the Victoria University of Wellington Students' Association, 1899–1999*. Wellington: Victoria University of Wellington Students' Association, 2002.

HARRIS, Jose, 'Thucydides Amongst the Mandarins: Hancock and the World War II Civil Histories', in D. A. Low (ed.), *Keith Hancock: The legacy of an historian*. Melbourne: Melbourne University Press, 2001, pp. 122–48.

HART, L. S., 'Disputed Island [review of *Crete*, by Dan Davin]', *New Zealand Listener*, 6 November 1953, pp. 12–13.

HASLUCK, Paul, *The Government and the People, 1939–1941*, 2 vols. Canberra: Australian War Memorial, 1952.

HASLUCK, Paul, *A Time for Building: Australian administration in Papua and New Guinea, 1951–1963*. Melbourne: Melbourne University Press, 1976.

HASLUCK, Paul, *Diplomatic Witness: Australian foreign affairs, 1941–1947*. Melbourne: Melbourne University Press, 1980.

HAY, Denys, 'British Historians and the Beginnings of the Civil History of the Second World War', in M. R. D. Foot (ed.), *War and Society: Essays in honour and memory of J. R. Weston, 1928–1971*. London: Elek, 1973, pp. 39–57.

HAYS, Terence (ed.), *Ethnographic Presents: Pioneering anthropologists in the Papua New Guinea Highlands*. Berkeley: University of California Press, 1992.

HEYWARD, Michael, *The Ern Malley Affair*. St Lucia: University of Queensland Press, 1993.

HEMPEL, Carl, 'The Function of General Laws in History', *Journal of Philosophy*, 39:2 (1942), pp. 35–48.

HEMPENSTALL, Peter, *The Meddlesome Priest: A life of Ernest Burgman*. Sydney: Allen & Unwin, 1993.

HEMPENSTALL, Peter, '"On Missionaries and Cultural Change in Samoa": Derek Freeman preparing for a "heretical" life', *Journal of Pacific History*, 39:2 (2004), pp. 241–50.

HEMPENSTALL, Peter, 'Overcoming Separate Histories: Historians as "ideas traders" in a trans-Tasman world', *History Australia*, 4:1 (2007), pp. 4.1–4.16.

HEMPENSTALL, Peter and Noel RUTHERFORD, *Protest and Dissent in the Colonial Pacific*. Suva: Institute of Pacific Studies of the University of the South Pacific, 1984.

HENSLEY, Gerald, *Beyond the Battlefield: New Zealand and its Allies, 1939–45*. Auckland: Penguin, 2009.

HETHERINGTON, John, *Blamey, Controversial Soldier: A biography of Field Marshal Sir Thomas Blamey, GBE, KCB, CMG, DSO, ED*. Canberra: Australian War Memorial and Australian Government Publishing Service, 1954.

HIATT, L. R. and Chandra JAYAWARDENA (eds), *Anthropology in Oceania: Essays in honour of Ian Hogbin*. Sydney: Angus & Robertson, 1971.

HILLIARD, Chris, *The Bookmen's Dominion: Cultural life in New Zealand, 1920–1950*. Auckland: Auckland University Press, 2006.

HINKSON, Melinda, 'Stanner and Makerere: On the "insuperable" challenges of practical anthropology in post-war East Africa', in Melinda Hinkson and Jeremy Beckett (eds), *An Appreciation of Difference: WEH Stanner and Aboriginal Australia*. Canberra: Aboriginal Studies Press, 2008, pp. 44–57.

HINKSON, Melinda, 'Thinking with Stanner in the Present', *Humanities Research*, 16:2 (2010), pp. 75–92.

HINSLEY, F. H. and John STRIPP (eds), *Codebreakers: The inside story of Bletchley Park*. Oxford: Oxford University Press, 1992.

HISTORY OF CANTERBURY, A. Christchurch: Canterbury Centennial Historical and Literary Committee, and Whitcombe and Tombs, 1957–65. *Volume 1: To 1854*, James Hight and C. R. Straubel (general eds); *Volume 2: General History, 1854–76 and cultural aspects*, W. J. Gardner (ed.); *Volume 3: 1876–1950*, by W. H. Scotter.

HOBSBAWM, Eric, *Interesting Times: A twentieth-century life*. London: Allen Lane, 2002.

HOBSBAWM, Eric, 'C (for Crisis)', *London Review of Books*, 6 August 2009, pp. 12–13.

HOFSTADTER, Richard, *The American Political Tradition and the Men who Made It*. New York: Knopf, 1948.

HOGBIN, H. Ian, *Law and Order in Polynesia: A study of primitive legal institutions*. London: Christophers, 1934.

HOGBIN, H. Ian, *Experiments in Civilization: The effects of European culture on a native community of the Solomon Islands*. London: Routledge & Sons, 1939.

HOGBIN, H. I., 'Our Native Policy [review of *Black Australians*, by Paul Hasluck, and *Papuan Achievement*, by Lewis Letts]', *Australian Quarterly*, 15:2 (1943), pp. 100–8.

HOGBIN, H. Ian, 'Native Councils and Native Courts in the Solomon Islands', *Oceania*, 14:2 (1944), pp. 257–83.

HOGBIN, H. Ian, 'Notes and Instructions to Native Administrators in the British Solomon Islands', *Oceania*, 16:1 (1945), pp. 61–9.

HOGBIN, H. Ian, *Transformation Scene: The changing culture of a New Guinea village*. London: Routledge, 1951.

HOGBIN, H. I. 'Developing New Guinea and the Future of the Natives', *Australian Journal of Science*, 5:5 (1953), pp. 133–5.

HOGBIN, H. Ian, *A Guadalcanal society: The Kaoka speakers*. New York: Holt, Rinehart & Winston, 1964.

HOGBIN, H. Ian, *Kinship and Marriage in a New Guinea Village*. London: Athlone Press, 1964.

HOGBIN, H. Ian, *The Island of Menstruating Men: Religion in Wogeo, New Guinea*. Scranton, Pa: Chander, 1970.

HOGBIN, H. Ian, *The Leaders and the Led: Social control in Wogeo, New Guinea*. Melbourne: Melbourne University Press, 1987.

HOGBIN, H. Ian and C. D. ROWLEY, 'Camilla Hildegarde Wedgwood', *South Pacific*, 8:6 (1955), pp. 110–12.

HOGBIN, H. Ian and C. H. WEDGWOOD, *Development and Welfare in the Western Pacific*. Sydney: Australian Institute of International Affairs, 1943.

HORNE, Donald, *The Education of Young Donald*. Sydney: Angus & Robertson, 1967.

HORNE, Donald, *Confessions of a New Boy*. Ringwood, Vic.: Penguin Books, 1985.

HORNER, David, *Inside the War Cabinet: Directing Australia's war effort, 1939–1945*. Sydney: Allen & Unwin, 1996.

[HURST, H. E.], *The Pacific Islanders: After the war what?* Geelong, Vic.: Pacific Islands Native Welfare Association, 1944.

HYAM, Ronald, *Understanding the British Empire*. Cambridge: Cambridge University Press, 2010.

IWAMOTO, Hiromutsu, 'Patrol Reports: Sources for assessing war damage in Papua New Guinea', in Yukio Toyoda and Hank Nelson (eds), *The Pacific War in Papua New Guinea: Memories and realities*. Tokyo: Centre for Asian Area Studies, Rikkyo University, 2006, pp. 349–61.

JEFFREY, Keith, 'The Second World War', in Judith M. Brown and Wm. Roger Louis (eds), *The Oxford History of the British Empire. Volume 4: The twentieth century*. Oxford: Oxford University Press, 2001, pp. 306–28.

JINKS, Brian, 'Alfred Conlon, the Directorate of Research and New Guinea', *Journal of Australian Studies*, 12 (1983), pp. 21–33.

JONES, Lawrence, *Barbed Wire and Mirrors: Essays on New Zealand prose*. Dunedin: University of Otago Press, 1987.

JOYCE, R. B., *Sir William MacGregor*. Melbourne: Oxford University Press, 1971.

KEESING, Felix, *The South Seas in the Modern World*. New York: John Day, 1941.

KEMPER, Robert, 'From Nationalism to Internationalism: The development of Mexican anthropology, 1934–1946', in June Helm (ed.), *Social Contexts of American Ethnology, 1840–1984*. 1984 Proceedings of the American Ethnological Society, 1985, pp. 139–56.

KENNEDY, Brian, *A Passion to Oppose: John Anderson, philosopher*. Melbourne: Melbourne University Press, 1995.

KENNEDY, Kett, 'Foreword: Brian James Dalton, 1924–1996', in Anne Smith and B. J. Dalton (eds), *Doctor on the Landsborough: The memoirs of Joseph Arratta*. Townsville, Qld: Department of History and Politics, James Cook University, 1997, pp. v–viii.

KERR, John, *Matters for Judgement: An autobiography*. Melbourne: Sun Books, 1978.

KERSHAW, Ian, *Making Friends with Hitler: Lord Londonderry and Britain's road to war*. London: Allen Lane, 2004.

KESSLER-HARRIS, Alice, 'Why Biography?', *American Historical Review*, 114:3 (2009), pp. 625–30.

KIPPENBERGER, Howard, *Infantry Brigadier*. London: Oxford University Press, 1949.

KISTE, Robert C. and Mac MARSHALL (eds), *American Anthropology in Micronesia: An assessment*. Honolulu: University of Hawai'i Press, 1999.

LAKE, Marilyn, 'Female Desires: The meaning of World War Two', in Joy Damousi and Marilyn Lake (eds), *Gender and War: Australians at war in the twentieth century*. Cambridge: Cambridge University Press, 1995, pp. 60–80.

LAL, Brij V. and Allison LEY (eds), *The Coombs: A house of memories*. Canberra: Research School of Pacific and Asian Studies, Australian National University, 2006.

LAMBERT, David and Alan LESTER (eds), *Colonial Lives Across the Empire: Imperial careering in the long nineteenth century*. Cambridge: Cambridge University Press, 2006.

LARACY Hugh, 'World War Two', in K. R. Howe, Robert C. Kiste and Brij V. Lal (eds), *Tides of History: The Pacific Islands in the twentieth century*. Honolulu: University of Hawai'i Press, 1994, pp. 149–69.

LARSON, Magali Sarfatti, *The Rise of Professionalism: A sociological analysis*. Berkeley: University of California Press, 1977.

LEE, J. M. and Martin PETTER, *The Colonial Office, War and Development Policy: Organisation and the planning of a metropolitan initiative, 1939–1945*. London: Maurice Temple Smith, 1982.

LEGGE, J. D., *Australian Colonial Policy: A survey of native administration and European development in Papua*. Sydney: Angus & Robertson, 1956.

LEGGE, J. D., 'Chance and Circumstance: A gradual journey towards Asian studies', in Nicholas Tarling (ed.), *Historians and Their Discipline: The call of Southeast Asian history*. Kuala Lumpur: Royal Asiatic Society, 2007, pp. 55–71.

LINDSTROM, Lamont and Geoffrey M. WHITE, *Island Encounters: Black and white memories of the Pacific War*. Washington, DC: Smithsonian Institution Press, 1990.

LOCKWOOD, Douglas, *Australia's Pearl Harbour: Darwin 1942*. Melbourne: Cassell, 1966.

LONG, Gavin, *The Final Campaigns*. Canberra: Australian War Memorial, 1963.

LUTKEHAUS, Nancy, '"She was *very* Cambridge": Camilla Wedgwood and British female anthropologists', *American Ethnologist*, 13:4 (1986), pp. 776–98.

LUTKEHAUS, Nancy, 'Review [of *Camilla: C. V. Wedgwood, 1901–1955*, by David Wetherell and Charlotte Carr-Gregg]', *Oceania*, 62:2 (1991), pp. 156–7.

LUTKEHAUS, Nancy C., *Zaria's Fire: Engendered moments in Manam ethnography*. Durham, NC: Carolina Academic Press, 1995.

McAULEY, James, 'John Kerr's Judgement', *Quadrant*, 20:1 (1976), pp. 25–8.

McGIBBON, Ian, '"Something of them is here recorded": Official history in New Zealand', in Jeffrey Grey (ed.), *The Last Word? Essays on official history in the United States and British Commonwealth*. New York: Greenwood, 2003, pp. 53–68, <http://www.nzetc.org/tm/scholarly/name-140760.html>

McGREGOR, Russell, 'The Concept of Primitivity in the Early Anthropological Writings of A. P. Elkin', *Aboriginal History*, 17:2 (1993), pp. 95–104.

MACINTYRE, Stuart, *The Poor Relation: A history of Social Sciences in Australia*. Melbourne: Melbourne University Press, 2010.

McKENNA, Mark, *An Eye for Eternity: The life of Manning Clark*. Melbourne: The Miegunyah Press, 2011.

McKINNON, Malcolm, 'The Uncompleted Centennial Atlas', in William Renwick (ed.), *Creating the National Spirit: Celebrating New Zealand's centennial*. Wellington: Victoria University Press, 2004, pp. 149–60, <http://www.nzetc.org/tm/scholarly/tei-RenCrea-t1-body-d3-d5.html#n149>

McLAREN-ROSS, Julian, 'I Had to Go Absent [with commentary by Paul Willetts]', *Times Literary Supplement*, 27 June 2008, pp. 13–15.

MacLEOD, Roy, 'Introduction', in Roy MacLeod (ed.), *Science and the Pacific War: Science and survival in the Pacific, 1939–1945*. Dordrecht: Kluwer, 2000, pp. 1–9.

McNALLY, Ward, *Aborigines, Artefacts and Anguish*. Adelaide: Lutheran Publishing House, 1981.

McNEISH, James, *Dance of the Peacocks: New Zealanders in exile in the time of Hitler and Mao Tse-Tung*. Auckland: Viking, 2003.

McNEISH, James, *The Sixth Man: The extraordinary life of Paddy Costello*. Auckland: Viking, 2007.

McPHEE, Peter, *'Pansy': A life of Roy Douglas Wright*. Melbourne: Melbourne University Press, 1999.

McPHERSON, Naomi (ed.), *In Colonial New Guinea: Anthropological perspectives*. Pittsburgh: University of Pittsburgh Press, 2001.

MADGE, Charles and Tom HARRISSON, *Britain by Mass-Observation*. Harmonsdworth, UK: Penguin, 1939.

MAIR, Lucy, *Australia in New Guinea*. London and Melbourne: Christophers, 1948; 2nd edn, Melbourne: Melbourne University Press, 1970.

MALINOWSKI, Bronislaw, *Argonauts of the Western Pacific: An account of native enterprise and adventure in the archipelagoes of Melanesian New Guinea*. London: G. Routledge, 1922.

MALINOWSKI, B., *Coral Gardens and their Magic: A study of the methods of tilling soil and of the agricultural rites in the Trobriand Islands*. London: Allen & Unwin, 1935.

MANDER, Linder [sic] A., 'Review [of *Island Administration in the South West Pacific*, by Cyril S. Belshaw]', *Pacific Historical Review*, 19:3 (1950), pp. 315–16.

MANDER, Linden A., *Some Dependent Peoples of the South Pacific*. Leiden and New York: Macmillan, 1954.

MARSHALL, S. L. A., *Men Against Fire: The problem of battle command*. Norman: University of Oklahoma Press, 2000 [1947].

MARTIN, Sylvia, *Ida Leeson: A life*. Sydney: Allen & Unwin, 2006.

MAY, Ernest R., *Strange Victory: Hitler's conquest of France*. New York: Hill & Wang, 2000.

MAY, Philip Ross, *The West Coast Gold Rushes*. Christchurch: Pegasus Press, 1957; 2nd edn, 1962.

MEAD, Margaret, 'Anthropological Contributions to National Policies During and Immediately After World War II', in Walter Goldschmidt (ed.), *The Uses of Anthropology. A special publication of the American Anthropological Association*, no. 11 (1979), pp. 145–57.

MEGGITT, M. J., 'Social Organization: Morphology and typology', in Helen Sheils (ed.), *Australian Aboriginal Studies*. Melbourne: Oxford University Press for the Institute of Aboriginal Studies, 1963, pp. 211–17.

MEIN SMITH, Philippa, Peter HEMPENSTALL and Shaun GOLDFINCH, with Stuart McMILLAN and Rosemary BAIRD, *Remaking the Tasman World*. Christchurch: Canterbury University Press, 2008.

MELLEUISH, Gregory, 'Conceptions of the Sacred in Australian Political Thought', *Political Theory Newsletter*, 5:1 (1993), pp. 39–51.

MILLAR, Paul, *No Fretful Sleeper: A life of Bill Pearson*. Auckland: Auckland University Press, 2010.

MILLS, David, 'Anthropology at the End of Empire: The rise and fall of the Colonial Social Sciences Research Council, 1944–1962', in Benoit De L'estoile, Federico Neiburg and Lygia Sigaud (eds), *Empires, Nations, and Natives: Anthropology and state-making*. Durham, NC: Duke University Press, 2005, pp. 135–66.

MILLS, David, 'How Not to be a "Government House Pet": Audrey Richards and the East African Institute for Social Research', in Mwenda Ntarangwi, David Mills and Mustafa Babiker (eds), *African Anthropologies: History, critique and practice*. London: Zed Books, 2006, pp. 76–98.

MILLS, David, *Difficult Folk? A political history of social anthropology*. New York: Berghahn Books, 2008.

MULGAN, John, *Report on Experience*. London: Oxford University Press, 1947.

MULGAN, John and D. M. DAVIN, *An Introduction to English Literature*. Oxford: Clarendon Press, 1947.

MULVANEY, D. J. (ed.), 'Donald Thomson's Report on the Northern Territory Coastal Patrol and the Special Reconnaissance Unit 1941–3', *Aboriginal History*, 16:1 (1992), pp. 1–57.

MULVANEY, D. J., 'Australian Anthropology: Foundations and funding', *Aboriginal History*, 17:2 (1993), pp. 105–28.

MULVEY, Paul, *The Political Life of Josiah C. Wedgwood: Land, liberty and empire, 1872–1943*. Woodbridge, UK: Boydell & Brewer, 2010.

MUNRO, Doug, 'J. W. Davidson—The making of a participant historian', in Brij V. Lal and Peter Hempenstall (eds), *Pacific Lives, Pacific Places: Bursting boundaries in Pacific history*. Canberra: Journal of Pacific History, 2001, pp. 98–116.

MUNRO, Doug, 'Becoming an Expatriate: J. W. Davidson and the brain drain', *Journal of New Zealand Studies*, 2–3 (2003–04), pp. 19–43.

MUNRO, Doug, 'J. W. Davidson and W. K. Hancock: Patronage, preferment, privilege', *Journal of New Zealand Studies*, 4–5 (2005–06), pp. 39–63.

MUNRO, Doug, 'On Being a Participant Biographer: The search for J. W. Davidson', in Brij V. Lal and Vicki Luker (eds), *Telling Pacific Lives: Prisms of process*. Canberra: ANU E Press, 2008, pp. 149–63.

MUNRO, Doug, *The Ivory Tower and Beyond: Participant historians of the Pacific*. Newcastle upon Tyne, UK: Cambridge Scholars Publishing, 2009.

MURPHY, W. E., 'Crete [review of *Crete*, by Dan Davin]', *Comment: A New Zealand quarterly review*, 33 (1967), pp. 28–30.

NAVAL INTELLIGENCE DIVISION [of the British Admiralty], *Pacific Islands*. Geographical Handbook Series, 4 vols, [no place of publication], 1943–45.

NELSON, Hank, 'Loyalties at Sword-Point: The Lutheran missionaries in wartime New Guinea, 1939–1945', *Australian Journal of Politics and History*, 24:2 (1978), pp. 199–217.

NELSON, Hank, 'The Swinging Index: Capital punishment and British and Australian administrations in Papua and New Guinea, 1888–1945', *Journal of Pacific History*, 13:3 (1978), pp. 130–52.

NELSON, Hank, '*Taim Bilong Pait*: The impact of the Second World War on Papua and New Guinea', in Alfred W. McCoy (ed.), *Southeast Asia under Japanese Occupation*. New Haven, Conn.: Yale University Press, 1980, pp. 320–48.

NELSON, Hank (ed.), *The War Diaries of Eddie Stanton: Papua New, 1942–45, New Guinea, 1945–1946*. Sydney: Allen & Unwin, 1996.

NELSON, Hank, 'Payback: Australian compensation to wartime Papua New Guinea', in Yukio Toyoda and Hank Nelson (eds), *The Pacific War in Papua New Guinea: Memories and realities*. Tokyo: Centre for Asian Area Studies, Rikkyo University, 2006, pp. 320–48.

NGATA, A. T., 'Anthropology and the Government of the Native Races in the Pacific', *Australasian Journal of Psychology and Philosophy*, 6:1 (1928), pp. 1–14.

NORMAN, Philip, *Douglas Lilburn: His life and music*. Christchurch: Canterbury University Press, 2005, pp. 78–9.

'NOTES AND NEWS', *Oceania*, 12:2 (1941), p. 187; 14:2 (1943), p. 182; 15:3 (1945), p. 276; 16:4 (1946), p. 353; 18:2 (1947), p. 176; 18:4 (1948), p. 358; 24:1 (1953), p. 78.

OGILVIE, Gordon, *Denis Glover: His life*. Auckland: Godwit, 1999.

OLLARD, Richard, *A Man of Contradictions: A life of A. L. Rowse*. London: Penguin Books, 2000.

O'SULLIVAN, Vincent, *Long Journey to the Border: A life of John Mulgan*. Wellington: Victoria University of Wellington, 2003.

OVENDEN, Keith, *A Fighting Withdrawal: The life of Dan Davin, writer, soldier, publisher*. Oxford: Oxford University Press, 1996.

OVERY, Richard, *The Morbid Age: Britain and the crisis of civilization, 1919–1939*. London: Allen Lane, 2009.

PALMER, William, *Engagement with the Past: The lives and works of the World War II generation of historians*. Lexington: University of Kentucky Press, 2001.

PARRISH, Michael E., *Felix Frankfurter and His Times: The reform years*. New York: Free Press, 1982.

PARTRIDGE, Francis, *A Pacifist's War*. London: Hogarth Press, 1978.

PETERSEN, Glenn, 'Politics in Postwar Micronesia', in Robert C. Kiste and Mac Marshall (eds), *American Anthropology in Micronesia: An assessment*. Honolulu: University of Hawai'i Press, 1999, pp. 145–96.

PHILLIPS, Jock, *A Man's Country?: The image of the Pakeha male: a history*. Auckland: Penguin, 1987.

PHILLIPS, N. C., 'Collectivism and the British Commonwealth', *Landfall*, 1:3 (1947), pp. 174–85.

PHILLIPS, N. C., 'The Referendum: A retrospect', *Landfall*, 3:3 (1949), pp. 307–20.

PHILLIPS, N. C., 'Burke and Paine: The conservative and radical minds', *Landfall*, 29 (1954), pp. 36–46.

PHILLIPS, N. C., *Italy. Volume 1: The Sangro to Cassino. Official History of New Zealand in the Second World War, 1939–1945*. Wellington: War History Branch, Department of Internal Affairs, 1957, <http://www.nzetc.org/tm/scholarly/tei-WH2-1Ita.html>

PHILLIPS, N. C., 'The British General Election of 1780: A vortex of politics', *Political Science*, 11:2 (1959), pp. 3–22.

PHILLIPS, N. C., *Yorkshire and English National Politics, 1783–1784*. Christchurch: University of Canterbury, 1961.

PHILLIPS, N. C., 'Edmund Burke and the County Movement, 1779–1780', *English Historical Review*, 76:254 (1961), pp. 254–78.

PHILLIPS, N. C., 'Namier and His Method', *Political Science*, 14:2 (1962), pp. 16–26.

PHILLIPS, N. C., 'Hight, James, 1870–1958', *Dictionary of New Zealand Biography. Volume 3*. Auckland and Wellington: Auckland University Press with Bridget Williams Books and Department of Internal Affairs, 1996, pp. 217–18, updated 22 June 2007, <http://www.dnzb.govt.nz/>

PINKOWSKI, Max, 'American Colonialism at the Dawn of the Cold War', in Dustin M. Wax (ed.), *Anthropology at the Dawn of the Cold War*. London/Ann Arbor: University of Michigan Press, 2008, pp. 62–88.

POPKIN, Jeremy D., *History, Historians, & Autobiography*. Chicago/London: University of Chicago Press, 2005.

POTTER, Simon, 'What Did You Do in the War, Professor? Imperial history and propaganda, 1939–45', in Robert Blyth and Keith Jeffery (eds), *The British Empire and its Contested Pasts*. Dublin/Portland: Irish Academic Press, 2009, pp. 24–42.

POUND, Father John, 'The Marist Brothers, Invercargill', in Janet Wilson (ed.), *Intimate Stranger: Reminiscences of Dan Davin*. Wellington: Steele Roberts, 2000, pp. 25–9.

POWELL, Alan, 'The Darwin "Panic", 1942', *Journal of the Australian War Memorial*, 3 (1983), pp. 3–9.

POWELL, Alan, *War By Stealth: Australians and the Allied Intelligence Bureau, 1942–1945*. Melbourne: Melbourne University Press, 1996.

POWELL, Alan, *The Third Force: ANGAU's New Guinea war, 1942–46*. Melbourne: Oxford University Press, 2003.

PRICE, David, 'Lessons from Second World War Anthropology: Peripheral, persuasive and ignored contributions', *Anthropology Today*, 18:3 (2002), pp. 14–20.

PRICE, David H., *Threatening Anthropology: McCarthyism and the FBI's surveillance of activist anthropologists*. Durham, NC: Duke University Press, 2004.

PRICE, David H., *Anthropological Intelligence: The deployment and neglect of American anthropology in the Second World War*. Durham, NC: Duke University Press, 2008.

PUGH, Patricia, *Educate, Agitate, Organize: 100 years of Fabian socialism*. London: Methuen, 1984.

PYBUS, Cassandra, *The Devil and James McAuley*. St Lucia: University of Queensland Press, 1999.

RAVENSCROFT, Mona, 'The Housing Problem', *Social Horizons*, (July 1943), pp. 48–53.

RAYNES, Cameron, 'Ooldea, Boxing Day, 1941: Part two', *recordSArchives* [official newsletter of the State Records of South Australia], 23 (November 2002), pp. 4–5.

READ, Kenneth E., 'Effects of the War in the Markham Valley, New Guinea', *Oceania*, 18:1 (1946), pp. 95–116.

READ, Kenneth E., *The High Valley*. London: Allen & Unwin, 1966.

REAY, Marie, 'A Half-Caste Aboriginal Community in North-Western New South Wales', *Oceania*, 15:4 (1945), pp. 296–323.

REAY, Marie, 'Review [of *Camilla: C. V. Wedgwood, 1901–1955*, by David Wetherell and Charlotte Carr-Gregg]', *Canberra Anthropology*, 14:2 (1991), pp. 120–3.

RENWICK, William (ed.), *Creating the National Spirit: Celebrating New Zealand's centennial*. Wellington: Victoria University Press, 2004, <http://www.nzetc.org/tm/scholarly/tei-RenCrea-t1-front-d4.html>

RISEMAN, Noah, 'Australian [Mis]treatment of Indigenous Labour in World War II Papua and New Guinea', *Labour History*, 98 (2010), pp. 163–82.

ROBERTSON, John, *J. H. Scullin: A political biography*. Perth: University of Western Australia Press, 1974.

ROBINSON, Neville, *Villagers at War: Some Papua New Guinea experiences in World War II*. Pacific Research Monograph No. 2. Canberra: Australian National University, 1979.

ROSS, Angus, *23 Battalion. Official History of New Zealand in the Second World War, 1939–1945*. Wellington: War History Branch, Department of Internal Affairs, 1959, <http://www.nzetc.org/tm/scholarly/tei-WH2-23Ba.html>

ROSS, Margot and Angus ROSS, 'Writing about the War', in Janet Wilson (ed.), *Intimate Stranger: Reminiscences of Dan Davin*. Wellington: Steele Roberts, 2000, pp. 63–5.

ROWLEY, C. D., *The Australians in German New Guinea, 1914–1921*. Melbourne: Melbourne University Press, 1958.

ROWLEY, C. D., *The New Guinea Villager*. Melbourne: Melbourne University Press, 1965.

ROWSE, Tim, *Australian Liberalism and National Character*. Melbourne: Kibble Books, 1978.

ROWSE, Tim, *Obliged to be Difficult: Nugget Coombs' legacy in Indigenous affairs*. Melbourne: Cambridge University Press, 2000.

ROWSE, Tim, *Nugget Coombs: A reforming life*. Melbourne: Cambridge University Press, 2002.

ROWSE, Tim, 'After the Dreaming: The Boyer lecturer as social critic', in Melinda Hinkson and Jeremy Beckett (eds), *An Appreciation of Difference: WEH Stanner and Aboriginal Australia*. Canberra: Aboriginal Studies Press, 2008, pp. 251–70.

RYAN, Peter, *Fear Drive My Feet*. Sydney: Angus & Robertson, 1959. Republished by Melbourne University Press, 1960.

RYAN, Peter, 'The Australian New Guinea Administrative Unit (ANGAU)', in K. S. Inglis (ed.), *The History of Melanesia: Second Waigani Seminar*. Port Moresby and Canberra: University of Papua New Guinea and Research School of Pacific Studies, Australian National University, 1969, pp. 531–48.

RYAN, Peter, 'Conlon, Alfred Austin Joseph (Alf) (1908–1961)', *Australian Dictionary of Biography. Volume 13*. Melbourne: Melbourne University Press, 1993, pp. 479–80, <http://adbonline.anu.edu.au/biogs/A130529b.htm>

RYAN, Peter, *Brief Lives*. Sydney: Duffy & Snellgrove, 2004.

SALAMONI, Frank A., 'In the Name of Science: The Cold War and the direction of scientific pursuits', in Dustin M. Wax (ed.), *Anthropology at the Dawn of the Cold War*. London/Ann Arbor: University of Michigan Press, 2008, pp. 89–107.

SARZIN, Anne, 'Review [of *Profiles: Australian women scientists*, by Ragbir Bhathal]', viewed 22 April 2011, <http://www.wisenet-australia.org/issue52/bookrev.htm>

SCOTT, Jonathan, *Harry's Absence: Looking for my father on the mountain*. Wellington: Victoria University Press, 1997.

SHANKMAN, Paul, *The Trashing of Margaret Mead: Anatomy of an anthropological controversy*. Madison: University of Wisconsin Press, 2009.

SHINEBERG, Dorothy, 'The Early Years of Pacific History', *Journal of Pacific Studies*, 20 (1996), pp. 1–15.

SIMMINGTON, Margot, 'The Southwest Pacific Islands in Australian Interwar Defence Planning', *Australian Journal of Politics and History*, 32:2 (1977), pp. 173–7.

SINCLAIR, Keith. *Walter Nash*. Auckland: Auckland University Press, 1976.

SINCLAIR, Keith, *Halfway Round the Harbour: An autobiography*. Auckland: Penguin, 1993.

SISMAN, Adam, *Hugh Trevor-Roper: The biography*. London: Weidenfeld & Nicolson, 2010.

SOFFER, Reba N., *History, Historians, and Conservatism in Britain and America: From the Great War to Thatcher and Reagan*. Oxford: Oxford University Press, 2009.

SORRENSON, M. P. K., 'Polynesian Corpuscles and Pacific Anthropology: The home-made anthropology of Sir Apirana Ngata and Sir Peter Buck', *Journal of the Polynesian Society*, 91:1 (1992), pp. 17–23.

SPATE, O. H. K., 'And Now There Will Be A Void: A tribute to J. W. Davidson', *Journal of Pacific Studies*, 20 (1996), pp. 21–2.

STANNER, W. E. H., 'New Guinea under War Conditions', *International Affairs*, 20:4 (1944), pp. 481–94.

STANNER, W. E. H., 'Observations on Colonial Planning', *International Affairs*, 25:3 (1949), pp. 318–28.

STANNER, W. E. H., 'Review [of *Australia in New Guinea*, by L. P. Mair]', *International Affairs*, 25:3 (1949), p. 394.

STANNER, W. E. H., *The South Seas in Transition: A study of post-war rehabilitation and reconstruction in three British Pacific dependencies*. Sydney: Australasian Publishing Company, 1953.

STANTON, John E., 'Obituary: Ronald Murray Berndt 14 July 1916–2 May 1990', <http://www.berndt.uwa.edu.au/generic.lasso?token_value=berndt>

STAR, Leonie, *Julius Stone: An intellectual life*. Sydney/Melbourne: Oxford University Press, 1992.

STOCKING, George W. jr, *After Tylor: British social anthropology 1888–1951*. Madison: University of Wisconsin Press, 1995.

STONE, Julius, *Colonial Trusteeship in Transition*. Sydney: Australian Institute of International Affairs, 1944.

STURM, Terry (ed.), *Whim Wham's New Zealand: The best of Whim Wham, 1937–1988*. Auckland: Auckland University Press, 2005.

SUMMERFIELD, Penny, 'Mass-Observation: Social research or social movement?', *Journal of Contemporary History*, 20:3 (1985), pp. 439–52.

SUZUKI, Peter, 'Lessons from WWII', [Letter], *Anthropology Today*, 18:6 (2002), p. 26.

SYMONDS, Richard, *Oxford and Empire: The last lost cause?* Basingstoke, UK: Macmillan, 1986.

TAYLOR, Nancy M., *The New Zealand People at War: The home front. Official History of New Zealand in the Second World War, 1939–1945*. Wellington: War History Branch, Department of Internal Affairs, 1986, <http://www.nzetc.org/tm/scholarly/tei-WH2-1Hom.html>

TAYLOR, Nan, 'Human Rights in World War II in New Zealand', *New Zealand Journal of History*, 23:2 (1989), pp. 109–23.

THOMPSON, John (ed.), *Alfred Conlon: A memorial by some of his friends*. Sydney: Benevolent Society of New South Wales, 1963.

THOMPSON, John (ed.), *Five to Remember*. Melbourne: Landsdown Press, 1964.

THOMPSON, Joyce A., *The WAAAF in Wartime Australia*. Melbourne: Melbourne University Press, 1991.

THOMPSON, L. H., *New Zealanders with the Royal Air Force. Volume 1: European Theatre. Official History of New Zealand in the Second World War, 1939–1945*. Wellington: War History Branch, Department of Internal Affairs, 1953, <http://www.nzetc.org/tm/scholarly/tei-WH2-1RAF.html>

THOMPSON, Roger C., *Australia and the Pacific Islands in the 20th Century*. Melbourne: Australian Scholarly Publishing, 1998.

TONKINSON, Robert and Michael HOWARD (eds), *Going It Alone? Prospects for Aboriginal autonomy: essays in honour on Ronald and Catherine Berndt*. Canberra: Aboriginal Studies Press, 1990.

TOYODA, Yukio and Hank NELSON (eds), *The Pacific War in Papua New Guinea: Memories and realities*. Tokyo: Centre for Asian Area Studies, Rikkyo University, 2006.

TRÄBING, Gerhard, 'Wolfgang Rosenberg', in James N. Bade (ed.), *Out of the Shadow of War: The German connection with New Zealand in the twentieth century*. Melbourne: Oxford University Press, 1998, pp. 162–8.

TUZIN, Don, 'Derek Freeman (1916–2001)', *American Anthropologist*, 104:3 (2002), pp. 1013–15.

WALKER, Alan, *Coaltown: A social survey of Cessnock*. Melbourne: Melbourne University Press, 1945.

WALKER, Richard and Helen WALKER, *Curtin's Cowboys: Australia's secret bush commandos*. Sydney: Allen & Unwin, 1986.

WARD, R. Gerard, 'Davidson's Contribution to the "Admiralty Handbooks"', *Journal of Pacific History*, 29:2 (1994), pp. 238–40.

WAX, Dustin M. (ed.), *Anthropology at the Dawn of the Cold War: The influence of foundations, McCarthyism and the CIA*. London: Pluto Press, 2008.

WAX, Murray, 'Rosalie H Wax (nee Rosalie Amelia Hankey), 1911–1998', *Anthropology Today*, 19:1 (2003), p. 25.

WEBSTER, Steven, *Patrons of Maori Culture: Power, theory and ideology in the Maori renaissance*. Dunedin: University of Otago Press, 1998.

WEDGWOOD, Camilla, 'The Contribution of Anthropology to the Education and Development of Colonial Peoples', *South Pacific*, 4:5 (1950), pp. 78–84.

WEST, F. J., 'Review [of *Italy. Volume 1: The Sangro to Cassino*, by N. C. Phillips]', *Landfall*, 11:1 (1958), pp. 84–7.

WEST, Francis, *Hubert Murray: The Australian pro-consul*. Melbourne: Oxford University, 1968.

WETHERELL, David (ed.), *The New Guinea Diaries of Philip Strong, 1936–1945*. Melbourne: Macmillan, 1981.

WETHERELL, David and Charlotte CARR-GREGG, *Camilla: C. H. Wedgwood, 1901–1955: a life*. Sydney: University of New South Wales Press, 1990.

WHIM WHAM [Alan Curnow], *A Present for Hitler and Other Verse*. [Christchurch]: Caxton Press, [1941].

WHITE, Geoffrey M. (ed.), *Remembering the Pacific War*. Honolulu: University of Hawai'i Press, 1991.

WHITE, Geoffrey M. and Lamont LINDSTROM (eds), *The Pacific Theater: Island representations of World War II*. Melbourne: Melbourne University Press, 1990.

WILKES, Owen, 'New Zealand and the Atomic Bomb', in John Crawford (ed.), *Kia Kaha: New Zealand in the Second World War*. Melbourne: Oxford University Press, 2002, pp. 264–75.

WILLIAMS, F. E., *Native Education: The language of instruction and intellectual education*. Port Moresby: Government Printer, 1928.

WILLIAMS, Kathleen Broome, *Improbable Warriors: Women scientists and the U.S. Navy in World War II*. Annapolis: Naval Institute Press, 2001.

WILLIAMSON, David, *Heretic: Based on the life of Derek Freeman*. Melbourne: Penguin, 1996.

WILMOT, Chester, *Tobruk, 1941: Capture, siege, relief*. Sydney: Angus & Robertson, 1945.

WILSON, Jane S. and Charlotte SERBER (eds), *Standing By and Making Do: Women of wartime Los Alamos*. Los Alamos, NM: Los Alamos Historical Society, 2008 [1988].

WILSON, Janet (ed.), *Intimate Stranger: Reminiscences of Dan Davin*. Wellington: Steele Roberts, 2000.

WILSON, Janet (ed.), *The Gorse Blooms Pale: Dan Davin's Southland stories*. Dunedin: Otago University Press, 2007. First published London: Nicholson & Watson, 1947.

WILSON, Ormond, *An Outsider Looks Back: Reflections on experience*. Wellington: Port Nicolson Press, 1982.

WINKS, Robin W., *Cloak & Gown: Scholars in the secret war, 1939–1961*, 2nd edn. New Haven, Conn.: Yale University Press, 1996.

WINTER, Christine, 'The Long Arm of the Third Reich: Internment of New Guinea Germans in Tatura', *Journal of Pacific History*, 38:1 (2003), pp. 85–108.

WINTER, Christine, '"A Good-Will Ship": The light cruiser *Köln* visits Rabaul (1933)', *Australian Journal of Politics and History*, 54:1 (2008), pp. 44–54.

WINTER, Christine, 'The NSDAP Stronghold Finschafen, New Guinea', in Emily Turner-Graham and Christine Winter (eds), *National Socialism in Oceania: A critical evaluation of its effect and aftermath*. Frankfurt am Main: Peter Lang, 2010, pp. 31–47.

WISE, Tigger, *The Self-Made Anthropologist: A life of A. P. Elkin*. Sydney: Allen & Unwin, 1985.

WOOD, F. L. W., *The New Zealand People at War: Political and external affairs. Official History of New Zealand in the Second World War, 1939–1945*. Wellington: War History Branch, Department of Internal Affairs, 1958, <http://www.nzetc.org/tm/scholarly/tei-WH2Poli.html>

WOODBURN, Susan, *Where Our Hearts Still Lie: A life of Harry and Honor Maude in the Pacific Islands*. Adelaide: Crawford House, 2003.

WOODMAN, Dorothy, *An A. B. C. of the Pacific*. Harmondsworth, UK: Penguin, 1942.

WRIGHT, Donald, *The Professionalization of History in English Canada*. Toronto: Toronto University Press, 2005.

YOUNG, Michael, 'Review [of *Camilla: C. V. Wedgwood, 1901–1955*, by David Wetherell and Charlotte Carr-Gregg]', *Journal of Pacific History*, 26:1 (1991), pp. 121–3.

Oral History Interviews (in public repositories)

FREEMAN, Derek, Interviewed by Frank Heiman, 2 February 2001, Oral History Collection, TRC 4660, National Library Australia, Canberra.

HOGBIN, H. Ian, 25 April 1971, AC33/10, University of Papua New Guinea Library, Port Moresby.

McAULEY, James, Interviewed by Catherine Santamaria, 5–7 May 1976, Oral History Collection, TRC 576, National Library of Australia, Canberra.

McINTOSH, A. D., Interviewed by F. L. W. Wood and Mary Boyd, 2 December 1975, OHColl-0163/1, typescript accessioned as 80-413, Alexander Turnbull Library, Wellington.

PASSMORE, John, Interviewed by Stephen Foster, 17 May 1991, Series 44/20, Australian National University Archives, Canberra.

STRONG, P. N. W., Interviewed by D. J. Dickson, 1 February 1969, University of Papua New Guinea Library, Port Moresby.

Index

Abbott, Charles Lydiard Aubrey, 51, 144
Abel, Russell William, 128
Alexander, Frederick (Fred), 161
Alomes, Stephen, 53
Amis, Kingsley, 240
Anderson, Francis, 37
Anderson, John, 36, 88, 153, 155
Anderson, W P, 209
Andrews, John, 60, 67-8, 155
Annan, Noel, 117
Armstrong, Wallace Edwin, 117
Ashley, William Patrick (Bill), 35, 42-3
Baldwin, Stanley, 204
Bamford, Harry Dean, 210
Barnes, John Arundel, 86, 91-3, 114, 147, 164
Barry, John Vincent, 81, 93
Barth, Charles George Lange, 45
Barwick, Diane Elizabeth (née MacEachern), 97, 116
Beaglehole, Ernest, 5-6, 18, 20, 172, 174-5, 178, 181
Beaglehole, John Cawte, 167, 172-3, 195, 212-3, 231
Beckett, Jeremy, 26, 74, 83, 91, 93, 96-7, 116
Beethoven, Ludwig van, 189
Belich, James, 13, 165, 174
Bell, Jim, 11
Belshaw, Cyril, 6, 13, 23-4, 31, 84, 93
Benedict, Ruth, 1, 7
Bennett, Jack, 240
Benson, James, 126
Berndt, Alfred Henry, 137
Berndt, Catherine Helen (née Webb), 8-10, 12, 15-6, 18-9, 112, 133-46
Berndt, Elisabeth, 229, 231
Berndt, Minna (née Schulze), 137
Berndt, Patricia Katarina (Patty), 229, 231
Berndt, Ronald Murray, 2, 8-10, 12, 15-19, 27, 31, 92-3, 112, 114, 133-47
Berry, Joe, 218-21
Biggs, Bruce, 6
Bingle, Alison Seymour, 143-4
Bird, Clara, see Phillips, Clara
Black, John Russel, 103
Blamey, Thomas, 5, 33, 35, 60-1, 64-5, 67-71, 77, 99, 102, 120, 154, 159
Bowen, Charles Synge Christopher, 117
Bowen, Elizabeth, 240
Bowen, Ethel Kate, see Wedgwood, Ethel Kate
Bray, Frank I, 137
Brittain, Vera Mary, 190
Britton, Theresa, 132
Brock, Margaret (née Freeman), 171
Brooke, Charles Vyner de Windt (Rajah of Sarawak), 65
Brooke, Rupert, 177
Brown, John Macmillan, 178
Bruce, Stanley Melbourne, 108
Buck, Peter Henry (Te Rangi Hiroa), 20, 175, 178
Burfitt family, 128
Burgmann, Ernest Henry, 37
Burke, Edmund, 212, 223
Burton, John Wear, 24, 59, 84, 90
Cadogan family, 128
Calvocoressi, Peter John Ambrose, 190, 194
Cameron, Donald Charles, 52-3
Capell, Arthur, 88-9

Carlyle, Thomas, 210

Carrodus, Joseph Aloysius, 143

Chadwyck-Healey, Edward, 220

Chamberlain, Arthur Neville, 119, 187, 192, 204-5, 216

Chifley, Joseph Benedict (Ben), 51, 71

Chinnery, Ernest William Pearson, 3-4, 20, 30, 50-1, 111, 138, 143-5

Churchill, Winston, 198, 222

Cleland, Donald Mackinnon, 79, 101, 160

Cleland, John Burton, 133, 135-6, 140-2

Clunies Ross, William Ian, 48, 110, 112

Cole, George Douglas Howard, 204, 215

Conde, Harold Graydon, 32-3

Conlon, Alfred Austin Joseph (Alf), 3-4, 22, 27, 32-4, 48-9, 58-72, 75-9, 82-6, 97-100, 102-7, 110, 120, 127, 149, 152-4, 159-60

Cook, James, 172

Coombs, Herbert Cole (Nugget), 10, 12-3, 22, 59, 66, 76, 98, 116

Copland, Douglas, 9, 89, 91

Cornford, Rupert John, 174

Costello, Desmond Patrick (Paddy), 230-3, 235-7, 240

Cottrell, Leonard, 241

Cowan, James, 213

Cox, Geoffrey, 230, 232-5

Craig, Jean, 10-1, 18, 140

Cranswick, George, 24, 84

Crawford, Raymond Maxwell, 149-52

Crossman, Richard Howard Stafford (Dick), 204

Curnow, Allen, 210, 213

Curtin, John, 13, 35, 42-4, 48-9, 58-9, 61, 64-5, 69-70, 97, 133, 138-9, 152

Dalton, Brian James, 163

Darwin, Charles, 37, 117, 174

Davidson, Edith Mable (née Brown), 187-90, 192-3, 196-7, 199, 201

Davidson, George Wightman, 187-9, 191, 193-8, 201

Davidson, James Wightman (Jim), 2, 13-6, 162-7, 181, 187-205, 212-3

Davidson, Ruth, 195-6

Davin, Anna Deirdre, 229

Davin, Daniel Marcus (Dan), 2, 16, 26, 164-7, 225-41

Davin, Delia (Helen), 229

Davin, Katharine Brigid, 229

Davin, Tom, 229

Davin, Winifred (née Gonley), 229, 233, 240

Davis, Norman, 240

Davis, Stan, 174

Deacon, Bernard, 118, 131

Deacon, Desley, 2

Dolla family, 128

Dowling, Norman, 174

Drakeford, Arthur Samuel, 52

Eggleston, Frederic William, 109

Elkin, Adolphus Peter, 2, 4, 9-16, 18-20, 22, 24, 27, 29-30, 32, 35-54, 58, 64, 67-8, 73-7, 79, 81-92, 95-6, 102-4, 106-8, 111-6, 118, 130, 132-5, 137-147, 158

Emerson, Harrington, 45

Epstein, Arnold Leonard (Bill), 114

Evans-Pritchard, Edward Evan, 14, 113

Evatt, Herbert Vere (Bert), 22, 41, 53, 62-3, 70, 105, 112, 161

Evennett family, 128

Fa'imoto, Loani (John), 178

Fadden, Arthur William, 40

Farish, Matthew, 3

Firth, Raymond, 4, 6, 9, 14-6, 31, 38, 74, 84, 87-92, 95-7, 103-5, 107-111, 113-6, 118, 139, 161, 183-4, 199-202
Fitzpatrick, Brian, 59
Fitzpatrick, Kathleen (née Pitt), 149
Florey, Howard, 14, 67
Foot, Michael Richard Daniell, 163, 190
Ford, Edgar, 60
Forde, Darryll, 14, 113
Forde, Frank Michael, 53, 68, 70-1,
Forsyth, William Douglass, 110
Fortes, Meyer, 185
Fortune, Reo Franklin, 113, 202
Foxwell, Roland, 220
Franco, Francisco, 174
Frankfurter, Felix, 209
Freedman, Maurice, 92
Freeman, John Derek, 2, 6, 12, 14, 16, 29, 92, 116, 164-5, 167, 169-185, 203
Freeman, Monica (née Maitland), 171, 184-5
Freud, Sigmund, 175
Freyberg, Bernard Cyril, 222, 227-8, 230, 233, 236, 240
Gantt, Henry Laurence, 45
Gardiner, Noel (Wig), 231, 238, 240
Gasking, Douglas, 150, 157-8
Geddes, William Robert (Bill), 6-7, 31, 93, 114
Gibbings, Robert, 184
Gibson, Alexander James, 140
Ginsburg, Morris, 172
Glover, Denis, 210-1, 213
Gluckman, Max Herman, 90, 113
Gonley, Winifred (Winnie), *see* Davin, Winifred
Gordon, Sir Arthur Hamilton (Lord Stanmore), 162

Göring, Hermann, 218
Gorman, Eugene, 60
Gramsci, Antonio, 55
Green, Harrie E, 136-7, 142
Greene, Graham, 240
Greenwood, Miles, 187-9, 192-3, 196, 200-1, 204
Groves, William Charles, 4, 20, 30, 123, 131-2
Guise family, 128
Haddon, Alfred Cort, 14, 117
Hailey, William Malcolm, 102, 112
Hall, Richard, 13, 17, 62, 99
Halligan, James Reginald (Reg), 53, 64, 90, 115
Hamilton, Bruce, 208-9
Hancock, William Keith, 9, 12-6, 161-3, 191, 201-2
Harding, Florence, 11
Harlow, Vincent Todd, 162
Harris, Max, 63, 155
Harrisson, Tom, 38
Hasluck, Paul, 13, 20, 22-3, 40-1, 59, 98-99, 115, 160-1
Heenan, Joseph (Joe), 166, 196
Hellenthal, Walter, 173
Henderson, Andrew Kennaway, 211
Herbert, Alan Patrick, 210
Herring, Edmund Francis (Ned), 98
Hess, Rudolf, 198
Hight, James, 167, 210-1, 215-6, 220
Hilliard, Chris, 166, 211
Hindenburg, Paul von, 135
Hinsley, Francis Harry, 163, 203
Hitler, Adolf, 173, 187, 189-90, 192, 203-5, 209-10, 216, 230
Hogben, George, 208

Hogbin, Herbert Ian Priestley, 2, 4, 15-6, 18, 22, 24, 26-7, 30-2, 53, 55, 58, 61-5, 67-8, 73-93, 101-7, 110, 113, 120-3, 125, 128, 130, 155, 157
Hole, Winifred Vere, 11
Holland, William Lancelot, 6, 31
Hope, Alec, 75
Horne, Donald, 55-8, 72, 75
Housman, Alfred Edward, 209
Hunter, Thomas, 174-5
Hutley, Frank, 60
Huxley, Thomas Henry, 117
Hyam, Ronald, 203
Isles, Keith, 61, 63, 66, 110
Jackson, R F, 85
Jinks, Brian, 4-5, 86, 98-9, 120, 160
Johnston, Thomas Harvey, 133
Jordan, W K, 214
Julius, Charles, 19-20
Kaberry, Phyllis, 9, 16
Karloan, Albert, 139
Keesing, Felix Maxwell, 23-4
Kelly, Caroline Tennant, 11, 140
Kerr, John Robert, 17, 32-4, 55, 59-60, 62-5, 69-70, 72, 79, 83, 98-106, 109-10, 120, 130, 154, 160
Keynes, Geoffrey Langdon, 117
Keynes, John Maynard, 117
Kingsley, Charles, 37
Kippenberger, Howard Karl, 226-7, 233
Krämer, Augustin, 178
Krishnamurti, Jiddu, 174, 180
Lauvi Vainu'u, 178
Layard, John, 131
Leach, Edmund, 184
Lee, Roy Stuart, 37
Leeson, Ida, 33, 62, 69, 154, 157, 159

Legge, John D, 2, 17, 26, 32, 67, 70, 78, 81, 120, 149-62
Lewin, Ernie, 208
Lewin, Jack, 208
Lewis, Clive Staples, 119
Lilburn, Douglas Gordon, 174, 187-9, 191-2, 194-5, 197-8, 201, 213
Lloyd, Charles Edward Maurice, 60, 99, 154
Lorenz, Konrad, 169
Lugard, Frederick John Dealtry, 162
MacArthur, Douglas, 61, 65, 70, 78
Macaskie, Charles Frederick Cunningham, 103
MacCallum, Mungo William, 14
MacDonald, Donald Peter, 48
MacGregor, William, 158
MacLeod, Roy Malcolm, 2, 4, 8, 26, 29, 163
Madden, A Frederick, 162
Madge, Charles, 38
Mair, Lucy, 15, 24, 33, 67, 81, 85, 99, 103, 106, 110, 120, 131-2, 157-8, 160, 162
Makinson, Rachel, 8
Malinowski, Bronislaw, 9, 14-5, 73-4, 82, 118-9, 121-2, 124, 129, 132, 155, 183
Malley, Ern, 63, 155
Mander, Linden Alfred, 23, 110, 113
Manning, Olivia, 231
Mara, Kamisese Ratu, 162
Martin, Jean (née Craig), *see* Craig, Jean
Mata'afa Iosefo, 179
Maude, Henry Evans (Harry), 89, 110, 131, 203
Maurice, Frederick Denison, 37
Maxwell, Ian, 75
May, Philip Ross, 223
Mazarin, Jules (Giulio Raimondo Mazzarino), 210

McAuley, James, 33-4, 55, 59, 62, 67-8, 70, 72, 75, 78, 87, 99, 102-3, 105, 120, 132, 154-5, 159
McCarthy, Fred, 30
McClymont, W G (Monty), 226
McDonald, John, 11
McKay, Wattie Horton, 230
McKenna, Jack, 158
McNeish, James, 225, 230-3, 235-6, 241
McRae, Christopher, Ralph, 48
Mead, Margaret, 1, 4, 7, 11, 67, 169-70, 174, 177-8, 180-2, 184-5, 202
Mein Smith, Philippa, 13
Melleuish, Gregory, 37, 48,
Melville, Leslie Galfreid, 9
Menzies, Robert, 23, 41, 97, 115
Mill, John Stuart, 54
Mills, Richard, 56, 59, 66
Mitchell, Philip Euen, 76
Morris, Basil Moorhouse, 79, 101, 121-2, 126, 156
Morrison, Heather, 175
Mulgan, John Alan Edward, 165, 188, 213, 227, 241,
Murray, Hubert, 121, 158
Murray, Jack Keith, 5, 19, 31, 61, 66-7, 84-6, 93, 99, 105, 113, 120, 130, 157, 159-60
Nadel, Siegfried Frederick, 11, 14-5, 90-3, 114-5
Nash, Walter, 214
Nelson, Jim, 213-20
Nelson, Patricia (née Palmer), 213-20
Neumann, Hans, 179
Nixon, Pamela, 12
Noel, Owen C, 77
Oliphant, Mark, 14
Ovenden, Keith, 226-7, 229-34, 237-8, 240-1

Palmer, Pauline, 213-5, 217, 217, 220, 224
Parascos family, 128
Patience, John Delmont, 81, 100-1
Paul, George, 150, 155
Pease, Helen Bowen (née Wedgwood), 117-9, 122, 126, 131-2
Pease, Michael Stewart, 119
Perham, Margery Freda, 199-202
Phillips, Clara (Claire) (née Bird), 207-8
Phillips, David, 208
Phillips, Elizabeth, 217
Phillips, Frederick Beaumont, 83
Phillips, Jock, 166, 207-224
Phillips, Neville Crompton, 2, 16, 26, 164-7, 187, 202, 207-24
Phillips, Pauline (née Palmer), *see* Palmer, Pauline
Phillips, Samuel (Sam), 207-9
Piddington, Ralph O'Reilly, 14-5, 30, 49, 67-8, 113, 157, 185
Pilcher, Charles Venn, 48
Plimsoll, James (Jim), 33, 55, 154
Powell, Alan, 4, 51, 80, 99, 101-2, 121
Powell, Enoch, 232
Power, Eileen Edna LePoer, 189
Prichett, Victor Sawdon, 240
Pybus, Cassandra, 5, 22, 34, 75, 99, 103, 105, 120
Radcliffe-Brown, Alfred Reginald, 4, 14-5, 73-4, 95, 108, 114, 118, 140
Rajah of Sarawak, *see* Brooke, Charles Vyner de Windt
Ravenscroft, Mona, 11, 18, 140
Read, Kenneth Eyre (Mick), 81-2
Reay, Marie, 12, 97, 124, 139
Richards, Audrey, 9, 15, 90, 96, 103, 111, 132
Richelieu, Armand-Jean du Plessis de, 210

Roosevelt, Franklin Delano, 62, 222
Rosenberg, Wolfgang, 175-6, 185
Ross, Angus, 227
Ross, Julian McLaren, 240
Rowell, Sydney Fairbairn, 61
Rowley, Charles Dunford, 102, 115, 121, 125, 156, 160
Rowse, Alfred Leslie, 204
Russel, Penny, 2
Ryan, John, 60
Ryan, Peter, 26, 33-4, 68, 80, 100, 121, 130, 152, 155
Sapir, Edward, 172
Sargeson, Frank, 213, 236-7, 240-1
Sarzin, Anne, 8
Sayers, Dorothy Leigh, 119
Schroder, John Henry Erle, 167
Scullin, James Henry, 48-9
Seddon, Richard John, 213
Shaw, Mary Turner, 76, 90
Shevill, Ian Wotton Allnutt, 24, 84
Shineberg, Dorothy, 33, 82
Sinclair, Keith, 6, 14, 181-4, 213, 215
Sisi, 179, 182
Skinner, Henry (Harry) Devenish, 7, 9, 31
Smart, Amy, 231
Smart, Walter, 231
Smith, Grafton Elliot, 14
Smith, Reggie, 231
Smith, Stephenson Percy, 178
Spate, Oskar Hermann Khristian, 205
Spender, Percy Claude, 97
Stafford Cripps, Richard, 214
Stanner, William Edward Hanley, 2, 4, 5, 16, 22, 24, 27, 30, 32, 51, 61, 63-7, 79-80, 81, 84, 86, 88, 90-2, 95-116
Stantke, Victor Paul Hildebrand, 57, 59-60, 77, 98-9, 153-4

Stanton, Eddie Allan, 64-5
Steven, Bertram Sydney Barnsdale, 95, 115
Stevenson, Robert Louis, 177
Stewart, Harold Frederick (Hal), 33, 55, 62-3, 75, 154-5
Stewart, Helen, 208
Stone, Julius, 17, 22, 24, 33, 56, 58, 61-4, 66, 76, 83-4, 120, 130, 152
Stout, Alan, 56, 58, 66, 76
Strehlow, Theodor George Henry (Ted), 30, 157
Strong, Philip, 126-8
Syme, Ronald, 232
Taylor, Alan John Percivale, 201
Taylor, Dorothy Griffith, 73-4
Taylor, Frederick Winslow, 45
Taylor, James (Jim), 81-2, 103, 157
Taylor, Thomas Griffith, 74
Temple, William, 119
Tennant-Kelly, Caroline, *see* Kelly, Caroline Tennant
Tennyson, Alfred Lord, 211, 222
Thomson, Donald Fergusson, 5, 30
Trevor-Roper, Hugh Redwald, 203-4
Tupua Tamasese Lealofi III, 176
Turnbull, Alfred Clarke, 180
Tuzin, Donald Francis (Don), 171, 174, 180, 182
Vaughan Williams, Ralph, 117
Wakefield, Edward Gibbon, 210
Walker, Eric Anderson, 192, 198
Ward, Edward John (Eddy), 23, 31, 53, 64-6, 78, 81, 83-4, 93, 102, 105, 110, 112, 156, 158-60
Webb, Catherine Helen, *see* Berndt, Catherine Helen
Webb, Jessie Stobo Watson, 149
Wedgwood, Cicely Veronica, 117

Wedgwood, Ethel Kate (née Bowen), 117, 131

Wedgwood, Helen Bowen, *see* Pease, Helen Bowen

Wedgwood, Camilla Hildegarde, 2, 9, 15, 22, 24, 27, 30-1, 61, 63, 65-8, 73, 78-9, 83-8, 95, 102, 104, 117-32, 154, 157

Wedgwood, Josiah Clement, 117, 132

Wentworth, William Charles (Bill), 25, 95, 115

White, Thomas Walter, 68

Williams, Edgar Trevor (Bill), 162, 226, 231-2

Williams, Francis Edgar, 3-4, 20, 30, 82, 123, 130

Williams, Kathleen Broome, 8

Williams, Ralph Vaughan, 117, 188

Williams, Robin M, 164

Wilmot, Chester, 43

Wilson, Edward Osborne, 169

Wilson, James Thomas, 14

Wilson, Ormond, 217

Wise, Tigger, 32, 35-9, 45, 48-9, 68, 76, 85, 106

Wittgenstein, Ludwig, 150

Woollacott, Angela, 2

Wright, Roy Douglas (Panzee), 33, 57-8, 66, 76, 152

Wurm, Stefan (Stephen), 20

Wurth, Wallace Charles, 45-6, 50

Zohrab, Amyas Constantine, 209-10

www.ingramcontent.com/pod-product-compliance
Lightning Source LLC
Chambersburg PA
CBHW060928170426
43192CB00031B/2866